35·00

The Impact of the Edwardian Castles in Wales

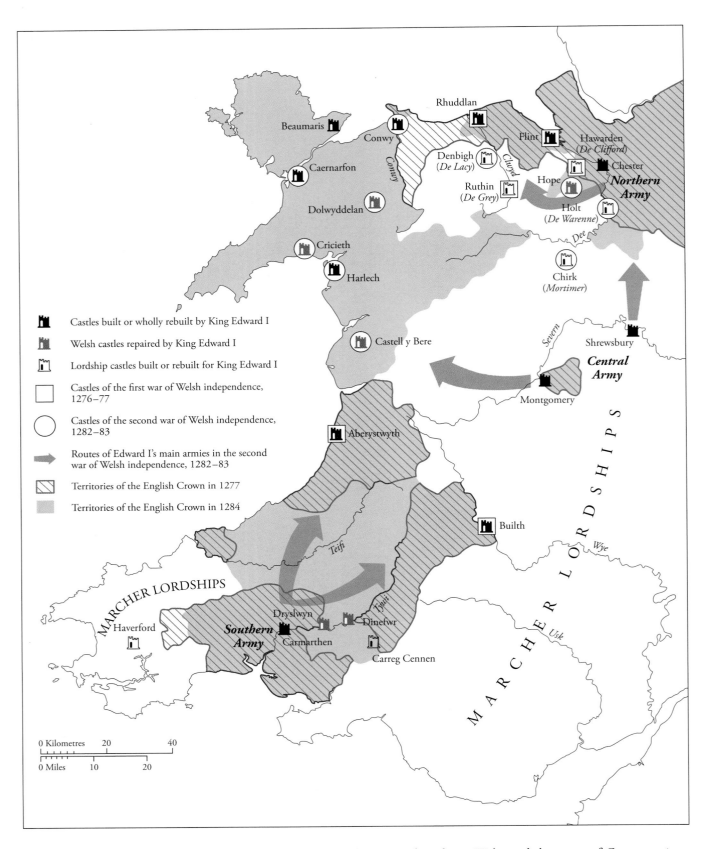

Frontispiece: Map showing the castles built or commissioned by King Edward I in Wales and the extent of Crown territory in 1277 and 1284. (Cadw, Welsh Assembly Government: Crown Copyright).

The Impact of the Edwardian Castles in Wales

The proceedings of a conference held at
Bangor University, 7–9 September 2007

*Edited by Diane M. Williams
and John R. Kenyon*

Llywodraeth Cynulliad Cymru
Welsh Assembly Government

The Castle Studies
Group
Grŵp Astudiaethau
Cestyll

Oxbow Books

Oxford and Oakville

Published by
Oxbow Books, Oxford

ISBN 978-1-84217-380-0

A CIP record for this book is available from the British Library

This book is available direct from

Oxbow Books, Oxford, UK
(Phone: 01865-241249, Fax: 01865-794449)

and

The David Brown Book Company
PO Box 511, Oakville, CT 06779, USA
(Phone: 860-945-9329; Fax: 860-945-9468)

or from our website

www.oxbowbooks.com

Library of Congress Cataloging-in-Publication Data

The impact of the Edwardian castles in Wales : the proceedings of a conference held at Bangor University, 7-9 September 2007
/ edited by Diane M. Williams and John R. Kenyon.
    p. cm.
  Includes bibliographical references and index.
  ISBN 978-1-84217-380-0
  1. Wales--History--1284-1536--Congresses. 2. Edward I, King of England, 1239-1307--Relations with Welsh--Congresses. 3.
Castles--Wales--History--Congresses. 4. Great Britain--History--Edward I, 1272-1307--Congresses. I. Williams, Diane M. II.
Kenyon, John R. III. Bangor University.
  DA715.I47 2009
  942.9'035--dc22
                        2009043939

*Front cover: (left to right) Beaumaris Castle, Caernarfon Castle, Conwy Castle, Harlech Castle
(Cadw, Welsh Assembly Government: Crown Copyright).
Back cover: Dolwyddelan Castle (Cadw, Welsh Assembly Government: Crown Copyright).*

Printed in Great Britain by
Gomer Press
Llandysul
Wales

Contents

Editors' Preface

The Impact of the Edwardian Castles in Wales was a conference organized by Bangor University, Cadw (the historic environment service of the Welsh Assembly Government) and the Castle Studies Group. It was held at Bangor University between 7 and 9 September 2007, a year that marked the seventh centenary of the death of King Edward I.

The conference not only marked this anniversary, but also acknowledged that Edward I's most enduring monuments are the castles that he built in north Wales after two wars, 1277 and 1282–83, and completed following a Welsh uprising in 1294–95. More than this, however, the conference aimed to review recent scholarship on these castles and rethink the effect that their building had upon Wales in the past, present and future.

It set out first to build upon the seminal work of Arnold Taylor, whose study of the buildings and documentary evidence has been pivotal to Edwardian castle studies for more than fifty years. Already, in 2003, one of our contributors, Nicola Coldstream, had called into question the role of Master James of St George as the architect of the king's new castles, whilst Jeremy Ashbee, in his study of royal accommodation in the thirteenth century, had been examining more closely the inner ward of Conwy. Likewise, Peter Brears has been making a notable contribution to our knowledge of how households worked, especially in the kitchen and accounting departments.

New approaches to castle studies are encouraging a more holistic understanding of the Edwardian castles and their context and to this end the conference looked at their impact on Welsh society and its princes in the thirteenth century, notably Llywelyn ab Iorwerth (Llywelyn Fawr, Llywelyn the Great) and his grandson, Llywelyn ap Gruffudd, prince of Wales. The castles still have powerful resonance and we are especially grateful to Alun Ffred Jones AM, Minister for Heritage in the Welsh Assembly Government, for his paper which considers their role and presentation in Wales today and in the future.

As well as the Minister for Heritage's contribution, four additional papers were commissioned to enhance the contents: David Browne on the castles of Aberystwyth and Builth, Adam Chapman on Welsh soldiers in the armies of Edward I, John Kenyon on Arnold Taylor's seminal work in north Wales, and Graham Lott on the buildings stones. Huw Pryce very kindly contributed the Foreword. Unfortunately, Dr Pamela Marshall was unable to submit her conference paper for family reasons.

The weekend was also an acknowledgement of the work of the late Richard Avent, a colleague and friend to many of the contributors, who died in an accident whilst on holiday in 2006. Much was written in the national press of Richard's contribution to archaeology in Wales and beyond in his position as chief inspector of ancient monuments and historic buildings at Cadw. He also played a leading role in the process that saw the inscription of the four great Edwardian castles as a World Heritage Site in 1986, and was noted in particular for his work on the castles of the Welsh princes. This volume is dedicated to his memory.

The very successful conference would not have been realized without the hard work of Nancy Edwards and Linda Jones of Bangor University, Helen and Rick Turner of Cadw and Pamela Marshall of the Castle Studies Group. The editors would like to thank all the contributors for responding so promptly to requests for their papers, and for nobly bearing with patience the various queries that inevitably arise from editing papers for publication. We would also like to thank Pete Lawrence for drawing many of the maps and plans in this volume and Huw David for his work on the photographs. *Diolch yn fawr!*

Diane M. Williams
Cadw, Welsh Assembly Government
John R. Kenyon
Amgueddfa Cymru – National Museum Wales

Contributors

Jeremy Ashbee MA, PhD, FSA is head properties curator for English Heritage and has written a number of guidebooks and papers on castle studies, including the recent Cadw guidebook to Conwy's castle and town walls.

Richard Avent BA, MA, FSA, who died in 2006, was the chief inspector of ancient monuments and historic buildings for Cadw, and wrote extensively on castles, notably those of the Welsh princes.

Peter Brears DipAD, FSA, FMA is a food historian and former museum curator. He has advised bodies such as Cadw, English Heritage and the National Trust on culinary matters, and his book on cooking and dining in medieval England was published in 2008.

David Browne BA, MA, FRAI, FRGS is head of publications and outreach at the Royal Commission on the Ancient and Historical Monuments of Wales. He is preparing the final report on the excavations at Aberystwyth Castle.

Lawrence Butler MA, PhD, FSA was a senior lecturer in medieval archaeology at the University of York. He excavated Llywelyn ap Gruffudd's castle of Dolforwyn and has published a number of books and papers on castles, as well as on other medieval subjects.

Adam Chapman BA, MA is a doctoral researcher on 'The Welsh soldier', University of Southampton, as part of the team working on *The Soldier in Later Medieval England* project.

Nicola Coldstream MA, PhD, FSA is an architectural historian. She is the author of a number of publications, including *The Decorated Style: Architecture and Ornament 1240–1360* and *Builders & Decorators: Medieval Craftsmen in Wales*.

Dylan Foster Evans MA, PhD is a senior lecturer in the School of Welsh at Cardiff University and has published widely on medieval literature and culture. His particular interest is the poetry of the Welsh gentry.

John Goodall BA, MA, PhD, FSA is the architectural editor of *Country Life*. Formerly at English Heritage, he has written a number of guidebooks and articles on castles, as well as other publications. Yale University Press is to publish his book *English Castle Architecture, 1066–1640*.

Alun Ffred Jones AM, BA is the Minister for Heritage in the Welsh Assembly Government.

John R. Kenyon BA, MCLIP, FSA, FRHistS, FSA (Scot) is the librarian of Amgueddfa Cymru — National Museum Wales. He has published extensively on castles and later fortifications, and contributed to the series *The Buildings of Wales*. His bibliography of publications on fortifications in the UK and Ireland appeared in 2008.

Robert Liddiard BA, MA, PhD, FSA is a lecturer in the School of History, University of East Anglia. He is the author of a number of papers on castles and *Castles in Context: Power, Symbolism and Landscape, 1066 to 1500*.

Keith D. Lilley BA, PhD is a lecturer in the School of Geography, Queen's University Belfast. He has published widely on the urban landscape and has worked on the project that has led to the creation of an interactive online atlas of medieval towns.

David Longley BA, FSA is the director of the Gwynedd Archaeological Trust and has published papers on a wide range of multi-period aspects of Gwynedd's archaeology and history.

Graham Lott BSc, PhD is a petrologist and building stone specialist with the British Geological Survey. He is the co-author of the two BGS guides *Geology and Building Stones in Wales* and contributed to *Stone in Wales: Materials, Heritage and Conservation*.

Marc Morris MA, DPhil, FRHistS is a historian and broadcaster, and the author of a number of books, including *A Great and Terrible King: Edward I and the Forging of Britain*, published in 2008.

Michael Prestwich MA, DPhil, FRHistS, FSA has recently retired as professor of history at the University of Durham. Amongst his books are *War, Politics and Finance under Edward I* and *Edward I* in what is now the Yale English Monarchs series.

Huw Pryce MA, DPhil, FRHistS is professor of Welsh history at Bangor University. His most recent book is *The Acts of Welsh Rulers 1120–1283*.

David Stephenson MA, DPhil, Grad Cert Ed is an honorary research fellow in the School of History and Welsh History, Bangor University. The author of *The Governance of Gwynedd*, he is currently researching the Welsh Marches in the twelfth and thirteenth centuries.

Chris Tabraham BA is principal historian with Historic Scotland and the author of a number of publications on the history of Scotland and its castles.

Rick Turner MA, FSA is an inspector of ancient monuments at Cadw. He has worked extensively and published on Chepstow Castle and St Davids Bishop's Palace, and is the author of a number of Cadw guidebooks.

Abigail Wheatley MA, PhD is a castle historian and the author of *The Idea of the Castle in Medieval England*.

Diane Williams BA, MA, PhD, FSA is head of publications at Cadw and guidebook series editor.

Foreword

Huw Pryce

The Edwardian castles of Wales are remarkable monuments of European significance. Most obviously, their unprecedented scale and consummate design represented the determination of Edward I to secure the Welsh territories he had conquered in 1277 and 1282–83 by imposing a new military and political order. As such, the castles set the seal on the final phase of an age of conquest that had commenced two centuries earlier in the reign of William I, and thereby marked not only an important turning point in the history of Wales, but also a graphic instance of a much broader phenomenon of territorial expansion by the powerful polities of medieval Europe. This collection of papers throws valuable new light on the construction of the castles and their role in the conquest of Wales, and also includes comparisons with Edward I's activities in Gascony and Scotland. Yet in presenting the fruits of recent research, the volume also seeks to offer fresh perspectives by setting the castles in their multiple contexts. In part, this is a matter of moving away from a predominantly military focus by considering some of the domestic and symbolic aspects of the castles and the planning of their adjacent towns. In addition, though, several contributors shift the emphasis from the conquerors to the conquered through exploring the Welsh background and context, notably the expansionist ambitions and castle building of the thirteenth-century princes of Gwynedd. This serves as a reminder that the castles of Edward I reflected both a drastic response to the resilience of Welsh rulers, over whom previous kings of England had achieved only a partial and temporary dominance at best, and the latest chapter of an old story: the exercise of power over the people of Gwynedd and other lands in Wales. Nor is the significance of the castles restricted to their role in the Middle Ages, for they remain a powerful presence in the landscape that can still evoke strongly diverse reactions. It is therefore fitting that the volume also assesses how these monuments have been regarded in the modern period, with respect to both popular perceptions and scholarly interpretations, notably the seminal studies of Arnold Taylor, and concludes with suggestions as to how we may develop our understanding of them in the future. In looking anew at the Edwardian castles and their contexts, the contributions assembled here provide a valuable overview of the current state of scholarship and thus an important point of departure for further work.

1

Edward I and Wales

Michael Prestwich

In the thirteenth century there were many conquests. The Mongols made spectacular gains, establishing a vast empire. In Spain, the Christian kingdoms advanced into the Moslem territories of the peninsula. The Fourth Crusade saw the capture of Constantinople, which was followed by the establishment of Frankish rule in Greece. The Mamluks conquered the Latin kingdom in the east. Beside such triumphs, Edward I's conquest of Wales may seem small in scale. It was, however, exceptional in its totality, with the destruction of the ruling native dynasties, the introduction of English methods of administration and law, and above all the building of the great castles. This all stood in clear contrast to previous Anglo-Norman activity in Wales, which had been a matter of staged piecemeal expansion, rather than full-scale conquest.

Edward's involvement in Wales began in 1254, when the grant made to him at the time of his marriage to Eleanor of Castile included the earldom of Chester. With this came the Four Cantrefs (*Perfeddwlad*), the lands between the rivers Dee and Conwy. Harsh rule by Edward's officials, notably Geoffrey de Langley, provoked rebellion in 1256. The rising brought Llywelyn ap Gruffudd, prince of Gwynedd, immense success not only in the north, but also in mid- and south Wales. Edward's forces were defeated in the Tywi valley in 1257. A royal expedition in the same year reached Deganwy, but was forced to withdraw, faced by famine and harassed by the Welsh. Edward was present in the army, and must have learned a hard lesson from the campaign.[1]

Llywelyn was well placed to take advantage of the English civil war of the 1260s.[2] An expedition led by Edward in 1263 succeeded in revictualling Dyserth and Deganwy, but nothing more. After his triumph at Lewes in 1264, Simon de Montfort looked to his ally, Llywelyn, for support. Montfort was defeated at Evesham in the following year, but the Welsh prince played his cards well, and in the settlement after the civil war negotiated the favourable terms of the Treaty of Montgomery of 1267. This saw the English recognize him as prince of Wales, and acknowledged that the Four Cantrefs were his. Edward had already given his lands in south Wales, Carmarthen and Cardigan, to his brother Edmund; with the treaty, he now had no remaining territorial interest in Wales. This must have rankled, and a desire to undo the Treaty of Montgomery was surely part of the motivation behind his policies towards Wales after he became king.

Edward went on crusade in 1270, and did not return to England until 1274. There were difficulties in these years between Llywelyn and the lords of the March, and the English government in vain ordered the Welsh prince to cease building his new castle at Dolforwyn in Montgomeryshire. When Edward returned, the issue that predominated was that of Llywelyn's failure to perform fealty and homage to him. The Welsh prince did not appear at Edward's coronation, and ignored a stream of summonses requesting his presence. His plans to marry Simon de Montfort's daughter, Eleanor, must have been seen by Edward as highly provocative. Equally, Llywelyn was understandably resentful when his rebellious brother, Dafydd, was received at the English court. Edward's refusal to release Llywelyn's bride after she was captured at sea in 1275 could only be read as a hostile move. Relations continued to deteriorate, and in 1277 Edward led an army into north Wales. There are no memoranda which set out Edward's war aims in explicit terms, but it seems certain that he hoped to destroy Llywelyn's authority, break up his principality, and regain the Four Cantrefs. The rest of Gwynedd would be divided between Edward and Llywelyn's brothers, Dafydd and Owain. Full-scale conquest was not yet the objective.[3]

The war began in the Marches. The earl of Warwick, Roger Mortimer and Payn de Chaworth were appointed as captains, and the earl of Lincoln also had an important force under his command. There were many successes, notably the capture of Dolforwyn Castle. Much of the work had been done by the time that Edward's own army advanced from Chester in July. By late August the royal army was at Rhuddlan, and soon it reached Deganwy. Numbers were impressive, with some 15,000 men, of whom about 9,000 were from south Wales and the Marches; there was an element of civil war to the campaign. Some troops were sent by sea to Anglesey, where they harvested the crops in a move intended to starve out the Welsh. The campaign was brief, for Llywelyn soon realized that resistance was fruitless. On 9 November terms were agreed.

In contrast to the war of 1277, it was the Welsh who started the conflict of 1282–83. They had many grievances. Legal issues were important. Edward's handling, characterized by lengthy delays, of a major dispute between Llywelyn and Gruffudd ap Gwenwynwyn of southern Powys over the *cantref* of Arwystli proved particularly significant. Aggressive behaviour by English officials, particularly that of Reginald de Grey, justiciar of Chester, was deeply resented. There were other matters. What may seem a minor issue about some honey impounded by English officials from a wreck, which Llywelyn claimed took place on his land, clearly rankled. A letter from the warden of the friary at Llanfaes to the king emphasized this grievance, along with Llywelyn's problems with Gruffudd ap Gwenwynwyn.[4] There was, however, no question, of Edward deliberately goading the Welsh into war; he simply miscalculated. In particular, he failed to provide Llywelyn's brother, Dafydd, with the level of rewards he expected after he had supported the English in the previous war.

It was Dafydd who led the rebellion with an attack on the castle at Hawarden at Easter in 1282. Edward had to mobilize his troops quickly. The initial plan, set out in writs on 5 April, was for a royal muster at Worcester, and presumably a march into mid-Wales, but this was changed on 20 May for a muster at Rhuddlan. By the end of August the king had some 750 cavalry and about 8,000 foot under his command there. Once again, forces were sent to Anglesey, and an elaborate pontoon bridge was constructed so they could cross to the mainland, a remarkable piece of engineering. Meanwhile, troops under Marcher leadership were operating in mid- and south Wales, though not with unmitigated success, for the earl of Gloucester was defeated in one engagement. In November the Welsh achieved a small triumph, with the defeat of a force which Luke de Tany led across the Anglesey bridge. In November, Llywelyn moved south from Snowdonia, a gamble that ended in disaster for him when he was slain in a battle near Builth, on 11 December. This was a war on a much larger and longer scale than that of 1277. Edward wintered in Wales, at Rhuddlan. In January, Dolywddelan surrendered. In March, the headquarters was shifted to Conwy. Final mopping up was completed early in the summer of 1283 when Dafydd ap Gruffudd was eventually captured.

This campaign in 1282–83 was one of conquest. Dafydd was executed at Shrewsbury and the remaining members of the princely family of Gwynedd sent to imprisonment or nunneries in England. Important landholding families in north Wales vanished; it was only Gruffudd ap Gwenwynwyn, lord of Powys, and an ally of Edward, who retained his possessions. A major territorial settlement took place even before the war was completed, in 1282, with grants of lands in the Four Cantrefs to Earl Warenne, the earl of Lincoln, and Reginald de Grey. In 1284 the Statute of Wales was issued, in which Edward stated that Wales was 'wholly and entirely transferred to our proper dominion'.[5] A new structure of local government was set up, with the creation of the shires of Flint, Anglesey, Caernarvon and Merioneth.

The first rebellion against Edward's rule came in 1287, when Rhys ap Maredudd, lord of Dryslwyn, a former loyal ally of the English, attempted to take advantage of the king's absence in Gascony. This was put down without too much difficulty or expense; but in September 1294 a much more serious uprising took place, which was both widespread and popular. There is, unfortunately, no surviving statement of the Welsh grievances, but it is likely that the introduction of English-style taxation in Wales was a significant element. The timing of the rising was intended to take advantage of the king's preoccupation with his French war, and a planned expedition to Gascony. The English campaign in response did not begin until November, far later in the year than was normal. Edward marched once again from Chester, reaching Conwy by Christmas. In January he conducted a rapid raid into the Llŷn peninsula. Marcher forces operated from Montgomery and Carmarthen. The rebel leader, Madog ap Llywelyn, was defeated by the earl of Warwick at Maes Moydog in mid-Wales in March. Edward launched an attack on Anglesey in April, and then began a march on a circuit south to Cardigan and Carmarthen, before returning northward through the Marches. The overall number of troops employed by the English in this war was highly impressive, with up to 35,000 at one time in the various armies.

Although there was a major difference in the aims of the first and second wars, the strategy the English adopted throughout was remarkably similar, with royal armies advancing from Chester into Gwynedd. Some historians have written in scathing terms about strategy in this period, considering tactical success the best that could be expected of medieval commanders. 'However good a tactician he may have been, he was a pitiable strategist', was one comment on Edward I.[6] One difficulty facing historians is that there was little contemporary writing about military strategy. Exceptionally, in the twelfth century Gerald of Wales had given advice as to how the English should plan their campaigns. Internal divisions among the Welsh were to be encouraged. An economic blockade was needed. Lightly armed troops were appropriate, recruited in the Welsh Marches and in Ireland, and supplemented by mercenaries from across the Channel.[7] If Gerald's work was known to the king and his advisers, its advice was not followed. Nothing similar was written in the thirteenth century; the only tract discussing strategic issues that can be connected with Edward I's circle is one probably written by his Savoyard friend, Otto de Grandson, on how a crusade might best be conducted. The king did possess a translation of the late Roman treatise on warfare by Vegetius, but there is no way to know whether he took the advice it contained to heart.[8] Although there is no indication of what discussions may have taken place in Edward I's councils about the way in which his wars in Wales should be conducted, it would however be foolish to think that there were no strategic ideas in this period. Edward's French war, which began in 1294, saw the king adopt an ambitious strategy, which was surely carefully thought through. English forces would maintain their position in Gascony, while the main attack would come from invasion from the north, where Edward planned to operate with the aid of a vast allied coalition. This was not a new concept; it dated back to the last days of the Angevin empire, but it was no less a strategy for that.

At the core of Edward's strategy for Wales was the immense advantage that he had over his opponents in terms of resources. He could recruit massive armies, mobilizing up to 30,000 men, who he could back up with naval forces. He was able to raise taxes on a massive scale to pay for his wars. In addition to forces recruited directly by the Crown, he was able to rely on the support of the lords of the Welsh March. In contrast, Llywelyn ap Gruffudd was probably little wealthier or more powerful than an average English earl, though he did have the advantage of defending difficult terrain. Edward's basic plan was for forces under the leadership of major magnates to engage the Welsh in mid- and south Wales, while the royal army advanced into north Wales from Chester. Woodcutters could create new routes for the march. Seizing Anglesey was an important objective, for it was there that grain was produced. By harvesting it, Edward was able to put added pressure on Llywelyn.

A key element in Edward's strategy was the building of his new castles. Existing Welsh castles did not, for the most part, meet the required criteria, for they were relatively small and remote. Cricieth was the only one that could be supplied by sea, and if that were not possible, English-held castles were vulnerable to blockade. Edward had seen for himself in 1262 the difficulties involved in supplying Dyserth and Deganwy. Nor were the sites of Welsh castles convenient for the establishment of new towns.

The first war saw the beginning of construction at Flint and Rhuddlan, along with Builth (a refortification of an existing site) and Aberystwyth. The main new castles of the war of 1282–83 were Conwy, Caernarfon and Harlech, while the rebellion of 1294–95 saw the construction of Beaumaris in Anglesey. It was, of course, nothing new to link campaigns and castles. William I, on his route north in 1070, had ordered castles to be built at the major centres he passed through. King John's Irish expedition of 1210 saw a fine new castle started at Limerick. Campaigns in Wales early in Henry III's reign (1223, 1228 and 1231) achieved little, and demonstrated the difficulties involved in launching expeditions from the central Marches. The first of these campaigns, however, did see a new castle at Montgomery, and the third extensive work at Painscastle. In 1241 Dafydd ap Llywelyn was swiftly defeated, and a new castle constructed at Dyserth. Four years later Henry III's forces marched along the coast, and reached Deganwy, where much work was done on the refortification of the castle.[9] The scale of operations was much smaller than it would be under Edward I, but the pattern was established for armies to advance into north Wales, and for gains to be secured by castle building.

In addition to these precedents, Edward's own experience was surely relevant. Before he came to the throne, he had campaigned in Wales in 1257, and he had gained ample experience of warfare in the conflict with Simon de Montfort in the mid-1260s. That was a war dominated by two great battles, Lewes and Evesham. Sieges, however, also had their part to play. Edward was involved in the capture of some castles in the Welsh Marches early in 1264, and in concluding the siege of Gloucester with a truce. After the defeat of Simon de Montfort's forces at Evesham, Henry de Hastings and a number of die-hard opponents of the Crown held out for nearly a year at Kenilworth. This was the last major siege of the Middle Ages to take place on English soil. Edward would have learned from this just how easy it was for a relatively small number of men to maintain resistance from behind stout walls and wide water defences.

Edward must also have learned from his crusading

expedition of 1270. He embarked for North Africa from Aigues Mortes, St Louis' new crusading port. This was surely important, for there are obvious parallels to the castle-building operation in Wales. Here was a new walled town, carefully planned with a regular grid pattern of streets. It was connected to the sea by a newly excavated channel, and in the Tour de Constance it possessed a remarkable keep, independent from the town walls, yet positioned so as to guard them effectively. A twin-towered gatehouse made for an impressive entry.

Edward's brief stay in North Africa was disillusioning; the French king, Louis IX, died before Edward landed, and he was appalled to discover that an agreement had been reached with the Tunisian emir. Of the crusade leaders, Edward was the most determined to continue the expedition. He went next to Sicily, where he may have seen Frederick II's fine Castel Ursino at Catania, a rectangular round-towered construction. When he eventually reached the East, the most impressive fortifications he would have seen were those of the city of Acre, to which he added a new tower. He never reached any of the great crusader castles. Krac des Chevaliers, for example, had fallen shortly before his arrival in the East. Edward's return from the East saw him take a very different route from his outward journey. He landed in Sicily, at Trapani, and then made his way north through Italy. His precise route to Rome is not known; it is very possible that he could have seen Frederick II's celebrated Castel del Monte, with its polygonal towers. From Rome he went to Orvieto, and then on through Lombardy. He crossed the Alps via the Mont Cenis pass, and spent some time in Savoy. His main stay was at the count's new castle of St Georges-d'Espéranche; this had concentric defences, rather like Harlech, and octagonal towers, anticipating Caernarfon.[10] The importance of his travel through Savoy for the castle-building programme in Wales was the contact that he surely made with Master James of St George in Savoy. Arnold Taylor's brilliant work on the role of Master James and the other Savoyard masons who worked for Edward in Wales is so convincing, and his thesis so well established, that it is easy to forget how surprising the king's choice of Master James was in many ways.[11]

The new castles in Wales were not the first indication of Edward's enthusiasm for castle building. His first great project, begun soon after his return to England, was a massive extension of the Tower of London. The castle was converted into full concentric form, with the digging of a new moat, a new outer wall, a grand water gate, called St Thomas's Tower, and new gates with a barbican forming the landward entrance. The chief mason involved was Robert of Beverley, with clerical assistance provided by

Giles of Oudenarde. Brother John of Acre, along with a Flemish expert, Master Walter, were responsible for the moat.[12] Robert of Beverley would have been the obvious man to advise on the new castles in Wales, but work on the Tower was not halted because of the Welsh campaigns, and the king had to look elsewhere. Arnold Taylor suggested that he may have turned to the veteran Master Bertram as his first supremo on the Welsh castles. The Gascon Bertram was an expert in siege machines, rather than castle building. One element of Taylor's argument was the apparent striking similarity between two towers at Blanquefort in Gascony and the twin-towered gates of Rhuddlan. This was perhaps an imaginative leap too far. There is no evidence of Bertram's involvement at Blanquefort, and Taylor's carefully selected camera angle disguises the fundamental dissimilarities between the castles.[13] Bertram, however, was certainly involved in Wales, though there were doubts about him. A letter of April 1277, which Taylor plausibly argued was from Otto de Grandson, reported that Dolforwyn Castle was likely to be surrendered, and that it would then need considerable repair. Someone was needed to take responsibility for the works, and the writer feared that if Master Bertram was employed, he 'will devise too many things, and perhaps the king's money will not be so well employed as it needs to be.'[14] It is very likely that Otto's influence was important in the choice that Edward made of the Savoyard Master James of St George to play a leading role in the castle-building programme in Wales.

From the very outset, castles and campaigning went hand in hand for Edward in Wales; it was not a matter of building only once victory had been achieved. A letter from Henry de Lacy, earl of Lincoln, as early as May 1277 is indicative of the importance attached to castles. He had mustered his forces for an attack on Dinas Brân, only to find that the garrison had set fire to the castle and abandoned it. The houses within were destroyed, but the walls and keep were intact. His advice was clear: 'As the castle is good and strong, he suggests that it be repaired and garrisoned, and asks for instructions.'[15] In all three major campaigns, castle building was planned at an early stage. Aberystwyth and Builth were both begun in the initial stages of the war of 1277, and work at Flint, where the siting of the keep was a little reminiscent of Aigues Mortes, began almost as soon as the army reached there in July of that year. It is less clear when Rhuddlan was started, but the diversion of the river Clwyd was well under way in the autumn. This was important, for by cutting the new canal ships could reach the castle. In this, there was a clear parallel to Aigues Mortes.

Recruitment of workmen started at the very beginning

of war in 1282, and work at Hope Castle began in June, well before the main royal army mustered at Rhuddlan early in August. The great castle at Conwy seems to have been planned as soon as the king arrived there in March 1283, and very soon after that, in April, work started at Harlech. Caernarfon soon followed, in June. When the Welsh rebelled in 1294, workmen as well as soldiers comprised the first force sent to Anglesey in December, though full-scale work on Beaumaris, the last of Edward's great castles, did not start for another four months.

The military context of castles is not a fashionable topic. Much recent work on castles, led by Charles Coulson, has emphasized their many roles, but has largely excluded consideration of their military function, save perhaps to denigrate their capability in war. The weak points of Bodiam have been analysed with care, and even Henry II's great keep at Dover is seen as a building more symbolic than strong, despite its immensely thick walls. Castles are viewed as symbols of status, not as defensive structures.[16] Edward's castles, however, have to be seen as strongholds designed for war. They were, by any standards, remarkable in terms of their strength. The southern wall of Caernarfon, for example, with its triple tiers of arrowloops, provided a highly ingenious solution to the problem of how to incorporate aggressive elements into a massive defensive structure. A list of pieces of armour and other equipment, including fifty-two bacinets and thirty iron-tipped lances, acquired by the constable of Beaumaris in about 1307, provides another form of testimony to the military character of the castles.[17]

The proof of the success of Edward's castle-building policy lay, at least in part, in their performance in war. At the start of the war in 1282 Aberystwyth fell, its constable victim to a ruse when invited to dine by Gruffudd ap Maredudd. Rhuddlan came under attack, and although it held out, the castle was unable to provide protection for the little settlement under its walls.[18] Flint also survived Welsh attack. When Edward advanced into north Wales, Flint and Rhuddlan proved their value as staging posts; the latter was the king's headquarters base until late in the war.

In the rebellion of 1294–95, the royal castles all held out, with the exception of the grandest of them all, Caernarfon, which was only half-complete. Flint played little part in the war; Edward's march into north Wales took him via the earl of Lincoln's castle at Denbigh on to Conwy. It was Conwy that served as the main royal base for the campaign, though there were also significant numbers of troops based at Rhuddlan. The strong walls of Conwy made it possible for Edward to remain in Wales over the winter. He was for a time besieged by the Welsh

there, but the fact that the wine ran out was probably as much of a problem to the defenders as any attacks the Welsh were able to mount. Victualling was a difficulty, if not as much so as in the past: Harlech and the old Welsh castle of Cricieth were only saved when ships from Ireland brought much needed supplies in April 1295. Aberystwyth also received supplies by sea, from Bristol.[19]

War in the late thirteenth century was a costly business. The bill for the second Welsh war came to about £80,000. At the start of the war of 1294–95 over £55,000 in cash was sent to Wales.[20] It is in this context that the expense of castle building needs to be set. The cost of the castles was worked out long ago by Goronwy Edwards, and by 1301 came to some £80,000.[21] That equates, roughly, to a successful tax (the fifteenth of 1275 raised about this sum, as did the tenth and sixth of 1294), or perhaps to a single campaign against the Welsh. There is no evidence, however, to suggest that Edward or his advisers thought in such terms. Budgeting, such as it was, was primitive; an estimate of income was produced in 1284, but no attempts appear to have been made to match plans such as those for the castles to projected income. Nevertheless, the expense of the castles, great as it was, was not unreasonable when set against the cost of campaigning.

The strategy of Edward's castle building was not purely military. It also had a strong colonial element, linked to the construction of new towns. One reason for the decision to abandon Henry III's site at Deganwy, militarily strong though it was, was no doubt that Conwy offered the opportunity for urban development in a way that Deganwy had not done. The thirteenth century was a great age of urban expansion, with many new towns created. Hull is one notable example; Edward's interest in towns was demonstrated by the way that he took over the new town from Meaux Abbey. New Winchelsea, necessary because coastal erosion had annihilated the original town, was an important royal foundation, carefully planned with a typical regular grid pattern of tenements. The establishment of new towns, or bastides, in Gascony was an important part of royal policy in the duchy. It was very rare for the Gascon bastides to be linked to castles. Bonnegarde, an unsuccessful foundation dating from 1283, is one possible exception. What was distinctive about the new towns in Wales was the way in which they were an integral part of the castle-building programme, a reflection of English insecurity. Only at Caerwys, between Flint and Rhuddlan, and at Newborough in Anglesey, did Edward create towns without a castle overlooking them.[22]

The success of the new towns varied. Beaumaris was the largest; by 1305 it had 132¼ burgage tenements.

Conwy had 124 in 1312. Caernarfon had 59 in 1298, a number which had scarcely risen by the mid-fourteenth century. Flint was a success, with seventy-six taxpayers in 1292; in contrast, the borough at Harlech was tiny, with a dozen taxpayers and a total population of forty-four.[23] As instruments intended to encourage large-scale English settlement in north Wales, the castle towns were probably less of an achievement than Edward I had hoped.

The castles have been described as 'the seats of civilian governance, the headquarters of a new administrative, financial and judicial dispensation.'[24] This is true in a sense, but it was in the towns they dominated that the business of government was conducted, not within the castles themselves. Plans changed with time. Initially, after the first war, Rhuddlan was intended as the seat of English royal authority in north Wales; it was there that the case over Arwystli was heard in 1278. There were even plans for a new cathedral to be built there, but nothing came of this. The second Welsh war changed all this, with the focus moving further west. At Conwy, administrative affairs were conducted in the king's hall and the justiciar's hall in the town, while the chamberlain's lodgings were above one of the town gates. It was, however, Caernarfon that became pre-eminent in administrative terms; this was the seat of Edward's first justiciar of north Wales, Otto de Grandson. His court house, however, was not in the castle itself, but lay in the town, while his exchequer was in one of the gatehouses of the town.[25]

From the first, the castles were intended to provide impressive and comfortable accommodation. At Rhuddlan there was a fishpond surrounded by seats, and the lawn that required 6,000 turves. A lawn for the queen was created at Caernarfon in the very earliest stages of the castle's construction. At Flint the 'noble and beautiful' circular wooden structure, or *carola*, which surmounted the great tower in the early fourteenth century was surely an enhancement of the living quarters, not a defensive hoarding.[26] The extensive domestic buildings at Conwy, with hall and ancillary structures in the outer ward, and a magnificent royal suite in the inner, provide obvious testimony to the residential purpose that was envisaged for the castle. Beaumaris, had it been fully completed, would have had sumptuous halls and apartments, as well as ample living space in its two great gatehouses.

There was a propaganda element to Edward's building programme. The castles, it has been said, 'proclaimed proudly, almost extravagantly, the quasi-imperial character of Edward's vision of his conquest of Wales.'[27] At Conwy, the new castle and the new town used part of the site occupied by the Cistercian abbey, which provided the burial place for the princes of Gwynedd, and by a princely

residence. It was obviously convenient that there were residential buildings that could be pressed into use while building work went ahead on the castle, but the use of this site also made a very emphatic statement about the way in which Edward was determined to destroy the traditions of the line of Llywelyn ab Iorwerth (the Great).

Caernarfon was particularly remarkable. The way in which the castle made allusion to the Roman past, and in particular to the legend of Maxen Wledig, is well known thanks to the work of Arnold Taylor.[28] There was a belief, which was of course wholly erroneous, that Maxen (or Maximus) was the Emperor Constantine's father, and a chronicle reported that in 1283 Maximus's body was discovered at Caernarfon, and reburied on Edward's instructions. Taylor argued that Caernarfon was built in deliberate imitation of the defences of the imperial city of Constantinople. There, the Theodosian walls have some polygonal towers, and dark bands run through the masonry. Abigail Wheatley has argued for some qualifications to Taylor's thesis, suggesting that while the banded masonry makes allusion to the Roman past, this may not be specifically to Constantinople.[29] Edward himself had never visited Constantinople, and Taylor could only identify one member of his household who had. One possibility is that the building style of Caernarfon made allusion to the walls of York, the city where Constantine was proclaimed emperor, and where there is a polygonal tower with a dark band of tile.[30] Taylor identified Caernarfon with the castle described in the Welsh tale of Maxen Wledig; the new castle was a physical embodiment of a legendary story. While symbolism is by far the best explanation for the very different appearance of Caernarfon from the other Edwardian castles, it is unlikely that many who saw the castle would have had the awareness and knowledge to decode its meaning.

The building style of Caernarfon with its Roman allusions certainly suggests that Edward had romantic ideas about conquering Wales in pursuit of an imperial concept; that he perhaps saw himself as a new Arthur. He undoubtedly had an interest in the mythical British king, for he had what were thought to be the bodies of both Arthur and his queen reburied in a splendid ceremony at Glastonbury in 1278.[31] There is nothing, however, more than the date to suggest that this had any connection with the recent campaign in Wales. Nor is there anything in the writs produced by the royal chancery to suggest that Edward saw his war of conquest of 1282–83 in an Arthurian or imperial light. Caernarfon, with its eagle-topped triple turrets, stands effectively alone as evidence for an imperial dream. It should also be noted that not all the elements of the vision were complete by the time of Edward I's death in 1307. The eagles themselves were installed in the next reign, and the statue which stands on the King's Gate looking out over the town is of the ineffective Edward II, who was certainly not a man to have grandiose ideas of empire.[32]

Edward's strategy in Wales worked, and the castles he built stand as an astonishing monument to the power of the thirteenth-century English state. The majesty of Conwy, Caernarfon and the other castles should not, however, disguise the fact that the achievement was in some senses flawed. The scale of the building programme was excessive. The stumpy towers of Beaumaris, carried no higher than the curtain wall, provide vivid evidence of the failure to carry out the grand plans in full. The Welsh did not have the military capability to threaten or besiege castles on the scale of Conwy or Caernarfon, save by means of a lengthy blockade, and it can be argued that smaller castles would have been more than adequate. More seriously, the English did not have the resources to maintain the castles properly; surveys made in around 1340 show that by then they were already in a poor condition.[33] Nor were there sufficient funds to provide them with the garrisons that they needed. In 1284 arrangements were made for William Cicon at Conwy to receive £190 a year, out of which he was to maintain a garrison of thirty, in addition to himself and his household. John of Havering at Caernarfon would get £166 13s. 4d. a year, and have a garrison of forty. The sum for Harlech was £100.[34] These sums were adequate but little more, and as time went on the sums allocated to the constables of the castles were much lower. In the 1380s the fee paid to the constable of Conwy was £66 13s. 4d., but in the following decade the sum was down to

£40. In 1391 the fee granted to the constable of Harlech was raised from £13 6s. 8d. to £20, a fifth of the amount paid a century earlier.[35] The magnificent accommodation suites were not needed, and indeed were never built at Caernarfon or Beaumaris. The fourteenth century passed without a royal visit until 1399, when Richard II, a broken man, passed through Harlech and Caernarfon on his way to Conwy and Flint.

The great Edwardian castles were not tested during the fourteenth century. They had, however, an important part to play in Owain Glyndŵr's rebellion, when their performance was no more than partially successful. The Welsh did not have the resources, particularly in terms of siege equipment, to be able to challenge the English garrisons as they no doubt wished. Caernarfon withstood a siege, even though the attackers had the assistance of some French soldiers who doubtless had greater expertise in castle warfare than their Welsh allies. Conwy fell to the Welsh, but this was possible only because the garrison was in church, and the great castle was unguarded. The garrisons of both Aberystwyth and Harlech, blockaded by the Welsh, surrendered, and the castles then served the rebel cause well.[36]

The sad reality of the castles a little later in the fifteenth century is suggested by a request made by the constable of Conwy, John Bolde, in 1423. He had a staff of six valets with him, so that he could keep the castle. Now he was ordered to dismiss them, but he pointed out that if he did this, it would not be possible to guard the three French knights held in captivity. He asked if he could either keep the valets, or be relieved of the prisoners.[37] So much for the grand vision of Edward I's day; the castle had become no more than an understaffed prison.

Notes

1. For Edward's early involvement with Wales, see M. C. Prestwich, *Edward I* (London 1988), 16–19. I am very grateful to Marc Morris for his valuable comments on an earlier draft of this paper.
2. Llywelyn's career is admirably discussed and analysed by J. B. Smith, *Llywelyn ap Gruffudd, Prince of Wales* (Cardiff 1988).
3. For the events of the wars, see J. E. Morris, *The Welsh Wars of Edward I* (Oxford 1901); R. R. Davies, *Conquest, Coexistence and Change: Wales 1063–1415* (Oxford 1987), 333–54, 380–85; Smith, *Llywelyn ap Gruffudd*, 414–38, 511–81; Prestwich, *Edward I*, 170–201, 220–32.
4. *Calendar of Ancient Correspondence Concerning Wales*, ed. J. G. Edwards (Cardiff 1935), 99–100. See also Llywelyn's letter, ibid., 90–91.
5. *Statutes of the Realm*, I (London 1810), 55.
6. H. G. Richardson, in a review of *The History of the King's Works*, *English Historical Review*, 80 (1965), 556.
7. *Giraldi Cambrensis Opera*, ed. J. F. Dimock, VI (Rolls Series XXI, London 1868), 218–22.
8. Prestwich, *Edward I*, 75, 123.
9. For these castles, see R. A. Brown, H. M. Colvin and A. J. Taylor, *The History of the King's Works: the Middle Ages*, II (London 1963), 624–26, 644–45, 739–41, 775–76.
10. For Edward's career in the civil war, and for his crusade, see Prestwich, *Edward I*, 42–84.
11. See in particular A. J. Taylor, 'Master James of St George', *English Historical Review*, 65 (1950), 433–57, and the various articles in A. J. Taylor, *Studies in Castles and Castle-Building* (London 1985).
12. *King's Works*, II, 715–22. The National Archives (TNA): PRO E 101/468/5 shows that, curiously, one of the workmen at the Tower was known as 'Plein de Amore'.
13. A. J. Taylor, 'Master Bertram, *Ingeniator Regis*', in *Studies in Medieval History Presented to R. Allen Brown*, eds C. Harper-Bill, C. Holdsworth and J. L. Nelson (Woodbridge 1989), 289–315.

14. *Calendar of Ancient Correspondence Concerning Wales*, 31; Taylor, 'Master Bertram', 296, 309.

15. *Calendar of Ancient Correspondence Concerning Wales*, 83.

16. C. A. Coulson, 'Fourteenth-century castles in context: apotheosis or decline?', *Fourteenth Century England I*, ed. N. Saul (Woodbridge 2000), 133–51, is one of a number of publications in which Coulson substantially revises traditional interpretations. For an assault on Coulson's position, see C. Platt, 'Revisionism in castle studies: a caution', *Medieval Archaeology*, 51 (2007), 83–102.

17. TNA: PRO SC 6/1211/28. These levels of equipment were not maintained for long; TNA: PRO E 101/17/11 shows that by the mid-1320s Beaumaris contained armour for only sixteen men.

18. It has been suggested that the castle may have fallen to the Welsh; see *King's Works*, I, 323. It seems more likely that the reference in a letter of 8 April to a castle having been occupied by the Welsh is to Aberystwyth, which fell on 24 March; see *Calendar of Ancient Correspondence Concerning Wales*, 56. See also Smith, *Llywelyn ap Gruffudd*, 519.

19. *Book of Prests of the King's Wardrobe for 1294–5*, ed. E. B. Fryde (Oxford 1962), xxxv; J. Griffiths, 'Documents relating to the rebellion of Madoc, 1294–5', *Bulletin of the Board of Celtic Studies*, 8 (1935–37), 149–55.

20. Prestwich, *Edward I*, 200 (where castle building is included with the costs of the 1282–83 campaign), 225.

21. J. G. Edwards, 'Edward I's castle-building in Wales', *Proceedings of the British Academy*, 32 (1946), 62–63, 66–73; *King's Works*, II, 1027–28.

22. M. W. Beresford, *New Towns of the Middle Ages: Town Plantation in England, Wales and Gascony* (London 1967), 187.

23. J. Given, 'The economic consequences of the English conquest of Gwynedd', *Speculum*, 64 (1989), 11–45: 21; Beresford, *New Towns*, 46, 550.

24. Davies, *Conquest, Coexistence and Change*, 360.

25. Smith, 473–74; *King's Works*, I, 323, 353, 377; A. J. Taylor, *Caernarvon Castle and Town Walls*, 2nd edn (London 1969), 41.

26. *King's Works*, I, 318, 324, 372.

27. Davies, *Conquest, Coexistence and Change*, 360.

28. *King's Works*, I, 369–71.

29. A. Wheatley, *The Idea of the Castle in Medieval England* (Woodbridge 2004), 112–40.

30. I am very grateful to Deirdre Mortimer for this suggestion, which derives from her discussions with Christopher Norton. Edward had been in York in 1284 for the translation of the body of St William of York, and the consecration of Anthony Bek as bishop of Durham. The parallel to York is noted by M. Fradley, 'Space and structure at Caernarfon Castle', *Medieval Archaeology*, 50 (2006), 165–78: 165.

31. Prestwich, *Edward I*, 120.

32. *King's Works*, I, 388; Taylor, *Caernarvon Castle and Town Walls*, 20–21, where the possibility that the eagles echoed the arms of the count of Savoy is discussed.

33. *King's Works*, I, 352, 367, 389.

34. *Calendar of Various Chancery Rolls 1277–1326* (London 1912), 291.

35. *Calendar of Patent Rolls, 1381–85*, 183; ibid., *1389–91*, 419; ibid., *1391–96*, 208, 501.

36. R. R. Davies, *The Revolt of Owain Glyn Dŵr* (Oxford 1995), 103, 116–17, 236.

37. *Proceedings and Ordinances of the Privy Council of England*, ed. N. H. Nicolas, III (London 1834), 81.

2

From Llywelyn ap Gruffudd to Edward I: Expansionist Rulers and Welsh Society in Thirteenth-Century Gwynedd

David Stephenson

The castles that Edward I caused to be built in central and north Wales in the aftermath of the wars of 1277, 1282–83 and 1294–95 were the most spectacular part of a more general scheme for the control of the conquered territories. That scheme embraced in addition the establishment of the fortified boroughs sheltered by the new castles as well as by their own impressive walls and towers. It involved, at the highest levels of government, a new structure of administration and the dispensing of favours, rewards for service in the cause of conquest. At the head of the list of recipients of such rewards were of course many of the great figures of the English baronage. But the rewards were not confined to men of such exalted rank, nor were they confined to Englishmen. Welsh magnates who had sided with Edward, men such as Gruffudd ap Gwenwynwyn of southern Powys, and, for a time, Rhys ap Maredudd of Ystrad Tywi, also shared the fruits of the king's victory.

Sometimes the beneficiaries of Edward's combination of largesse and political realism were representatives of the burgeoning ministerial aristocracy that had developed in Gwynedd in the thirteenth century. Gruffudd ap Tudur, the son of one of Llywelyn ap Gruffudd's most prominent courtiers in the late 1240s and the 1250s, appears as constable of Dolwyddelan after 1284, a post for which he received 40 marks per year. His brother Tudur Fychan was granted the town of Nantmawr for life in 1284 and in 1290 received an additional grant of £20 for his good service to the king.[1] A significant number of members of the most famous of the ministerial lineages, the descendants of Ednyfed Fychan, were also associated with the king's administration in the years after conquest.[2]

On occasion, the terms in which the king's will was expressed betray something of the tensions which must often have lain behind the distribution of rewards: Ednyfed ap Goronwy, for example, was to have a bailiwick in place of someone who had not served Edward I.[3] We should recall, of course, that Edward's administration was not simply marked by generosity. Those who had opposed the king often had to face the forfeiture of their lands and of any prospects of royal favour in the future. Amongst those who died against the king's peace was Goronwy ap Heilyn, once a courtier of Llywelyn ap Gruffudd, subsequently a royal servant and finally, as the prince's steward, one of the band of die-hards who were with Dafydd ap Gruffudd in the desperate days of 1283. Goronwy's lands escheated upon his death and his son, Llywelyn, was imprisoned in Chester Castle for years.[4] As the new Edwardian order of governance was introduced it was perhaps inevitable that in many respects it should prove to be burdensome. By the early 1290s the sheriffs of the three shires of Gwynedd west of the Conwy were reporting significant arrears in payment of rents 'on account of the poverty of the landholders'. The situation was then seriously exacerbated by the collection in 1292–93 of the lay subsidy of a fifteenth of movable property, which had been requested by the king in 1291.[5] The collection of the fifteenth seems to have been the final factor that drove the Welsh of north Wales to the great revolt of 1294–95 under the leadership of Madog ap Llywelyn. As we shall see, however, the population of Gwynedd had had experience of exorbitant financial demands before the Edwardian conquest.

Edwardian government might on occasion be heavy handed; it also appeared, in many respects, to be novel. Thus established offices within the commote or *cantref*, such as those of *rhaglaw* and *rhingyll*, remained and were filled overwhelmingly by Welshmen, often themselves drawn from families with a history of service to the native princes. But above those offices a new hierarchy of officials was imposed. These included, in Gwynedd west of the Conwy, the sheriffs of the newly created shires of Anglesey, Caernarvon, and Merioneth. At the very summit of the administration were to be found the justiciar of north Wales, the treasurer, the chamberlain and the controller, all based at Caernarfon. For the whole of Edward's reign these offices were filled, almost entirely, by non-Welshmen.[6] If the senior offices of the principality were symbols of an alien regime so too in general were the new boroughs, particularly after the revolt of 1294–95. Ordinances apparently issued after that date stipulated that no Welshman was to reside in the English boroughs of north Wales; no Welshman was to trade outside those boroughs, and no Welshman was to carry arms within them.[7]

And yet for all the novelty of the Edwardian structure, there were strong links to the past. Even the office of justiciar of north Wales evoked the memory of the principal officer of the native princes, the *distain*. This officer had on occasion under Llywelyn ap Gruffudd styled himself *Justiciarius* and it was this office that was recalled in 1305 when Prince Edward's council referred to '*sustentatio hospicii Principis vel Justiciarii sui qui est loco destein*'.[8] Again, Llywelyn had had his treasurer and his chamberlain.[9] The people of Llywelyn's principality, moreover, had become used to change and, sometimes, rapid change, in the course of the century and more before the Edwardian conquest. At the highest level of the polity, not only had new officials appeared in the prince's court, but old offices had developed new functions. The foremost local official of the prince, the *rhaglaw*, had replaced the earlier officers known as the *maer* and the *canghellor*, whose titles survived only occasionally, in fossilized form, in the records of post-conquest administration.[10] The field of law and legal administration had seen constant change, as exemplified in the comment of a witness before Edward I's enquiry into the use of the laws of Hywel Dda in 1281 that Prince Dafydd ap Llywelyn had abolished *galanas* – kin compensation for killing – throughout north Wales. It seemed, said the witness, to the prince and his council that responsibility for the offence should lie with the perpetrator rather than with others who had not offended, as had been the case with the collection of *galanas*.[11] And in the case of the obligations imposed by the prince upon both laity and clerics, the records of the final third of the thirteenth century abound with reports of the inventiveness of Llywelyn ap Gruffudd and his advisers.

Like Edward I, Llywelyn ap Gruffudd had been a conqueror and had behaved like one. He had made himself supreme in Gwynedd by overcoming his rivals and his adversaries – amongst them the young Edward himself. He had extended his control over much of Wales by means of force. In the process many of his compatriots had suffered.[12] Like Edward I Llywelyn had developed an apparatus of control and exploitation. Even the lay subsidy collected in 1292–93 seems to have been foreshadowed by fiscal innovations associated with Llywelyn. Bishop Anian

of St Asaph reported, probably in 1275, that Llywelyn had levied a tax of 3d. on each head of cattle and other animals at his pleasure throughout his dominions. Here we see an indication that Llywelyn was beginning to tax on the basis of goods rather than lands: this was a point picked up in the grievances of the community of Gwynedd against the former prince in 1283.[13]

In many other respects Llywelyn's efforts seem to foreshadow those of Edward I. For instance, it suited Edward's purpose to commute obligations in kind into cash payments, and post-conquest records make it clear that this process developed rapidly after 1284. But it is also clear that commutation of renders was no new phenomenon of the Edwardian period. Particularly in areas where renders in kind were not required by the itinerant court of the prince, commutation was far advanced by 1282.[14] Again like Edward, Llywelyn understood the importance of rewarding service. Even those members of the community of Gwynedd who were loud in their condemnation of his rule in 1283 admitted that he had been capable of showing generosity to his entourage and to his subjects.[15] Leading figures in his administration were granted lands on privileged terms, but it seems fairly clear that Llywelyn was unwilling or unable to make such grants as often as his grandfather had done. Professor Beverley Smith has raised the suspicion that Llywelyn ap Gruffudd's endowments may have been grudgingly made.[16] It seems indeed that Llywelyn's rule was more often characterized by the forceful assertion of power than by a widespread distribution of patronage.

Llywelyn was associated with the development of stone castles in Wales. These were, it has been well established, usually sited in locations quite separate from the old demesne centres, unlike many earlier earth-and-timber structures. He was possibly the founder of Ewloe in the territory facing Chester, whilst in the fastnesses of Gwynedd he refashioned others including Castell y Bere and Cricieth and, possibly, Carndochan.[17] This list is surely not exhaustive. Beyond Gwynedd he built Dolforwyn in Cedewain in the 1270s, and was probably responsible for adding to Castell Bryn Amlwg at the junction of the lordships of Ceri, Maelienydd and Clun, and for building Rhyd-y-briw, Sennybridge, in Brecon.[18] Elsewhere lords closely associated with Llywelyn's rule also engaged in castle building or development. Thus, his staunchest lieutenant, Gruffudd ap Madog of northern Powys, constructed one of the most spectacular native castles, at Dinas Brân above the Dee near Llangollen.[19] The castles, of course, had a military potential but also served a political purpose as symbols of the prince's power and as prisons. Like the castles of Edward I they were part of an apparatus of control. Thus in 1259 Maredudd ap

Rhys of Deheubarth was incarcerated in Cricieth whilst Llywelyn's brother, Owain, was held in a tower, probably that of Dolbadarn, from 1255 until, at the earliest, the end of 1277.[20] Not only prisoners, but also valuables might be lodged in the castles – as in the case of the use of Dolwyddelan for storing Llywelyn's treasure.[21] Castles acted as relatively safe, comfortable and, certainly, prestigious places at which the prince and his entourage might rest, entertain and conduct business. It is clear that the decline of the old *llysoedd* or courts that is evident in the late thirteenth and early fourteenth centuries was already under way in some instances in the pre-conquest period. This process may be exemplified by the case of Dolbenmaen, possibly replaced in most respects by Cricieth Castle in the course of the thirteenth century.[22] Llywelyn's itinerary included not only *llysoedd*, but also stone castles and the granges of the generally supportive Cistercian abbeys. What is perhaps particularly striking is that a prince with the aspirations and evident pride of Llywelyn ap Gruffudd was not responsible for raising more stone castles, particularly in the period of his ascendancy in Wales, from the early 1260s through to the mid-1270s. There is perhaps an implication here that he limited his castle building in view of other calls upon his finances.

There is little sign that Llywelyn stinted himself in the development of effective field armies. We know that he had siege engines at his disposal. He was able to destroy castles such as Gilbert de Clare's first structure at Caerphilly, whilst in the middle March the castle of Knucklas surrendered when it was approached by Llywelyn's men, 'for fear of the siege engines'.[23] And if Llywelyn's ambitions involved his forces in pitched battles, he had also made great efforts to be well prepared. He had developed an effective force of cavalry: in 1260 we hear of 240 horses both armoured and uncovered and, in 1263, the bishop of Hereford reports the appearance in the March of Llywelyn at the head of 300 cavalry and a mass of foot soldiers.[24] Not all of Llywelyn's military successes were the result of simple force. We learn, for example, in 1260 that 'three English lookouts who were keeping the castle of Builth handed it over to the men of the Lord Llywelyn ap Gruffudd shortly before dawn for a great sum of money'.[25] As in many contemporary military campaigns bribery had its place in Llywelyn's advance through Wales. And sometimes bribery took a political rather than a military form. We can perhaps read this between the lines of the comment in *Annales Cambriae* under 1260 that Owain ap Maredudd (of Elfael) came to Llywelyn, who freed his son Madog and gave him £300.[26]

The development of castles, military effectiveness and the extension of lordship all came at a price as did,

notoriously, Llywelyn's quest for royal recognition of his conquests. In 1257 he offered Henry III £1,000 for a seven-year truce or £3,000 for a permanent peace. By 1259 he had increased the offer to £16,000 (payable over eighty years) for a permanent peace and recognition of his conquests. In 1265 his agreement with even a desperate Simon de Montfort involved him in promising 30,000 marks for recognition of his principality of Wales, whilst two years later in the Treaty of Montgomery Llywelyn accepted an obligation to pay Henry III 25,000 marks within a decade for a similar recognition. In 1270 Llywelyn added a further 5,000 marks to his obligation in order to purchase the homage of Maredudd ap Rhys of Deheubarth, the one Welsh ruler who had been excepted from the 1267 agreement.[27]

We may well ask how Llywelyn contrived to meet these very significant demands upon his resources. The agreements that he made with them make it clear that members of the ruling houses of Wales who made common cause with the prince or who accepted his leadership were expected to help him in his military designs, as do entries in the Welsh chronicles.[28] We have already seen that his lordly lieutenants built or developed castles that served his purposes as much as theirs. And his armies must frequently have been composed of troops drawn from the lands of, and funded by, the lords of Powys, Deheubarth and the middle March. We do not know how far such lords were compelled in addition to pay tribute. We may perhaps catch a glimpse of possible obligations to the prince when Gruffudd ap Madog of Bromfield, granting Maelor Saesneg to his wife, Emma, for her life, probably about 1268, stipulates that the land may not be withdrawn from the 'lord of Wales'.[29]

From his own dominions he could, of course, rely upon traditional renders, most of which had originally been assessed in kind but had, in some instances, been commuted into cash payments by the later thirteenth century. These included the various food renders due from freemen and the bond population and the circuit dues (*cylchoedd*) of the household, the huntsman, the falconers and so forth. Then there were revenues such as *amobr*, the payment to a lord upon a woman's marriage or loss of virginity, *ebediw*, a form of death duty, or the investiture fee known as *gobr estyn*.[30] To such traditional dues may be added a growing range of market tolls. We have already noted that novel exactions such as the 1275 levy on cattle and other beasts were being introduced. A source of revenue that was of great – and literally incalculable – importance was constituted by the profits of justice. From the limited evidence available it is clear that penalties in cash rather than in kind were on the increase in the thirteenth century and that they were not insubstantial. Offences such as theft or receiving stolen goods might involve fines of £1 5s. or £1 10s. whilst other misdeeds – or vindictive, rapacious or pressurized officials – might give rise to fines of £5, £6 or even more.[31] It would not take many such offences to meet the building costs of Dolforwyn which in the year 1273–74 apparently amounted to £174 6s. 8d., a surprisingly low figure that suggests that the obligation of the bond, and perhaps even the free, community to provide unpaid labour was being exploited and extended.[32] At the top end of the scale were the *douceurs* that might be extended to the prince in order to obtain a hearing in his court. Thus, presumably not long after 1262, Owain ap Madog ap Gruffudd, who claimed membership of the ruling house of Cedewain, offered the prince 300 marks to hear his claim to the lordship of the *cantref*. His later claim to Cedewain before Edward I's justices after 1277 turned in part on the question of whether Llywelyn had told him that he had no right to the lordship or – as argued by Owain – the prince had merely told him that he would do nothing for him. At any rate, the claim in the prince's court failed and Llywelyn retained Cedewain for himself.[33] It was a valuable territory in which he would later build Dolforwyn Castle and an adjacent borough. For many, Llywelyn's castle must have symbolized far more than simply a determination to counter the royal castle and borough of Montgomery.

Yet another source of revenue was constituted by confiscations or fines for disloyalty. Thus in December 1281 Rhys ap Gruffudd, a grandson of Ednyfed Fychan, was forced to acknowledge his obligation to pay Llywelyn £100 whenever he was required to do so. It was the price of obtaining the prince's goodwill following some act of disobedience and contempt that Rhys had shown to Llywelyn at the court of Aberffraw.[34] And when it was discovered that Llywelyn's brother, Dafydd, had conspired with Gruffudd ap Gwenwynwyn of southern Powys against Llywelyn's life in 1274, both men were forced to flee into England. The result was that Dafydd lost extensive territories in Gwynedd east of the Conwy and Gruffudd lost his large lordship of southern Powys, the value of which will be considered a little later.[35]

There is every possibility that the conspirators of 1274 may have believed that the assassination of Llywelyn ap Gruffudd would be well received by many of his countrymen. The admittedly limited body of evidence gives the strong impression that the burdens of governance grew heavier in the principate of Llywelyn ap Gruffudd. The most striking instance of this is the collection of *Gravamina* against the late prince put forward by those purporting to represent the community of Gwynedd assembled before the bishop of Bangor in 1283. The grievances expressed were wide ranging. They covered,

inter alia, an increase in the number of local officials, novel exactions in cash and increased exactions in kind – some of these linked to increases in the volume of measures used in the assessment of renders. Also mentioned are heavier obligations of service, such as the duty to provide horses for carrying the prince's goods, the seizure of lands, a rapacious attitude towards rights of wreck involving novel and oppressive interpretation of the traditional rules governing the prince's rights. The prince was also accused of having obscured the distinction between the free and bond population in the interests of exacting more revenue and service.[36] Some of these complaints can be corroborated from other evidence. For example, one of them seems to relate to the bishop of St Asaph's 1275 report of Llywelyn's levy of 3d. on each head of cattle. Again, the allegation relating to the change in measures seems to be reflected in post-conquest references, such as that in the 1284 Extent of Anglesey to the *cranoca Lewelini*.[37] It is likely that the articles relating to the confusion of bond and free status reflect a process that was particularly resented by the more substantial members of Venedotian society, and for many of these the end of Llywelyn's rule may have come as a relief. We must be cautious in accepting these and other complaints as faithful representations of the nature of Llywelyn's governance and its impact.[38] But, even when allowances for special pleading, exaggeration and distortion have been made the accusations remain powerful.

Further evidence of Llywelyn's exactions emerges from an examination of his relationship with ecclesiastical magnates and institutions. Some ecclesiastical protestations are limited to single instances of the prince's alleged oppressions. Thus the abbot of Basingwerk claimed that Llywelyn ab Iorwerth and Dafydd ap Llywelyn had been accustomed to levy food renders for 300 men from the abbey's grange when they came hunting in Penllyn, and took nothing in years when they did not come to hunt. This situation changed under Llywelyn ap Gruffudd who levied dues for 500 men and in addition took two yearling foals; furthermore in years when he did not come to hunt he took money in lieu of the food render. Again, the abbot of Basingwerk protested to the bishop of St Asaph that Llywelyn ap Gruffudd had allowed some of his men to make significant encroachments upon the lands of the abbey '*accepta magna pecunie summa*'.[39] This was not apparently a unique occurrence. It seems probable that Llywelyn's relationships with perhaps the most significant representatives of ecclesiastical authority in Gwynedd, the bishops of Bangor and St Asaph, were marked by a conciliatory attitude on the prince's part during the early years of his rule. Important agreements were reached with both of them at the start of the 1260s, though the fact that there were significant matters to be resolved was perhaps ominous.[40] In subsequent years Llywelyn's relationship with the bishops was frequently strained. By the spring of 1269 Llywelyn was ordering his bailiffs in the *Perfeddwlad* (the Four Cantrefs) to respect the rights of the bishop of St Asaph: it is possible that by this date the prince's officials were feeling the pressure of their master's demands.[41] It is in the statements of grievances against the prince issued by Anian II of St Asaph in late 1274 and 1276 that we can glimpse the extent to which Llywelyn was alleged to have trespassed upon episcopal rights. In article after article the prince is accused of ruthlessly extending his capacity to exact money and goods. In some instances he may indeed have acted in accordance with the precepts of law books constructed long before he came to power. But the explicit accusations that he had acted contrary to the ordinances of earlier rulers and that he had ignored episcopal rights derived from old and hitherto accepted custom have considerable cumulative force.[42] Regarding one important topic, namely the sharing of fines between princely and episcopal authorities, particularly in cases of theft by an episcopal tenant, the bishop was able to present, in furtherance of his case, a formidable array of supporting evidence. Cases indicating adherence to a traditional practice of sharing fines and penalties in kind were cited in 1274 from the years of Llywelyn ab Iorwerth, Dafydd ap Llywelyn, the period when Henry III controlled Gwynedd east of the Conwy, and even from the principate of Llywelyn ap Gruffudd himself up to, it seems, the early 1270s.[43] The implication is that Llywelyn's conduct had changed relatively recently. Detailed analysis of the nature and magnitude of the penalties recorded in the cases cited points, firstly, to the conclusion that an important stage in the availability of cash in eastern Gwynedd had been reached by the 1240s, when cash fines rather than seizures of goods begin to predominate. It suggests, secondly, that in the period up to the early 1270s the level of fines exacted under Llywelyn ap Gruffudd was not unusually exorbitant. Indeed, fines exacted in the period of English control of Gwynedd east of the Conwy, from the mid-1240s to the mid-1250s, seem to have been particularly heavy.[44] By the early 1270s Llywelyn's governance may have been heavy handed, but it seems that there may still have been scope for an intensification of the pressure.

Until 1267 Llywelyn's policies – military, political and diplomatic – had been costly but not, perhaps, ruinous. With his acceptance of the obligation to pay to the English government at least 25,000 marks within eight years, he may have committed himself to more than his principality could bear. This has been the contention of most commentators. Keith Williams-Jones believed that 'to support his pretensions, Llywelyn II required a firmer

economic base for his principality' and, more tartly, he criticized Llywelyn's 'over-weaning ambition and ill-conceived policies'; the prince had 'grossly over-estimated his fiscal resources'.[45] This approach has in essence been followed, but expressed in more cautious terms, by Professor Beverley Smith who notes that Llywelyn began to default on his payments at the end of 1270 and that he defaulted altogether after late 1272. He raises the possibility that 'Llywelyn's failure to deliver the money was due, less to any desire to withhold payment on an issue of principle, than to the fact that he faced a financial crisis which made it difficult for him to meet his obligations'.[46]

I have taken, and still take, a more optimistic view of Llywelyn's capacity to fulfil his obligations. This is not the place to review the whole argument, but I would stress that Llywelyn's defaults began at the time when he also started to complain about failures on the English side to honour the Treaty of Montgomery.[47] By the end of 1272 Llywelyn had paid some 15,000 marks out of the 25,000 that he had initially agreed. At this point he was apparently some 5,000 marks in arrears and was therefore incurring financial penalties as specified in the Treaty of Montgomery.[48] He had in 1270 increased his obligation by agreeing to pay an additional 5,000 marks for the homage of Maredudd ap Rhys of Deheubarth. But in the course of negotiations with Edward I in 1274 Llywelyn had made it clear that he would pay all arrears immediately if the king would ensure that the Treaty of Montgomery was observed. In a far more desperate situation at the end of 1276, attempting to stave off an attack by Edward, Llywelyn had promised to pay promptly all arrears and in addition a further 6,000 marks by way of indemnity.[49]

It is indeed difficult to see how Gwynedd alone could have supported such payments. Most analyses of Llywelyn's financial resources concentrate, perhaps inevitably, on his northern territories. Thus Professor Beverley Smith comments that 'the resources of Gwynedd bore the burden of the apparatus of the wider principality' and notes 'his dependence on the resources of his patrimonial land'.[50] But this is to ignore the fact that from the early 1260s onwards Llywelyn possessed very extensive territories in mid-Wales: Gwerthrynion, Builth, Brecon, Cedewain and part of Ceri as well as part of Elfael.[51] He had also made encroachments into the Shropshire March, into the bishop of Hereford's large manor of Lydbury North, and into the fitz Alan territory of Temsiter.[52] Between 1258 and 1263 and again between 1274 and late 1276 he controlled the large lordship of southern Powys.[53]

It is difficult to establish exactly how valuable these territories were. We do not possess the same sort of detailed post-conquest extents that we have for Gwynedd, but we do have some indications of worth. We have numerous indications that Llywelyn was resolved to exploit his lands in mid-Wales to the utmost. When he visited his new castle of Dolforwyn in 1274, it was reported that he would bear part of the cost of his stay, but in addition each of the bailiffs of Wales was to supply him for two days.[54] Llywelyn kept his officials in those territories apparently under close supervision and there are signs of a dangerous readiness on his part to extort money from leading figures in those lordships.[55] The *Brut* hints at the pressures of his governance when it notes that after the flight of Gruffudd ap Gwenwynwyn from southern Powys at the end of 1274 Llywelyn entered the lordship and installed his own officers.[56]

In the case of southern Powys, the 1293 inquisition post mortem of Owain ap Gruffudd, lord of most of that land, provides an indication of its value to Llywelyn. The inquisition provides similar information in summary form to that obtained earlier in the extents of the lands of Gwynedd and later in those of the lordships of northern Powys. It suggests an ordinary revenue of a little over £215 per year.[57] This does not include lands held by Hawise Lestrange, Owain's mother, in dower, nor does it include a figure for the disputed territory of Gorddwr, the relatively poor commote of Mawddwy or Mochnant uwch Rhaeadr. This last part of the lordship was valued at nearly £16 per year in the inquisition post mortem of Gruffudd ab Owain in 1309 and the lands of Hawise were valued at her death in 1311 at a little over £73 per year.[58] Mawddwy was apparently of little value, though we should recall that it had sustained Gruffudd ap Gwenwynwyn's brother, Madog, in the years around 1263. Gorddwr, when not war torn, was far richer.[59] The 1293 inquisition included revenues from towns, Llanidloes and Machynlleth, which are normally regarded as having developed only after 1277. The inclusion of these sums is perhaps balanced by the absence of those for Gorddwr. In other words, it would not be unreasonable to assume that the annual sums accruing from fixed rents and renders in southern Powys in the second half of the thirteenth century amounted to around £300.

It is worth noting at this point that the post-conquest extents and similar documents are imperfect instruments for gauging the real value to Llywelyn ap Gruffudd of the lands under his control. They do not, for example,

cover the bulk of the profits of justice nor do they cover extraordinary taxation. The value of Anglesey to Edward I recorded in the 1284 extent was a little over £430, but the account of the chamberlain of north Wales for 1305–06 shows a revenue of over £820.[60] 1305–06 was a year when revenues were plentiful but nevertheless the figure shows what was possible. Again, the 1332 extent of the lordship of Chirk gives a total valuation of £137 11s. 7d. for a land that produced, according to Rees Davies's reckoning, an annual income for its lord of over £300 in the 1320s, and was capable of producing much more.[61] By scaling up accordingly the sums already noted in the inquisitions post mortem for southern Powys we may well postulate a real income of some £500–600 per year. It is certainly to be emphasized that lordships such as Brecon, Builth and Cedewain were regarded as valuable commodities. Thus a report on the lordship of Brecon by a royal commissioner in 1302 notes that 'there is a very fine and great lordship in these places which will be worth at least 2,000 marks a year if it is well managed.'[62] They had been eagerly snapped up by Marcher lords in the twelfth and early thirteenth centuries and were snapped up again after the demise of Llywelyn. Even though the prince's hold on some territories such as Brecon had not been unchallenged, it was nevertheless a valuable addition to his resources from the early 1260s to the mid-1270s.[63]

Llywelyn's fiscal capacity in his wider principality was not negligible and the indications are that he knew this and exploited it. His financial needs were felt in territories far beyond Gwynedd and his rule in those territories does not seem to have been an indulgent one. But even if we recognize that Llywelyn was generating a significant income from his wider dominions we cannot assume that he found it at all easy to raise the sums demanded of him, or that those sums were raised without causing great tension and even despair within his principality. Musing on the death of Llywelyn in battle in December 1282, the Welsh chronicle *Brenhinedd y Saesson* considered that 'Wales was then cast to the ground'.[64] But though some might on occasion revolt, and some might petition for redress, the people of Wales generally endured, and in some cases profited from, the post-conquest regime. They had in significant measure been taught to do this by Llywelyn ap Gruffudd.

Notes

1. *Calendar of Various Chancery Rolls, 1277–1326* (London 1912), 288–89, 324–25.
2. D. Stephenson, *The Governance of Gwynedd* (Cardiff 1984), 106 n. 53, 127, 218.
3. *Calendar of Various Chancery Rolls,* 176.
4. Stephenson, *Governance,* 214; *The Survey of the Honour of Denbigh, 1334,* ed. P. Vinogradoff and F. Morgan (London 1914), 297; J. B. Smith, *Llywelyn ap Gruffudd, Prince of Wales* (Cardiff 1998), 577 and n. 228.

5. *The Merioneth Lay Subsidy Roll, 1292–3*, ed. K. Williams-Jones (Cardiff 1976), xxiv–xxxv, esp. xxxi.

6. W. H. Waters, *The Edwardian Settlement of North Wales in its Administrative and Legal Aspects (1284–1343)* (Cardiff 1935), 25 and 171–75.

7. *Registrum Vulgariter Nuncupatum 'The Record of Caernarvon'*, ed. H. Ellis (London 1838), 131–32.

8. ibid., 213.

9. Stephenson, *Governance*, 20–23.

10. See for example *Record of Caernarvon*, 215.

11. *Calendar of Various Chancery Rolls*, 199.

12. For a specific case of particular interest see D. Stephenson, 'The Arwystli Case', *Montgomeryshire Collections*, 94 (2006), 1–13: 6.

13. *A Calendar of Ancient Correspondence Concerning Wales*, ed. J. G. Edwards (Cardiff 1935), 105; Ll. B. Smith, 'The *Gravamina* of the community of Gwynedd against Llywelyn ap Gruffudd', *Bulletin of the Board of Celtic Studies*, 31(1984–85), 158–76: see especially articles XIII and XXIII.

14. See Stephenson, *Governance*, 64–69; Smith, *Llywelyn ap Gruffudd*, 241–46.

15. Smith, '*Gravamina*', 174 (article VI).

16. Smith, *Llywelyn ap Gruffudd*, 263.

17. ibid., 252 and n. 288.

18. On Bryn Amlwg see L. Alcock, D. J. C. King, W. G. Putnam and C. J. Spurgeon, 'Excavations at Castell Bryn Amlwg', *Montgomeryshire Collections*, 60 (1967–68), 8–27, at 25; D. Stephenson, 'Llywelyn the Great, the Shropshire March and the building of Montgomery Castle', *Shropshire History and Archaeology*, 80 (2005), 52–58. For Rhyd-y-briw see Smith, *Llywelyn ap Gruffudd*, 416–17, n. 99.

19. D. Stephenson, '*Potens et prudens*: Gruffudd ap Madog, Lord of Bromfield 1236–1269', *Welsh History Review*, 22 (2005), 409–31, at 427–28.

20. *Annales Cambriae*, ed. J. Williams ab Ithel (Rolls Series XX, London 1860), 97; Smith, *Llywelyn ap Gruffudd*, 74.

21. ibid., 231 n. 206.

22. D. Longley, 'The royal courts of the Welsh princes of Gwynedd, AD 400–1283', in *Landscape and Settlement in Medieval Wales*, ed. N. Edwards (Oxford 1997), 41–54; N. Johnstone, 'The location of the royal courts of thirteenth-century Gwynedd', ibid., 55–69: 60–61.

23. Smith, *Llywelyn ap Gruffudd*, 351–53; *Annales Cambriae*, 100.

24. *Calendar of Ancient Correspondence*, 15–16.

25. *Annales Cambriae*, 98.

26. ibid.

27. *The Acts of Welsh Rulers 1120–1283*, ed. H. Pryce (Cardiff 2005), nos 327, 330, 338 and 363; Smith, *Llywelyn ap Gruffudd*, 364.

28. *Brut y Tywysogyon, or The Chronicle of the Princes. Red Book of Hergest Version*, ed. T. Jones (Cardiff 1955), 247, 249, 251; *Annales Cambriae*, 96 and 100, *Calendar of Ancient Correspondence*, 52.

29. *Acts of Welsh Rulers*, no. 515.

30. For the range of dues available to the princes see Stephenson, *Governance*, 64–94.

31. ibid., 83–85; H. Pryce, *Native Law and the Church in Medieval Wales* (Oxford 1993), 224–29.

32. *Littere Wallie*, ed. J. G. Edwards (Cardiff 1940), 23–24.

33. *The Welsh Assize Roll, 1277–84*, ed. J. C. Davies (Cardiff 1940), 254–55.

34. *Littere Wallie*, 31.

35. Smith, *Llywelyn ap Gruffudd*, 373–74.

36. ibid., 259.

37. ibid., 256 n. 305.

38. ibid., 267, 271.

39. *Calendar of Inquisitions, Miscellaneous*, I, no. 1357; *Councils and Ecclesiastical Documents relating to Great Britain and Ireland*, ed. A. W. Haddan and W. Stubbs, I (Oxford 1869), 515.

40. Stephenson, *Governance*, 172; *Acts of Welsh Rulers*, nos 345–46.

41. ibid., no. 369.

42. *Councils and Ecclesiastical Documents*, 491–92, 511–16.

43. National Library of Wales, Peniarth Ms. 231B, 116–125. Five cases, on 123, relate to the early episcopate of Anian II, which began in 1268.

44. ibid., 123–24.

45. *Merioneth Lay Subsidy Roll*, xvii–xix.

46. Smith, *Llywelyn ap Gruffudd*, 364.

47. *Acts of Welsh Rulers*, nos 372 (before 24 July 1270); 373 (before 13 October 1270); 375 (November 1271). Llywelyn had complained bitterly about the conduct of Gilbert de Clare in December 1267 but agreement was reached in September 1268: ibid., nos 365–66. See R. R. Davies, *Conquest, Coexistence and Change: Wales 1063–1415* (Oxford 1987), reprinted in paperback as *The Age of Conquest: Wales 1063–1415* (Oxford 1991), 322–23.

48. Smith, *Llywelyn ap Gruffudd*, 364 n. 91; *Littere Wallie*, li n.1.

49. *Acts of Welsh Rulers*, nos 380, 398.

50. Smith, *Llywelyn ap Gruffudd*, 251 (but cf. 295).

51. ibid., 125–27, 141, 150; *Acts of Welsh Rulers* no. 364; D. Stephenson 'The lordship of Ceri in the thirteenth century', *Montgomeryshire Collections*, 95 (2007), 23–31. A study by the author of Cedewain in the twelfth and thirteenth centuries is currently in progress.

52. *Acts of Welsh Rulers*, no. 365; *Calendar of Inquisitions Post Mortem*, I, no. 812; *Registrum Thome de Cantilupo Episcopi Herefordensis*, introduced by W. W. Capes (London 1907), 9, 10, 29.

53. D. Stephenson, 'The politics of Powys Wenwynwyn in the thirteenth century', *Cambridge Medieval Celtic Studies*, 7 (1984), 39–61.

54. *Calendar of Ancient Correspondence*, 49.

55. See for examples *Littere Wallie*, 24, 26, 28, 30, 33, 35, 41–42, 44, 126.

56. *Brut y Tywysogyon, Red Book of Hergest*, 262–63.

57. G. T. O. Bridgeman, 'The princes of upper Powys', *Montgomeryshire Collections*, 1 (1868), 5–194: 142–48.

58. ibid., 159–60; the inquisition post mortem of Hawise is at 166–68.

59. For Mawddwy, see *Acts of Welsh Rulers* no. 358 (clause 11), and for Gorddwr, the discussion by R. Morgan, 'The territorial divisions of medieval Montgomeryshire', *Montgomeryshire Collections*, 69 (1981), 9–44: 38–44, and ibid., 70 (1982), 11–39: 11–22.

60. A. D. Carr, *Medieval Anglesey* (Llangefni 1982), 88.

61. *The Extent of Chirkland 1391–1399*, ed. G. P. Jones (Liverpool 1933), 90–91; Davies, *Conquest, Coexistence and Change*, 403 and idem, *Lordship and Society in the March of Wales 1282–1400* (Oxford 1978), 143.

62. Davies, *Lordship and Society*, 92.

63. Davies, *Conquest, Coexistence and Change*, 321–22.

64. *Brenhinedd y Saesson*, ed. T. Jones (Cardiff 1971), 258–59.

3

Gwynedd Before and After the Conquest

David Longley

The kingdom of Gwynedd during the earlier medieval centuries was, more often than not, a significant entity in the endemic political jostling of Welsh politics. In the early sixth century, Maelgwn Gwynedd was singled out by Gildas as one of the most powerful if not the most powerful of the kings of western Britain. Cadfan's seventh-century epitaph describes the ruler as the wisest and most renowned of all kings. Rhodri, in the tenth century, was one of the very few kings to be styled 'Great'. He had, before his death, extended the boundaries of his kingdom to Ceredigion in the south and close to Offa's Dyke in the east. Gruffudd ap Llywelyn went a few steps further. Harassing the borders of England, he was recognized as the undisputed overlord of almost all the Welsh territories. His death in 1063, at the hands of his own men in the war of Harold Godwinson,[1] and the success of William of Normandy, changed the situation dramatically.

With the establishment of a palatine earldom in the northern march at Chester, Earl Hugh and his *magister militum*, Robert, extended Norman control along the north Wales coast during the 1070s and 1080s. By 1086 Robert held Rhos and Rhufoniog in fee from King William. Robert is also described as holding 'North Wales' directly from the king at farm for £40.[2] The implication is that lands west of the Conwy were also in Norman hands by that date. An indication of the extent of the Norman hold on Gwynedd, quite apart from a string of earthwork castles running from Rhuddlan to Aberlleiniog on Anglesey, is that the revenues of two Anglesey manors and fishing rights in the Menai Strait could be diverted to support the building works at St Werburgh's, Chester, in 1093.[3]

During the maelstrom of the late eleventh century, Gruffudd ap Cynan, a legitimate claimant to the throne of Gwynedd, born and brought up in exile at the Viking court at Dublin, now sought to regain his inheritance. Almost at the point of Gwynedd's eclipse, Gruffudd's campaign succeeded in breaking the Norman stranglehold, largely through the suspiciously fortuitous intervention of Magnus Barelegs' Viking fleet in the Menai Strait.[4] By 1100 the Normans had been pushed back east of the Conwy and during the last thirty-eight years of his long life Gruffudd succeeded, through skilful diplomacy, in establishing a stable foundation for expansion and administrative reform. Gruffudd's son, Owain, built on his father's success. The pattern of royal administration that characterizes the last century and a half of Gwynedd's independence may, very possibly, be a product of Owain Gwynedd's achievement.

A very schematic presentation of the hierarchical association of different components in the administrative landscape is presented in the various redactions of the 'Law of Hywel Dda'. These do not constitute the promulgation of law; they represent jurists' test-case illustrations of an ideal scenario against which real-life situations could be judged. The redaction which most closely reflects the north Wales experience is the thirteenth-century 'Llyfr Iorwerth'.[5] The framework of Llyfr Iorwerth, albeit superficially schematic, nevertheless reflects a pattern identifiable in several areas of the Gwynedd landscape and deserves closer consideration.

We begin with the concept of the *cantref*, literally one hundred townships. The term township (*tref*) might originally have designated a stake in the soil, a homestead, but by the twelfth and thirteenth centuries a township occupied a variable area encompassing individual homesteads and possibly one or more nucleated hamlets. In area, a township might be very broadly equivalent to a later ecclesiastical parish.

The lawbooks identify a division of the *cantref* into two commotes (*cymydau* pl.). The neat schema of two commotes to each *cantref* did not always apply. Nevertheless, in the Anglesey *cantrefi* (pl.) of Cemais, Aberffraw and Rhosyr we meet with textbook conformity.

On the mainland, in Arfon, Arllechwedd and Llŷn, the pattern is familiar and is carried through less formally into Eifionydd, Meirionnydd and Penllyn.

Each theoretical commote is populated by twelve *maenolau* (pl.). A *maenol* defines a dynastic territorial lordship, with its component parts having strong kinship links. The lawbooks specify four townships (*trefi* pl.) in each *maenol* of perhaps the homestead or hamlet type rather than the larger rural townships referred to above, although there are, exceptionally, *maenolau* that extend across two or three townships. The progeny of Cenythllyn and Dwyrig in the commote of Afloegion on the Llŷn peninsula, for example, had roots in the townships of Ystradgeirch, Bodfel and Llangian.[6]

Where it is possible to judge, the boundaries of Anglesey's commotes seem to have been drawn around the boundaries of pre-existing interests. The boundaries of the commote of Twrcelyn, for example, encompass the lands of the great free *maenolau* of Llysdulas and Bodafon, while at the same time including the king's demesne at Penrhos and the *clas* township of Llaneilian. The northern part of Dindaethwy (north of the Afon Nodwydd) reflects the extent of the freeholding townships of the Mathafarns, Castellbwlchwyn and Llanddyfnan. Similarly, the eccentric boundary of Menai, with its eastward salient on the south side of Cors Dygai, seems to have taken account of the limits of the large *maenol* of Porthamel. On the mainland the administrative geography is a little less mechanistic and the boundaries of commotes are a little more organic in taking their line from landscape features. The *maenolau* comprised an extensive network of farmlands and hamlets. The heads of families within these clan lands might have their own bondmen. In an earlier period the king's '*gwestfa*' or hospitality render would be levied on each *maenol*, but, by the thirteenth century, it would appear that the *maenol* no longer constituted an administrative component in the hierarchy of royal administration and the commuted renders were paid in cash at the *maerdrefi* (pl.).[7]

The jurists' lawbooks are clearly conscious of the numerical implications of their hierarchical division and subdivision of the units of land. Four townships in each *maenol*, twelve *maenolau* in each commote and two commotes in each *cantref* suggest a total of ninety-six townships; four townships short of the ideal of the expected one-hundred-townships in the *cantref*. This is schematic and theoretical of course, but, nevertheless, the lawbooks square the equation by identifying two very distinct settlements in each commote, set aside for the king's use (Fig. 3.1). The king's two townships are, firstly, the king's *maerdref* or, to apply the term loosely, his manorial centre and demesne lands and secondly, the king's *ffriddoedd* (pl.)

or *hafodydd* (pl.); his summer cow-pastures on uncultivated ground (for *ffridd* compare middle English *frith* / old English *fyrhthe, freyth* – 'land overgrown with brushwood, scrubland on the edge of forest').[8] At first reading, the scheme of the lawbooks may seem to have little relevance to real-world situations, identifying as they do a pattern of hierarchical and artificial relationships in the terminology of landholding. On closer observation, however, there is a marked concordance. Anglesey provides the best example in the pattern of *cantrefi* and, more importantly, its six commotes; it may be no coincidence that Anglesey was the core area of Gwynedd's resurgence and expansion during the twelfth century (Fig. 3.2).

Closely corresponding to the precepts of the jurists we may identify a royal *maerdref* in almost every commote, each with several distinctive components that are more or less replicated. At the core of the *maerdref* there would be a royal hall, or halls, provision for the accommodation of guests and the officials and stewards responsible for the operation of the demesne, and for the management of the king's interests in the commote generally. These would include the collection and supervision of rents and dues owed to the king by his bond and free tenants throughout the commote. At the *maerdref* itself there would be a settlement of tied estate workers who held their tenancies under a particularly restrictive bond tenancy *trefgyfrif* or 'register land'. The nature of *trefgyfrif* involved a redistribution of the plots of bond land on the death of the head of a tenant family. This arrangement was conducive to the formation of nucleated hamlets within the royal township. At Aberffraw there were seven such hamlets spread across the *maerdref* lands. Beyond the core there might be occasional enclaves of demesne tenants performing specialized functions as, for example, the half-*gafael* of the prince's tenants operating the ferry boats at Porthaethwy in the commote of Dindaethwy on the Menai Strait.

We now turn to the second component of royal administration identified in the lawbooks: the king's summer pasture lands. Here, the best evidence is to be found on the mainland and, in particular, in the commotes of Arllechwedd Uchaf, Nanconwy, Is and Uwch Gwyrfai and Dinllaen. In the commote of Arllechwedd Uchaf, where the royal *maerdref* is at Aber, the *hafodydd* extend across the high ground in an arc above the valley bottom and mostly, if not entirely, lie within the royal township. In Nanconwy and Is Gwyrfai, on the other hand, the royal pasturelands lie in separate and relatively distant townships. The *ffriddoedd* or *hafodydd* of Nanconwy lie in the township of Dolwyddelan. Ten *hafodydd* range from the valley bottom to the upper slopes on both sides of the Lledr

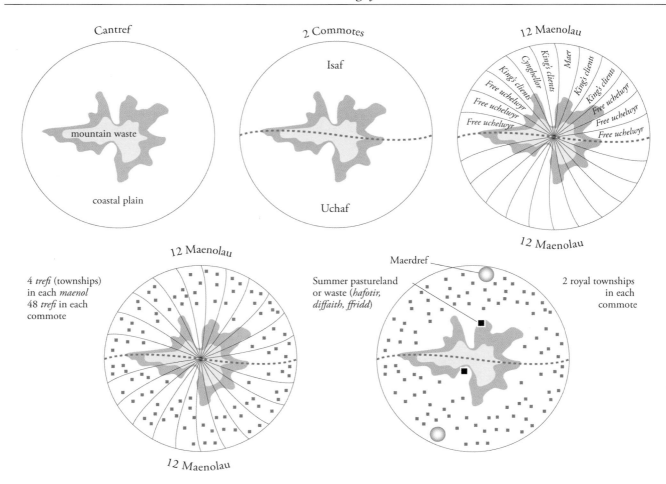

Figure 3.1: Schematic outline of cantrefi, *commotes,* maenolau, *townships (*trefi*) and* maerdrefi *(royal townships) in Llyfr Iorwerth (David Longley).*

valley and extend over 7,500 acres (3,000ha). Llywelyn ab Iorwerth's stone castle at Dolwyddelan was built on one of these *hafodydd* at Ffriddgelli. The *maerdref* of the same commote stood on the left bank of the river Conwy at Trefriw (a corruption of *trefgyfrif*, indicating demesne tenure) some 7 miles (11km) distant (Fig. 3.3).

The *ffridd* of Is Gwyrfai lay across the north-western slopes of Snowdon, within the township of Dolbadarn. In similar fashion, but different style, Llywelyn ab Iorwerth built a round-towered stone castle on the *ffridd* at Dolbadarn on the valley floor between the two lakes of Padarn and Peris. The commotal *maerdref* stood just under 10 miles (16km) to the west on or close to the future site of Edward I's walled town at Caernarfon. The documented *trefgyfrif* bond hamlet of the princes was at Llanbeblig, on the outskirts of Caernarfon, adjacent to the Roman fort at Segontium.

The valley of Nantgwynant, formerly the township of Nanhwynan, lies along a north-east–south-west axis in central Snowdonia, between the valley of the Lledr (Dolwyddelan) and Nant Peris (Dolbadarn). At the southern end of Nanhwynan, there once stood a rectangular stone castle on the rock of Dinas Emrys, a comparable context to the towers of Dolwyddelan and Dolbadarn. The valley with its *hafodydd* was granted to the Cistercian monks of Aberconwy around 1200 by Llywelyn ab Iorwerth. Formerly royal land, this total resource, from the Lledr to Nant Peris, would have constituted a swathe of cow pastures extending for just over 10 miles (16km), unbroken except for the highest slopes of Snowdon and Moel Siabod. These and other *ffriddoedd* in the king's hands were carefully managed resources, operated as cattle ranches on an all-year-round basis rather than simply providing opportunities for summer grazing.

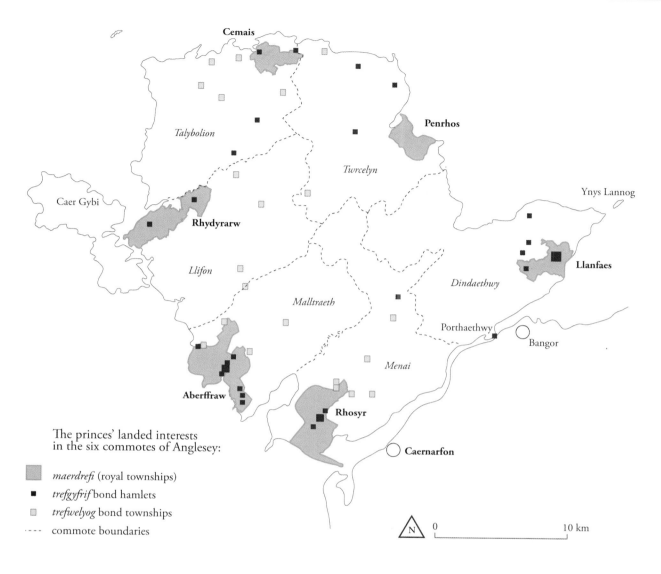

Figure 3.2: The princes' landed interests in the six commotes of Anglesey (David Longley).

It should also be noted that the freeholding clans had access to extensive, but less well-documented, *friddoedd* in the free townships. The detailed sixteenth-century record of Bodfaeo in Arllechwedd Uchaf, in which several lands and acres were said to have been enclosed out of the queen's waste of the Forest of Snowdon, is an exception. The largest of these *friddoedd* extended over an area of 940 acres (380ha) immediately to the south and south-west of the bond *gafael* of Cwm Eigiau in the adjacent commote. Gerald of Wales was surely right in observing that, 'If all the herds in Wales were driven together, the mountains of Snowdonia could supply them with pasture'.[9]

Finally, in each commote there might be certain tenants of the king who held their land on a hereditary basis. Each future generation would expect to inherit his father's house and lands under the rules of partible inheritance, or a share in the inheritance in the case of more than one heir. The name of this tenure is *trefwelyog*. These arrangements are not dissimilar to the inheritance rules applied to freeholders with the exception that the bond *trefwelyog* tenants could not leave the land without the lord's permission. The *gwely* referred to in the tenurial designation *trefwelyog* describes the kinship or lineage interests, or associations, in the land in the way that *tref* defines a stake in soil. By the twelfth and thirteenth centuries the *gwely* had become the regular usage for a

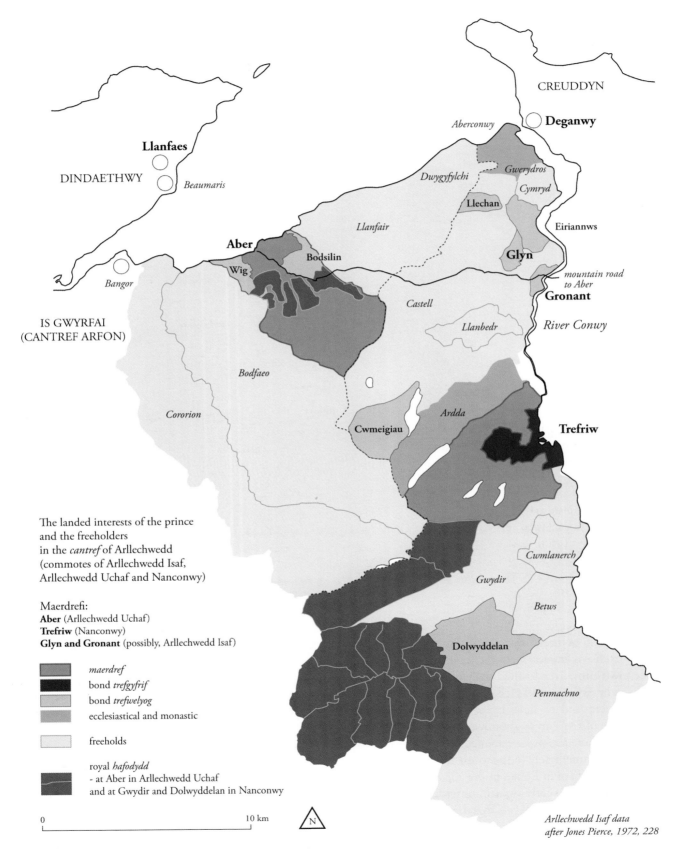

Figure 3.3: Freeholders' landed interests compared with royal interests in the cantref *of Arllechwedd (David Longley).*

subdivision of the *tref* at a time when the boundaries of townships would seem to have become fixed. Partible inheritance ensured that these *gwelyau* of both the bond tenants and the freeholders were further divided into the smallholdings of successive heirs. All were constrained within the township boundaries and taxed at the level of the *gwely*, regardless of the fluctuating number of smallholders within them.[10] In general, bond *trefwelyog* tenancies lie closer to rather than distant from the *maerdref* whereas freeholding townships occupy large tracts of the remainder of commotes, a counterpart to the king's landed interests (Fig. 3.1).

In addition to a royal manorial centre with demesne land adjacent, the nucleated hamlets of tied estate workers, hereditary bond tenants occupying their own smallholdings and extensive tracts of freely held land, there might be alienated land in the tenure of ancient quasi-monastic *clas* communities and communities of the newer pan-European orders, invariably Cistercian. The network of royal commotal centres was convenient in a number of ways. They provided a regional focus at which renders and dues were paid and accommodated the prince and his entourage when on circuit. The retinue could be large; when Llywelyn ab Iorwerth went to hunt in Penllyn, for example, he required maintenance for 300 men. Llywelyn ap Gruffudd took maintenance for 500 men and the cash equivalent if he did not hunt in that year. The peripatetic nature of governance allowed the prince to utilize the resources of each commote and to do business and keep abreast of regional issues.[11]

Charters are known to have been issued from commotal centres and the princes also made use of the facilities and clerical expertise of monastic houses.[12] Every one of the six Anglesey *maerdrefi* was responsible for issuing at least one charter between 1200 and 1283 (if we can accept Rhydyrarw at the estuary of the Alaw as a component of the 'lost' *maerdref* of Llifon). The royal presence at these locations confirms the peripatetic regime of the court. Charters issued by the prince and the royal family are recorded at the mainland *maerdrefi* of Aber, Caernarfon, Nefyn, Ystumanner, Talybont and Bala (Fig. 3.4).

The pattern of administration was not static. During the later thirteenth century stone castles were increasingly resorted to, usurping some of the functions of the traditional *maerdrefi*. By the time of the Edwardian conquest, for example, the traditional rents and dues from the commote of Is Gwyrfai were channelled into the support of Dolbadarn Castle in that commote, rather than to Caernarfon. This pattern is reflected in royal charters issued at Dolbadarn (actually Llanberis), Dolwyddelan and Cricieth Castles in the 1270s and 1280s.

Many of the *maerdrefi* survived into the later thirteenth century, but their role and focus were changing. Aber, in the commote of Arllechwedd Uchaf, continued to operate as a royal palace and it would seem that the prince and his family regularly resorted there right up to the final days of the war of 1282–83. The royal *maerdref* of Arllechwedd Isaf, plausibly thought to have been centred at the townships of Glyn and Gronant in the Conwy valley where the ferry crossed the river at Tal-y-Cafn, had been rendered redundant by the time of the conquest and the dues of the commotal tenants were channelled across the watershed to Aber. Similarly, the *maerdref* of Llifon on Anglesey was defunct before 1284 and the first Edwardian extent of that year accounts for the townships of Llifon within the *cantref* of Aberffraw, rather than the parent commote.

From the beginning of the thirteenth century, the increasing costs of administration and external politics caused the princes to find ways of translating the traditional resources available to them into hard cash. In particular, the rents and dues of the *maerdrefi* of Pwllheli and Nefyn in the commotes of Afloegion and Dinllaen, and Llanfaes in the commote of Dindaethwy were commuted to cash payments. This strategy was particularly successful where the geographical context provided a favourable basis for the development of trade. Llanfaes controlled the northernmost of the Menai ferries and access to the northern coastline of Arllechwedd Isaf, Uchaf and Creuddyn. Its trade was not purely local; its fairs and markets flourished, supplemented by seaborne traffic. Immediately after the conquest it is recorded that around eighty trading ships a year put into the port of Llanfaes.[13] Llanfaes was a proto-town, its urban status confirmed by the establishment of a Franciscan friary on the shoreline there in the late 1230s.[14]

In 1282 Llywelyn ap Gruffudd was killed near Builth and his brother, Dafydd, was captured and executed in 1283, at the culmination of the second of two devastating wars with England. The shire counties of Anglesey, Caernarvon and Merioneth were created across the former kingdom of Gwynedd. Nevertheless, the framework of commotes and the associations of township, hamlet and *gwely* persisted and continued to be useful for administrative purposes into the seventeenth century. In some respects little changed, in others the changes were far reaching and were ultimately, over the longer period, to bring about the fragmentation of the old social geography. The lands in the tenure of Llywelyn ap Gruffudd and the rights, dues and rents owed to him now passed into the hands of the English Crown. At one level this process simply saw a change of landlord. The royal commotal centres lost their administrative status, but continued to

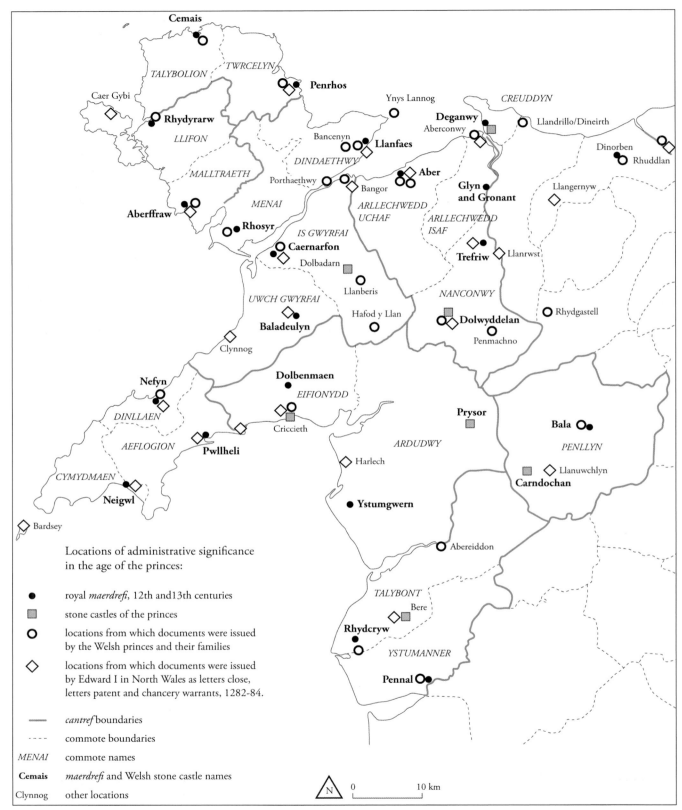

Figure 3.4: Map showing maerdrefi and places where charters were signed by the Gwynedd dynasty in the twelfth and thirteenth centuries (and itinerary of Edward I, in 1283–84). These sites show the location of places of administrative significance (David Longley).

be run on estate lines for the benefit of the Crown and its lessees. The buildings of the *llys* could still be useful and in 1305 the community of Rhosyr petitioned for resources to repair the hall there. A structure occupying a smaller footprint than the fullest extent of the hall complex may represent the last phase of building works at Rhosyr. The published report, however, interprets the feature as a component of the pre-conquest hall (Fig. 3.5).[15]

Elsewhere, on the other hand, royal halls were dismantled and their components reused at a different location. At Ystumgwern, Ardudwy, the hall of the *llys* was removed in its entirety and re-erected in Harlech Castle. At Aberffraw, 198 lengths of good timber, from the hall and other buildings, were taken for building works at Caernarfon in 1317.[16] At Aber, the former *maerdref* of Arllechwedd Uchaf was granted to Sir William Sutton and ceased to be accounted for in Crown rentals. Building accounts, however, record extensive repairs to the hall in 1303–04, which may be the winged hall, excavated immediately adjacent to the earthwork castle there, but not for certain.[17]

Llanfaes, the commercial centre and *maerdref* of the commote of Dindaethwy, suffered a sudden demise in 1295. This followed Madog's rebellion against the exactions of Roger Puleston, Edward's sheriff in Anglesey, in 1294.[18] Edward moved swiftly to establish a new castle at the northern approach to the Menai Strait on the Anglesey side, at the southern boundary of Llanfaes, and to provide alongside it the commercial support of a new town. This was to be Beaumaris. Buildings in Llanfaes had been burnt in 1294 and were not repaired. Beaumaris appropriated the Llanfaes ferry and its trade, and the tenants of Llanfaes were forcefully encouraged to decamp and re-establish their community at a purpose-built location on the demesne of Rhosyr in the commote of Menai. Both communities, as it turned out, prospered. The 'New-borough' at Rhosyr was necessarily a Welsh borough. The new English castle boroughs of Beaumaris, Conwy and Caernarfon were initially English frontier communities populated by incomers from Cheshire and Lancashire, many of whom were to make a significant impact on their adopted towns.[19]

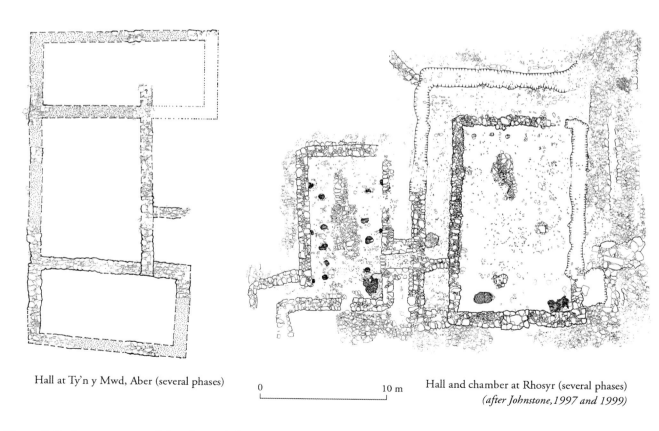

Hall at Ty'n y Mwd, Aber (several phases)

0   10 m

Hall and chamber at Rhosyr (several phases)
(after Johnstone, 1997 and 1999)

Figure 3.5: A comparison of the plans of the excavated halls at the last phase of use at the maerdrefi *of Rhosyr and Aber (David Longley).*

In time, asset stripping was to transform the traditional social landscape. An example is the dislocation of those former bond townships within which lay extensive *ffriddoedd* and the separation of the *ffriddoedd* from the townships. During the fourteenth century, inquisitions '*in quo warranto*', confirmed and defined rights in respect of the former royal *ffriddoedd*, which had been transferred to petitioners of the royal interest. In Merioneth, Walter de Mauny, constable of Harlech Castle and sheriff of Merioneth, claimed the fee-farm of Harlech and Bala together with other perquisites including the *hafodydd* of Ystumanner, Talybont, Ardudwy and Penllyn. A similar pattern is seen in the new county of Caernarvon. By 1338, Walter de Mauny had also been granted the manor of Aber, which brought with it the *ffriddoedd* of Arllechwedd Uchaf.[20] Thomas Missenden claimed the *hafodydd* of Uwch and Is Gwyrfai, Eifionydd and Llŷn; Robert Pollard, chamberlain, held Bryntyrch in Gwydir, and John Chirbury had the *ffriddoedd* of Dolwyddelan in Nanconwy. These fee-farms, often divorced from townships within which they lay, were leased for their revenue value to English and foreign petitioners. During the fifteenth century however, locally based prominent Welshmen began to acquire such leases in the Conwy valley, Penllyn, Talybont, Nanconwy and Eifionydd. Towards the end of the fifteenth century Maredudd ap Ieuan, ancestor of the Gwydir family, obtained rights in the *ffriddoedd* of Dolwyddelan 'to find elbow room for himself in that waste country among the bondmen'. He took up residence in the castle and may even have made repairs before removing a short distance to Penamnen, 'being the principal best ground' in the township.[21] Maredudd's reach was extensive, with leases, mostly drawn from Crown and monastic land. Maredudd and his descendants set about redefining the nature of 'these barren pastures and mountain'. He improved the economic potential by 'filling every empty tenement with a tenant or two, whereof most was the king's land'.[22] He established smallholdings, occupied on a year-round basis, where no permanent settlement had been seen before. Two generations later, the *ffridd* of Bryntyrch contained 4 acres (1.6ha) of arable, 40 acres (16ha) of moorish ground, meadow and woodland, 'with the commodity of the mountains containing by estimation 600 acres [243ha], but marvellous barren, whereon is built one dwelling house and 5 cottages for cattle'.[23] These tenants' leases stipulated that substantial slate-roofed buildings should be erected, enclosed with walls, ditches and quick-set hedges.[24]

The sixteenth century provided many opportunities for the acquisition of leases in bond townships and monastic lands. For example, the abbey of Aberconwy had leased out tenements in Nanhwynan (Nant Gwynant) and Penmynydd (Dindaethwy) before the dissolution. After 1537 the opportunities increased. On Anglesey the township of Penmon, formerly a part of the landed endowment of Penmon Priory, passed, firstly into the hands of John Moore of Crabbet and, by 1565, to the Bulkeley family of Beaumaris. Similarly, after passing through the hands of Thomas Seymour and John, duke of Northumberland, John Wyn ap Hugh Bodfel acquired Bardsey.

Leases were placed with prominent individuals across the former bond lands, including the commotal centres and their hamlets. The *maerdref*, or manor, of Arllechwedd Uchaf at Aber, was leased very soon after the conquest, as the *maerdref* of Llifon may have been. The probable location of the Llifon *maerdref* is the township of Cleifiog, together with Llanllibio, at the estuary of the river Alaw at Rhydyrarw. Cleifiog was in the hands of Llywelyn Foel ap Gruffudd ap Gwgan in 1289, but escheated on his death.[25] In 1352, Cleifiog included one carucate of demesne land. A marginal entry in the Crown survey of that year made a point of noting the demesne component and the presence of bond tenants.[26] The adjacent township of Llanllibio was exclusively of the nature of *trefgyfrif* and indicative of demesne tenure. In the late sixteenth century, 261 acres (105ha) of the 'manor' of Cleifiog and Llanllibio were granted by charter of Elizabeth I to Richard Meyrick and five others to hold as freeholds. Sixty-eight individually rented tenancies are identified, sub-let in blocks, and show clear evidence of an even earlier parcelling of smaller holdings. In the 1560s, Richard Bulkeley acquired the bond lands of these townships by letters patent. Whereas the freeholds created were relatively small, we see that the former demesne and its tenants were now comprehensively exploited across 631 acres (255ha) of Llanllibio and 1,408 acres (570ha) of Cleifiog. A similar process can be observed in the *maerdrefi* of the commotes of Menai and Malltraeth.[27]

The *maerdref* of Aberffraw was granted by royal charter to Sir Hugh Owen as a free tenant together with fifteen other freeholders. The demesne hamlets of the *maerdref* had previously been leased by letters patent of Elizabeth. Hugh Owen held the hamlets of Trecastell, Maerdref and Garddau; Richard Meyrick held Treberfedd, Cefn Treffraw, Dinllwydan and Trefri. The former bond *trefwelyog* townships beyond the limits of the *maerdref* were similarly leased; Rhosmor and its hamlet, Treiddon, to Owen Wood and Jane Owen, and Dindryfwl to Richard Meyrick, again by letters patent. Inevitably the process of estate building generated considerable complaints and litigation regarding boundary disputes and encroachment on customary tenurial rights.[28] A comparable process in the commote of Menai saw the manor of Rhosyr pass as freeholds to Owen Wood and thirty-one other free tenants. The hamlets at the core of the *maerdref*, 'Hendre, Rhosfaire and Maerdref' were leased by letters patent to William Owen of Fron Deg and sub-let '*ex demissione supra*' to forty-eight tenants across 464 acres (188ha). The outlying demesne hamlets of Hirdrefaig and Dinan were leased in 1587 and 1588 respectively.

Transactions and conveyances in the property market were also undertaken between freeholders. Free land in the Middle Ages should not, in theory, be legally alienated, but devices resembling a perpetually recurring mortgage were employed to circumvent this restriction, as were the payments of retrospective fines and licences, from the early fourteenth century. An example from the mid-fifteenth century concerns the career of a notable Lancastrian gentleman based at the castle town of Beaumaris, Thomas Norres of West Derby. Norres was constable of the castle. He was also an alderman of the town with significant properties in and around the borough and had taken a lease on the Beaumaris shoreline, close to Ferryman Warth. Hafoty, a tenement occupying half the hamlet of Bodarddar in the township of Crymlyn Heilin, was acquired by Norres in the 1440s. He employed two clerics, John and Robert Taverner, to acquire a licence, who paid a retrospective fine to do so.[29]

The amalgamation of holdings, so clearly seen among the demesne hamlets and gaining pace during the sixteenth century, was not, therefore, confined to the former bond tenements of the prince. One of the clearest instances concerns the accumulation, through purchase, of several hundred acres of smallholdings, arable, meadow and pasture in the free township of Castell in the Conwy valley by another Lancastrian, Bartholomew Bolde, a burgess of Conwy, in the early fifteenth century. Bolde's estate was 'one of the earliest regroupings of tenant rights', as Jones Pierce observed, 'heralding the last stage in the decay of tribal institutions, … of tribal holdings becoming concentrated in private hands.'[30]

We may leave the last words with the Crown surveyor, Robert Fludd (Llwyd), writing in 1608:

'We find the township of Cemmais to have been sometimes the kings maiesties manor, and part of ye principality of North Wales: As by a certain reccorde called the Extent book of North Wales, it dooth and may appear. And also we find that there was a patent granted of the said manor of Kemmais, by the late Kinge Henry the eighth of famous memory to one Nicholas Hurlton, Clerk. And that nowe one Sir Willm Thomas, Knight dooth holld and enjoy the said manor as his free holld; and hath so doon by himself and his Ancestors, for the space of forty years and upwards … but by what right or title, we know not.'[31]

and Henry Rowlands in the early eighteenth century:

'Through necessity or neglect … it is hardly possible at the present day to distinguish amidst the common mass what might be a villeinage from a freehold. Indeed in the present state of conducting matters, they have all become freeholds indiscriminately'.[32]

Notes

1. *The Anglo-Saxon Chronicle*, trans. and ed. M. J. Swanton (London 1996), 191, s.a. 1063.
2. *A History of the County of Cheshire. 1. Physique… and Domesday*, eds B. E. Harris and A.T. Thacker (Oxford 1987) 369–70.
3. J. E. Lloyd, *A History of Wales*, II (London 1911), 387–88; *The Chartulary or Register of the Abbey of St. Werburgh, Chester*, 1, ed. J. Tait, Chetham Society, new ser. 79 (Manchester 1920), 14; A. D. Carr, *Medieval Anglesey* (Llangefni 1982), 41.
4. Florence of Worcester, *Chronicon ex Chronicis*, ed. B. Thorpe (London 1849), 41–42; *The Chronicle of Florence of Worcester*, trans. T. Forester (London 1854), 204; *Brut y Tywysogyon or the Chronicle of the Princes. Peniarth Ms. 20 Version*, trans. T. Jones (Cardiff 1952), 20–21, s.a. 1096/98.
5. *Llyfr Iorwerth: a Critical Text of the Venedotian Code of Medieval Welsh Law*, ed. A. R. Wiliam (Cardiff 1960); *The Law of Hywel Dda: Law Texts from Medieval Wales*, trans. and ed. D. Jenkins (Llandysul 1986).
6. *Registrum Vulgariter Nuncupatum 'The Record of Caernarvon'*, ed. H. Ellis (London 1838), 27–28.
7. ibid., *extentae, passim*.
8. M. Gelling, *Place-Names in the Landscape* (London 1984), 191–92; M. Gelling and A. Cole, *The Landscape of Place-Names* (Stamford 2000), 225.
9. Gerald of Wales, *The Journey through Wales and The Description of Wales*, trans. L. Thorpe (Harmondsworth 1978), 230.
10. *Record of Caernarvon, extentae, passim*.
11. *Calendar of Inquisitions Miscellaneous*, I (London 1916), 392 (1357, dated at Llanfor, 1285).
12. *The Acts of Welsh Rulers 1120–1283*, ed. H. Pryce (Cardiff 2005).
13. F. Seebohm, *The Tribal System in Wales* (London 1895), Appendix A, 3–4; Carr, *Medieval Anglesey*, 112.
14. *Brut y Tywysogyon*, 104, s.a. 1237.
15. N. Johnstone, 'Cae Llys, Rhosyr: a court of the princes of Wales', *Studia Celtica* 33 (1999), 251–95; *Record of Caernarvon*, 214.
16. A. Taylor, *The Welsh Castles of Edward I* (London 1986), 94, n. 6.
17. The National Archives (TNA): PRO E 101/485/30; N. Johnstone, 'An investigation into the location of the royal courts of thirteenth-

century Gwynedd', in *Landscape and Settlement in Medieval Wales*, ed. N. Edwards (Oxford 1997), 64.

18. Carr, *Medieval Anglesey*, 56–57.

19. ibid., 237–58.

20. *Calendar of Patent Rolls, 1338–1340*, 56, dated April 29, 1338, at Westminster.

21. Sir John Wynn, *The History of the Gwydir Family and Memoirs*, ed. J. G. Jones (Llandysul 1990), 52; R. Avent, *Dolwyddelan Castle, Dolbadarn Castle, Castell y Bere* (Cardiff 2004), 20–21.

22. Wynn, *Gwydir*, 56–57.

23. *Records of the Court of Augmentations Relating to Wales and Monmouthshire*, ed. E. A. Lewis and J. C. Davies (Cardiff 1954), 276 (6/5/9, about 1550).

24. National Library of Wales, Llanstephan Ms. 179b, 12–19.

25. Seebohm, *Tribal System*, Appendix A (escheats), 22.

26. *Record of Caernarvon*, 52.

27. TNA: PRO LR 2/205.

28. *An Inventory of the Exchequer Proceedings (Equity) Concerning Wales, Henry VIII–Elizabeth*, comp. E. G. Jones (Cardiff 1939), 21 (58/35, 35 Eliz.); 23 (58/39, 37–39 Eliz.); T. J. Jeffreys Jones, *Exchequer Proceedings Concerning Wales in Tempore James I* (Cardiff 1955), 7 (144/60/6 Jac. I); 13–14 (144/73/9, Jac. I); 17 (144/81/11, Jac. 1).

29. D. Longley, 'Hafoty and its occupiers', *Anglesey Antiquarian Society and Field Club Transactions*, (2007), 24–39.

30. T. Jones Pierce, 'The *gafael* in Bangor Manuscript 1939', in *Medieval Welsh Society: Collected Essays*, ed. J. B. Smith (Cardiff 1972), 195–228.

31. TNA: PRO LR 2/205, 128.

32. H. Rowlands, 'Antiquitates parochiales. No. IV', *Archaeologia Cambrensis*, 2 (1847), 7–8.

4

The Castles of the Princes of Gwynedd

Lawrence Butler

All scholars working on castles in Wales are constantly aware of the debt they owe to the work of David Cathcart King, Arnold Taylor and Richard Avent. All have assiduously promoted the study of castles in Wales; all wrote eloquently about them, and all took active steps to protect them. Taylor and Avent, in their capacity as Chief Inspectors for Wales, initiated programmes to conserve the fabric of the castles in State care and protected the setting of the great Edwardian strongholds from insensitive modern development. All three wore their scholarship lightly and happily collaborated with their fellow workers. In the last fifteen years, in particular, Richard Avent made the topic of the native Welsh castle his speciality not only by writing the valuable series of Cadw guidebooks to many of the Welsh-built castles of north and mid-Wales, but also by promoting their conservation and presentation to the public.[1]

The Welsh princes built their castles on craggy outcrops with lines of irregular perimeter walls following the contours of the hills. These strongholds are in marked contrast to Anglo-Norman structures with their massive great towers, high keeps or donjons, and expansive levelled baileys. It is therefore tempting to see a specifically Welsh ancestry for the native castles in the early Christian period forts at Dinas Emrys, near Beddgelert in the Nantgwynant valley, and at Deganwy at the mouth of the Conwy. On both summits later stone towers were erected on sites that were associated with early princely occupation and redolent with literary traditions.

All the major developments in Welsh castles are compressed within two centuries and it is the development and characteristics of those castles associated principally with the princes of Gwynedd that this paper seeks to address.

The Twelfth Century

The Norman invasion of Wales was characterized by the castle – both motte and ringwork, with and without a bailey – hastily constructed of timber, and easily burnt when captured. The Welsh also adopted this type of defence and took the functional name *castell* into the Welsh language (though the descriptive *tomen* meaning mound was also used) (Fig. 4.1). Documentary evidence for castle building by the Welsh occurs as early as 1111 when the Powys prince, Cadwgan ap Bleddyn, was killed whilst building a castle at Welshpool. In 1116 his cousin, Uchdryd ab Edwin, is recorded constructing a castle at Cymer in Meirionnydd.[2] In Gwynedd, the substantial motte and bailey at Tomen y Rhodwydd (Fig. 4.2) was erected by Owain ap Gruffudd ap Cynan in 1149 to defend the eastern border of his territory from Norman penetration, though ironically it was burnt down in 1157 by his neighbour Iorwerth Goch ap Maredudd of the Powys dynasty.[3] This site is predominantly of earth construction, but some other mottes were built around rocky knolls, which were then covered by soil or shale; for example, Cynfal, which was both built and destroyed by the Welsh in 1147.[4]

From here it is but a short progression to revet a knoll of rock with a stone batter or plinth and erect a stone tower on it. Twelfth-century Welsh towers took various forms: round, for example at Prysor, east of Trawsfynydd; rectangular at Dinas Emrys and sub-rectangular at Tomen Castell on the valley floor near Dolwyddelan. These last two sites are on the southern flanks of Snowdonia and may well be linked to the expansionist policies of Owain Gwynedd (d. 1170).[5] Two other castles are known from this period through the writing of Gerald of Wales who, in 1188, recorded them as newly built. One, which belonged to the sons of Conan, controlled the river crossing of Deudraeth and was situated in Eifionydd looking towards the northern mountains. This was identified by Wilfrid Hemp as Aber Iâ where there is a knoll of rock strengthened by revetting and topped with a tower, probably a square one; there are, however, other claimants to be the site, notably Pen y garn, Pren-teg and Moel y gest, Ynyschynhaiarn. The second castle mentioned by Gerald belonged to the sons of Owain Gwynedd and was on the

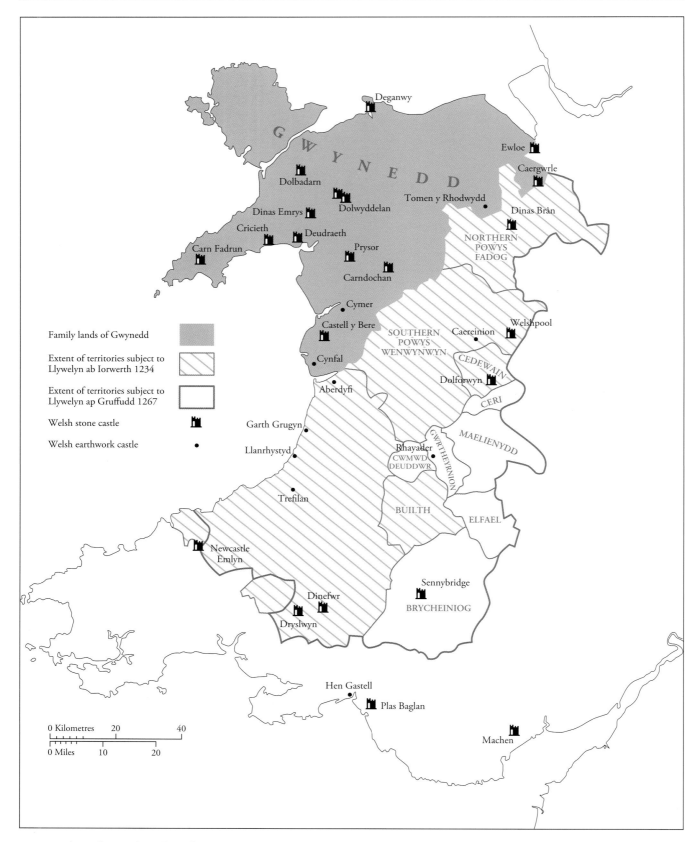

Figure 4.1: The earthwork and stone castles of the Welsh princes (Cadw, Welsh Assembly Government: Crown Copyright).

Figure 4.2: Tomen y Rhodwydd – aerial view of motte and bailey, from the south-east (Cadw, Welsh Assembly Government: Crown Copyright).

summit of Carn Fadrun, a prominent hillfort in Llŷn.[6]

We see in several of the sites mentioned above, especially where masonry is used, constructional characteristics more akin to previous centuries; certainly, without Gerald's comment on the castles built about 1188, archaeologists would not have interpreted the central stronghold on Carn Fadrun, with its drystone walling, as anything but part of the hillfort.

The Early Thirteenth Century

Although Prysor may have twelfth-century origins, it lay to the south of those described above and can perhaps be seen as the first stage by Llywelyn ab Iorwerth to secure the gateway to Ardudwy and his south-western frontier in the early thirteenth century.[7] If so, then Carndochan would be the second stage in dominating the south-eastern frontier, controlling the *cantref* of Penllyn from 1202, by enhancing a craggy site with a square tower enclosed by an oval enclosure.[8]

Wherever possible, the policy of the Normans had been to plant their castles beside the centre of a *cantref* or commote and to dominate physically the undefended Welsh court or *llys*. By contrast the Welsh princes almost invariably made a distinction between the location of a castle and that of a *llys*. This has been demonstrated by Goronwy Edwards in Ceredigion, and can also be observed in Powys and Gwynedd.[9] In the heartland of Gwynedd, which contained the princes' granary and their mountain pastures, there are no Welsh castles on Anglesey and only four major castles in and around Snowdonia. All four can be linked to Llywelyn ab Iorwerth. Only at Deganwy do the castle and the commotal centre of Creuddyn stand near each other in the same vicinity.[10] This quartet may well have had a practical purpose in controlling routes by land and water, the mountain passes and the river crossings. However, they may also have been symbolic of Llywelyn's role as lord of the mountains (Dolbadarn and Dolwyddelan, Plates 15 and 16) and as protector of the coasts (Deganwy and Cricieth, Plate 15).[11] Although written a century earlier, the white limewashed churches of Gwynedd were said to 'glitter … like the firmament with stars', a description that was just as apt for the thirteenth-century castles. [12]

The Welsh princes were war-leaders, protecting their own kindred from outside invasion, either by fellow Welshmen or by would-be alien conquerors. Indeed, we have seen already that the Welsh used castles in areas where there was no Norman threat. In a society based on partible inheritance they needed secure prisons, often for scheming brothers or cousins – though this does beg the question as to what they had been using before. In a society based on a barter economy the castle could also serve as a strong centre to house a treasury and armoury.

The main distinguishing features of the castles of the Welsh princes are their irregular perimeter walls, the small size of their enclosed courtyards and towers that rarely exceeded one storey over a basement. They did not need to contain a large mounted garrison to overawe the countryside or any pre-existing town; nor did the princes anticipate withstanding prolonged sieges, as indicated by the lightly defended entrances. Only Cricieth and the later Dinas Brân have twin-towered defensive gate-passages. The plan of Cricieth's gatehouse was probably based on that of Beeston, which dominates the Cheshire plain.[13] This lack of defence is also shown by the lack of provision for flanking fire, even though most castles have towers which protrude from the curtain walls (Fig. 4.3).

At three of the four castles the symbolism, as well as

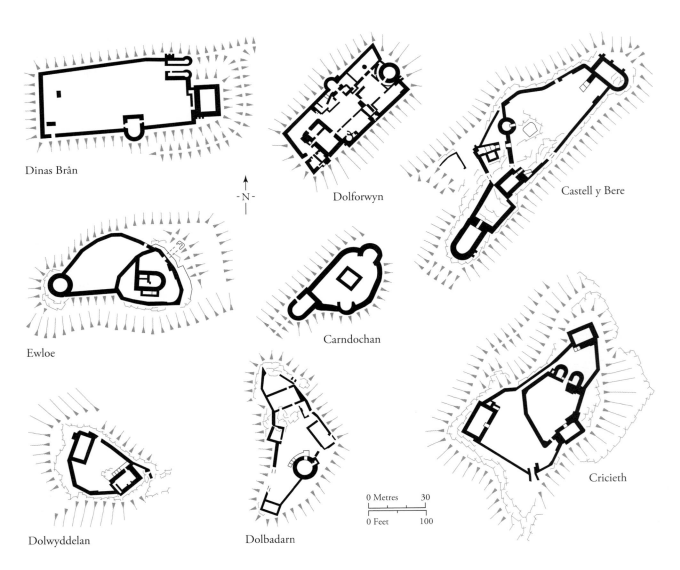

Dinas Brân

Dolforwyn

Castell y Bere

- N -

Ewloe

Carndochan

Dolwyddelan

Dolbadarn

Cricieth

0 Metres 30

0 Feet 100

Figure 4.3: Comparative ground plans of stone castles of the Welsh princes (Cadw, Welsh Assembly Government: Crown Copyright).

the accommodation, was based initially on a single tower. The towers are rectangular at Deganwy and Dolwyddelan; the latter is two storeys high with an outside stair and an internal latrine. At Dolbadarn there is an impressive three-storey round tower, which rises above the buildings in the courtyard, and at Cricieth the first phase is dominated by both the apsidal twin-towered gatehouse and also by a rectangular south-east tower (Fig. 4.4).

Dolbadarn, with its defended outer stair and an encircling mural stair, has the most sophisticated domestic arrangements, even though the latrine outlet compromises its defensive character by discharging outside the curtain (Plate 15). Whilst the great tower at Dolbadarn was placed inside an existing enclosure with two small square perimeter towers, Cricieth is more complicated and has links to the later castles of Llywelyn ab Iorwerth (d. 1240) and his grandson, Llywelyn ap Gruffudd (d. 1282). Here, the gatehouse opens into an inner courtyard with a rectangular tower at its south-east corner, which seems to be work of 1230–40, though much repaired (Plate 15).

Llywelyn ab Iorwerth also built Castell y Bere, which is scenically stunning, in the latter part of his reign after he took control of the *cantref* of Meirionnydd in 1221 (Fig. 4.5). The roughly triangular courtyard is bounded by the rectangular middle tower, a circular west tower and an impressive apsidal north tower.[14] All three towers were of two storeys; two had outside stairs and none had evidence of a latrine. The nearest model for the apsidal tower – Hemp's

Figure 4.4: Cricieth Castle – reconstruction of the castle as it may have appeared in about 1240 (Illustration by Ivan Lapper, Cadw, Welsh Assembly Government: Crown Copyright).

Figure 4.5: Castell y Bere – aerial view of the castle, south is at the top.

characteristic 'Welsh Tower' – seems to be the first version of the apsidal Well Tower at Montgomery Castle (Fig. 4.6), another semi-detached tower finished by 1234.[15] Only at Cricieth and Castell y Bere is there any evidence of decorative sculpture (plus a single decorative corbel from Deganwy, which is believed to represent Llywelyn ab Iorwerth, see Fig. 21.3). At both sites Cefn y Fedw sandstone was brought from a distance; otherwise local stones were used for building material though lime for mortar had to be imported if there was no adjacent source.

In contrast to the Gwynedd princes, developments by other rulers in Ceredigion and Powys were more modest with a single rectangular tower at Ystrad Meurig (and possibly at Plas Crug near Aberystwyth, if it really is medieval as argued by Ralph Griffiths), and probably two rectangular towers and a courtyard in the earliest phase at Powis, near Welshpool. [16]

The proliferation of towers, often of different plan form, is a feature of the mid-thirteenth-century castles in Gwynedd and Powys. Each tower could have fulfilled a separate function and each may well have stressed a separate aspect of the prince's role – to house his justiciar, his chamberlain, his castellan and his wife.

The latter aspect is significant: Llywelyn ab Iorwerth wished to meet the Anglo-Normans on equal terms and be socially acceptable at the English court. He pursued an active policy in forging marriage alliances with the major Anglo-Norman families of the Marches: Blundeville, Clifford, Braose, Lacy and Mortimer. His own wife was a daughter of King John and he required his castles to reflect his status and meet the expectations of his new-found peer group. The prince's neighbours in Powys did likewise, with marriages to the Audleys of Cheshire and the Corbets and the Lestranges of Shropshire.[17] His own grandson, Llywelyn ap Gruffudd, married Eleanor de Montfort, and her prolonged detention by Edward I was a source of sustained grievance.

The Later Thirteenth Century

Just as several castles in England underwent considerable improvements at this time, both in terms of defences as well as domestic accommodation and services, so we see similar improvements being made in the castles of Gwynedd under Llywelyn ap Gruffudd.

Dolwyddelan received a second rectangular tower with latrines on the edge of a modest courtyard (Plate 16). Cricieth also received a second rectangular tower, larger and better appointed, at the south-west angle of an outer courtyard added on the seaward side of the existing castle. Carndochan had a modest circular tower around a rocky knoll, and a well-built apsidal tower guarding the easiest approach route. These additions are likely to be the work of Llywelyn ap Gruffudd. He also added a second apsidal tower at the south end of Castell y Bere (Fig. 4.7): the deep ditch with its flanking walls and the latrine passage in the wall thickness can be paralleled at the later Dolforwyn.

Figure 4.6: Montgomery Castle – the apsidal Well Tower, looking north-east (Cadw, Welsh Assembly Government: Crown Copyright).

Figure 4.7: Castell y Bere – the later southern apsidal tower, looking south-west (Cadw, Welsh Assembly Government: Crown Copyright).

The gate, stair and barbican at Castell y Bere are also later additions creating an impressive entrance in front of the curtain wall.[18]

Llywelyn built two new castles in the early 1260s. Ewloe, in a corner of a wood between Chester and Holywell, was built soon after 1257. Its position, close to the border with England, emphasizes the extent of Llywelyn's power at this time.[19] Ewloe's main strength was a freestanding apsidal tower in the upper ward, two storeys high, with an outside approach stair and an internal stair in the thickness of the wall (Fig. 4.8). It commanded a bridge over a deep rock-cut ditch and was set within a modest enclosure. As at Cricieth, a second ward of oval shape was added, focused on a circular tower at its western extremity set upon a boss of rock. The two phases were probably immediately consecutive. Sennybridge, Llywelyn's 'new castle above Brecon', was started soon after 1262. It has a strongly built apsidal tower, which still survives, placed centrally on the south 'show' front across a brook. There are possibly two other towers, also facing south, at the angles of a roughly square enclosure.[20]

Two other castles mark a significant departure in planning, though not in their hilltop position, or in the vocabulary of designed features. Dinas Brân in northern Powys (Powys Fadog) (Fig. 4.9) and Dolforwyn in Cedewain, mid-Wales (Plate 16), both have rectangular courtyard plans imposed upon a deliberately scarped summit. Dinas Brân is undated but is likely to have been built for Llywelyn ap Grufudd's ally, Gruffudd ap Madog (d. 1269).[21] It dominates the

Figure 4.8: Ewloe Castle – the apsidal tower and curtain wall of upper ward, from the south (Cadw, Welsh Assembly Government: Crown Copyright).

Figure 4.9: Castell Dinas Brân – aerial view looking west, gatehouse and square tower in foreground (Cadw, Welsh Assembly Government: Crown Copyright).

Figure 4.10: Dolforwyn Castle – reconstruction of the castle under siege in 1277, looking north (Illustration by Ivan Lapper, Cadw, Welsh Assembly Government: Crown Copyright).

Dee valley just before it opens out into the Cheshire plain. A massive inner ditch was cut within the existing hillfort except on the north where a precipice forms an impregnable defence. There is a well-designed, though rather compact, gatehouse, with a rectangular tower beside it, unusually placed outside the courtyard wall. On the opposite side of the enclosure, there is a small apsidal tower alongside a single-storey hall. In similar fashion Llywelyn ap Gruffudd built Dolforwyn between 1273 and 1277 (Fig. 4.10) to command a stretch of the Severn valley on the edge of his lands in Cedewain and Ceri before the river flows into southern Powys (Powys Gwenwynwyn) at Welshpool on its north bank and English lands around Montgomery on its south bank.[22] The rectangular courtyard contains a square tower and a circular tower at opposite ends. An inner ditch, leading from the south entrance to a two-storey hall alongside a small apsidal tower, bisects the courtyard.

Beyond, to the west lay an outer ditch protected by flanking walls and then a town built to challenge Montgomery. It is one of the few castle-towns founded by the Welsh; there are others at Dinefwr and Dryslwyn in Deheubarth to the south-west.

After Edward I's campaign of 1277 and the enforced contraction of the lands held by Llywelyn ap Gruffudd, a Gwynedd prince built one last castle and that must have been with the king's permission and perhaps also with English guidance. Llywelyn's duplicitous brother, Dafydd ap Gruffudd, built Hope or Caergwrle after he had been granted the commote or lordship in 1277 (Fig. 4.11). Raised within an existing hillfort, and with a new strong ditch on its most vulnerable north-east side, it has a substantial curtain wall with an English-looking buttress to mask a change in wall direction.[23] Parts of two apsidal towers of different internal designs remain. John Manley in 1990 found evidence of

Figure 4.11: Caergwrle Castle – aerial view (© Crown Copyright: Royal Commission on the Ancient and Historical Monuments of Wales; NPRN 93–CS-1393; GTJ25749).

a secondary more elaborate bridge approach. The round tower was unfinished but its internal diameter exceeds that of Llywelyn ab Iorwerth's great tower at Dolbadarn – perhaps a deliberately defiant gesture against his brother and his grandfather. Manley, and before him Cathcart King, assumed that the west curtain wall was defined by the present edge of the quarry, but it seems preferable to place it further west and assume greater English influence on the gateway with a third apsidal tower at the north-west angle to provide a stronger if widely splayed gatehouse.

Conclusion

This survey of the Gwynedd princes' castles provides a benchmark against which to set the efforts of Edward I in his conquest of Wales. The princes were resilient and resourceful forcing the English king to muster money and men in a hitherto unprecedented building campaign. Although the Welsh castles may not rival the thirteenth-century strongholds built by the English in terms of their architecture, they were formidable obstacles in terms of their structure and physical location. Edward's strategy during the Welsh wars confirms this: his commanders knew only too well that the Welsh castles had to be taken as part of their advance into Gwynedd, not simply bypassed and isolated. Indeed, not only were they captured, but many were repaired and reused, no doubt as symbols of conquest as well as centres of administration and defence.[24] Nor were they bleak strongholds in a harsh landscape: some of the finest stone carving from thirteenth-century Wales was recovered from Castell y Bere. Taken together the castles and religious foundations of the Welsh princes throughout Wales provide us with an image of a flourishing and vibrant society.

Notes

1.　His more general surveys are *Cestyll Twysogion Gwynedd / Castles of the Princes of Gwynedd* (Cardiff 1983) and 'Castles of the Welsh princes', *Château Gaillard*, 16 (1994), 11–20.

2.　*Brut y Tywysogyon or The Chronicle of the Princes. Peniarth Ms. 20 Version*, trans. T. Jones (Cardiff 1952), 35, 45–46. D. J. C. King with J. R. Kenyon, 'The castles: a study in military architecture', in *Merioneth County History*, II, eds J. B. Smith and Ll. B. Smith (Cardiff 2001), 411 (386–421, esp. 404–08, 418).

3.　*Brut y Tywysogyon. Peniarth Ms. 20 Version*, 57, 60; *Brut y Tywysogyon or The Chronicle of the Princes. Red Book of Hergest Version*, trans. T. Jones, 2nd edn (Cardiff 1973), 137; *Brenhinedd y Saesson or the Kings of the Saxons*, trans. T. Jones (Cardiff 1971), 159.

4. *Brut y Tywysogyon. Peniarth Ms. 20 Version,* 56.

5. H. N. Savory, 'Excavations at Dinas Emrys, Beddgelert (Caerns.), 1954–56', *Archaeologia Cambrensis,* 109 (1960), 13–77. J. E. Jones, 'Tomen Castell, Dolwyddelan', *Archaeology in Wales,* 3 (1963), 16 and op. cit., 4 (1964), 13.

6. Gerald of Wales, *The Journey through Wales and The Description of Wales,* trans. L. Thorpe (Harmondsworth 1978), 183. W. J. Hemp, 'Castell Aber Ia', *Archaeologia Cambrensis,* 100 (1949), 311–12. King with Kenyon, 'The castles', 409, n. 46, where Pen y garn, Pren-teg is suggested as an alternative site. Another could be Moel y gest in Ynyscynhaiarn: Royal Commission on Ancient and Historical Monuments in Wales and Monmouthshire, *An Inventory of the Ancient Monuments in Caernarvonshire,* II (London 1960), 256–57.

7. M. de Lewandowicz, 'A survey of Castell Prysor, Meirionnydd', *Archaeology in Wales,* 38 (1998), 36–42. King with Kenyon, 'The castles', 408–09.

8. A. H. A. Hogg, 'Castell Carndochan', *Journal of the Merioneth Historical and Record Society,* 2 (1953–56), 178–80. King with Kenyon, 'The castles', 404–08.

9. J. G. Edwards, 'The Normans and the Welsh March', *Proceedings of the British Academy,* 42 (1956), 155–77.

10. L. Alcock, 'Excavations at Degannwy Castle, Caernarvonshire, 1961–6', *Archaeological Journal,* 124 (1967), 190–201.

11. R. Avent, *Dolwyddelan Castle, Dolbadarn Castle, Castell y Bere* (Cardiff 2004); R. Avent, *Criccieth Castle, Pennarth Fawr Medieval Hall-house, St Cybi's Well* (Cardiff 1989).

12. This phrase was used to describe newly built churches in Gwynedd by the biographer of Gruffudd ap Cynan: *The History of Gruffydd ap Cynan,* trans. A. Jones (Manchester 1910), 155.

13. R. Avent, *Criccieth Castle,* 11–13.

14. R. Avent, *Dolwyddelan Castle,* 37–40. L. A. S. Butler, 'Medieval finds from Castell-y-Bere', *Archaeologia Cambrensis,* 123 (1974), 78–112.

15. W. J. Hemp, 'The castle of Ewloe and the Welsh castle plan', *Y Cymmrodor,* 39 (1928), 4–19, though Hemp's comparison with the then recently excavated keep at Helmsley (Yorkshire) now seems far less convincing. L. Butler and J. K. Knight, *Dolforwyn Castle, Montgomery Castle* (Cardiff 2004), 45–46.

16. P. R. Davis, *Castles of the Welsh Princes,* 2nd edn (Talybont 2007), 82–83; R. A. Griffiths, 'The three castles at Aberystwyth', *Archaeologia Cambrensis,* 126 (1977), 74–87; C. J. Arnold, 'Powis Castle: recent excavations and observations', *Montgomeryshire Collections,* 73 (1985), 30–37. Further refinement of Arnold's dating of the structural evidence is offered by D. Stephenson, 'Powis Castle: a reappraisal of its medieval development', *Montgomeryshire Collections,* 95 (2007), 9–21, esp. 14–20.

17. Gwenwynwyn (d. 1216) of southern Powys married Margaret Corbet and his son, Gruffudd (d. 1286), married Hawise Lestrange. Gruffudd ap Madog Maelor (d. 1269) of northern Powys married Emma Audley.

18. In an earlier brief version (1997) of the guide Richard Avent suggested that the gateway defences were Edwardian work, but he later revised his opinion. However, there are few diagnostic features to enable this entrance complex to be assigned to one particular phase.

19. D. Renn and R. Avent, *Flint Castle, Ewloe Castle,* revised edn (Cardiff 2001); Hemp, 'The castle of Ewloe'.

20. D. J. C. King, 'Camlais and Sennybridge castles', *Brycheiniog,* 21 (1984–85), 9–11. P. Remfry, *The Castles of Breconshire* (Almeley 1999), 126–27; Davis, *Castles of the Welsh Princes,* 68, but suggesting a different site.

21. D. J. C. King, 'Two castles of northern Powys: Dinas Brân and Caergwrle', *Archaeologia Cambrensis,* 123 (1974), 113–39, esp. 119–31.

22. L. A. S. Butler, 'Dolforwyn Castle, Montgomery, Powys. First report: the excavations 1981–1986', *Archaeologia Cambrensis,* 138 (1989), 78–98; idem, 'Dolforwyn Castle, Montgomery, Powys. Second report: the excavations 1987–1994', *Archaeologia Cambrensis,* 144 (1995), 133–203; idem, 'Dolforwyn Castle, Montgomery, Powys. Third report: the excavations 1995–2000', *Archaeologia Cambrensis,* (forthcoming). Also idem, 'Dolforwyn Castle: prospect and retrospect' in *The Medieval Castle in Ireland and Wales,* eds J. R. Kenyon and K. O'Conor (Dublin 2003), 149–62.

23. King, 'Two castles of northern Powys', 131–39; J. Manley, 'Excavations at Caergwrle Castle, Clwyd, north Wales: 1988–1990', *Medieval Archaeology,* 38 (1994), 83–133.

24. Seven of the Welsh-built castles continued in use: three as royal castles – Criciech until Glyndŵr's revolt in 1404, Castell y Bere until Madog's revolt in 1294 and Caergwrle more briefly. Two were centres of local administration – Dolbadarn and Dolwyddelan; two were lordship castles – Dolforwyn for the Mortimers until about 1390 and Powis has remained in continuous occupation by the descendants of Gruffudd ap Gwenwynwyn. All the rest were abandoned.

5

James of St George

Nicola Coldstream

Late in 1277 or early in 1278 a mason named Master James of St George set out from the Alpine County of Savoy on a journey to England, whence in April 1278 Edward I sent him to Wales 'to ordain the works of the castles there'.[1] By the time of his death in 1308/09 James had spent thirty years working for the king on the castles in Wales and Scotland. He was master of the King's Works in Wales, had acted as constable of Harlech Castle, and had been granted manors and a pension above his normal salary, showing that he was much trusted by the king.[2]

This was a remarkable career, notable less for its geographical reach, which was not unique at the time, than for James's rise to high status. Although Richard of Chester, his colleague in Wales, also achieved both status and a fortune, these were not the usual lot of a late thirteenth-century mason, although they were becoming more common by the fifteenth.[3] That we know so much about Master James is thanks mainly to inspired and painstaking research by the late Arnold Taylor, and also the accident of James's working for administrations whose records were preserved down the centuries. James of St George's activities in Wales had long been known from the building accounts of the royal works; but it was Arnold Taylor who discovered the link with Savoy.[4] He noticed similarities between buildings there and in north Wales, and subsequently found documents in the archives at Turin that named Master James as a mason working in Savoy for Count Philip, who was building a series of castles and new towns. Taylor conjectured that James may have originated in St Georges-d'Espéranche, a village now in France, where Philip had a castle-palace. Taylor's intimate knowledge of the buildings in question and his discoveries in the archives led him to propose that James of St George designed the castles in north Wales. He never deviated from the view that James was 'a master of military design' who produced at Beaumaris 'a consummate example of his art'.[5]

A man thus described ought to be an innovator after the mould of such later figures as the seventeenth-century military architects Menno van Coehoorn and Sébastien Vauban. These men did not wait for orders but devised new designs and sold them to their patrons. The sheer splendour and apparently consistent design in the castles in north Wales invite the idea that a presiding genius was responsible for the concept. Yet their reputation as classic statements of late thirteenth-century castle design is derived less from innovation than from generations of accumulated experience and consolidated ideas that went into their final form. One essential question, therefore, is whether James of St George had the necessary experience. This paper looks at the arguments in favour of Taylor's view; at the arguments against it; at who else might have been involved; and, finally, it suggests what Master James was really doing in Snowdonia, and why he remains a significant figure.

Given the documentary record, which is rich in comparison with those of most medieval buildings, it may seem odd that there should be any doubt. The name of the designer should be evident. Unfortunately the process of design is one of the few aspects that does not emerge from the building accounts. The accounts include the supply of materials and wages lists, but the master masons, who were responsible for design, were paid annual salaries, and appear in the wages lists only for odd jobs performed at task. Their design work, not done at task, goes undescribed. Thus the process of design, not only in these but in most other sets of building accounts, remains obscure owing to a technicality in accounting.

The arguments in favour of Master James as designer of the castles are numerous. His title, master of the works in Wales, attests that he was in charge of the building programme as a whole; and in the 1290s he was specifically in charge at Beaumaris, where he is described as master of the works. This title would normally imply that he designed the building as well as supervising its construction.

Figure 5.1: Walls and towers of Saillon (Peter Humphries).

What caught Taylor's eye and started him on his research was the resemblance as he saw it between the cylindrical towers of such buildings in the upper Rhône valley as Saxon, La Bâtiaz at Martigny and Saillon, and the castles of north Wales, Conwy in particular (Figs 5.1 and 5.2). His further investigations in Savoy produced parallels for a number of architectural details that appear in Wales but cannot be found in earlier buildings in Britain.[6] The following list is not exhaustive, but includes: the use of semi-circular arches in doorways, evident at Harlech and Saillon in Savoy (Figs 5.3 and 5.4); distinctive, wide windows with segmental arches and tracery, built at Chillon Castle on Lake Geneva and at Harlech and Conwy (Figs 5.5 and 5.6);[7] crenellations adorned with pinnacles, which appear at Conwy (Fig. 5.7) and are a prominent feature of San Giorio in the Val de Susa in north Italy; and two kinds of latrine shaft, a flat one in the angle of a tower and curtain wall, at Harlech and the castle-palace of St Georges-d'Espéranche, and a structure corbelled out of the curtain, at Harlech and La Bâtiaz (Figs 5.8 and 5.9). Finally, Taylor found putlog holes arranged in a sloping

Figure 5.2: Conwy Castle (Cadw, Welsh Assembly Government: Crown Copyright).

Figure 5.3: Harlech Castle, semi-circular arch (Cadw, Welsh Assembly Government: Crown Copyright).

Figure 5.4: Saillon, semi-circular arch (Peter Humphries).

Figure 5.5: Window at Chillon Castle (Peter Humphries).

Figure 5.6: Window at Harlech Castle (Cadw, Welsh Assembly Government: Crown Copyright).

Figure 5.7: Pinnacles on the north-west tower, Conwy Castle (Cadw, Welsh Assembly Government: Crown Copyright).

Figure 5.8: Corbelled latrine at Harlech Castle (Cadw, Welsh Assembly Government: Crown Copyright).

line up a flat wall, as at Conwy, or spiralling round a tower, as at Harlech, Conwy and Saxon (Fig. 5.10). This latter arrangement is not peculiar to Savoy, but it does seem to make its first appearance in Britain in Edward's castles.

Master James was not the only Savoyard mason to work in north Wales. He summoned a number of colleagues, whom Taylor found in the records of both Wales and Savoy.[8] The strong Savoyard presence, close architectural parallels and Master James's evident status led naturally to the conclusion that James of St George was a military architect.

Yet this conclusion presents difficulties. We can substitute Taylor's subjective judgment on the similarity of towers with a subjective judgment of our own, namely the difference in quality between the work in Wales and that of Savoy. However splendid the castles in Wales may be, the walls and towers of the upper Rhône valley are serviceable at best. Any comparison reveals at once that – to adapt Pevsner's famous contrast of Lincoln Cathedral with a bicycle shed – while in Wales we have architecture, in Savoy we have building.[9] Although the quality of construction at St Georges-d'Espéranche is a little higher, it is difficult to argue that Master James was chosen for his

fine designer's eye. Edward I had seen the work in Savoy; he had stopped there on his way home from the Holy Land in 1273 in order that Count Philip could do him homage for some castles that guarded the Alpine passes, of which Edward was feudal overlord. It was there that Edward had become aware of the mason's existence, and when he summoned Master James to Britain he knew what was being built in Savoy.

There are, however, less subjective considerations. The apparent similarities of planning that Taylor also emphasized are less persuasive in the buildings themselves than they are on paper.[10] All the architectural parallels with Savoy are either constructional, as in the putlog holes, or such elements as windows, ornaments and latrine shafts. These are details, hardly fundamental to strategic design. In addition there is one obvious omission. This is the defining characteristic of many of Edward's castles: the strengthened, towered gatehouse. The gatehouse combines civilized living with formidable defensive capability, and

Figure 5.9: Corbelled latrines at La Bâtiaz, Martigny (Peter Humphries).

it appears in all the new castles except Flint and Conwy. Rhuddlan, which was under construction before Master James arrived, has two gatehouses (Fig. 5.11). Yet this type of gatehouse did not exist in Savoy. When James of St George came to Britain he had never seen a gatehouse and cannot have known how to build one.

Castles are not, however, all about form; or rather, their form embraces aspects other than construction techniques, which need to be taken into account. Two of the castles in Wales have, or had, a festive appearance: Conwy has its pinnacles and once gleamed with whitewash, while Caernarfon outstrips even Conwy. Caernarfon has polygonal, as distinct from circular, towers, and has bands of masonry in contrasting shades. Some crenellations of the towers are adorned with carved heads, and some towers have turrets, although both heads and turrets may date from after the reign of Edward I (Fig. 5.12). Caernarfon nevertheless seems to have been marked out in some special way. Historians are agreed that these details and others are not purely decorative, and the symbolic interpretation of Caernarfon Castle has been the subject of several recent publications.

Taylor's original suggestion that the banded walls of Caernarfon were based on the Theodosian walls of Constantinople, with their connotations of Constantine and a Christian *imperium,* has been questioned by Abigail Wheatley.[11] She argues for a Roman symbolism based on Britain's legendary past, including an Arthurian element. The Arthurian theme was explored by Richard Morris,[12]

Figure 5.10: Sloped and spiralling putlog holes, Conwy town walls, between towers 15 and 16 The windows probably mark the site of Llywelyn's Hall. (Cadw, Welsh Assembly Government: Crown Copyright).

Figure 5.11: Rhuddlan Castle, west gatehouse (Cadw, Welsh Assembly Government: Crown Copyright).

Figure 5.12: Caernarfon Castle, Eagle Tower with banded masonry (Cadw, Welsh Assembly Government: Crown Copyright).

who offered Caernarfon as an Arthurian fantasy castle. He noted that in 1284 Edward had held a Round Table very near Caernarfon at Nefyn, and, as an enthusiastic Arthurian, Edward would have known of Arthur's influence in Wales. Already in 1278 Edward had attended the entombment of the remains of Arthur and Guinevere at Glastonbury Abbey, perhaps to remind the Welsh that Arthur was not after all asleep in his cave, waiting to rise and lead them to victory. Presented with the so-called Crown of Arthur, Edward despatched it to the royal treasury in London. The Crown was handed over at Aberconwy Abbey, where Llywelyn ab Iorwerth was buried. Edward moved the abbey upstream to Maenan and built Conwy Castle on its original site. From now on Arthur was to be associated not with the princes of Wales but with the kings of England.

These interpretations may differ and others may be proposed, but they all demonstrate that symbolism is inherent to the design. Deciding what symbolism to build into a structure was not the responsibility of the master mason. Given the castles' extreme political as well as symbolic importance we can postulate that others besides the masons played a prominent role in the early planning. Taylor himself recognized this.[13] The king's intimate circle included household knights and clerical officials of the Wardrobe, the department that financed the

building programme. Household knights were appointed administrators of the works, and James of St George, like any master mason, worked closely with the administrators in both Savoy and Wales. Several Savoyards, notably John de Bevillard and William de Cicon, were appointed to senior duties in north Wales.[14] Yet, as with such Wardrobe clerks as William de Perton, evidence for their advice on castle design is neutral.

A similar neutrality surrounds most of the senior Wardrobe figures who made up Edward's inner council, the treasurers, keepers and stewards who were part of his *familia* or close household. They were all clerics rather than fighting men, either occupying senior positions in the Church or anticipating such posts. Nothing rules them out of advising on the castle-building programme in the 1270s and 1280s, but nothing associates them with it.[15] The only official whom we can associate with Edward's buildings is Robert Burnell, bishop of Bath and Wells and Edward's chancellor and close companion until his death in 1292. While there is no evidence that Burnell gave advice on castle design, his own house, at Acton Burnell in Shropshire, has domical vaults that betray the influence of vaults at Caernarfon.[16]

Edward's intimates included the men who did fight, of whom the greatest seem to have been his two Savoyard friends, his cousin Amadeus of Savoy and Otto de

Grandson, both of whom played active parts in the conquest of north Wales. Otto de Grandson was a man of exceptional importance in Edward's life. He was Edward's closest friend; they took the Cross together twice, went to the Holy Land in 1268, and Otto went again at Edward's behest in 1290.[17] Prestwich surmised that Otto 'had a part to play' in the planning of the castles.[18] Together with John de Vescy and Roger de Clifford, Otto travelled with Edward to Savoy in 1273. Taylor speculated that Robert Tibetot and Payn de Chaworth, builder of Kidwelly Castle, were also present at the ceremonies of homage at St Georges-d'Espéranche.[19] All these men were involved in both military and diplomatic exercises in Wales, and their supposed presence in Savoy helped Taylor to strengthen his ideas about the transmission of forms.

Most of this is, however, inference, and it would be as well not to exaggerate the significance of their possible advice. In 1273 war in Wales was not inevitable, and there was no particular reason why the party that went to Savoy should interest itself in Count Philip's castles. We can imagine Edward, Otto and their friends whiling away dull periods of inactivity in the heat of Palestine with discussions about attack, defence and military hardware, but any intimate of Edward I would do well to tell the king what he wanted to hear.

A more persuasive contributor to the design of the castles in Wales is Edward I himself. He had a direct interest in any symbolic message that the castles might convey, and was a considerable patron of architecture, both building and enabling others to build churches, castles and new towns. The records show that he kept a close eye on the building programmes in Wales. He ensured that special diggers be sent from East Anglia to Rhuddlan to make the harbour works there.[20] In 1282 Master James was sent to Aberystwyth, where the gatehouse was causing concern, but it is recorded that the masons were to do 'what the king shall enjoin upon them'.[21] In 1283 Edward wrote to his clerk, William de Perton, that he should 'cause to be brought divers tools and other necessaries, as our beloved Richard the Engineer will tell you, for making ditches at Aberconway. You are also to cause to come to Conway masons and quarry-breakers, as the same Richard will tell you.'[22] During the Scottish campaign Edward specified the exact features he wanted built at Linlithgow Castle.[23] In all these instances he gave direct orders not only to Master James but to other trusted masons, including Richard of Chester.

Yet issuing instructions is one thing; the technical expertise required for designing and building a complicated structure is quite another. For this Edward needed his trained masons, for only a master mason could set out the plan, draw the templates for all the mouldings, and apply his experience to ensure that the building would stand up. Edward was surrounded by competent masters: such men as Richard of Chester and Walter of Hereford, who were second only to James of St George in privileges and perquisites, and, unlike James, arrived in Wales already familiar with the kind of castle that the king wanted.[24] Gatehouses may have been unknown in Savoy, but they had been part of the Anglo-French world since the twelfth century. They were built throughout the thirteenth, especially in the Welsh Marches. Most recently the Clare earls of Gloucester had built magnificent examples at Tonbridge in Kent and Caerphilly on the southern March; and Edward himself had built two at the Tower of London.[25] There was no shortage of masons who could design and build a strengthened gatehouse; and if James of St George did finally design Beaumaris, he no doubt learned how to do it from his English colleagues.

The details that came from Savoy arrived either with Master James or the masons who followed him over. Such men as Gilet of St George, Beynardus and John Francis, discovered by Taylor in both the Savoyard and Welsh records, were active professionals, building castles in Savoy that Master James only visited. They also came with fresh ideas, since the corbelled latrine at La Bâtiaz that inspired the one at Harlech was built only in 1282, long after Master James had left Savoy.

All this suggests an alternative view of the way the castles were designed. Instead of a genius acting alone we may postulate a collaboration between the king, the Savoyards and the English masons, the masons all working on the front line, urged on by directives from a monarch who knew clearly what he wanted. Yet if Master James is to be deprived of his role as a military architect, his honours, salary and pension must be explained. The explanation is evident in the records, a nice irony in view of the opacity that lies under their transparent surface. Edward did not summon Master James because of his genius as an architect. The merest glance at the buildings in Savoy reveals no signs of genius, and in any case James was hardly responsible for them; he is recorded working on only a few buildings, in a subordinate capacity. Where he mostly appears is as a co-ordinator, charged with supervising, over an extensive, mountainous area, a large number of important building programmes including castles and castles-with-towns.[26] Controlling a project that was divided by lakes, rivers and the Alps was a huge problem, which Master James seems to have overcome. This kind of supervision is exactly what he was called to do in Wales. The genius that Edward required was that of a consummate organizer with practical building knowledge.[27]

Although the king could call on many English masons who were competent builders, he evidently did not trust any of them to supervise the works as a whole. So we find Master James generally overseeing the proceedings, writing to the king and appearing at different buildings to do occasional pieces of work at task. The design features and symbolic ornament of the castles were decided by the king, with or without his clerical and military advisers; at every site an under-master from England or Savoy, each a master mason in his own right, was in charge of day-to-day building. These masons used their own familiar methods, whether English or Savoyard. Over the project as a whole bestrode the figure of James of St George, master mason and organizer *par excellence*.

This group of castles demonstrates what the lack of documents conceals in most medieval building campaigns: the necessary collaboration between the patron and the master masons on site. Taylor played down the contributions of the king, the English masons and the other Savoyards, not deliberately or indeed probably even consciously, but because he was wedded to the idea of a single architect who brought his genius to the service of a grateful patron. The idea of the architect as a solitary hero, working without the benefit of colleagues or collaboration, was current in academic circles of the mid-twentieth century when Taylor began his long voyage round James of St George. John Harvey's biography of the master mason, Henry Yevele, had apparently shown that it was legitimate to see a medieval mason in the same light, and gave Taylor's approach its legitimacy.[28] But more recent research has demonstrated the collaborative nature of medieval building enterprises, even – or perhaps especially – when the master mason himself was much in demand at several sites simultaneously.[29] The danger of seeing the architect as a solitary hero is not only that the picture becomes distorted, but that many other contributors are written out of history. Writing back in the people who built the castles in Wales does not deny James of St George's achievements or his significance: it redefines them.

Acknowledgement

This text is a reduced version of N. Coldstream, 'Architects, advisers and design at Edward I's Castles in Wales', *Architectural History*, 46 (2003), 19–36. I am grateful to the Society of Architectural Historians of Great Britain for permission to draw on material in that article. In it will be found a more detailed analysis than space allows here.

Notes

1. A. J. Taylor, 'Master James of St. George', *English Historical Review*, 65 (1950), 433–57. Master James's documented names include Jacobo Ingeniatori, Jakes de Seint Jorge and Jacqueto di Sancti Jorio, but he is Anglicized as James of St George.
2. Taylor, 'Master James'. Most of Taylor's articles on Master James and the castles in north Wales have been collected in A. J. Taylor, *Studies in Castles and Castle-Building* (London 1985). Useful accounts of Master James's documented career can also be found in R. A. Brown, H. M. Colvin and A. J. Taylor *The History of the King's Works: the Middle Ages*, I (London 1963), 203–05; J. Harvey, *English Mediaeval Architects: a Biographical Dictionary down to 1550*, rev. edn (Gloucester 1984); *The Dictionary of Art*, ed. J. Turner, 34 vols (London 1996); *Oxford Dictionary of National Biography*, 60 vols (Oxford 2004).
3. See the article by R. Turner in this volume.
4. A. J. Taylor, 'Castle building in thirteenth-century Wales and Savoy', *Proceedings of the British Academy*, 72 (1977), 265–92.
5. Taylor, 'Master James', 448–49.
6. Taylor, 'Castle-building'.
7. The windows at Chillon and Harlech have very similar measurements: Taylor, 'Castle-building', 274, fig. 2.
8. *King's Works*, II, 1036–39.
9. N. Pevsner, *An Outline of European Architecture*, 7th edn (London 1973), 15.
10. For example, Yverdon may resemble Flint in a printed ground plan, but the two buildings did not resemble each other: Taylor, 'Castle-building', pl. 13a and b.
11. Taylor in *King's Works*, I, 370–71; A. Wheatley, *The Idea of the Castle in Medieval England* (Woodbridge 2004), 112–22; A. Wheatley in this volume.
12. R. K. Morris, 'The architecture of Arthurian enthusiasm: castle symbolism in the reigns of Edward I and his successors', in *Arms, Chivalry and Warfare in Medieval Britain and France*, ed. M. Strickland, Proceedings of the 1995 Harlaxton Symposium (Stamford 1998), 63–81.
13. Taylor, 'Castle-building'; A. J. Taylor, 'Castle-building in Wales in the later thirteenth century: the prelude to construction', in *Studies in Building History: Essays in Recognition of the Work of B. H. St J. O'Neil*, ed. E. M. Jope (London 1961), 104–33.
14. *King's Works*, I, 341–42.
15. Taylor, 'Castle-Building in Wales'; T. F. Tout, *Chapters in the Administrative History of Mediaeval England*, II (Manchester 1920), 56; M. Prestwich, *Edward I* (London 1988), 138.
16. J. M. Maddison, 'Decorated architecture in the north-west Midlands – an investigation of the work of provincial masons and their sources', (unpublished PhD thesis, University of Manchester, 1978).
17. *Oxford Dictionary of National Biography*, 23 (Oxford 2004), 269–70 (under Grandson).
18. Prestwich, *Edward I*, 209.
19. Otherwise known as Tiptoft; A. J. Taylor, 'The castle of St. Georges-d'Espéranche', *Antiquaries Journal*, 33 (1953), 33–47: 33.
20. *King's Works*, I, 319.
21. ibid., 305.

22. Taylor, 'Castle-building in Wales', 121; *King's Works*, I, 341.
23. *King's Works*, I, 413.
24. Harvey, *English Mediaeval Architects*. See R. Turner in this volume.
25. D. Renn, 'Tonbridge and some other gatehouses', in *Collectanea Historica: Essays in Memory of Stuart Rigold*, ed. A. Detsicas (Maidstone 1981), 93–103.
26. Taylor, 'Master James'.
27. W. D. Simpson, 'Harlech Castle and the Edwardian castle plan', *Archaeologia Cambrensis*, 95 (1940), 163, n. 4, argued that Master James was not a mason but a civil servant; Taylor demonstrated unequivocally that he was a mason in Taylor, 'Master James of St George'. For further suggestions of Master James's activities in Wales, see K. Lilley in this volume.
28. J. Harvey, *Henry Yevele c. 1320–1400: the Life of an English Architect* (London 1944).
29. e.g. S. Murray, *Building Troyes Cathedral: the Late Gothic Campaigns* (Bloomington and Indianapolis 1987); R. Goy, *The House of Gold: Building a Palace in Medieval Venice* (Cambridge 1992).

6

The Life and Career of Richard the Engineer

Rick Turner

Introduction

It has been the fate of many worthy men to be remembered as the faithful lieutenant of someone more famous: in history, for example, Captain Hardy and Admiral Nelson. In architecture, such fine designers as Nicholas Hawksmoor and Herbert Baker are often remembered as the jobbing partners of the more celebrated Christopher Wren and Edwin Lutyens.

The same fate seems to have befallen Richard the Engineer, or *Lenginour* (about 1240–1315), who appears in the royal records as one of the key figures in the building of the Edwardian castles in north Wales.[1] These records have been taken to imply that he was in the second tier of master craftsmen employed by the royal works. Above him was the presiding genius and principal designer, James of St George, bringing with him the apparently superior military engineering of Savoy. Arnold Taylor's view of James has been the subject of re-evaluation.[2] Perhaps the time is right to do the same for Richard the Engineer. In his case, the royal records are complemented by those from Chester, Richard's home city. Here he was employed both before and after the Welsh wars; he had substantial business interests, built an elaborate town house and a country retreat close by.

This paper aims to combine these two sets of records to describe the career and life of a successful, and ultimately wealthy, royal servant, who was involved in one of the greatest projects of the Middle Ages. Beyond the records, many of the places associated with Richard the Engineer and even some of his works survive to illustrate his life and times (Fig. 6.1).

Career

Richard is most regularly referred to in the records as *Lenginour* or *ingeniator*.[3] Whilst other master craftsmen involved in the Edwardian building campaigns are also referred to as *ingeniatores* (for example James of St George

and his Savoyard colleague, Bertram),[4] no other took this particular title as their name. Other records refer to him as Master Richard of Chester, probably Master Richard *socio suo* and even Master R. His chosen title of 'engineer' strongly suggests he did not consider his primary skills as masonry or design. The evidence for his career shows that he acted in many roles: as project manager; the organizer of groundworks and the setting out of castles; master carpenter, particularly of complex structures around the tops of towers; the builder of temporary and permanent bridges; and the maker of siege engines. In addition, he undertook both masonry and carpentry contracts for fixed price sums, suggesting he was willing to take financial risks as well as the regular salary he received from the royal works.

He first appears as the superintendent of work on the outer bailey of Chester Castle (Fig. 6.2) in 1265.[5] The earldom of Chester was a palatinate, at that time a part of the estate of Lord Edward. Richard was therefore working for and was potentially known to the future King Edward I. It is unlikely he was less than twenty-five years old to have held such responsibility. His career prospered for by 1272/73 he is described as Richard *ingeniator* of Chester, a title he was to hold until his death.[6]

His first mention in the royal records appears in July 1277. Richard was put in charge of 1,850 men mustered at Flint to begin work on the castle there and at Rhuddlan. The trades represented were diggers (970), carpenters (330), woodmen (320), masons (200), smiths (12) and charcoal burners (10).[7] The make-up of this substantial workforce suggests that Richard oversaw the construction of the workmen's bases,[8] the clearance of the two sites, and the excavation of the moats and ditches. He may also have superintended the canalization of the river Clwyd from the sea to the site of Rhuddlan Castle.[9]

James of St George did not leave Edward's court to go to Wales until April 1278, 'to ordain the works of the castles there'.[10] By this date building materials had been delivered to Rhuddlan, and 10,000 stones were being

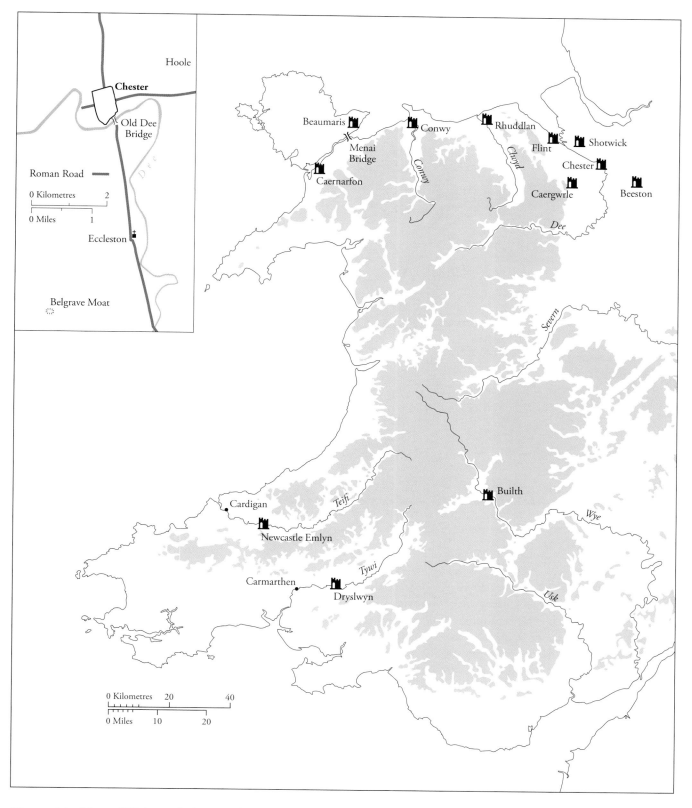

Figure 6.1: Map of Wales and the March showing the location of places mentioned in the text (Cadw, Welsh Assembly Government: Crown Copyright).

Figure 6.2: Plan of Chester Castle, about 1745, by Alexander de Lavaux (PM 18/1; by kind permission of Cheshire County Council and Chester City Council).

obtained for Flint from a quarry near Shotwick (Fig. 6.1). However, the king was at Rhuddlan, intermittently between 19 August to 27 September, and continuously then until 18/19 November 1277.[11] This re-opens the question of who designed Flint and Rhuddlan Castles (Plates 9 and 10). No doubt the king will have taken a great interest in this, but how much was left to Richard the Engineer and his colleague, Master Bertram, is a matter of speculation.[12]

Once Master James took overall charge of work at Flint and Rhuddlan in April 1278, Richard may have moved on to other works for he disappears temporarily from the records. At Builth Castle, from 9 May 1278 'Master R' and Master 'W' of Bromborough were paid 3s. 0d. and 2s. 6d. per week respectively and were described as master

carpenters.[13] The work was under the control of the master mason, Henry of Leominster, so if it is our Richard, his presence may have been to complete a specific task rather than to take overall charge. An alternative explanation for Richard's disappearance from the royal records can be found in the annals of St Werburgh's Abbey, Chester. They record that on 15 May 1278: 'Almost the whole of Chester within the walls of the city was burned down.'[14] As Chester's master mason, Richard may have been put in charge of a programme of reconstruction work in the city.

On 16 March 1281, Master Richard of Chester joined Master James of St George at Flint.[15] He was the second highest paid person at 10d. per day, compared with James at 2s. 0d. per day. However, events again in Chester that year may have brought him back to the city for the Dee Bridge was swept away.[16] Richard disappears from the records until 16 June 1282 when he was despatched with a team of 340 carpenters to Hope (Caergwrle) Castle. This was to repair damage caused by Dafydd ap Gruffudd when he slighted his own castle, an act of rebellion which helped fuel Edward's second Welsh campaign.[17] Richard's role was limited to this rapid response making the castle defensible and habitable using wood, leaving the large-scale reconstruction of the stone castle under Master James's direction. Two months later Richard was in Anglesey where he supervised the construction of a bridge of boats, partly manufactured and sent out from Chester.[18] The bridge was to cross the Menai Strait to Bangor, held at that point by the Welsh.

Richard's initial role was to set up the beachhead and construction camp near Llanfaes. He and his team of sixty were soon joined by Master Henry of Oxford with an additional 100 men and together they assembled the bridge in concert with Master Bertram. When the work was done Bertram *et R. socio suo* (his aide) were rewarded with a tun of wine each and wine was distributed amongst the whole workforce. The ship, *La Blithe* of Hastings, had engines placed in it, and these may also have been designed by Richard. The bridge was ready for use on 6 November 1282, but the first military expedition to cross it was a disaster, when sixteen knights and 300 infantry were lost in a Welsh ambush. The bridge was maintained over the winter, and a Bangor bridgehead became established. This work remained under the supervision of Henry of Oxford whilst Richard's whereabouts are unknown.

During the early years of the construction of Caernarfon Castle and town walls, beginning in the summer of 1283, Richard acted as Master James of St George's second-in-command; on 21 October 1284, the king granted James a life pension of 3s. per day and Richard 1s. per day.[19] He also had a complementary role in the building of Conwy Castle and town walls. On 30 March 1284, Richard was sent from Conwy to Chester and later to Newcastle-under-Lyme to procure the tools and workmen necessary to cut the rock ditches of the castle.[20] During 1284–85, he and Henry of Oxford were responsible for the carpentry and Master James the masonry of the hall, king's and queen's chambers built within the masonry shell of the castle.[21] This is an early example of payment for task work, rather than payment for all staff on day works. This change may reflect a desire to try to contain the costs more effectively now that the conquest had been successfully completed and the control of the hinterland had been established.

The records for Richard's activities again fall silent until the revolt of the Welsh prince, Rhys ap Maredudd,

Figure 6.3: View of Dryslwyn Castle (Cadw, Welsh Assembly Government: Crown Copyright).

in June 1287. Within weeks an army totalling 11,400 men had been mustered from the whole of Wales and the Marcher lordships. It was under the command of the king's cousin, Edmund, earl of Cornwall. Rhys had taken refuge in his castle of Dryslwyn (Carmarthenshire) when this force arrived to mount a siege in mid-August (Fig. 6.3). Master Richard the Engineer probably came with the contingent sent from Chester, and he began to build a siege engine (almost certainly a trebuchet) at Carmarthen (Fig. 6.4). Materials had been obtained before his arrival and payments were made for large quantities of timber, hides, ropes, pulleys, nails and lead with a total recorded cost of £17 9s. 3d.[22] In addition, Master Adam and nineteen others spent a fortnight in a quarry making stone balls for the siege engine. These were delivered between 22 August and 8 September – when the castle surrendered – during which time the engine was probably firing.[23]

Richard will also have overseen the attempts to undermine the castle walls by sapping. Though this was ultimately successful, a party of knights led by William

Figure 6.4: View of the trebuchet in action at Caerphilly Castle (Cadw, Welsh Assembly Government: Crown Copyright).

de Moncensey was killed when the tunnels collapsed on them during an inspection of the works.[24]

Rhys ap Maredudd escaped from Dryslwyn and fled to Newcastle Emlyn Castle, where a second siege took place. The siege engine was first hauled to Cardigan by forty oxen, and then onto Newcastle Emlyn by sixty oxen, under escort from 500 soldiers, where it was used in the capture of that castle.[25]

For the following few years, Richard seems to have concentrated on his business interests in Chester and supervision of works at the city's castle (Fig. 6.5).[26] However, it was a second revolt, more widespread and threatening than that of 1287, which brought Richard back into the king's service. The revolt broke out in the autumn of 1294 under the leadership of Madog ap Llywelyn and saw the capture of such major castles as Caernarfon, Denbigh and Ruthin. Edward I was trapped in Conwy Castle from Christmas 1294 until spring 1295.[27] Despite this, preparations were put in place for building the new castle of Beaumaris. This was to be facilitated by the construction of a second bridge

of boats across the Menai Strait, this time beginning on the Bangor side. James of St George and Richard the Engineer ordered the felling of 2,300 oaks on the lands owned by the abbot of St Werburgh and elsewhere in Cheshire and the boats were constructed in the Dee Estuary in March 1295. The bridge was ready for use by 10 April after which the building of Beaumaris began in earnest, though Richard seems to have taken no further part in the project.[28]

After this rebellion, the king's attention turned to the conquest of Scotland.[29] This led James of St George to take responsibility for the military engineering there,[30] leaving Richard the Engineer to undertake a range of repairs and improvements at Edward's castles in north-east Wales and Cheshire in the years 1301–04.[31] At Flint, works to the value of £146 were undertaken. The main item was the addition of *una carola lignee nobili et pulchra*, a noble and beautiful timber gallery added to the top of the Great Tower. The contract was assigned to Richard, who probably designed it, but the work was carried out by a deputy, the Chester carpenter, Master

Figure 6.5: The outer bailey, Chester Castle, with the hall to the left and the square Agricola Tower beyond, by Moses Griffith (Grosvenor Museum, Chester City Council).

Henry de Rihull (Rhyl?). A programme of works was also undertaken at Rhuddlan. Here, Richard supervised a range of craftsmen occupied in repairs and additions, including the construction of a timber oriel at the top of the north tower of the inner ward. This may have been a similar if less complex structure to the *carola* at Flint. These works were prompted by the king's grant of royal lands in Wales to his son Edward of Caernarfon, when he became prince of Wales. It may have been Prince Edward who ordered the work to be carried out through the justiciar and chamberlain of Chester.[32]

Richard was also instructed to undertake a series of repairs at Chester Castle following a fire in 1303. This involved works inside the Agricola Tower and to the hall and great kitchen (Figs 6.2 and 6.5). Similar tasks were undertaken at Beeston Castle.[33]

The king did call on Richard for one major piece of work in his Scottish campaigns. This drew on one of his particular specialisms, for he was summoned to Windsor in January 1303 to discuss the building of three bridges to outflank the Scottish garrison at Stirling Castle. He

returned to Chester to muster a squad of carpenters and these were sent off under his deputy, Master Henry de Rihull, to King's Lynn, Norfolk. Here they prefabricated the bridges, with remarkable speed, in the same manner as the two Menai Strait bridges. They were carried on floating pontoons and were each defended by a brattice, containing a drawbridge raised by hawsers running over brass pulleys. Their total cost was £938 9s. 6d. and the fleet sailed on 24 May.[34]

By this time Richard the Engineer was well into his sixties. His final recorded commission was at the Benedictine abbey of St Werburgh, now Chester Cathedral.[35] Richard received two substantial payments or recognizances from the abbot of £40 in 1310 and another of £20 13s. in 1312/13.[36] These sums are more than he would have received as a designer and are more likely to represent payment for works. The rebuilding of the choir of St Werburgh's in the late thirteenth and early fourteenth century is very complicated and involved a number of designers. Richard played a part, but his exact role is not clear.[37]

Figure 6.6: The Old Dee Bridge and Chester Castle, by Moses Griffith (Grosvenor Museum, Chester City Council).

Business and life in Chester

Tracing Richard the Engineer's business interests in Chester is more difficult than following his career in Wales. He is best recorded as the lessee of the mills alongside the Old Dee Bridge and the fishtraps set between the arches of the bridge (Fig. 6.6). These he leased from Edward I in the king's capacity as the earl of Chester. All the corn to make bread for sale within Chester had by law to be ground in the Dee Mills, and the proprietor took one-sixteenth of all the flour produced in the mills.[38] In 1275, Richard paid £140 to the king for the right to operate the mills for a year. At this time the mills seem to have been the subject of an annual lease as Master Bertram, another royal mason/*ingeniator*, leased the mills from 1277 until 1282 when the lease was retaken by Richard.[39] In 1284 he took a twelve-year lease of the mills and fishery for £200 per year. Under the terms of the lease, he was responsible for repairs, but not if the bridge or causeway was carried away by a flood, or the mills destroyed through war or fire. During this period he received a number of rebates worth a total of £154 because he was kept away from Chester in the king's service at Rhuddlan and Caernarfon. Richard also asserted his rights under the lease, for in 1290 he

seized a cartload of bread brought from Warwick for sale in Chester. Also, in 1290, he built two new mills and in 1298 he carried out substantial repairs on all five mills.[40] The millers were amongst the richest citizens of Chester, for at the same time the total of other farms or businesses let from the king in Chester amounted to only £100 per annum; half the amount Richard had paid for the lease of the mills and fishery.[41]

Throughout the Welsh campaigns, Chester was the focal point through which men, materials and money flowed. Richard would have been well placed to make the most of these opportunities. He had a permanent salary as master mason for the city and from 1284 a life pension from the king. On top of that regular income he had the profits from the mills and fishery. He was also willing to undertake projects as task work for the royal works, and design and direct operations, when he was too old to take control on site. These activities betray an entrepreneurial spirit, which seems to have flourished in Chester in the last quarter of the thirteenth century.

It is interesting to speculate what role Richard played in the design and construction of individual merchant's houses in the Rows or even for this unique system as a whole. A number of reasons have been given for the development of this two-tier system of commercial premises. These include topographic, commercial and the issue of a now lost comital decree. No single explanation is widely held.[42] Richard the Engineer owned houses in Bridge Street and Watergate Street, but his own residence was a major stone house within the Row system, occupying the site of 57–71 Lower Bridge Street (Fig. 6.7).[43] In the later seventeenth century, Randle Holme, the Chester Herald, noted that: 'This in ancient tyme was a famous structure of ston much like a castle or ffort having an high tower'. This part of Chester, east of the castle in the parish of St Mary's, seems to have contained the homes of a number of palatinate officials. Richard's house, with its high tower, had a barn forming a south range along Claverton Lane (modern Duke Street). This suggests that his house and business premises were combined around a courtyard. It was known as Pareas Hall, after its sale by Richard's son, Almaricus, to Robert Pares or Praers.[44] Large stone town houses with high towers are very rare in English medieval cities compared with their ubiquity in contemporary Italy. The only known parallel to Richard's house in England was the Manor of the Rose, Pountney Lane, London, built by Sir John Pultney (d. 1349), who was mayor in 1336. Its battlemented tower was shown still standing in a drawing of 1550.[45]

Richard was married to Agnes and had at least two sons, with the names Giles, Aymer, Egidius and Almaricus appearing in different records, and a daughter, Agnes. Lawsuits in the Chester Courts refer by name to a number of Master Richard's servants and he clearly had a considerable household centred on his home in Chester.[46] He acquired land and houses at Hoole, a suburb of Chester, and farmed cattle.[47] More surprisingly, he built for himself a country retreat at Belgrave (NGR SJ 390 605), 3.7 miles (6km) south of the city.[48] The name first appears about 1290 and it lies in the parish of Eccleston. Richard began acquiring land in Eccleston in 1284 and added to his holdings in the area over the next ten years. The first mention of a house at Belgrave comes in 1309 when Richard grants his 'messuage called Belgrave' to his son Egidius. What survives is a well-preserved trapezoidal moat with an internal platform about 280 feet (85m) across covering an area of 1.66 acres (6,750sq m) (Fig. 6.8). The main ditch is about 40 feet (12m) wide and about 8 feet (2.5m) deep. There is no evidence for buildings surviving on the platform, but what is most unusual is a group of secondary earthworks on the western and northern sides. These focus on a circular and triangular mound in the north-west corner. Small-scale excavation in 1986 suggested that they were garden features, with

shallow flowerbeds linked by flimsy wooden bridges contemporary with the main earthworks.[49]

If so, then this is evidence for Richard the Engineer's garden at his country house. Richard the Engineer is likely to have been familiar with gardens, for in 1283 Queen Eleanor had a herber made at Conwy Castle and there was a king's garden, ditched and hedged at Caernarfon Castle by 1295. Even closer to home he would have overseen the making of gardens, orchards and vegetable plots at Chester Castle between 1287 and 1302.[50] Moreover, the plan of the Belgrave Moat and its secondary works echoes very closely that of Flint Castle, if the latter is rotated through 180 degrees (compare Fig. 6.8 with Fig. 6.9). Perhaps this was Richard's whimsical reference to the project that really launched him on his successful career in royal service.

Other royal officials and merchants developed both town and country houses when they became rich during the reign of Edward I and his successors. For even more successful men than Richard, one can look at the wool merchant, Laurence of Ludlow (d. 1294), who had a substantial stone house, Bennett's Hall on Pride Hill, in Shrewsbury,[51] and built the remarkable Stokesay Castle, near Craven Arms, on a site he had acquired in 1281.[52] As we have seen, Sir John Pultney, merchant and mayor of London, later built the Manor of the Rose in the city; he also built the impressive hall surviving at Penshurst Place, Kent, in the country.[53]

Conclusion

John Harvey, in his comprehensive entry on Richard Lenginour in *English Mediaeval Architects*, concluded:

> Master Richard was clearly a craftsman of great importance, notwithstanding the higher fees accorded to James of St George, and if the latter was the expert designer of the extraordinary series of fortifications built in North Wales, it was Richard who was for many years in charge of the routine supervision and upkeep of these works.[54]

Harvey's summary, however, hardly gives Richard the credit he deserves: he had the confidence of Lord Edward, later King Edward I, before Master James of St George arrived. He was almost certainly a carpenter by training and not primarily a mason. He was a prototype Royal Engineer, specializing in bridge building and groundworks. He had a remarkable skill in organizing very large groups of men from different trades and delivering complex projects expeditiously in the aftermath of conflict or under the gaze of potential enemies.

He was also a designer of siege engines and siege works, a skill which the name 'Engineer' seems to celebrate. Nevertheless he was also capable of designing and

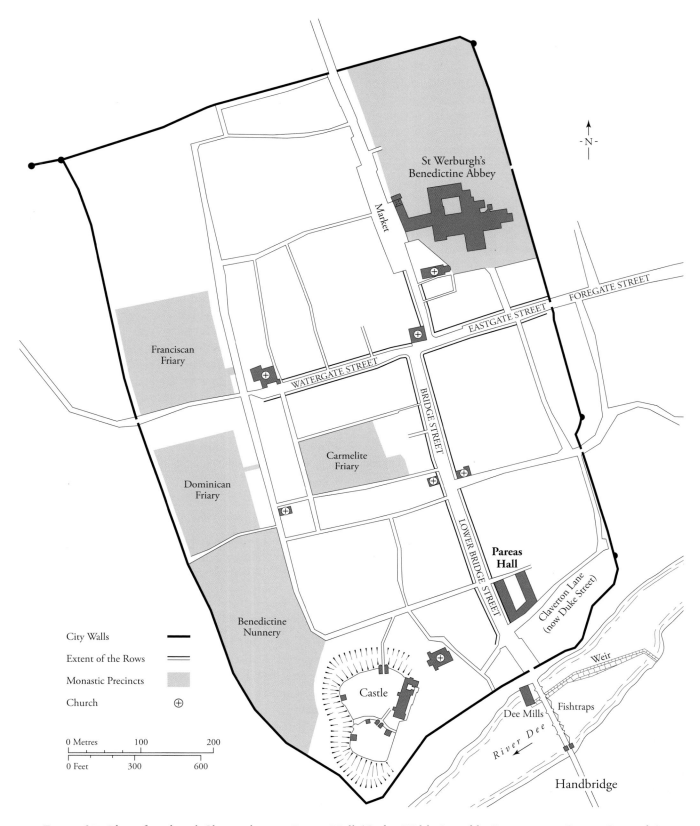

Figure 6.7: Plan of medieval Chester showing Pareas Hall (Cadw, Welsh Assembly Government: Crown Copyright).

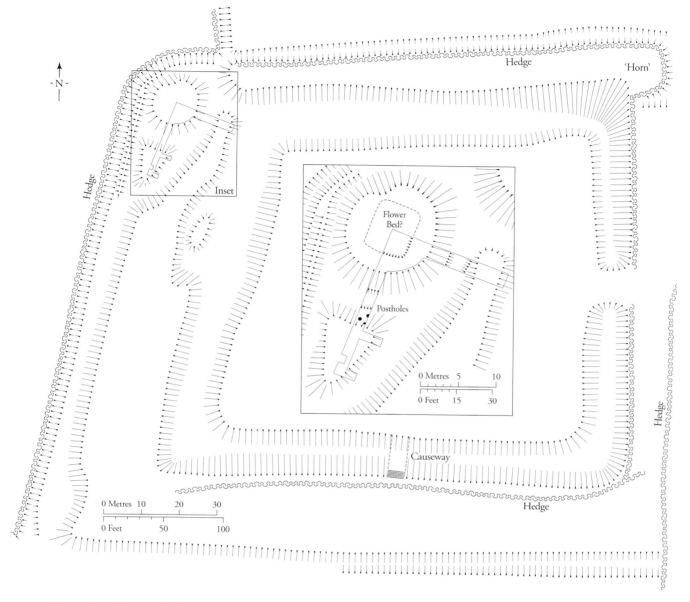

Figure 6.8: Plan of the Belgrave Moat (Cadw, Welsh Assembly Government: Crown Copyright, after B. Sale).

overseeing the erection of complex and high decorative structures such as the timber *carola* on the Great Tower at Flint.

There are gaps in his career for which no records survive. He may have had greater involvement in Chester, perhaps working on the town walls and bridge as well as the castle. It is tempting to assign him more of a role in building houses within the Rows or even in laying out this unique system. He must have remained a fit and active man for he was travelling extensively into his sixties and still at work in his seventies. The opportunities for excitement, adventure, professional

glory and advancement offered by the two Welsh wars and their aftermath were seized by Richard the Engineer and helped him prosper.

It is the other side of the surviving records that help to fill out the picture of the man, like few other master craftsmen of this day.[55] As well as being a royal official, he was a businessman. We know about the leasing of the Dee Mills and fishery, but this cannot be all for with the men, materials and money passing through Chester on an unprecedented scale, there would no doubt have been other opportunities. From November 1284, he received an annual pension of £18 4s., which provided security. To this

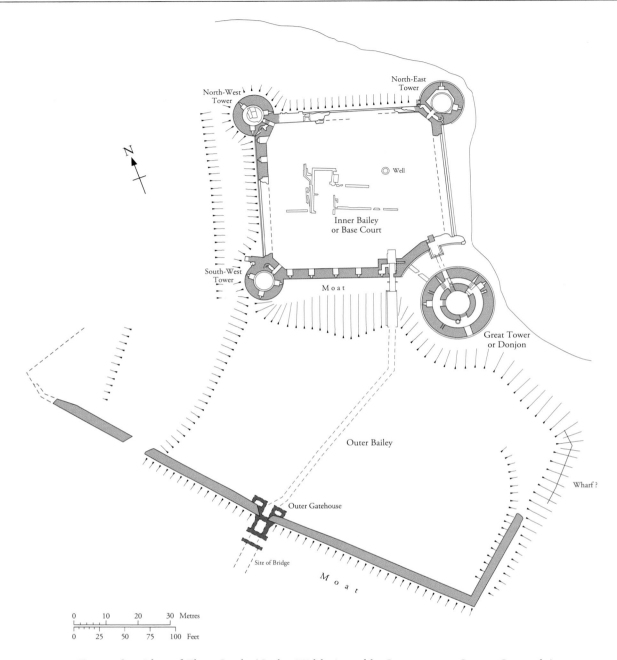

Figure 6.9: Plan of Flint Castle (Cadw, Welsh Assembly Government: Crown Copyright).

he could add income from business ventures and building contracts, as well as fees earned from his patrons.

Some of this wealth was put into the building of a large, stone town house in Lower Bridge Street, Chester, which provided a home and office for his family and his household. Other profits were used to acquire land in the beautiful Dee valley, south of the city, where he built his extensive moated manor house and gardens at Belgrave. The name implies it was a beautiful place of retreat for this busy man to relax with his family and reflect on his remarkable life and career.

Acknowledgements

I would particularly like to thank Brian Crossley of the Institution of Civil Engineers for encouraging my research into Richard the Engineer, and to Bevis Sale and Pete Lawrence (Welsh Assembly Government) for preparing the line drawings.

Notes

1. J. Harvey, *English Mediaeval Architects: a Biographical Dictionary down to 1550*, rev. edn (Gloucester 1984), 178–80, and indexed entries to Richard the Engineer in R. A. Brown, H. M. Colvin and A. J. Taylor, *The History of the King's Works: the Middle Ages* (London 1963).

2. N. Coldstream, 'Architects, advisers and design at Edward I's castles in Wales', *Architectural History*, 46 (2003), 19–36, and Coldstream (this volume).

3. The relevant entries for the Edwardian castles of Wales in the *King's Works* are gathered together, and updated, in A. Taylor, *The Welsh Castles of Edward I* (London 1986) and the page references in this work are used below.

4. Taylor, *Welsh Castles*, 29.

5. F. Simpson, 'Chester Castle, A.D. 907–1923', *Journal of the Chester & North Wales Archaeological & Historical Society*, new ser. 26 (1925), 71–132.

6. R. Stewart-Brown, 'Cheshire Pipe Rolls 1158–1301', *Record Society of Lancashire and Cheshire*, 92 (1938), 108–09.

7. Taylor, *Welsh Castles*, 17–18; The National Archives (TNA): PRO E 101/350/25; E 101/3/19.

8. The initial encampment may have formed the basis for the later town; see Lilley, this volume.

9. Though Taylor credits this to Master William, the *fossator*, his table on p. 17 shows that the master diggers were under Richard's command.

10. Taylor, *Welsh Castles*, 3.

11. ibid., 27.

12. ibid., 25, 28.

13. ibid., 4; TNA: PRO E 101/486/22.

14. R. C. Christie (ed.), 'Annales Cestrienses; or, Chronicle of the abbey of St. Werburgh, at Chester', *Record Society of Lancashire and Cheshire*, 14 (1887), 104–05.

15. Taylor, *Welsh Castles*, 20; TNA: PRO E 101/674/23.

16. Richard was also credited with supervising the building of Rhuddlan Bridge in 1281/2. E. Jervoise, *Ancient Bridges of Wales and Western England* (London 1936), 36.

17. Taylor, *Welsh Castles*, 39, TNA: PRO C 47/2/3, and J. Manley, 'Excavations at Caergwrle Castle, Clwyd, north Wales: 1988–1990', *Medieval Archaeology*, 38 (1994), 83–133.

18. Taylor, *Welsh Castles*, 62–65; TNA: PRO E 101.3.26.

19. Taylor, *Welsh Castles*, 82; *Calendar of Patent Rolls 1281–1292*, 137.

20. Taylor, *Welsh Castles*, 49; TNA: PRO SC 1/1/3/152.

21. Taylor, *Welsh Castles*, 52; J. Ashbee, 'The royal apartments in the inner ward at Conwy Castle', *Archaeologia Cambrensis*, 153 (2004), 51–72, and this volume; TNA: PRO E 372/131, rot. 26.

22. *Records of the Wardrobe and Household 1286–1289*, eds B. F. Byerly and C. R. Byerly (London 1986), 438, no. 3637.

23. C. Phillpotts and C. Caple, 'History of the revolt and siege (1287–97)', in C. Caple, *Excavations at Dryslwyn Castle 1980–95* (Leeds 2007), 185–190. TNA: PRO E 372/132 m1, E 101/4/16. In addition, the Dryslwyn Castle report has sections on the archaeological evidence for the siege, contemporary trebuchet balls and other weaponry.

24. A. J. Taylor, 'Who was 'John Pennardd, leader of the men of Gwynedd'?', *English Historical Review*, 91 (1976), 79–97.

25. R. A. Griffiths, 'The revolt of Rhys ap Maredudd, 1287–88', *Welsh History Review*, 3.2 (1966), 121–43.

26. For a list of works undertaken at Chester Castle from 1275 to 1301 see *A History of the County of Chester, V, part 2: The City of Chester: Culture, Buildings, Institutions*, eds C. P. Lewis and A. T. Thacker (Woodbridge and London 2005), 208–09. The twin-towered gatehouse of the outer bailey of Chester Castle was built in 1292–93 by Master William Marlow, showing Richard used assistants for daily supervision.

27. R. R. Davies, *Conquest, Coexistence and Change: Wales 1063–1415* (Oxford 1987), 380–82.

28. Taylor, *Welsh Castles*, 104; *Cal. Chancery Warrants*, 53; *Cal. Inquisitions Misc.* I, 475.

29. M. Prestwich, *Edward I* (London 1988).

30. Harvey, *Mediaeval Architects*, 267.

31. ibid., 179.

32. For Flint see Taylor, *Welsh Castles*, 26; TNA: PRO SC 6/771/1; A. Jones (ed.), 'Flintshire ministers' accounts 1301–1328', *Flintshire Historical Society Publications*, 3 (1913), 15–16, 32–35 and 45. For Rhuddlan see Taylor, *Welsh Castles*, 34; TNA: PRO SC 6/771/1, 2 and 4; Jones, 'Flintshire ministers accounts', 16–17, 36–37, 46–47.

33. Harvey, *Mediaeval Architects*, 179.

34. ibid., 179; *Calendar of Documents relating to Scotland*, ed. J. Bain, II (London 1884), 352–53; A. Z. Freeman, 'Wall-breakers and river-bridgers: military engineers in the Scottish wars of Edward I', *Journal of British Studies*, 10.2 (1971), 1–16.

35. R. V. H. Burne, *The Monks of Chester: the History of St Werburgh's Abbey* (London 1962). For a full architectural analysis see J. M. Maddison, 'The choir of Chester Cathedral', *Journal of the Chester Archaeological Society*, 66 (1983), 31–46.

36. Harvey, *Mediaeval Architects*, 179–80.

37. Maddison, 'Chester Cathedral' and J. Maddison, 'Problems in the Choir of Chester Cathedral', in ed. A. Thacker, *Medieval Archaeology, Art and Architecture at Chester*, British Archaeological Association Conference Transactions 22 (Leeds 2000), 66–80.

38. H. J. Hewitt, *Cheshire under the Three Edwards* (Chester 1967), 24–27.

39. Taylor, *Welsh Castles*, 127.

40. *A History of the County of Chester, V, part 2*, 105–06.

41. Hewitt, *Cheshire*, 26.

42. See 'Origins of the Rows', in A. Brown ed., *The Rows of Chester: the Chester Rows Research Project* (London 1999), 55–62.

43. *A History of the County of Chester, V, part 1: The City of Chester: General History and Topography*, eds C. P. Lewis and A. T. Thacker (Woodbridge and London 2003), 53 and 218.

44. Brown, *The Rows*, 15, 33, 166; London, British Library, Harleian Ms. 7568, f. 154: J. H. E. B[ennett], ' 'Pares Place or Hawarden's Hall', Chester', *Cheshire Sheaf*, 3 ser. 19 (1922) 72–73.

45. J. Schofield, *The Building of London from the Conquest to the Great Fire*, 3rd edn (Stroud 1999), 81–82 and fig. 83.

46. R. H. Morris, *Chester in the Plantagenet and Tudor Reigns* (Chester 1894), 101–04; R. Stewart-Brown, 'Calendar of the County Court, City Court and Eyre rolls of Chester 1259–1297', *Chetham Society*, new ser. 84 (1925); A. Hopkins, 'Selected rolls of the Chester City Courts', *Chetham Society*, 3 ser. 2 (1950).

47. *A History of the County of Chester, V, part 1*, 53.

48. R. C. Turner, C. B. Sale and J. A. A. Rutter, 'A medieval garden at the Belgrave Moat, Cheshire', *Journal of the Chester Archaeological Society*, 69 (1986), 59–77.

49. ibid.

50. J. Harvey, *Mediaeval Gardens* (London 1981), 84.

51. N. J. Baker, J. B. Lawson, R. Maxwell and J. T. Smith, 'Further work on Pride Hill, Shrewsbury'. *Shropshire History and Archaeology*, 68 (1993), 3–64.

52. J. Munby and H. Summerson, *Stokesay Castle, Shropshire* (London 2002).

53. C. Platt, *The Architecture of Medieval Britain: a Social History* (London 1990), 151.

54. Harvey, *Mediaeval Architects*, 180.

55. ibid., xl.

Builth Castle and Aberystwyth Castle 1277–1307

David M. Browne

Introduction

Builth Castle and Aberystwyth Castle remain little known compared with the Edwardian castles of the north Wales coast. However, sited on the southern and western flanks of Llywelyn ap Gruffudd's Gwynedd, they were of considerable strategic and political importance with work beginning at both sites in 1277.

The purpose of this paper is to review the work at these castles since Arnold Taylor compiled his entries in *The History of the King's Works*. At Builth a comprehensive earthwork survey took place in 1977 and at Aberystwyth there was an extended programme of archaeological excavation between 1975 and 1988. This paper is an opportunity to compare the results of this archaeological fieldwork with a comprehensive review of the documentary sources to put the development and final plans of the castles alongside those of the better-known sites in Cadw's care.

The period between 1274 and November 1276 witnessed increasingly dangerous tensions in the relationship between Llywelyn ap Gruffudd, acknowledged as prince of Wales by Henry III by the Treaty of Montgomery in 1267, and subsequently by the new king of England, Edward I. The political situation was exacerbated by Llywelyn's avoidance of paying homage to Edward, an act required of him for the provisions of the treaty of 1267 to be effected. It is likely that Edward had harboured the intention of bringing Llywelyn to submission for some time and the latter's recalcitrance played into his hands. In November 1276 Edward decided on war, and large-scale preparations were put underway for a three-pronged assault. Soldiers and construction workers massed at Chester, Montgomery and Carmarthen.

Much of the south of Wales was pacified during the first months of 1277, the royal army being under the command of Payn de Chaworth of Kidwelly. Dinefwr Castle was taken by April; the first accounts of work at Builth date from 3 May. In June Edmund of Lancaster, the king's brother, took charge of the army based at Carmarthen and he was joined shortly by a large number of labourers and craftsmen recruited in south-west England and transported by sea from Bristol. The southern campaign effectively ended when Edmund arrived at Llanbadarn (Aberystwyth) on 25 July and building of the castle began on 1 August. The war as a whole came to an end with Llywelyn's submission in November.

The dispositions of the royal castles of Builth, Aberystwyth, Flint, Rhuddlan, Ruthin and Hawarden, as well as the works at other frontier sites, show that Edward had decided to subdue the Welsh by colonizing their land with permanent, strongly defended castles and associated fortified settlements. It could be argued that the scheme of 1277 was the first stage of a longer-term plan which needed the political excuse given by the revolt of 1282 to implement. The authors of *The King's Works,*[1] and subsequent writers, did not believe that Edward intended to conquer all of Wales at the time of his 1276–77 campaign. Instead, they suggest that his strategy was to pen in a dependent prince and this required, in addition to pre-existing garrisons, new castles at the strategic locations of Aberystwyth, Builth, Flint and Rhuddlan and elsewhere.

Builth Castle (Plate 7)

Builth Castle (Fig. 7.1) is sited on the edge of a terrace on the south side of a right-angled loop of the river Wye at between 427 feet and 459 feet (130m–140m) above sea level. It commands an important crossing of the Wye, half a mile (0.8km) south-east of its confluence with the river Irfon. Edward's castle was raised on the site of an earlier Norman stronghold that was thoroughly demolished in 1260 by Llywelyn ap Gruffudd in a show of force to back up his diplomatic moves to obtain a peace treaty with

Figure 7.1: An aerial view of Builth Castle (© Crown Copyright: Royal Commission on the Ancient and Historical Monuments of Wales; NPRN 92025; GTJ25808).

Henry III as well as recognition of his principality.[2]

When Arnold Taylor wrote his analysis of Builth Castle, the earliest of Edward I's fortress-building programme, he began by observing that 'not one stone … is now to be seen above ground.'[3] The situation has hardly changed since. Jack Spurgeon, however, has carried out a detailed re-appraisal of the site on which this account is based (Fig. 7.2).[4]

Documentary Evidence

Some information about the main buildings of the castle can be derived from Taylor's documentary analysis.[5] Works began in early May 1277 with the construction of temporary timber buildings for use as a chapel, hall, chamber, kitchen and smithy; Taylor, reasonably, placed the hall and chamber on the pre-existing motte. By mid-November all the structures had been dismantled and a

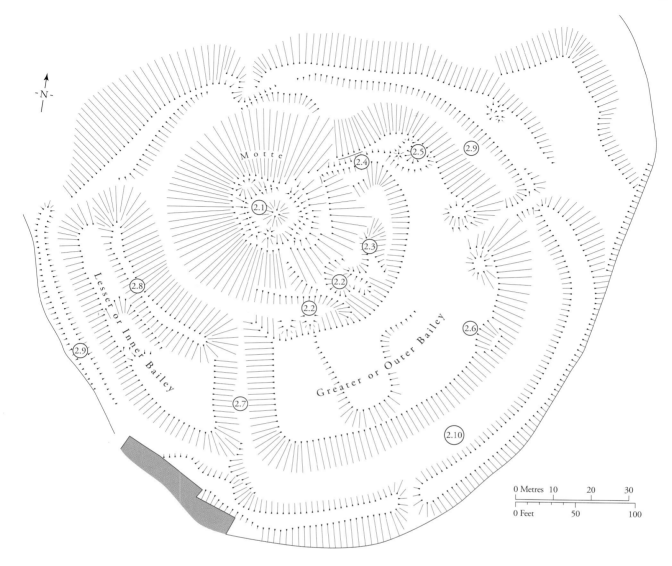

Figure 7.2: Plan of Builth Castle (Cadw, Welsh Assembly Government: Crown Copyright).

new hall, kitchen, brewhouse and stable had been built in stone. Considerable progress was also made in the latter half of 1277 in building a keep or great tower. In 1278 several structures were finished and a large palisade was erected around the lesser or outer bailey. The curtain that replaced the palisade was begun in 1279 or 1280, but progress was slow up to October of the latter year.

The account of October 1280 lists several buildings then in existence: the great tower, a stone wall with six towers around the castle, a 'turning' bridge with two large towers, a stone wall around the greater or inner bailey, a ditch in advance of the inner bailey wall, and the beginnings of the stone wall around the outer bailey.

Taylor suggests that the great tower took the form of a shell keep.[6]

Building continued at a reduced pace over the next couple of years and seems to have come to a finish towards the end of 1282 with important parts of the castle, such as the gatehouse, incomplete.

Description of the Site

Spurgeon was of the view that 'the existing earthworks … essentially represent the pre-existing motte-and-bailey castle of the Braose family which was probably raised before 1100.' Also 'Builth appears to have exploited the pre-existing earthworks to the full to create a castle quite unique in the [Edwardian] series.'[7] The arguments put forward to support these positions are reasonable.

Spurgeon makes several suggestions about the visible remains of the castle in relation to the Edwardian documentary evidence cited by Taylor. The only possible trace of the great tower (Fig. 7.2.1) is the sub-rectangular embankment on the top of the motte. Such remains would accord with the suggestion that the great tower was a shell keep. The mounds in the south-east part of the motte ditch probably represent substantial deposits of masonry and rubble, which may be derived from the twin-towered gatehouse referred to in 1280 (Fig. 7.2.2). The north–south shelf on the upper third of the slope of the motte on its east side might mark the site of the stone wall, which the documents state had six towers (Fig. 7.2.3). The bank that separates the motte ditch from the main ditch on the north-east is the remains of a mortared wall (Fig. 7.2.4); it may have terminated in a round tower at the north end of the bailey, marked by a circular bank (Fig. 7.2.5). Spurgeon believed these features belonged to the Edwardian period. He makes a very tentative identification of another tower with a scoop and shelf, 148 feet (45m) south of the possible north tower (Fig. 7.2.6).

Spurgeon suggests that the ditch (Fig. 7.2.7), which sub-divides the original crescentic bailey, was constructed for the Edwardian castle, and by implication that the wall recorded around the bailey was within its inner eastern lip. Spurgeon doubts that the narrow segment of the original bailey north-west of the ditch was walled. Instead, he draws attention to a steep bank along its north-east side above the motte ditch which he interprets as a strengthening obstacle erected in the Edwardian phase (Fig. 7.2.8).

The main outer ditch on the west and south-west, west of the ditch sub-dividing the original bailey, is shorter and shallower than the ditch east of the sub-dividing ditch and which is dug around the rest of the circuit (Fig. 7.2.9). Spurgeon associates the obvious widening and deepening on the south and east with the cutting of the sub-dividing ditch, which he believes took place in Edward's reign (Fig. 7.2.10). Builth did not have wet ditches.[8]

Other than point to some irregularities in the earthworks on the northerly side it is impossible to be sure of the location of the main entrance without excavation.

Conclusion

Builth Castle, as far as it is possible to judge from the available evidence, stands apart from the other Edwardian castles built as part of the first war. Indeed, it also stands apart from those castles erected after the rebellion of 1282. It was part of the 'fence' of castles erected to confine the prince of Gwynedd, but unlike Rhuddlan, Flint and Aberystwyth it was not accessible from the sea. Such accessibility, with its positive implications of lower costs for supply and reinforcement, was an important part of Edward's military strategy. But, in the case of Builth, for Edward this imposition of a new castle on this site was much more than a military act. It was a very firm assertion of ownership and overlordship, and a humiliation of Llywelyn who had destroyed the Anglo-Norman stronghold there in 1260 in an equally politically charged action. Henceforth the prince would have no recognized claim to the central lordship of Builth; the relevant sections of the Treaty of Montgomery were abrogated. The niceties of military architecture came second in this scheme of things.

The plans of Aberystwyth, Flint and Rhuddlan (Plates 8, 9 and 10), whilst each rather different from the other, share some important similarities. There is an attention to symmetry in layout, the construction of a great focal keep tower is eschewed (the Great Tower at Flint is not of this kind), and projecting angle towers around the whole enceinte are basic features. The choice of a site with pre-existing massive earthworks, which were too expensive to flatten, restricted the room for innovation of the builder initially in charge of the works. Builth, consequently, is unique among Edward's castles for the erection of a keep or tower on an elevated mound. The builder probably tried to incorporate up-to-date curtain and tower features as best he could, but he was clearly restricted in possibilities.

Aberystwyth Castle (Plate 8)

Aberystwyth Castle was built on a coastal promontory, with a south-east to north-west axis, rising to just over 66 feet (20m) above sea level. The site was easily approachable from the east, but was defended by steep cliffs on its other sides. The position gives broad views of the whole sweep of Cardigan Bay (Fig. 7.3).

Documentary Evidence

Arnold Taylor's analysis of the documentary sources allowed him to deduce a building sequence for Aberystwyth Castle.[9] Building began on 25 July 1277. The first action, probably, was to erect a stockade (*bretagium*) around the working zone. In 1278 a shortage of funds was hampering the progress of building, but it advanced considerably in the following year, judging from the amount of labour

Figure 7.3: An aerial view of Aberystwyth Castle (© Crown Copyright: Royal Commission on the Ancient and Historical Monuments of Wales; NPRN 86; DI2008_0928).

present, materials ordered and money spent. One record implies the construction of some internal buildings.

Bogo de Knovill, the newly appointed justiciar of west Wales and keeper of the castle, wrote a damning report on the state of the town and castle in early 1280. His account shows that work was underway on a main gate, but it had a major design fault as its footings were too close to the castle ditch and the proximity of the sea waves was making it unstable. His recommendations included appointing a high-ranking architect to oversee the works, increasing the labour force, improving the supply of victuals and materials, and the construction of a proper harbour. Despite this report, little seems to have been done in 1280 or 1281.

At the end of March 1282 the castle was captured by the Welsh and burned; the source implies that the curtain of the castle was also destroyed. The description of Master James of St George's mission in May 1282 to 'construct' the king's castle implies a major change of thinking and considerably more than repairs. The new works seem to have got underway in earnest in 1283 and Taylor suggests that the order for a large amount of lead in September

means that several buildings were advanced enough to be roofed. It may be supposed that considerable progress had been made by the time the king stayed at the castle between 10 and 16 November in 1284.

An account compiled in 1290, but referring to 1286, gives the first detailed record of the erection or refurbishment of particular buildings. New structures were: the outer wall of the castle on the north side over the sea; a stable and bakehouse under the same roof on the west side of the castle; a chamber and wall, adjacent to the latter under the king's chamber, and an outer barbican facing the town. Refurbishment included: doubling the chamber over the gate on the side towards the sea; renewing the roof of the latter; remaking the well; a porch over the door of the great chamber, and raising a tower over the middle of the gate facing the town and raising its flanking walls.

The second part of the 1290 account refers to work between 27 April 1287 and 1 August 1289. New buildings included: a wall flanking the bridge, two posterns in the outer bailey, a wall on the sea front, with a new tower, beyond the outer bailey, and a granary. Repairs included: blocking a postern in the outer bailey, the wall of a kitchen (outer bailey?), the castle ditches, 'houses' within the castle, and deepening a well.

A survey of the castle made in 1320 found it to be adequately manned and armed, but in urgent need of repair, particularly its timberwork and roofs. Roof repairs were required for the great chamber adjoining the chapel, which contained a long chamber, the king's and queen's chambers and the entrance way, the four towers in the second bailey, the corner tower of the second bailey, the three outer towers, and the two outer chambers above the outer gates on both sides of the castle. Especial attention was drawn to the bridge of the outer bailey which was rotting, putting the castle 'en grant peril'.[10]

Despite some attention having been paid to repairs early in Edward III's reign, the castle had deteriorated markedly by the time William of Embleton had arrived in Aberystwyth in August 1343 to receive a report on its condition, prior to it being handed over to the attorneys of the prince of Wales. The windows of the king's hall were rotten; the 'Derkchaumbre' lacked its lead roof and its timbers were rotten; six chimneys at various locations had been partly thrown down by the elements; roofs required repairing in the king's and queen's chambers, a turret by the old hall, the old hall, a chamber in a tower by the hall and a chamber in the tower by the kitchen; the kitchen, bakehouse, stable and two granaries were in a state of serious disrepair; the long chamber had collapsed; the Cnovyll Chamber and its drawbridge were ruinous; other roof repairs were needed at the two towers over the gate of the second bailey; the drawbridges of the inner and outer bailey required considerable renovation; lengths of wall above a postern of the inner bailey and the kichen in the inner bailey needed rebuilding. The survey draws attention to the fact that most of the defences of the third bailey 'per maris intemperiem sunt prostrati'.[11]

Physical Remains of Aberystwyth Castle, about 1975

To understand the progress that has been made in the interpretation of the castle's history since Arnold Taylor's analysis of 1963, it is instructive to give a brief description of the visible remains of the castle in 1975 (Fig. 7.4) and how they had come to that condition subsequent to the large-scale destruction of the fortress by parliamentary forces in 1649.[12]

The site suffered extensive depredations during the eighteenth century. Court Leet presentments report stone robbing in 1739, 1742 and 1743.[13] The chaotic ruins left by these illegal activities were tidied up at the very beginning of the nineteenth century by John Probert into a system of embankments and pathways which still covered much of the site in 1975.[14] Some repair and support work was carried out in 1835, but its location and extent are obscure, but probably included restoring the south-east outer curtain.[15]

In 1975 the general outline of the plan of the site could be discerned, reflected by the embankments and walks created by Probert; these same earthworks concealed many details, however. Essentially, the layout consisted of concentric inner and outer wards, with a third bailey on the headland to the north-west, though nothing remained visible of its perimeter or internal buildings, which had probably been destroyed by the sea and landscaping. Stretches of the outer curtain were visible on all four sides, along with the north and south towers. The outer ward and inner curtain were covered by embankments; large blocks of architectural masonry were grouped at certain breaks of alignment in the bank covering the inner curtain. The north-west gate, particularly its well-known tower, was visible, so too was part of the great gate. No medieval features of the inner ward were visible, although earthworks, later found to represent the upcast from robber trenches, indicated a hall-like building in its south corner.

The Outer Curtain

The outer curtain, in places heavily reconstructed, formed the prominent envelope of the castle, with several visible architectural features. Almost entirely absent on the north-east in Hughes's plan of 1903, it was revealed during the excavations of 1903 and subsequently rebuilt between the north outer tower (Fig. 7.4.1) and the north tower of the east outer gate (Fig. 7.4.2).[16] A long stretch of the north-west outer curtain running south-west of the north outer tower had been exposed in 1903.[17] The fourteen crude steps of the sally port from the north-west outer gate were excavated in 1906 (Fig. 7.4.3).[18] A wooden bridge was built across the ditch from the gatehouse at that time. A length of the outer face of the south-west outer curtain was exposed in 1902.[19] A further length was cleared in 1903.[20]

The angle towers of the outer curtain on the north and south had been substantially restored by 1975 (Fig. 7.4.1, 4). The batter of the north outer tower was exposed in 1903.[21]

The Castle Ditch

The castle ditch was also a prominent feature on most sides in 1975 with the exception of the north-east, where the area had been landscaped to form a mini-golf course. A section across the north-east ditch had been cut in 1903, when what was probably, at least in part, the counterscarp bank to the ditch was removed.[22] The north-east length of the ditch between the north-west outer curtain and

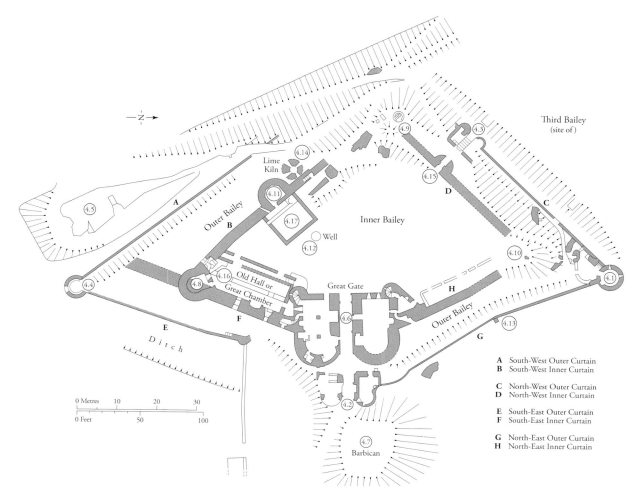

Figure 7.4: Plan of Aberystwyth Castle (Cadw, Welsh Assembly Government: Crown Copyright).

the third bailey was cleared in 1903.[23] The ditch in front of the southern half of the south-west outer curtain was a modification of a natural fissure between the main promontory and a detached cliff, known locally as 'Hill 99' (Fig. 7.4.5). Gardens beneath the south-east curtain occupied the site of the rock-cut ditch, but the original accompanying pond was defunct.

The East Outer Gate

The north tower of the east outer gate (Fig. 7.4.2) particularly its basement or 'dungeon', was a major feature of the site in 1975; it had been cleared and exposed in 1845.[24] The dungeon has been filled in since that time with masonry from the excavations that has potential use in any reconstruction or repair of the site. Spurgeon's speculation that the castle held other dungeons has not been borne out by excavation.[25]

The Great Gate

The great gate (Fig. 7.4.6), too, was a major feature of the site, but by 1975 only the front of the south chamber survived above ground-floor level. Some internal details of its south side were also exposed, presumably originally in 1845; it is also likely that at this time the passageway of the great gate was heavily and unintelligently restored.[26]

The Barbican

The east wall of the barbican (Fig. 7.4.7) could be seen as a revetment to a large mound of rubble. There have been no excavations of this feature, but it is badly in need of remedial action.

The Inner Curtain

In 1975 very little was known for certain of the extent to which the inner curtain had survived. This is one of the most noticeable features of the first archaeological plan, published by Harold Hughes and based on a visit in 1902.[27] Nevertheless the positions of the angle towers (Fig. 7.4.8, 9, 10) and the interval tower (Fig. 7.4.11) of the south-west inner curtain had long been suspected.[28] In Hughes's plan the latter is indicated as a small semicircular feature.[29]

Other Features

The well in the inner ward, 60 feet (18.3m) deep, was cleared out in 1845 (Fig. 7.4.12).[30]

The two most significant losses from the overall plan since the late thirteenth century were the curtain and internal buildings of the third bailey and the west angle of the main castle: the outer curtain and much of the west angle of the inner curtain. In both cases they had suffered from the ravages of the sea and the construction of the promenade, which was begun in 1901.[31]

Attached to the base of the north-east outer curtain, at a change of angle near its middle, is a short stub of wall that may be the remnant of a connection with the long-vanished town wall (Fig. 7.4.13).[32]

Excavations 1975–88

The initial excavations at the site, directed by Jack Spurgeon on behalf of the Archaeological Section of the Ceredigion Antiquarian Society, began as an investigation to find out how much of the original inner curtain was intact on the south-west side. They were subsequently taken over by Ceredigion District Council. From an archaeological point of view the principal aim was to understand the sequence of development of the castle from its foundation until the present, only very partially apparent from documentary analysis. From the local authorities' viewpoint the excavations would enhance local and visitors' enjoyment and appreciation of why the town was built in its spectacular coastal location. Both aims have been fulfilled, and the challenges for the future are to put in place an efficient, low-cost maintenance programme and to develop imaginative ways of presenting the history of the site to the public.[33]

Incidentally, in this context the excavations revealed some of the subtleties of the original landscapers. Several concentrations of large masonry architectural fragments disposed on the banks were shown to have been collected deliberately and placed to project from the uppermost layers of rubble forming the embankments of the promenades over the sites of the towers on the inner curtain. The landscapers were clearly aware of the presence of the towers and wished to mark their positions. Previously these large blocks had been interpreted as the remains of the Civil War destruction of the castle, lying where they had come to rest.[34]

Building Sequence

The excavation programme revealed an intriguing building sequence and considerable detail about individual structures, which will appear in the full excavation report.[35]

One of the first questions to be asked was whether there was an earlier castle on the site.[36] Spurgeon in 1977 had argued reasonably that as the land upon which Edward's castle stood was commandeered from Strata Florida Abbey no castle would have been on the site. Nevertheless, throughout the excavations a constant watch was kept for any possible trace of an earlier castle, but none was found; moreover, no artefacts were recovered that need pre-date 1277. This finding does not seem to deter the repetition of earlier speculations.[37]

Phase 1

The Outer Curtain

The evidence of the excavations suggests strongly that the south-west outer curtain was a primary structure (see below), as would be expected.[38] The remains of a limekiln were located immediately north of the south-west inner curtain interval tower (Fig. 7.4.14). They comprised a basal chamber with four flaring flues radiating from it. Clearly, the limekiln was erected before the inner curtain or tower and its base was backfilled after at least the foundations of these structures had been laid. It is reasonable to assume that the kiln was producing lime primarily for use in the construction of the nearby outer curtain wall. Although it seems to be totally inadequate for the needs of construction, with the exception of the western angle of the outer bailey, there is nowhere in the main castle where other kilns could have been located. Perhaps they were in the third bailey.

There were possible indications that a timber building (or buildings) was erected on the site of the interval tower, and dismantled when the latter was constructed. It was probably contemporary with or associated with the kiln, although on analogy with Builth (see above) it may represent temporary structures put up for a short while at the beginning of operations.

The North-West Outer Gate

The ground floor of the south-west tower of the north-west outer gate was excavated in 1976, revealing the lower steps of a newel stair within its semicircular outward projection. The rear of the tower projected internally, forming a rectangular guard-chamber with a straight flight of steps at its inner end, which led down to a concealed opening in the deep gap between the towers and beneath the site of the medieval bridge.[39]

The North-West Inner Gate

The north-west gate (Fig. 7.4.15) in the inner curtain was probably part of the original layout, given that the third bailey encompassing the headland must have been primary and there would have been a need for a fortified gate between it and the main castle. Nevertheless, it could have been part of a change of plan. The north-west gate tower retains part of the original wall-walk of the inner curtain, as shown in the reconstruction drawing (Fig. 7.5).[40] Unfortunately, it has been necessary for safety reasons to remove a small part of this since 1977, but the remainder has been stabilized and is still visible. It is sobering to look at this fragment of wall-walk and to calculate just how much of the original castle has been lost to stone robbing since the destruction of 1649.

The South-East Inner Curtain

The most surprising discovery of the excavations was at the south corner of the site. The south-east inner curtain had originally been intended to continue to form a junction with the south-west outer curtain, although the precise form this would have taken is uncertain. However high this had reached, it was levelled and the south tower (Fig. 7.4.8) of the inner curtain built over it. The remains comprised a basal course of clay-bonded masonry 9 feet 10 inches (3m) wide.[41]

This discovery demonstrated that the south-west inner curtain was a secondary feature. More importantly, it showed that the original plan was not intended to be fully concentric. This would have meant complete reliance on the natural defences and outer curtain on the south-west side. It is not clear if the south-east outer curtain was part of the original layout or whether it was constructed when the south-west inner curtain was erected.

The Great Gate and North-West Inner Curtain

In 1986–87 the southern chamber of the great gate (Fig. 7.4.6) was partially excavated.[42] Ground-floor access was gained from the inner bailey through a doorway at the north end of the rear wall, the heavily plastered lower rebates and drawbar hole of which survived. A latrine chamber was located in the body of the curving front (east) wall. The ceiling of the ground floor was supported by a triple arcade with two central piers; the springers for the arches survived internally on the front and rear walls. The alcove, mural passage and turret stairway in the south wall were already known.

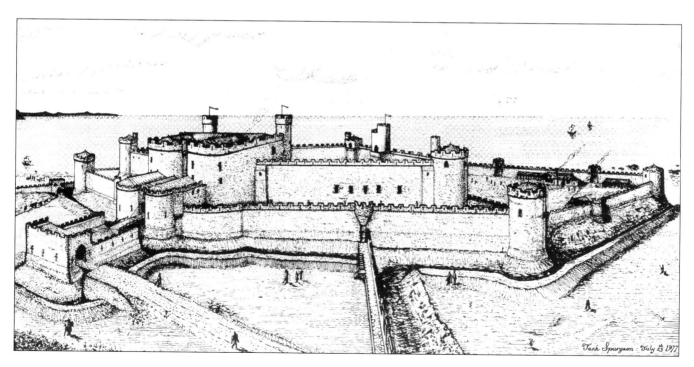

Figure 7.5: A reconstruction drawing of Aberystwyth Castle from the north-east, as it may have looked in the later thirteenth century (Drawing by Jack Spurgeon; © Crown Copyright: RCAHMW; NPRN 86; GTJ00059).

In 1987 substantial portions of the angle made by the northern chamber of the great gate and the north-east inner curtain were exposed.[43] Unfortunately the curtain only survived to a substantial height for 52 feet 6 inches (16m) north of this junction and was afterwards badly robbed; about halfway along its length it changed alignment, presumably in response to the topography. Part of the outline of the north tower (Fig. 7.4.10) of the curtain was exposed. A latrine drain arch in the wall was well preserved, 12 feet 6 inches (3.8m) north of the gate junction.[44] Hints of medieval buildings inside the north-east inner curtain were revealed below seventeenth-century structures, but full details were not recovered.[45]

Phase 2

The South-West Inner Curtain

As discussed above, the south-west inner curtain was shown to be a secondary feature in 1976 and 1985. In places it survived to a height of 7 feet 6 inches (2.3m). The facing masonry was of very variable quality, but bonded with a strong gravelly lime mortar. In contrast, its lower courses were built of rubble set in clay or mud, with only the faces mortared.[46]

In 1975 a diagonal culvert cut through the curtain to the south of the interval tower was revealed and in 1984 two arched culverts, through which latrines at higher levels in the curtain wall discharged into the outer ward, were recovered at its southernmost end. This was presumably not a well-frequented area.[47]

The interval tower (Fig. 7.4.11) was a large building, projecting from the curtain with a semicircular front and a six-sided interior at ground-floor level. Access to this level was through a doorway in its eastern corner, where the drawbar hole was still intact; a window gave light through the north-east wall. Ingress to the upper floors was gained via a wall-walk passage, the base of which was intact to the north-west of the tower, as suspected by Spurgeon.[48] The basal springing of a latrine chute survived in the northern angle between the tower and curtain. The tower's large dimensions suggest that it functioned as the main vantage point overlooking the harbour and sea lanes to the south.[49]

The south tower (Fig. 7.4.8) projected beyond the curtain with a semicircular front; internally it was originally circular. Access to its first floor was via a turret at its north-west corner.

Phase 3X

Work to expose the remains of the long-suspected hall (Fig. 7.4.16) in the south-east part of the inner bailey began in 1982, and continued the following year.[50]

Details of the south-west end were revealed in 1985.[51] A substantial part of its north gable wall had been visible for some time. Moreover, it could be seen to be blocking a light in the rear turret of the south chamber of the great gate, suggesting its construction was an afterthought. Indeed, excavation at the north-east end showed that the original plan for the great gate involved a symmetrical rear façade towering over the inner ward. However, the wall between the rear turret of the south chamber and the inner curtain was either never carried up far above its footings before the change in plan or was demolished to make way for the insertion of the north-east gable end of the hall. Nevertheless, there is no reason to doubt that the different internal arrangements for access by the rear turrets to the first floors of the great gate were original; access is direct from the south turret and indirect, through a triangular ante-chamber from the north.[52]

The hall had suffered considerable damage, but because its south-east wall was part of the inner curtain, several important features survived. In particular, a central fireplace and two windows, which had probably been inserted in an originally blank lower curtain. The north-western front was severely damaged, but appears to have had a narrow portico in front of the main wall. Part of the south entrance through the main wall survived in the form of a slab threshold and the bottom of a roll and fillet jamb moulding; there were two doors into the portico.[53] Some sort of access between the hall and the first-floor level of the south chamber of the great gate was formed by a flight of steps at the north end of the portico and a platform against the rear wall of the gate.[54]

The need to provide a satisfactory roof to the hall probably accounted for the alterations that were made to the rear of the south tower of the inner curtain.[55] The stair turret was demolished and the back wall squared up, creating an elongated D-shaped plan to the interior. Access to the ground floor of the tower was through a new door, the reveals, drawbar hole and slab threshold of which were still *in situ*; there was a small splayed light through the wall to the south-west. The new access to the first floor of the tower was probably by an open-sided staircase in the thickness of the inner curtain forming the other part of the south-west end of the hall.

Phase 3Y

A rectangular building (Fig. 7.4.17) was constructed behind the south-west interval tower, through which there was access to the ground floor of the tower. The building was of medieval date but its precise position in the structural sequence in relation to other buildings in the south-east part of the castle is uncertain. The nature of the association of several small hearths and a primitive oven with the rectangular building was uncertain.

Overall Dimensions

As a result of the excavations we now have a better idea of the overall dimensions of the site. The inner bailey measures 246 feet by 144 feet (75m by 44m) north–south, an area of about 0.8 acres (0.33ha). The distance between the inner and outer curtains varies: approximately 39 feet to 49 feet (about 12m to 15m) on the south-west; 25 feet (7.5m) on the south-east; about 40 feet (10m) on the north-west; and about 30 feet (9m) on the north-east. We cannot be certain about the dimensions, or even shape, of the third bailey, but it was probably at least 197 feet (60m) wide at its north-west to south-east base and at least 230 feet (70m) along its main axis, an area of about 0.52 acres (0.21ha).

Discussion

The two surveys of 1320 and 1343 assign names to various buildings, which R. F. Walker has identified in a recent paper, and are considered further here in relation to the excavated evidence.[56]

Walker suggests that the hall exposed in the south part of the inner bailey could be identified with 'the great chamber' referred to in the survey of 1320. This is not unreasonable, but the equation of the 'long chamber' with the portico of the excavated hall is less likely; it seems more probable that the 'long chamber' was the main chamber of the hall. If we accept Walker's principal identification of the great chamber, we can do the same for his location of the 'adjoining chapel' in the great gate. The 'king's chamber' and the 'queen's chamber' are likely to have been here, too. The 'four towers in the second bailey' are no doubt the towers of the inner curtain. The 'corner tower in the second bailey' must have been the now largely destroyed west tower of the inner curtain (Fig. 7.4.9), heavily exposed to the sea.[57] Walker also identifies, reasonably, 'the three outer towers' as those on the outer curtain and the 'two outer chambers' as being above the east outer gate and the north-west outer gate.

The survey of 1343 received by William of Embleton is much more detailed than the earlier one. However it is not possible to be sure of the location of all the buildings it mentions. For example, it is not clear where the 'dark chamber' was. The mention of two turrets either side of the 'king's and queen's chambers' is further evidence that Walker is correct in his identification of their location as the great gate. The document seems to identify two different buildings: 'the king's hall' and the 'old hall'. Walker suggests that the old hall maybe the same as the

'great chamber' of the 1320 survey and that the 'tower by the hall' was the south tower of the inner bailey. A complication to these identifications, however, is the reference to a collapsed 'long chamber'. Walker, holding to his idea that the 'old hall' was the 'great chamber' of 1320 (that is, the excavated hall), rejects the identification of the 1343 long chamber as being the same as that referred to in 1320; this author concurs with his view. If Walker is correct in his other suggestions the most likely position would be behind the north-east inner curtain.

The 1343 survey mentions a bakehouse and stable, which are most probably those referred to in 1286. In 1977 Spurgeon called attention to a building incorporating an oven uncovered by the excavations of 1975 behind the interval tower of the south-west inner curtain.[58] He identified this with the bakehouse documented as being built 'under the west wall' in 1286. Subsequent excavations have shown that the structures belong to the first half of the seventeenth century, but they were built on the site of a rectangular medieval building (Phase 3Y, see above), which might have housed them.[59] The 'tower by the kitchen', in this case, would have been the interval tower. The location of the two granaries mentioned is uncertain.

Before his 1995 paper Walker had already made the connection between the 'Cnovyll chamber' and Bogo (Bevis) de Knovill.[60] He makes a good case for locating the chamber in the north-west outer gate, which he suggests may have been a rebuild of the imperilled gate noted by de Knovill in his report of 1280.

We know very little of the third bailey. Walker is probably right in regarding 'the outer wall on the north over the sea' as part of it.[61] He is also probably correct in thinking that 'a wall on the sea front, with a new tower, beyond the outer bailey' in accounts for 1287–89 did not belong to the third bailey, but to works between the castle and harbour.[62]

Conclusion

The excavated evidence clearly indicates that the builders in the early months of the construction of Aberystwyth Castle did not intend to create a concentric plan on the south-west.[63] The discovery is certainly a surprise. At the beginning of the excavations Spurgeon could still express the then current belief that Aberystwyth and Rhuddlan 'were Edward's first concentric castles in the form first expressed in Gilbert de Clare's great fortress at Caerphilly'.[64] Instead, as was the case with all of Edward's new foundations, the form of its plan was strongly influenced by the topography of the chosen site.[65] In the case of Aberystwyth the place selected was expansive enough to accommodate a major change of plan early on.

The constructions of Phase 1 may be assigned to the period 1277–82. Phase 2 was probably initiated by Master James of St George and belonged to 1282–84. Phase 3 can be accommodated in the period 1286–89. After this, both archaeologically and according to documentary sources, there was little new building, merely repair, until the seventeenth century.

Dedication

The author would like to dedicate this paper to the memory of Clifford Jack Spurgeon.

Notes

1. R. A. Brown, H. Colvin and A. J. Taylor, *The History of the King's Works: the Middle Ages*, I (London, 1963), 293. J. B. Smith, 'Llywelyn ap Gruffudd and the March of Wales', *Brycheiniog*, 20 (1982–83), 9–22 (specifically 11–12). M. Morris, *A Great and Terrible King: Edward I and the Forging of Britain* (London 2008), 159; M. Prestwich, *Edward I* (London 1988), 170.
2. Smith, 'Llywelyn ap Gruffudd'.
3. A. J. Taylor, 'Builth', in *King's Works*, 293.
4. C. J. Spurgeon, 'Builth Castle', *Brycheiniog*, 18 (1978–79), 47–59. Spurgeon's work was inspired by the recent survey carried out by the Royal Commission as a staff-training exercise under the supervision of A. H. A. Hogg.
5. Details given below follow Taylor, 'Builth', 293–98.
6. Taylor, 'Builth', 296.
7. Spurgeon, 'Builth', 47; the discussion hereafter follows Spurgeon, 'Builth', *passim*.
8. Spurgeon, 'Builth', 51–52, reports the results of analyses by Dr B. L. Finlayson of the University of Oxford.
9. A. J. Taylor, 'Aberystwyth', in *King's Works*, 299–307. The author has examined all the documents in The National Archives used by Arnold Taylor to compile the account of Aberystwyth Castle in *The King's Works* and, with the exception of one entirely insignificant difference of reading, can confirm his transcriptions.
10. R. F. Walker, 'Two fourteenth-century surveys of Aberystwyth Castle', *Ceredigion*, 12.3 (1995), 3–22 (specifically 5).
11. ibid., 10–14.
12. Spurgeon gives a basic description of the then extant remains in his guide to the castle of 1973, updated in 1975 (C. J. Spurgeon, *The Castle and Borough of Aberystwyth* (Aberystwyth 1975)). He further reviewed the state of our knowledge of the castle in 1977, in a volume celebrating the seven hundredth anniversary of the founding of the castle and borough (C. J. Spurgeon, 'The castle and borough to 1649', in *Aberystwyth 1277–1977*, ed. I. G. Jones (Llandysul 1977), 28–45). His chapter updated, to a certain extent, what he had written in his guide, and in his later piece he was able to take account of the preliminary results of a campaign of excavations that had begun in 1975, though, inevitably, some of his interpretations have been superseded. For 1649: J. Morgan, *A Short History of the Castle of Aberystwyth* (Aberystwyth n. d.), 4; Spurgeon, *The Castle and Borough*, 13; some other sources misdate this event.
13. G. E. Evans, *Aberystwyth and its Court Leet, etc.* (Aberystwyth 1902), 91–96.
14. J. Morgan, *Morgan's New Guide to Aberystwyth and its Environs etc.* (Aberystwyth 1874); R. J. Silvester, 'John Probert and the map of Trefnant township', *Montgomeryshire Collections*, 89 (2001), 163–78; for the social context of these, see M.

Freeman, *Aberystwyth: a History & Celebration* (Salisbury 2005), 37; the author is grateful to Michael Freeman for references to manuscripts in the National Library of Wales relevant to the later history of the castle.
15. Morgan, *A Short History*, 18; H. Hughes, 'Excavations proposed to be carried out at Aberystwyth Castle', *Archaeologia Cambrensis*, 6 ser. 3 (1903), 273–79; H. Burnham, 'Test pits at Aberystwyth Castle, December 1989: results of archaeological recording', *Ceredigion*, 11.4 (1992), 337–56.
16. H. Hughes, 'Aberystwyth Castle. Excavations carried out in the year 1903', *Archaeologia Cambrensis*, 6 ser. 4 (1904), 317–23.
17. ibid., 319–20.
18. Morgan, *A Short History*, 14; National Library of Wales Ms. 13487, 189.
19. Hughes, 'Excavations proposed', 275.
20. Hughes, 'Aberystwyth Castle', 319–20.
21. ibid., 318–19.
22. ibid., 319–20; 317.
23. ibid., 319–20; Walker, 'Fourteenth-century surveys', specifically plan and 8–9 for terms used.
24. Morgan, *Morgan's New Guide*, 41; Hughes, 'Excavations proposed', 273, 277.
25. Spurgeon, 'Castle and borough to 1649', 36. Besides a small trench dug into the rubble filling the ground floor of the south tower to allow the insertion of a buttress to support a stub of its north wall, the outer gateway was not excavated and no new information has been revealed since 1975.
26. NLW Ms. 13483, 79, has a photo of the main entrance passage annotated 'cleared of rubbish ... 1844; Morgan, *A Short History*, 13, gives 1844–45 as the date of these excavations.
27. Hughes, 'Excavations proposed', 274.
28. ibid.
29. Spurgeon, 'Castle and borough to 1649', plan. In the early phases of the excavations of 1976 it had proved to be much larger, but the details of its interior were unknown, leading Spurgeon in 1977 to depict it as circular on analogy with the angle towers.
30. Morgan, *Morgan's New Guide*, 41; Hughes, 'Excavations proposed', 277.
31. Hughes, 'Excavations proposed', 278; for a somewhat fanciful attempt to suggest a plan for this area, see H. M. Madeley, 'The plan of Aberystwyth Castle', *Archaeologia Cambrensis*, 6 ser. 17 (1917), 82–85.
32. D. Stewart, D. M. Browne and C. J. Spurgeon, 'Aberystwyth Castle', *Archaeology in Wales*, 28 (1988), 69. Above it the excavations revealed the base of a bastion in a corresponding position against the front of the north-east inner curtain. Although seventeenth century in date, its purpose was most likely to have been to mount artillery to rake the then extant town defences.

33. D. M. Browne, 'The secrets of Aberystwyth Castle', in *Aberystwyth*, ed. I. Manning (Stroud 2001), 68–79.

34. Hughes, 'Excavations proposed', 273.

35. The reports of the excavations are to be published electronically by the Royal Commission, commencing in 2010. Access to the site records may be obtained by contacting the National Monuments Record Wales at RCAHMW at nmr.wales@rcahmw.gov.uk

36. Spurgeon, 'Castle and borough to 1649'; R. A. Griffiths, 'The three castles at Aberystwyth', *Archaeologia Cambrensis*, 126 (1977), 74–87.

37. Freeman, *Aberystwyth*, 14.

38. Spurgeon, 'Castle and borough to 1649', 36.

39. C. J. Spurgeon and D. M. Browne, 'Aberystwyth Castle', *Archaeology in Wales*, 16 (1976), 38.

40. C. J. Spurgeon's reconstruction of Aberystwyth Castle: postcard and original artwork in the National Monuments Record of Wales; Spurgeon, 'Castle and borough to 1649', 38. The opportunity has been taken to record photographically the interior of the gate's upper chamber; details are in the National Monuments Record of Wales.

41. A. Davis, 'Aberystwyth Castle', *Archaeology in Wales*, 25 (1985), 35; A. Davis, 'Aberystwyth Castle', *Archaeology in Wales*, 26 (1986), 51.

42. ibid.

43. D. Stewart, 'Aberystwyth Castle', *Archaeology in Wales*, 27 (1987), 56.

44. Stewart, Browne and Spurgeon, 'Aberystwyth Castle'.

45. ibid.

46. C. J. Spurgeon and E. Whatmore, 'Aberystwyth Castle', *Archaeology in Wales*, 15 (1975), 54–55.

47. A. Davis, 'Aberystwyth Castle', *Archaeology in Wales*, 24 (1984), 61–62.

48. Spurgeon, 'Castle and borough to 1649', 38–39.

49. ibid.

50. ibid., 37, 41; D. M. Browne, 'Aberystwyth Castle', *Archaeology in Wales*, 18 (1978), 54; J. Thorburn, 'Aberystwyth Castle', *Archaeology in Wales*, 22 (1982), 30; J. Thorburn, 'Aberystwyth Castle', *Archaeology in Wales*, 23 (1983), 51–52.

51. Davis, 'Aberystwyth Castle', 1985.

52. Spurgeon, 'Castle and borough to 1649', 39.

53. Thorburn, 'Aberystwyth Castle', 1983, 51.

54. Davis, 'Aberystwyth Castle', 1986, 51.

55. Davis, 'Aberystwyth Castle', 1985, 35; Davis, 'Aberystwyth Castle', 1986, 51.

56. Walker, 'Fourteenth-century surveys'. Walker's translations are used here.

57. ibid., 7.

58. Spurgeon, 'Castle and borough to 1649', 41; Spurgeon and Whatmore, 'Aberystwyth Castle'.

59. Walker, 'Fourteenth-century surveys', 15.

60. Spurgeon, 'Castle and borough to 1649', 42.

61. Walker, 'Fourteenth-century surveys', 16.

62. ibid.

63. ibid., 19. Walker has found it difficult to accept this as anything more than an error of the builders on the spot on account of his preconception about Edwardian fortifications.

64. Spurgeon, *Castle*, 6.

65. Spurgeon, 'Castle and borough to 1649', 34.

8

The King's Accommodation at his Castles

Jeremy Ashbee

Introduction

On 20 August 1332, Edward III's chancery sent a stiff letter to the chamberlain of north Wales reminding him to get on with his job.

> [You are] to cause the necessary repairs to be made to the houses within the castles of Karnarvan, Conewey, Beaumareys, Crukyth [Cricieth], and Hardelagh [Harlech] in North Wales… as the king understands that they are ruinous and not fit for him to dwell in if he should go there.[1]

The document is from a generation after Edward I's death, but it provides a useful reminder that castles in the conquered territory were seen as potential residences as well as military strongholds and centres of government. The choice of these particular sites is not significant: since Castell y Bere and Dolwyddelan had been abandoned, this was the complete list of royal castles in north Wales beyond the Conwy; Rhuddlan, Flint, Builth and Aberystwyth lay under other jurisdictions. As a collection of royal apartments built from scratch, albeit set inside fortresses and located a long way from London, castles like Conwy, Caernarfon, Harlech, Beaumaris and Rhuddlan have much to tell the modern student about residential planning at the highest social levels in the late thirteenth century (Fig. 8.1).

Much of this potential lies in the remarkable state of preservation of the buildings, exceptional for structures of such antiquity. From earlier periods, several Anglo-Norman great towers have survived in fairly complete states, but in almost all instances there are important unanswered questions about their function, notably the issue of whether they constituted the principal accommodation in their castles, or whether they stood behind other residential suites, now lost. From the earlier thirteenth century, structures like the *Gloriette* complex at Corfe give some idea of residential planning in a royal castle, but for the most part, the surviving buildings of John or Henry III, such as the great hall at Winchester and the Wakefield Tower in the Tower of London, stand isolated without the other structures which formerly stood around them. Only from the second half of the thirteenth century do a sizeable number of castles survive, both royal and baronial, in which something approaching the whole suite of buildings, residential and ancillary, can be traced in the visible fabric: several of the Edwardian castles lie within this group.

Partly through detailed examination, analysis and re-dating of baronial castles such as Caerphilly,[2] Goodrich[3] and Chepstow,[4] and partly through recent biographical work on the career of James of St George, it has been realized that some of the arguments which Arnold Taylor and others made for the contribution of Savoyard craftsmen to the design of the north Wales castles have been overstated.[5] Most of the principal design features for which the Edwardian castles are so celebrated, such as concentric curtain walls, regular disposition of mural towers, massive gatehouses combining defensive and residential features, and sophisticated use of water defences, were present in English castles for decades before James of St George and his fellow Savoyards came to Britain, and several of them are absent from the architectural traditions of Savoy. It is now permissible to argue that much of the architectural design of the north Wales castles comes directly from the cultural context of English castles built earlier in the thirteenth century. Taylor highlighted James of St George's role in designing the apartments at Conwy and inferred that the residential suites in the Edwardian castles imitated Savoyard prototypes such as Champvent and St Georges-d'Espéranche. However, in the general reassessment of architectural authorship, there is a need to assess whether the royal apartments too may owe more to England and the Welsh Marches than to Savoy.[6]

Figure 8.1: The inner ward at Conwy Castle facing south-east. This is the most complete set of apartments left by the medieval English monarchy (Cadw, Welsh Assembly Government: Crown Copyright).

Sources for Studying the North Wales Castles

The standing fabric of the castles is of course crucial to the study of their form and function in the Middle Ages. The good survival of walls, together with architectural features such as doors, windows, fireplaces, latrines and the sockets and scars left by missing floors, roofs and partitions means that large parts of the castles can be reconstructed conjecturally to an unusually complete degree, and with a high degree of confidence. Unfortunately in many cases, this exercise does not in itself resolve the questions of what the rooms were originally called, or how they were used. The buildings and rooms in the north Wales castles are mostly not distinctive and many of them look much like one another. Rooms in towers may be round or polygonal, and may appear grander or simpler through the size and elaboration of their fireplaces, the presence or absence of window seats, and the nearness or distance

of latrines, but generally there is little to choose between them; likewise most other rooms were simple rectangles, similarly provided with light, heat and sanitation. The physical fabric may still allow us to suggest how they functioned, particularly through reconstructing the ways in which they communicated one with another, but these are modern interpretations; there will always be a suspicion that they embody modern ideas about status, hygiene or privacy which Edward I would not have recognized.

For this reason, there is every motive to continue with an established methodology: the comparison of the fabric with the evidence of contemporary documents, a study which Arnold Taylor took from his mentor Bryan St John O'Neil, and made his own.[7] What the medieval exchequer accounts potentially offer is a set of authentic place-names, such as 'great hall', 'king's chamber' and 'queen's garden', and in some cases, further details of features within them, which may help with identification. It is almost irresistible, when given this kind of material, to connect a visible feature with a documented one: to point out in the gatehouse at Harlech Castle 'the chimney in the chamber of Sir John de Bonvillars', for which the masons, Master Peter Morel and Albert de Menz, were paid on 20 January 1286,[8] or 'three turrets in the garden at Conwy Castle', roofed in 1301 on the orders of the prince of Wales.[9] In fact honesty requires that there will always be some uncertainty about this kind of identification: we cannot be sure that Sir John de Bonvillars's room at Harlech lay in the gatehouse rather than one of the corner towers or a building in the bailey, and even if we could prove this, the gatehouse contains rooms with fireplaces on more than one floor.

Anyone studying the works accounts for the construction of the north Wales castles is also faced early on with an awkward and rarely stated truth: the documents are disappointingly light on detailed information of this kind.[10] The reasons for this are actually quite obvious: the exchequer was mainly concerned with the passage of money, and the clerks only described buildings in order to authenticate expenditure,[11] but most of all, they were documenting building sites rather than finished structures. On occasion, the accounts do give names to buildings under construction, such as 'the king's and queen's chambers' at Conwy,[12] but such references are very rare, outnumbered by payments for labour and the bulk purchase of materials. This silence may represent the clerks' disinterest in incidental details, but it may also reflect some uncertainty in what the buildings would be called when complete. This was true of Edward I's other castles: for example, the new apartments over the water gate at the Tower of London, begun in 1275, were originally called 'a hall with a chamber', but over the course of construction, the terminology changed, with 'hall' effectively being dropped in favour of 'great chamber'.[13]

Documents from after the completion of the castles are understandably much richer in detail, describing repairs (or their lack) to buildings for which a name or a function was well established. Particularly useful are dilapidation surveys in 1321 (in French)[14] and 1343 (in Latin),[15] which list the buildings in urgent need of maintenance, as well as documenting the generally parlous state of the castles' armouries and stores. The 1321 survey unfortunately says nothing about defects to the buildings of Caernarfon; otherwise both documents contain descriptions of Conwy, Beaumaris, Caernarfon, Cricieth, Harlech and Aberystwyth, and continue with castles in south Wales. For example, the topographical terms included in the two surveys of Aberystwyth are plentiful and invaluable for the study of the otherwise enigmatic physical remains

of buildings in the courtyard. They include entries for 'the great chamber adjoining the chapel, with the long chamber beside', 'the king's and queen's chambers and the walkway between them', 'the king's hall', 'two turrets to either side of the king's and queen's chambers, with a stair there' and 'a turret next to the old hall', all of which are potentially informative about the layout and function of the castle.[16]

From later in the fourteenth, sporadically in the fifteenth, and more plentifully in the first half of the sixteenth century, come repair accounts for the royal castles in north Wales, in which many useful details are given. These are more plentiful and more detailed for some sites than others: Conwy is particularly well covered, Beaumaris and Caernarfon less so. These accounts undoubtedly include repairs to some features of the thirteenth century, but being far removed in time from the period of Edward I, they describe a very different set of circumstances. Most obviously, the castles were clearly now being used for purposes unconnected with royal residence, principally storage of munitions and the imprisonment of local felons and debtors.[17] In such circumstances, the idea of the castles as accommodation for the court must have been at best a faint memory, and in most cases, something completely forgotten. This caveat must be borne in mind when considering the few sources that do hint at royal residence, such as the survey of Conwy Castle in 1627, which uses the terminology of contemporary royal apartments: great chamber, presence chamber, privy chamber and withdrawing chambers.[18] No monarch had used these apartments since 1399, when Richard II had been forced to stay at Conwy on several occasions for his own protection[19] (though in the 1540s, the castle was fitted up for a visit by the Lord President and the Council of the Marches).[20] The fact that in 1627 Conwy Castle was being sold by the Crown raises the possibility that these grandiose-sounding room names were revived or invented by a surveyor to make the property sound more impressive to the buyer and his friends. This is only speculation, but the survey makes it abundantly clear in descriptions of decaying stonework and collapsing roofs and floors that no-one had stayed in the supposed royal apartments for a long time.

The Royal Apartments at Conwy Castle

Conwy Castle is exceptional in the state of preservation of its royal apartments, and for the clarity with which its plan can be read today: it is no exaggeration that it contains the most complete set of royal apartments left by the medieval English monarchy anywhere (Fig. 8.2).[21] There also exists

Figure 8.2: Reconstruction drawing showing the meeting between Edward I and Archbishop Robert Winchelsey at Conwy Castle in February 1295. This was the only time Edward saw these apartments complete (Illustration by Peter Visscher; Cadw, Welsh Assembly Government: Crown Copyright).

documentary confirmation, however fleeting, that the site was built as a royal residence. In 1284–85, the third season of construction, James of St George was paid £320 in task work for the masonry of 'the hall and the king's and queen's chambers in Conwy Castle' (or alternatively 'the king's and queen's hall and chambers'), while Henry of Oxford and Richard the Engineer (of Chester) received £100 for the corresponding carpentry;[22] other task-work payments for the king's chamber are recorded on 29 September 1286.[23] The division of the castle into an outer ward, housing the castle's garrison and the main royal household, and an inner ward for the king and queen and their closest courtiers, is unmistakeable and beyond dispute. Yet there is nothing in the historical record to suggest that Conwy was intended for particularly intensive royal use (more than would be expected for Caernarfon, for example) and it is fair to wonder whether its apartments were typical of

the wider royal estate. Moreover, the detailed identification of rooms involves a combined use of fabric analysis, documentary information, and finally, conjecture.

Over the course of his career, Arnold Taylor explored several hypothetical identifications of the documented rooms with the physical spaces, before reaching his last conclusion in 1995:[24] this is the version accepted in the present paper (Fig. 8.3). Taylor felt that the 'hall' mentioned in 1284–85 lay in the outer ward, while the 'chambers' stood in the inner. The curving range against the south wall of the outer ward was divided into at least two principal spaces: a great hall in the centre, and partitioned off at its eastern end, a chapel. In addition to the fireplace in the great hall, the range contained two further fireplaces, in the north and west walls, and though the evidence for partitions has been lost through fourteenth-century alterations to the roof, it seems likely

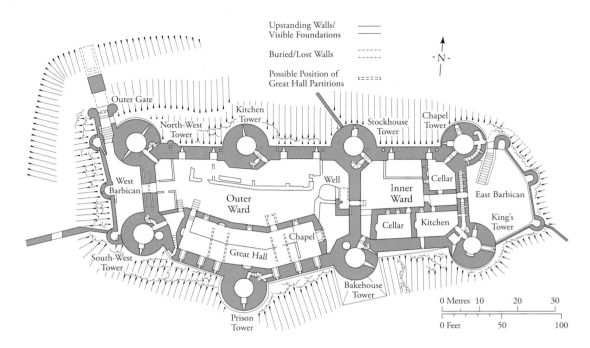

Figure 8.3: Plan of Conwy Castle, showing the division into the outer ward, for the garrison and greater household, and the inner ward for the king, the queen and their closest courtiers (Cadw, Welsh Assembly Government: Crown Copyright).

that two further rooms stood to the west of the great hall. These rooms could only be entered from the great hall and were passed through in sequence, with the westernmost room as a dead end. The layout accords with a reference in September 1286 to 'building the great hall and a pantry next to the small hall in the same great hall.'[25] Some of this layout is unique: with an entry on one side and a pantry on the other, the great hall had two 'low ends', while the small hall at the western end had no exit except for the pantry it shared with the great hall. However, the idea of a hall as a dead end does have contemporary parallels, in the bailey at Harlech and as originally built at Goodrich. The notion of a chapel adjoining the low end of a hall may also exist elsewhere: at Caerphilly, Kidwelly and perhaps in the original design for the bailey at Beaumaris. Across the outer ward from the great hall range stood ancillary buildings, identified in 1343 as a kitchen, brewhouse and bakehouse under one roof.[26] Several of these structures in the outer ward arguably duplicated others in the inner ward, including a chapel and a kitchen. This is explained by Edward I's household ordinances of 1279, which refer to a division between kitchen organizations serving the wider household and the king himself.[27] Finally, the outer ward contained four towers, each with two storeys of residential chambers over basements used for other

purposes: prison, bakehouse, storeroom and a probable larder, opening off the kitchen. The two western towers have sometimes been interpreted as part of the residence of the constable, but this seems less likely than a more varied use for the garrison[28] and occasional guests at the castle.[29]

The inner ward was a private royal enclave, separated from the outer ward by a drawbridge over a dry ditch and by a high cross-wall. In this respect it had clear parallels with other Edwardian castles, such as the *Gloriette* at Leeds Castle[30] and the *donjon* at Winchester,[31] but other near-contemporary examples, such as Restormel,[32] may suggest a functional derivation from much earlier prototypes, such as shell keeps, likewise separated from their main baileys by ditches. Within this enclosure at Conwy, the apartments lay on the first floor above storerooms and other services, including a royal kitchen (Fig. 8.4). They formed an L-shape of two ranges, fronting onto a small courtyard, from which two sets of wooden stairs rose to two first-floor doorways, interpreted as separate entrances to the great chamber and queen's chamber. Behind the ranges stood three corner towers of the inner ward, now seen as functionally separate from the royal apartments, a conclusion suggested by examining the patterns of circulation around the suite. This exercise shows particularly that the south-east tower, known since the nineteenth century as *Tŵr y Brenin* (King's Tower) and once believed to contain Edward I's chamber, was directly accessible from the goods entrance and king's kitchen, and was more plausibly intended for servants and household officers. This tower did communicate with the main range, however, by narrow mural passages, emerging discreetly in two window reveals of what was probably the king's chamber, which lay between the great chamber and the queen's chamber: these passages are best interpreted as servants' entrances. One tower alone was fully part of the suite: the north-east tower, the first floor of which contained the king's chapel, with a private watching chamber high in its west wall (provided with its own latrine behind). In the barbican to the east of the inner ward stood a small garden under the windows of the great chamber: described as a lawn (*herbarium*) in 1301[33] and 1316,[34] it contained wooden frames for vines or trailing plants in the 1390s[35] and in the 1540s, crab-apple trees around a turfed lawn.[36]

Caernarfon Castle (Fig. 8.5)

Like Conwy, Caernarfon Castle was planned with two baileys standing side-by-side, and this has led to an understandable desire to see its planning as essentially the same, with the western bailey as an outer or lower ward (containing the great hall and kitchens facing each other across the courtyard), and royal apartments in an upper enclosure towards the east, overlooking a royal garden.[37] This similarity can be overstated; most obviously, the relationship between the two parts of the castle was entirely different from Conwy. Since the main access from the town of Caernarfon lay between the two wards in a complex gatehouse and cross-range, the inner ward could be entered on foot without passing through the outer ward. As well as its different position, the Caernarfon gatehouse was planned to a size and elaboration far exceeding the relatively simple entrance at Conwy, with a chapel over the entrance passage and a large room on the second floor, described in 1343 as a hall.[38] The location corresponding to the gate at Conwy was filled by the Eagle Tower, an outsized decagonal tower of four storeys overlooking a small water gate, with three turrets, banded masonry and, famously, sculptures of human heads and eagles on the battlements.

The eastern or upper ward at Caernarfon poses particular difficulties (Fig. 8.6). Both documentary and physical evidence concur that the buildings were never finished, and in *The History of the King's Works*, Taylor suggested that they were not even begun.[39] He later

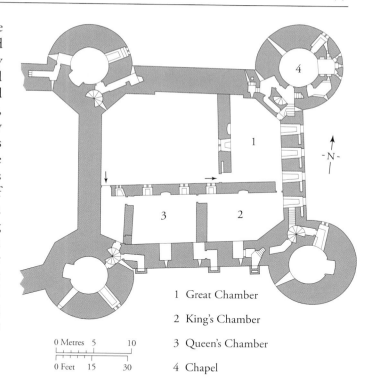

1 Great Chamber

2 King's Chamber

3 Queen's Chamber

4 Chapel

0 Metres 5 10

0 Feet 15 30

Figure 8.4: First-floor plan of the inner ward at Conwy as first configured, showing (1) great chamber, (2) king's chamber, (3) queen's chamber and (4) chapel (Cadw, Welsh Assembly Government: Crown Copyright).

qualified this judgment: the suspiciously neat toothings of incomplete cross-walls in the castle attested to a certain amount of tidying-up by Anthony Salvin in the mid-nineteenth century, and Taylor came to believe that more buildings had once existed than now survive.[40] Even had the buildings been finished as intended, they cannot have taken exactly the same form as those at Conwy. The enclosure was larger than the inner ward at Conwy and hexagonal rather than square, the disposition of the mural towers is very different, the area contains a major gateway at its eastern end – more substantial than the tiny riverside postern at Conwy, there were buildings on at least three sides rather than two, and most remarkably, the central space was filled with a huge mound, generally interpreted as the motte of an earlier castle first raised by Hugh of Chester in the late eleventh century.[41] Disappointingly, no medieval or Tudor documents have yet been found describing permanent apartments in Caernarfon Castle; the most substantial references are to temporary timber structures raised on the building site in 1283 as chambers for the king and queen.[42] What the accounts mention

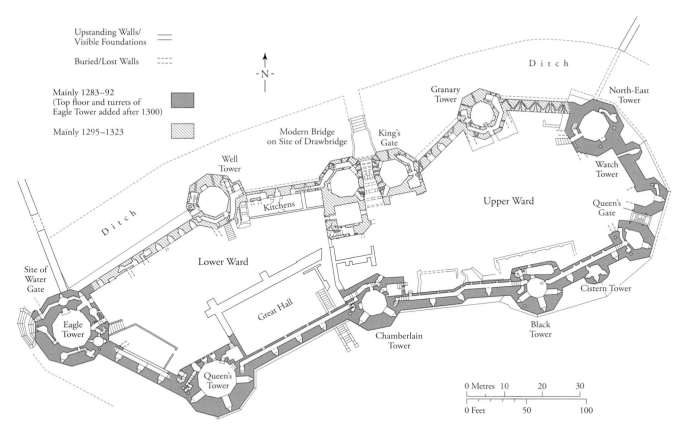

Figure 8.5: Plan of Caernarfon Castle (Cadw, Welsh Assembly Government: Crown Copyright).

regularly are buildings in the town, such as the shire hall, exchequer and the king's quay, and it seems entirely possible that Caernarfon Castle was never fitted up as a royal residence. As Taylor conceded, 'it is something of a paradox that this most lavishly conceived of all the king's works in Wales, costing probably over £20,000 and taking nearly half a century to build, should at the end of it all remain unfinished, and have been only once visited by a reigning sovereign from the time of Edward I to that of George V,'[43] but perhaps to the medieval burgesses of Caernarfon, there was not even an expectation that the monarch would stay in the castle.

Equally disappointing is that the documents do not resolve the question of who was meant to use the Eagle Tower, a building well provided with imposing rooms, surrounded by latrines, possible oratories and other mural chambers for ancillary purposes. The spectacular external embellishment of the building speaks eloquently of projecting royal or princely identity, and since in practice this was personified by the justiciar, it seems most likely that he was supposed to live in the building, at least in the absence of the royal court. For one of Taylor's most

appealing speculations, that a common heraldic source connected the prince of Wales's insignia of three feathers and the 'soaring *panache* of three six-sided turrets' on the tower's skyline, there is sadly as yet no supporting evidence.[44]

Concentric Castles – Rhuddlan (Plate 10)

The alternative plan type, and the one for which the Edwardian castles are better known, is the concentric fortress, represented by Rhuddlan, Aberystwyth, Harlech and Beaumaris. For the first two mentioned, there is documentary evidence from the 1280s that they contained accommodation for the royal court: references to 'the king's chamber' and 'great chamber' at Aberystwyth, discussed elsewhere in this volume,[45] (with fourteenth-century entries for an additional 'king's hall', an 'old hall', 'chapel' and a 'queen's chamber')[46] and at Rhuddlan to the 'queen's chamber', 'almonry' 'the king's hall, chamber and kitchen'.[47]

These buildings at Rhuddlan, most standing against the inner face of the curtain wall of the inner ward, were

Figure 8.6: View looking towards the eastern (upper) ward of Caernarfon Castle (Cadw, Welsh Assembly Government: Crown Copyright).

timber framed and daubed, roofed in lead (the queen's chamber)[48] or in turf (the almonry and possibly the king's hall). Taylor hypothesized, based on the prominent flashing of lead roofs in the standing fabric, that the most important buildings stood on the two northern sides of the courtyard, and that the king's and queen's suites occupied one wall apiece, meeting in a kitchen in front of the north tower,[49] though it is equally or more likely that the king's hall lay on one side, the chambers on the others. The 1282–83 account also mentions timber galleries or *aluras* next to the king's chamber,[50] almost certainly at first-floor level, running along the frontage of the buildings. It may be significant that the reference to these walkways also talks about what lay beneath them: the courtyard garden, which had among other features a lawn, and a fishpond beside the castle's well. On this occasion the garden is explicitly mentioned as created for the use of Eleanor of

Castile. Though the court stayed at Rhuddlan in 1283 solely for the prosecution of the war, it seems that they were not to be deprived of their comforts: Edward chose to spend first his birthday and later the Christmas of 1283 in the castle. In 1301 an account referred to the inner ward as '*le Dongoun*', in its common contemporary meaning of lordly enclosure, rather than its later sense of 'great tower.'[51] The whole inner ward at Rhuddlan seems to have been considered as an exclusive area, comparable to the inner ward at Conwy.

This last point raises a functional problem, which applies in some degree to all of the castles and has no perfect solution. The royal household could be extremely large, with as many as 500 people in Edward I's retinue and an additional 150–200 serving Eleanor of Castile.[52] Assuming that the castles of north Wales were built to house the royal family in 'normal' circumstances as well as wartime (which admittedly is a weighty assumption: most of the circumstances that would take the king to north Wales would probably be connected with fighting either in Wales or Ireland), we must believe that a way would have been found to accommodate them all. This problem becomes particularly acute if we are to believe that the greater part of a castle, the inner ward, was a royal enclave, out of bounds to the greater part of the household. At Rhuddlan, the second, outer ward is relatively spacious, but at the other concentric castles such as Aberystwyth, Harlech and Beaumaris, the narrow space between the two walls would have been good for little more than stables, workshops and perhaps barrack-like huts for the lowest-ranking figures. Part of the solution must lie either in accommodating some of the household in temporary buildings or tents, or in billeting them on the townspeople of the new boroughs beside the castles.

Apartments in Gatehouses – Harlech and Beaumaris

At several of the north Wales castles, important accommodation could have been provided on the upper floors of huge gatehouses. Three of these gatehouses are particularly difficult to interpret: Aberystwyth, because of the very fragmentary nature of the surviving fabric, Caernarfon (King's Gate) and Beaumaris because of the additional problem that it is unclear whether the buildings were formerly more complete than they are now, or whether they were simply never finished. Of the group, only Harlech stands effectively intact. Castle gatehouses had long been used for accommodation, and even the enlargement of the building into a major residential element had a long pedigree in the thirteenth century, with the Constable's Gate at Dover (1220s) being perhaps the earliest significant exemplar,[53] and with well-developed baronial examples at Caerphilly and Tonbridge.[54] An architecturally prominent and sophisticated type of building, the Edwardian gatehouse nevertheless had certain shortcomings as a residence, not least the need to provide for the defence of the gateway with portcullises and murder-holes, which needed to be operated from the apartments above the carriageway.

At all of the castles named, substantial buildings were designed for the castle bailey and it cannot be assumed that the gatehouse necessarily contained the main apartments. At Harlech, the great hall on the western side of the bailey had no chamber block at its upper (north) end, and formed a dead end, but at Beaumaris, the presence of two fireplaces in the eastern wall of the bailey indicates the intention to have more than one

room along this side, most probably a hall and chamber (Fig. 8.7). It is impossible to be categorical which was which, but it is more probable that the hall would have occupied the southern part of the range, with the chapel adjoining its lower end, and the chamber to the north, perhaps communicating with one or more levels in the north-east tower. There is, however, serious doubt that these buildings were ever completed as planned, and most writers have assumed that the hall mentioned in the 1343 survey lay inside the north gatehouse[55] While the courtyard buildings at Beaumaris may thus have been planned as a whole apartment, this seems not to have been true of Harlech, and the case for the Harlech gatehouse as the main chamber block in the castle is thus a stronger one than at the other castles.

Taylor naturally had views about how the rooms inside the gatehouse were used, and focused not on the royal person, but on the constables of Harlech. He imagined the knight, Sir John de Bonvillars, and later the master mason, James of St George, living in the building in state and domestic comfort with their respective wives, Agnes and Ambrosia (thus potentially introducing a gender dimension into the debate).[56] As has been mentioned above, one of the few points of architectural detail from the building accounts is an entry on a Sunday in January 1286 for two masons 'building a chimney in the chamber of Sir John de Bonvillars',[57] which Taylor quite understandably saw as one of the fireplaces in the rear range of the gatehouse, either on the first or the second floor. His description of the building is very succinct: '…the great gatehouse… was planned and designed to accommodate, one above the other, a pair of noble households. Each floor was self-contained and comprised a westward-facing hall and great chamber,[58] an orientated private chapel with flanking vestries, two large sleeping-rooms in the eastern towers, and latrines with access from all rooms except the chapels (Fig. 8.8). Evidently it was the lower floor that was intended for occupation by the constable, for from here was controlled the raising of the three portcullises closing the entrance passage, and from here alone there was direct access to the castle's courtyard when the innermost portcullis was down…'[59] He then added in a footnote, 'possibly the upper suite, with identical accommodation but greater privacy, was reserved for visits by the king or the justiciar…'[60]

This interpretation, while very useful, is not without its problems, as an examination of access arrangements shows. There was direct access to the first floor from the courtyard, via the predecessor of the present stone stair, but reaching the upper floor required one to pass through either the ground floor (guard-rooms?) or the first-floor

Figure 8.7: The remains of buildings against the east wall of the courtyard at Beaumaris Castle. These were probably, from right to left, the door to the chapel, the hall and the chamber (Cadw, Welsh Assembly Government: Crown Copyright).

suite, to reach the main access stairs, the spiral stairs in the rear turrets; neither of these routes was exactly stately, and the latter denied any privacy to the occupant of the first floor. There is an additional problem in that the top floor also had direct communication and shared latrines with the main castle wall-walks to either side. We might also doubt whether someone as important as the constable of Harlech would necessarily want a portcullis in his great chamber or indeed another in front of the altar of his domestic chapel. No solution for Harlech is entirely perfect (the chaplains serving in the upper floors of gatehouses must have put up with a certain level of inconvenience as part of their posting), but it seems most likely that the accommodation of royalty was not usually part of the regime of Harlech Castle: certainly no space seems to have been designed specifically with the royal household in mind.

The north gatehouse at Beaumaris – the more complete of the two – was clearly designed to resemble Harlech, but has several interesting points of difference in plan (Figs 8.9 and 8.10). The first floor was intended, like Harlech, to have its main range divided into two rooms, the larger towards the west, though it is clear from the positions of corbels for the roof that this division was never built, at least not in stone. Opening from this space were two large rooms in the drum towers, which also gave access to a central room over the gate-passage. Unlike the room in

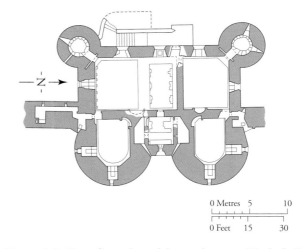

Figure 8.8: First-floor plan of the gatehouse at Harlech Castle (Cadw, Welsh Assembly Government: Crown Copyright).

this position at Harlech, the Beaumaris room was heated and like the rooms flanking it, contained a window with window seats: it is thus unlikely to have been a chapel, and an interpretation as a guard chamber may be more plausible. However, unlike Harlech, this room contained a spiral stair in the thickness of the wall, running up to a similar chamber above: a comparable stair also appears in the much more fragmentary south gatehouse. Thus

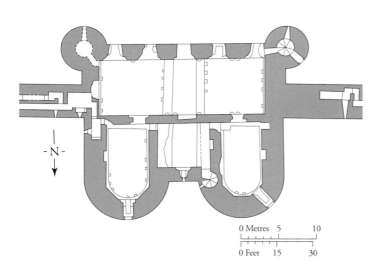

Figure 8.9: First-floor plan of the north gatehouse at Beaumaris Castle (Cadw, Welsh Assembly Government: Crown Copyright).

far the building was probably completed as planned, but it seems that the rear range of the gatehouse never rose above its first floor, and a corresponding suite on a second floor only contained the rooms in the drum towers and over the gate-passage before work was abandoned.

Conclusions

This résumé of the evidence for the grandest lodgings in the castles shows that little new material has come to light since Arnold Taylor published his surveys in *The History of the King's Works*, his articles and guidebooks. Most new findings have come from a refined understanding of the architectural context of the buildings, and from using arguments that Taylor might have rejected as overly conjectural. The medieval exchequer accounts on which Taylor based his research have yielded no new insights into subjects on which he could only pose questions, like the use of the Eagle Tower at Caernarfon, or the identification of the occupants of five complete suites and potentially

Figure 8.10: Reconstruction of the north gatehouse at Beaumaris Castle, showing the parts of the building that were eventually completed (Illustration by Chris Jones-Jenkins; Cadw, Welsh Assembly Government: Crown Copyright).

eleven more rooms at Beaumaris.[61] The discussion above has examined the sites individually, but it is clear that several patterns were common to more than one site, such as making chapels accessible to one side of the largest room in the suite, be it a hall or a great chamber, or the presence of gardens under the windows of the royal suites at Conwy and Rhuddlan, and at Caernarfon, even if the chambers themselves were never finished. The question of apartments for the queen has left tantalizingly slight evidence – all the more poignant in that Edward's plans in this regard were cut off by Eleanor's death in 1290 – though it is remarkable that the keepers of Aberystwyth Castle in 1321 and 1343 should remember to call a building 'the queen's chamber' in the forlorn hope that a queen might one day visit.

Taylor hypothesized that the apartments in Conwy Castle were planned by James of St George in imitation of those in Savoyard castles, and though modern scholarship has suggested that Master James's role as a designer was limited, this point of interpretation has been left unchallenged.[62] But there are several suggestions that this was not necessarily the case. The layout of the Conwy apartments was similar to that at Champvent, but it also had common elements with pre-existing English prototypes, such as the *Gloriette* at Corfe, built in 1205.[63] Moreover, this is only one apartment built by the master

of the works in north Wales: other building types were unknown in Savoy, such as the residential gatehouse, and it certainly does not follow that the planning of residential suites was left to the Savoyards. Most of the other 'imported' details are relatively minor, such as the design of latrines, windows, crenellations and constructional scaffolding, and it seems unlikely that such an important item as the planning of royal apartments would be left entirely to the discretion of the masons. Edward I and his courtiers should expect to have had at least an advisory role in defining what rooms would be needed and how they should be laid out.

In all the cases discussed in this paper, the apartment was internally compartmented, not the single barn-like space of the Normans or Angevins. This had not yet reached the formalized complexity of the second half of the fourteenth century, when places like Windsor Castle established something little short of what would appear in Henry VIII's Hampton Court or even that of William of Orange.[64] But if we are reading them correctly, the castle lodgings of Edward I and his most important barons give lie to the notion that segregation, or even privacy, are inventions of the modern world.[65] For that reason, they deserve to be considered seriously as mileposts in the development of social practice and attitude in the Middle Ages.

Notes

1. *Calendar of Close Rolls, 1330–33* (London 1898), 491.
2. Royal Commission on the Ancient and Historical Monuments of Wales, *An Inventory of the Ancient Monuments in Glamorgan. III. 1b. Medieval Secular Monuments: the Later Castles from 1217 to the Present* (Aberystwyth 2000), 51–104.
3. J. Ashbee, *Goodrich Castle* (London 2005).
4. R. Turner and A. Johnson eds, *Chepstow Castle: its History and Buildings* (Almeley 2006).
5. N. Coldstream, 'Architects, advisers and design at Edward I's castles in Wales', *Architectural History*, 46 (2003), 19–36.
6. A. J. Taylor, 'Castle-building in Wales and Savoy', reprinted in *Studies in Castles and Castle-Building* (London 1985), 8–9 and 15–16.
7. Taylor, *Studies*, foreword.
8. The National Archives (TNA): PRO E 101/485/26 and E 101/485/27.
9. TNA: PRO E 101/13/32, m2.
10. The principal documents are contained in Exchequer Accounts, King's Remembrancer, Various, (TNA: PRO Class E 101). Other useful sources include Pipe Rolls (E 372), Close Rolls (C 54), Inquisitions (C 145) and Ministers' Accounts (SC 6).
11. For the methodological problems posed by medieval works accounts, see B. Cunliffe and J. Munby, *Excavations at Portchester Castle*, 4 (London 1985), especially 134–35.
12. TNA: PRO 372/131, rot. 26.
13. TNA: PRO E 372/120, rot. 22, E 372/121, rot. 22, C 47/3/47; for a discussion, see J. A. Ashbee, 'The Tower of London as a Royal Residence, 1066–1400' (unpublished PhD thesis, University of London, 2006), 174.
14. British Library, Additional Roll 7198.
15. TNA: PRO E 163/4/42.
16. ibid.; BL, Additional Roll 7198.
17. e.g. TNA: PRO E 101/488/30, rot. 2 (felons held at Conwy), E 101/489/6 (gunpowder at Beaumaris), E 101/489/9 (debtors at Conwy), E 101/489/10, rot. 2 (ordnance at Conwy) and E 101/489/13 (debtors at Caernarfon).
18. TNA: PRO SP 16/89/25.
19. C. Given-Wilson ed., *Chronicles of the Revolution, 1397–1400* (Manchester 1993), 140–47.
20. TNA: PRO E 101/489/18.
21. For a detailed discussion of these apartments, see J. Ashbee, 'The royal apartments in the inner ward at Conwy Castle', *Archaeologia Cambrensis*, 153 (2006), 51–72; J. A. Ashbee, *Conwy Castle* (Cardiff 2007).
22. TNA: PRO E 372/131, rot. 26.
23. TNA: PRO E 101/485/28, m4.
24. A. J. Taylor, 'The town and castle of Conwy: preservation and interpretation', *Antiquaries Journal*, 75 (1995), 339–63.
25. TNA: PRO E 101/485/28, m4.
26. TNA: PRO E 163/4/42.
27. T. F. Tout, *Chapters in the Administrative History of Mediaeval*

England, 2 (Manchester 1937), 158–63.

28. Ashbee, *Conwy Castle*, 27.

29. Biblioteca Apostolica Vaticana, Ms. Latin 4015, fol. 193v. The 1301 miracle story of the child Roger of Conwy contains the detail that Nicholas of Havering, son of the justiciar of Wales, was lodged in the north-west tower at Conwy, beside the gate.

30. J. A. Ashbee, '"The Chamber called Gloriette': living at leisure in thirteenth and fourteenth-century castles', *Journal of the British Archaeological Association*, 157 (2004), 17–40.

31. TNA: PRO C 62/42, m4 and E 101/491/17, m3 and m4.

32. TNA: PRO E 120/1, rot. 8 contains a detailed description of the inner and outer wards at Restormel in 1337. The building is ascribed to Edmund, earl of Cornwall between 1272 and 1299; N. A. D. Molyneux, *Restormel Castle* (London 2003), 14.

33. TNA: PRO E 101/13/32, m2.

34. TNA: PRO SC 6/1211/7.

35. TNA: PRO E 101/487/14.

36. TNA: PRO E 101/489/17, rot. 1d.

37. A. J. Taylor, 'The king's works in Wales, 1277–1330', in R. A. Brown, H. M. Colvin and A. J. Taylor. *The History of the King's Works: the Middle Ages*, I (London 1963), 380, fig. 39.

38. TNA: PRO E 163/4/42.

39. Taylor, 'The king's works in Wales', 389.

40. A. J. Taylor, *Four Great Castles* (Gwasg Gregynog 1983), 21–22.

41. R. Avent, 'The conservation and restoration of Caernarfon Castle 1845–1912', in *The Modern Traveller to our Past: Festschrift in Honour of Ann Hamlin*, ed. M. Meek (Southport 2006), 344–52, and this volume.

42. Taylor, 'The king's works in Wales', 372.

43. ibid., 394.

44. Taylor, *Four Great Castles*, 27.

45. Taylor, 'The king's works in Wales', 306. See also Browne, this volume.

46. BL, Additional Roll 7198; TNA: PRO E 163/4/42.

47. TNA: PRO E 101/351/9, m2–m5.

48. ibid., m2.

49. A. J. Taylor, *Rhuddlan Castle* (Cardiff 2004), 7.

50. TNA: PRO E 101 351/9, m5.

51. Taylor, 'The king's works in Wales', 326, n. 4, citing TNA: PRO SC 6/1287/2, no. 9.

52. M. Prestwich, *Edward I* (London 1988), 134–36; J. C. Parsons, 'The court and household of Eleanor of Castile in 1290', *Pontifical Institute of Medieval Studies, Toronto. Studies and Texts*, 37 (1977).

53. J. Coad, *Dover Castle* (London 2007), 29.

54. D. Renn, 'Tonbridge and some other gatehouses', in *Collectanea Historica: Essays in Memory of Stuart Rigold*, ed. A. Detsicas (Maidstone 1981), 93–103.

55. TNA: PRO E 163 4/42. Note that the flashing lines for lead roofs are set very low and cut across the positions of the fireplace hoods suggesting that the hoods were not built as planned, and only ancillary buildings were built on this site.

56. Taylor, *Four Great Castles*, 51. Taylor later questioned whether Ambrosia of St George accompanied her husband to Harlech and hypothesized that she was the 'Dame Amboise de Saint Joire' who in 1288 became a Carthusian nun at Melan in Savoy. A. J. Taylor, 'St George, James (d. 1306 x 9)', *Oxford Dictionary of National Biography*, 48 (Oxford 2004), 606–07.

57. TNA: PRO E 101 485/27.

58. Cadw has since amended this in its interpretation materials to 'great chamber' and 'chamber'; see A. J. Taylor, *Harlech Castle* (Cardiff 2002), 25.

59. A. J. Taylor, 'Who was 'John Pennardd, leader of the men of Gwynedd'?', reprinted in Taylor, *Studies*, 221 onwards.

60. ibid., 224.

61. A. J. Taylor, *Beaumaris Castle* (Cardiff 2004), 32.

62. Coldstream, 'Architects', 33.

63. Royal Commission on the Historical Monuments of England, *An Inventory of the Historical Monuments in the County of Dorset. 2. South-east*, 1 (London 1970), 74–77.

64. C. Wilson, 'The royal lodgings of Edward III at Windsor Castle: form, function, representation' in eds L. Keen and E. Scarff *Windsor. Medieval Archaeology, Art and Architecture of the Thames Valley*, British Archaeological Association Conference Transactions 25 (Leeds 2002), 15–93.

65. e.g. D. Webb, *Privacy and Solitude in the Middle Ages* (London 2007), especially 47–59 and 97–117.

9

Food Supply and Preparation at the Edwardian Castles

Peter Brears

Introduction

The provision of food and drink was always of the greatest importance in the planning of any castle, since if these were to run out, the whole of the defences became virtually useless. This fact was particularly significant in the Edwardian conquest of Wales, when locally sourced supplies were virtually non-existent, transport overland was fraught with difficulties, and hence great reliance had to be made on provisions brought in by sea. For this reason, wharves and docks were essential features at the coastal castles. Once the supplies had arrived, they had to be carefully recorded and controlled as they were secured into their respective stores, and as they were rationed out to meet the daily requirements of those living within the walls.

The Edwardian castles of Wales are remarkable for the quality and variety of their plans, each individually designed to extract the best advantages from its site. They also vary considerably in their degree of completeness, either because they were never finished, or because of subsequent demolition and decay, both of which make their surviving fabrics additionally difficult to understand. However, it is clear that different castles were subject to different degrees of innovation in their domestic plans. At Harlech, and probably Flint and Beaumaris too, the service buildings and halls were set around the walls within their rectangular inner wards, in a very simple and straightforward manner. However, at Conwy and Caernarfon – both commenced in 1283 – the planning displayed a great degree of sophistication, apparently designed specifically to meet the requirements of their medieval administrators. This paper therefore concentrates on the service rooms of these castles, drawing attention to the manner in which they were planned to meet the organizational needs of their adminstrative officers as much as they were designed for defence. It commences with the smaller, but more complete suite at Conwy.

The Service Rooms, Conwy Castle

Documentary evidence for the service rooms of Conwy Castle is extremely sparse. There is little from the period of construction, 1283–87, except a reference to the great hall, pantry and small hall in a document of 29 September 1286.[1] The 1307–08 accounts for various works are limited to providing a bucket and chain of iron for the newly dug well for the hall kitchens, and the reparation of that building's walls and windows.[2] A survey by Sir William of Embleton taken in 1343 found the kitchen, bakehouse and garner in decay, but then there is nothing more until a programme of works completed for Henry VIII in 1525–40.[3] This included re-slating the well house, rebuilding the well winch, whitening and glazing the ale cellar, repairing the loft and chambers of the bakehouse tower, 'the chambre where harde corne used to be kept', the larder house and a chamber over the stockhouse, mending the kitchen oven with stones and red clay, and working on various drains. More detail, and the first real suggestions as to the positions of individual service rooms, is provided by a survey of 1627, which lists:[4]

1. [Hall] kitchen in the outer ward 10 x 8 yards, arched, the walls standing, but the roof timbers and lead totally collapsed.
2. Cellar, under the hall in the outer ward; above the floor is totally collapsed.
3. Draw well with 'water enough and singular good'.
4. Cellar, arched, in inner ward, with a stair up to a;
5. Buttery, a little room, to the north of the great chamber.
6. Kitchen, under the great and presence chambers.

Given this level of documentation, it is fortunate that the masonry of the castle still survives largely in its original late thirteenth-century state, offering considerable scope for unravelling its extremely efficient and innovative domestic planning.

The services required to cater for the household dining

in the great hall and small hall chamber (lesser hall), lining the south side of the outer ward (Fig. 9.1), were entirely separate from those serving the royal apartments in the inner ward. The 1627 survey confirms that the foundations flanking the curtain wall, to the north of the great hall, were the household or hall kitchen, close to the (modern-named) Kitchen Tower. The unheated basement room of this tower may have served as a larder for fresh and salt meats. In the early fourteenth century, the Conwy larders held eleven and a quarter salt beefs, eighteen 'quires' (quatonians or quarters?) more salt beef, four quarters and six bushels of coarse salt, and eight and a half quart of fine salt. However, there is no documentary evidence as to where the larder lay.[5]

Documentary references to 'a kitchen, brewhouse and bakehouse under one roof' and the order of service rooms listed in the 1343 survey indicate that the bakehouse and brewhouse each occupied the building represented by the foundations at one or other end of the kitchen.[6] The bakehouse oven still remains in the basement of the south-west tower, suggesting that this office was to the west of the kitchen (which lay at the centre of the north wall), while the location of the well would favour the brewhouse being to the east. Presumably all the flour and malt milling took place at the watermill on the river Gyffin outside the walls.

As for service into the halls, food would simply be carried across the outer ward into the extended porch, on into a screens passage, and through a door at each end directly into the great hall, or on into the probably higher status lesser hall beyond. Since the room to the east of the screens passage was used as a chapel, the buttery/pantry facilities had to be set most conveniently between the great and lesser halls, where the bread, table linen and tableware could be readily stored and then distributed (Fig. 9.1). This usage is confirmed by a payment of 30s. made in 1286 to Jordan of Canterbury for repairing the great hall and a certain pantry next to the small hall in the great hall, which exactly describes its location.[7]

The plan of the outer ward services is quite straightforward, but that of the inner ward is quite exceptional, since here the offices were designed as part of a fully equipped, if compact, royal palace (Fig. 9.2). In order to understand the plan, it is first necessary to consider the various individual rooms, before going on to see how they were inter-linked to form a coherent whole.

Since, like most of Edward I's coastal castles, Conwy was designed to be provisioned from ships, a wharf was constructed at the eastern tip of its rocky promontory. A bird's-eye view of the castle, drawn around 1600, shows that its river front had stairs ascending to a double-turreted water gate, and a battlement wall guarded by a round tower pierced with firing loops (Fig. 9.3).[8] The southern end was defended by a partially surviving wall, descending from the east barbican to the water's edge. This effectively enclosed the whole castle and town frontage along to the spur wall and round tower at the northern tip of the town walls. Its eastern end terminated in a steep staircase, its outer face defended by a battlemented wall, while its inner face clasped the northern tower of the east barbican, where its outline is still evident against the render. The narrow, arched gateway between this tower and the Chapel Tower appears to have been defended by a portcullis, winched up into a now destroyed superstructure. From here, stores would be carried through the broad passage beneath the great chamber and into their respective stores (Fig. 9.4).

The physical and administrative control of all stores was a major feature of medieval household management. Edward II's household ordinances of 1318, and those of Edward IV in 1474, both demonstrate a relatively conservative system of administration, probably continuing that already largely established when this castle was being constructed. In essence, a chief officer, either the lord steward, the lord treasurer, or the controller, had to attend the king at all times. He and his servants occupied their own chambers, and they directly supervised the counting house, whose staff included a cofferer and a receiver with seven clerks, to collect, hold and dispense funds, and fourteen clerks, including those of the pantry and buttery, the spicery, and the kitchen, to control the purchase, storage and distribution of foods and other goods. At Conwy, the so-called 'King's Tower' at the south-east corner of the inner ward was ideally constructed to house these administrators.

The principal first-floor room has a large hooded fireplace, and a wide window recess lined around three sides with masonry benches to form a well-lit carrel (Fig. 9.4.3). As the chief officer's chamber, this is where records from the counting house would be checked and their totals transcribed into separate rolls. This window appears to have been specifically positioned to give direct oversight of the stores as they were carried up into the east barbican, and on into the inner ward. From this chamber, a spiral stair goes up to the administrators' latrine, and down to a stair passage, which emerges at the back of the window seat in the king's chamber (Fig. 9.4.2). When this was masked behind tapestries, or painted cloths, it would be totally invisible. By this device, the king not only enjoyed direct communication with his chief officer, but could also have apparently completely private conversations, while his officers or soldiers were concealed only inches away.

Descending further, the main spiral stair reaches

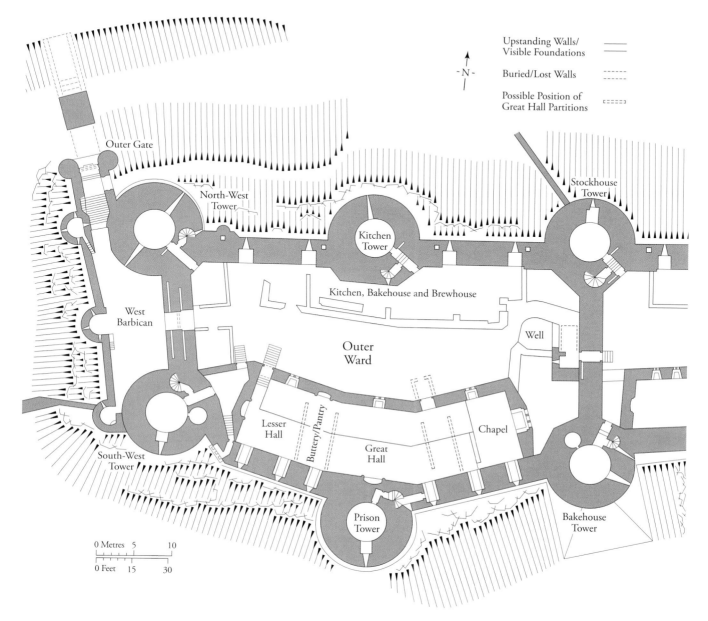

Figure 9.1: Plan of the outer ward of Conwy Castle (Cadw, Welsh Assembly Government: Crown Copyright).

a passage on the ground floor, with branches leading south-west into the king's wardrobe of beds and robes in a small room in the south curtain wall (Fig. 9.4.11), north-west into the kitchen, and north to the passage linking the inner barbican to the inner ward, or on into the rooms serving the great chamber. Turning to the south-east, meanwhile, an outwards-opening door led into the principal ground-floor room of this tower (Fig. 9.4.10). Almost certainly designed as the counting house, it too has a wide, hooded fireplace, and a deep window recess

lined with stone benches, which would serve as a carrel for entering records in the rolls. Since it faces east-south-east, it would receive direct sunlight from dawn to around 10am, the pre-dinner period when the counting house would be at its busiest. The really conclusive evidence for the use of this room lies directly beneath its timber floor, where there is a large, windowless chamber. Based solely on the opinions of romantic Gothick novelists, these features have traditionally been identified as prisons where the incarcerated were left to rot. The stench alone

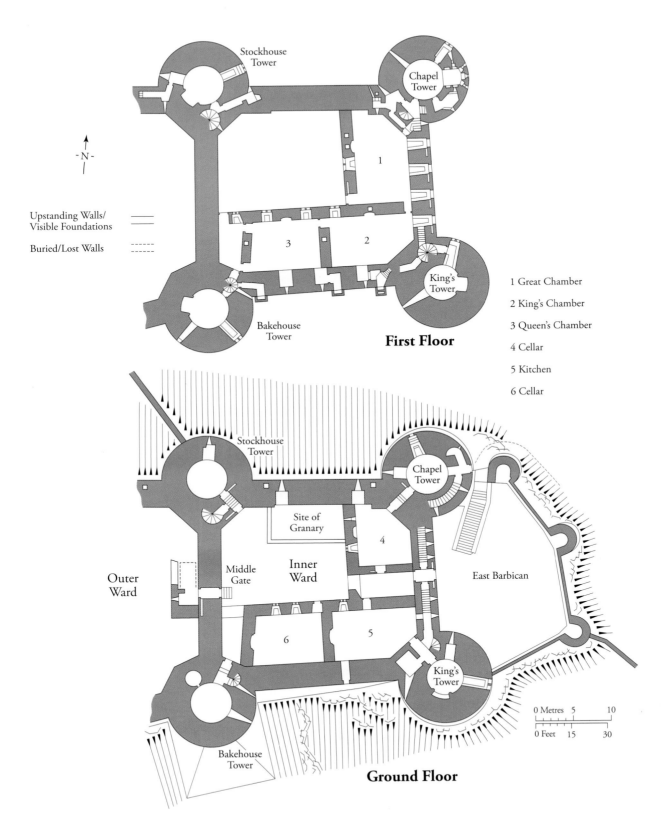

Figure 9.2: Plan of the inner ward of Conwy Castle (Cadw, Welsh Assembly Government: Crown Copyright).

of such a practice would have made the entire chamber suite totally uninhabitable. If without a latrine, they are, in fact, concealed under-floor strong rooms, ideal for keeping coinage for expenses and payrolls, along with other valuables, completely hidden from most of the household, and extremely secure.[9] Access would have been by way of a trapdoor and ladder, all disguised beneath floor coverings or furniture. Given its function, this tower would be more accurately described as a 'treasury tower' rather than the King's Tower, which it never was.

The first large ground-floor room proceeding clockwise around the inner ward is identifiable as the kitchen described in the 1627 survey (Fig. 9.4.13). Its position directly beneath the King's Chamber is one which was to be followed in later centuries, as in Henry VIII's Hampton Court Palace in the 1530s, since it provided the monarch with under-floor heating.[10] It was essentially a privy-cum-staff kitchen, designed both to serve those dining in the royal chamber suite when it was in active occupation, or the administrators who may have worked in the adjacent tower at other times. A number of physical features confirm its original function. The fireplace, for example, appears to be the largest in this ward, despite the robbing of its ashlar surround. Its floor is set at a slope, so that it could be brushed or washed down, draining through a doorway cut in the southern wall, by which rubbish could also be discharged onto the latrine middens on the Gyffin stream below. Even more conclusive is a row of original slots built into the south wall to hold the rails of built-in furniture. These suggest a long dresser board, 30–36 inches high (0.75m–0.9m), with a shelf above at a height of 65 inches (1.65m). These provide particularly rare evidence for medieval kitchen furnishings. Assuming that, as usual, the controller kept the keys to all the domestic offices, we may see the raw material being recorded and released from their various stores early in the morning, and carried into the kitchen via the eastern passageway. As cooking progressed, clerks in the counting house would oversee the entire kitchen from their hatch, cut high through the eastern wall, or the adjacent elevated doorway. When the food was ready, they could then survey and record it as it was carried along the eastern passage to emerge at the low end of the great chamber, up via the wardrobe into the king's chamber, or via external stairs into any of the three first-floor chambers.

Passing beyond the room described as the Low Parlour in 1627, the next service room is the bakehouse in the Bakehouse Tower (Fig. 9.4.14). This is entered by a wide, open-fronted passage, probably the wood-store for all the fires in this ward. The bakehouse here is essentially a privy bakehouse for baking bread and probably pastries too,

Figure 9.3: Detail from the 1600 'bird's-eye view' showing the east end of Conwy Castle (By permission of the marquess of Salisbury, Hatfield House, CPM 1/62).

entirely for those dining in this ward. Its large circular oven was built with a smoke-hood over its door, the flue above venting into the open air at wall-walk level.

Proceeding round by the door giving access to the outer ward and the well, the Stockhouse Tower lies in the north-western corner (Fig. 9.4.6). There is no evidence for any service use here, but its low, north-facing basement room would have been ideal for larder use, not available elsewhere in this ward. Adjacent to it stood a timber-framed granary building, its size being indicated by a low masonry sill wall and beam sockets in the walls above (Fig. 9.4.7).

The cellar, as described in the 1627 survey, was placed in the ideally cool and dark basement of the north-east, or Chapel Tower (Fig. 9.4.9). Casks of wine and so forth could be carried in through the entrance passages, through the heated, unidentified room in the north-east of the inner ward, and down a broad staircase to the basement. A doorway with a refaced exterior leads off the eastern side of this room, perhaps originally to the portcullis winch over the water gate. From the cellar, a narrow spiral stair may have permitted supplies to be brought up to an extremely complex arrangement of landings, stairs and passages at first-floor level. From this point, the stairs descend to the entrance passage, and ascend to the upper storey, presumably occupied by the chaplains and clerks of the king's chapel, while three doors lead into the chapel (Fig. 9.4.5), the great chamber (Fig. 9.4.1), and a small two-doored chamber (Fig. 9.4.8) respectively. From

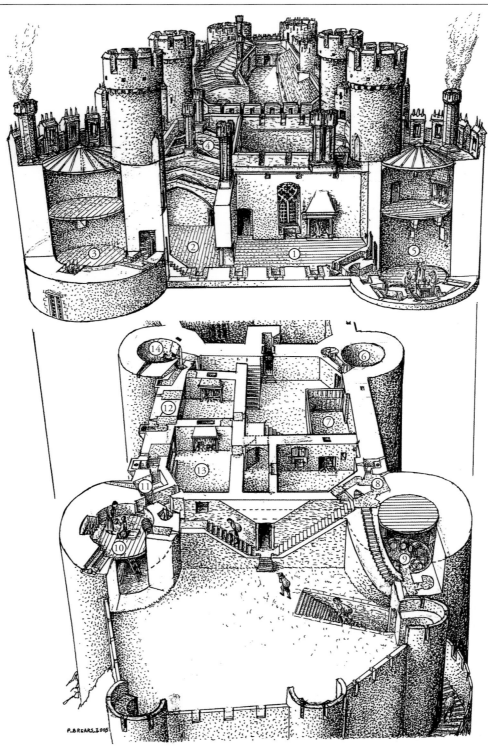

Figure 9.4: Exploded view of the inner ward of Conwy Castle viewed from the east. The rooms in the royal chamber suite have here been identified as: first floor (above): 1. great chamber; 2. king's chamber, with access to his wardrobe of robes and of beds, and latrines (11) as well as 3; 3. head officer's chamber with unheated chamber above; 4. queen's chamber with access to the wardrobe of robes and of beds (12); 5. chapel with chamber for chapel clergy above. Ground floor (below): 6. Stockhouse Tower, larder?; 7. granary; 8. buttery, with access to staff latrine; 9. cellar, with access to portcullis winch over back gate; 10. clerks' chamber or greencloth chamber with store room below; 11. & 12. king's & queen's wardrobes to their first-floor chambers; 13. kitchen with access to the clerks' chamber (10) and the entrance passage; 14. Bakehouse Tower, privy bakehouse with fuel store leading to the inner ward. Basement/external areas: Here the staircase ascends from the wharf to the water gate from where steps ascend to the entrance passage (P. Brears).

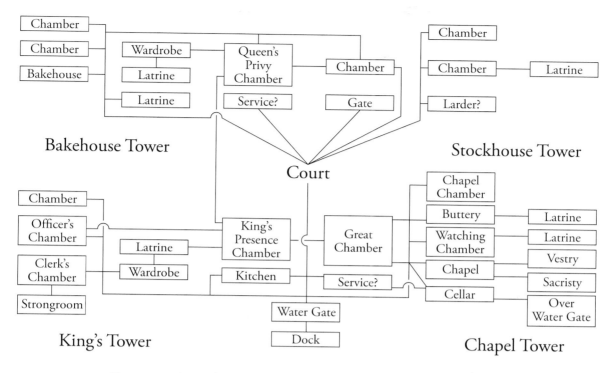

Figure 9.5: Access diagram of the inner ward of Conwy Castle (P. Brears).

its position, the latter may have been the 1627 'north end...little room used for a buttery'. It is certainly large enough to store the cups, pitchers etc, used to serve drinks from the cellar on into the great chamber, or the king's and queen's chambers beyond.

During this circular tour of the service rooms of the inner court, it will have been noted that they have been designed to establish the royal chamber suite as a complete, self-sufficient, defensible unit, which could be indefinitely provisioned by ship. This proved particularly important during the rebellion of Madog ap Llywelyn, when Edward I was effectively trapped here between Christmas 1294 and spring 1295. As the English baggage trains had been captured and re-provisioning overland was virtually impossible, the availability of a heavily defended dock proved invaluable. Even so, Walter of Guisborough records how the king of England refused the small quantity of wine kept back for him, insisting that it was shared out between all his troops.[11] At each point in the circuit of the inner ward rooms, locked or barred doors and convenient mural routes have been constructed to give the maximum combination of security and supervision required by the administrators. It was a building of great sophistication, representing the finest domestic planning in late thirteenth-century military architecture (Fig. 9.5).

The Service Rooms, Caernarfon Castle

There are many similarities between Conwy Castle and Caernarfon Castle. They were commenced almost simultaneously, both lay on rocky promontories with the sea on one side and their walled towns and town quays to the other. Both had upper and lower status wards, surrounded by high walls and higher mural towers. The great difference lies in their scale and aspirations. Caernarfon occupied over twice the area of Conwy, and was intended to provide accommodation for a major royal household of several hundred. Unfortunately, the full building programme was never brought to completion here, and there has been subsequent decay, but the substantial remains still contain much of interest. The phases of construction have been discussed elsewhere,[12] and so this paper will only discuss what survives, concentrating on the lower ward.

As at Conwy, there was a small wharf or landing at the seaward end of the castle, at the foot of the Eagle Tower. This was clearly intended to provide access into the lower ward (but not the tower) for royal visitors, personnel, and valuable stores such as wine (or bullion) in a basement cellar set against the adjacent curtain wall (Fig. 9.6). From the external north-west corner of the Eagle Tower, a water gate was to have provided access for sea-going ships into a dock extending up to 140 feet (43m) along the north curtain. Although never built, its portcullis slot and doorways still remain *in situ*.

The Well Tower, which dominates the landward end of the dock, was the direct equivalent of the King's Tower at Conwy. It was specifically designed to house the same group of administrative offices, and control the delivery of supplies into the castle (Fig. 9.7). The second floor is largely of nineteenth-century date, but may have been of high status to accommodate one of the chief officers (Fig. 9.7.1). The original first-floor room, with its fine hooded fireplace and traceried window, was designed for high-status use by a chief officer (Fig. 9.7.5). It had better administrative facilities than Conwy, including a

window/carrel overlooking the dock and water gate, and a staff kitchen (Fig. 9.7.6), where food could be cooked for those officers who either worked through the household's meal times in the great hall, or remained here during those long periods when the main household was absent. As at Conwy, the counting house was on the ground floor (Fig. 9.7.8). For security, it had only a single door, accessible from the passage linking the main spiral stair with the lower ward. Its window/carrel overlooks the dock. This visual supervision was extended by having direct control of the winch room for the portcullis of the back door, which opened onto the dockside quay at the Well Tower basement (Fig. 9.7.14). This meant that nothing could be either unloaded or carried into the castle without being

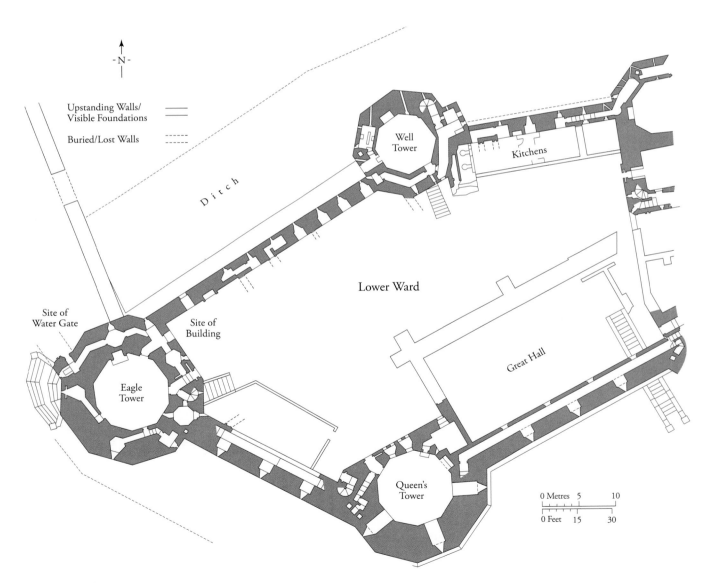

Figure 9.6: Plan of the lower ward of Caernarfon Castle (Cadw, Welsh Assembly Government: Crown Copyright).

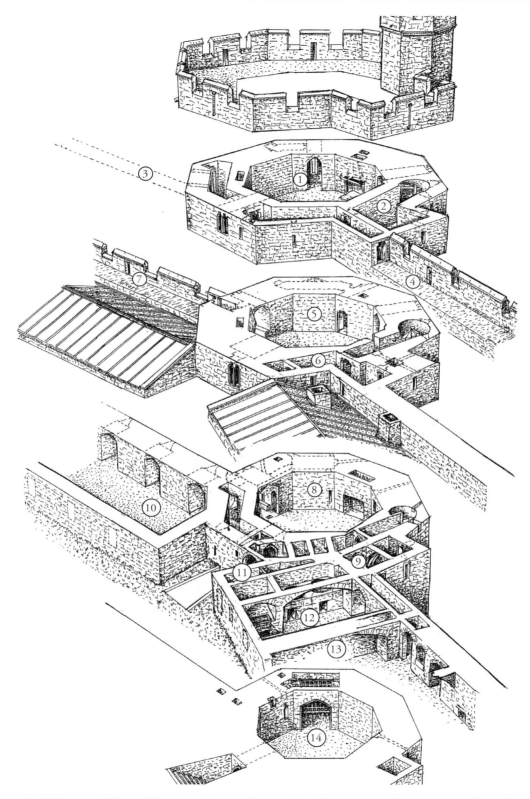

Figure 9.7: Exploded view of the Well Tower, Caernarfon Castle. The rooms in this tower are here identified as: third floor: wall-walk and turret. Second floor: 1. head officer's chamber with latrine; 2. mural chamber; 3. intended wall-walk to Eagle Tower; 4. wall-walk to King's Gate. First floor: 5. head officer's chamber with latrine; 6. staff kitchen; 7. wall-walk to Eagle Tower and water gate. Ground floor: 8. clerk's chamber or greencloth chamber with access to carrel and portcullis winch and to a latrine; 9. well chamber; 10. larders?; 11. dry store behind boiling furnaces; 12. boiling house; 13. hall place kitchen. Basement: 14. basement with door to dock and stairs up to lower ward (P. Brears).

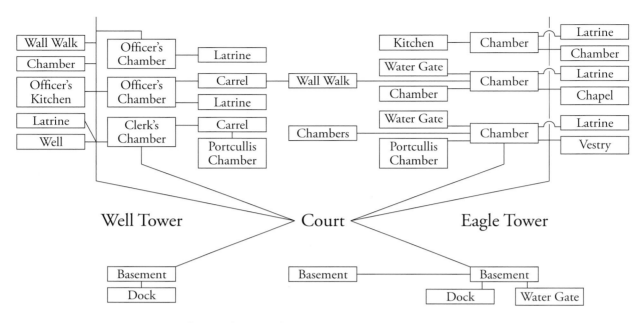

Figure 9.8: Caernarfon Castle access diagram of the Well Tower and Eagle Tower (P. Brears).

under the constant watch and control of the administrative officers and clerks.

Having been transferred into the basement of the tower, provisions may have been housed in this cool, dark and secure room, before being carried up its steep staircase into the lower ward, and on into the appropriate stores. Presumably grain was taken to the Granary Tower in the upper ward, while salt meats, fish and so forth would be more conveniently kept in larders, perhaps along the curtain wall towards the Eagle Tower.

As at Conwy, the kitchens and great hall were set on opposite sides of the lower ward. The kitchens of the mid- to late 1280s were set against the north curtain wall, between the Well Tower and the King's Gate. Proceeding from the west, the first feature of note is a narrow chamber in the thickness of the west wall, probably entered by a doorway in the passage leading into the tower (Fig. 9.7.11). Formerly identified as a smoking chamber for meat,[13] even though there was never any access for smoke, and meat smoking was three hundred years into the future, it must have been a store intended for dry materials, either records or expensive foodstuffs. Later examples are known elsewhere, as in the pastry at Slingsby Castle, North Yorkshire.

Immediately east of this dry store lay the boiling house (Fig. 9.7.12), the earliest architectural or archival evidence for the separation of this department from the main household kitchen (Fig. 9.8). Boiling houses were

intended for production of the bulk of the food served in the great hall. Early each morning joints of meat (or fish on fish days), each sufficient to feed a 'mess' of four people, were simmered here until tender. The joints were then removed using flesh-hooks, and pre-chopped and cooked vegetables, usually with oatmeal, stirred into the remaining stock to rapidly convert it into pottage. This was always served as the first course, being followed by the rested meat or fish. Here, the pair of boiling furnaces is in a remarkable state of preservation. They take the form of a high masonry bench pierced by two, hourglass-shaped holes. A firemouth into the lower half enabled a substantial wood fire to be built up across its large, flat base, the flames there being channelled through the narrow central hole, two-thirds the area of the base, directly onto the base and up the sides of a hemispherical boiling vessel supported from above (Fig. 9.9).

Springers and projecting tie-stones on the adjacent curtain wall show that a large stone-arched smoke-hood was to have bridged over the front of the furnaces to extract the rising smoke and steam into a chimney above. A window through the curtain wall provided both illumination for those working here and, by means of a shutter, a way of controlling draught up the chimney. The substantial supplies of water required in the boiling house were probably conducted into a cistern at the south end of the furnaces, the duct for the lead pipe from the well chamber cistern running through their back wall to this point,

Figure 9.9: Caernarfon Castle: reconstruction of the boiling house (P. Brears).

above a major drain. The blank wall opposite the furnaces would have provided an ideal location for a long dresser board where joints might be trimmed before boiling, or rested afterwards, and where cooked vegetables might be chopped, or the pottage dished ready for serving.

From the boiling house, a mural passage leads through the curtain wall to the main kitchen (Fig. 9.7.13). Once again, springers and tie-stones show that a large cooking fireplace was intended to back against the boiling house wall. Here the pottage vegetables might be boiled and other processes such as frying or broiling on gridirons carried out. A cistern, with parts of its lead lining still in place, again supplied water from the well house cistern by way of a lead pipe, the duct for which has been cut open in antiquity to extract the lead. From here, water could be baled out as and when required; a drain, a little further out, allowed surplus water, waste, and dirty water from floor-washing to be swilled down into the moat. Set into the centre of the kitchen wall are the springers for a substantial transverse arch showing that the roof above was to have been bridged by long east–west purlins, extending to the masonry end walls.

A short staircase in the eastern of the two window recesses gives access to a short stair leading both to a latrine, and to a square room in the angle between the curtain wall and the King's Gate. Its floor joists would have rested on the stone ledge running along the west face of the King's Gate. The position of this room, elevated some 5 feet (1.5m) above the kitchen floor, would make it an ideal office for the clerk of the kitchen. Openings in its intended west wall enabled him to oversee the whole of the kitchen, while a southern window would supervise the route from the kitchen across to the great hall. There was a semi-basement room below, apparently having no connection to the kitchen, but perhaps entered by a door in its southern wall, where an adjacent door at the same level leads into the basement of the King's Gate. We should expect to find a surveying place in this area, with hatches from which the food was recorded and dispatched, but the surviving masonry offers no clues in this direction.

This description of the boiling house and kitchen is based on the foundations and tie-stones in the mid-1280s curtain wall. By the time this wall was being raised to its full height in the later 1290s, following the 1294 attack by Madog ap Llywelyn, the decision had already been taken to abandon the original scheme. As a result, the rising flues, walls and springers were left truncated, and never brought to completion. As such, they still represent particularly rare and revealing evidence for kitchen planning and services of the late thirteenth century.

Since later surveys confirm that the great hall was completed, a practical kitchen was certainly required in this position. It was, however, of a far flimsier construction, but apparently followed the same division into boiling house, kitchen, and clerk's office. Its floor level was some 3 feet (0.9m) below that proposed in 1283, while its internal wall was only 15 feet (4.6m) south of the curtain wall, where the narrow masonry sill for its timber-framed façade stands in great contrast to the massive 1280s foundations seen everywhere else around the castle. The new boiling house extended from the original furnaces to the site of the intended transverse arch. An oval cobbled boiling hearth suitable for freestanding boilers occupies the centre of the floor, perhaps once beneath a louvre, while the foundations of a chimney stack completely close its eastern end. When complete, this apparently provided a boiler furnace (and oven?) for the boiling house to the west, and a conventional wide, cooking hearth for the kitchen to the east.

It is probable that the wall originally proposed for the east end of the kitchen was now built in stone up to its full height. The best evidence for this is to be seen in the west wall of the King's Gate. Here the ledge to support the proposed clerk's office was modified by forming six massive beam sockets, lined with a rather ginger-coloured stone, quite different to that used in the original build. They only extend as far as the new timber-framed south wall, the top of which had its wall plate fitted into a new beam slot, still to be seen directly above. There is no strong evidence for the form of the new roof, but a low single pitch of lead-covered boards would be most likely for a narrow building such as this. Perhaps no other part of the castle so clearly demonstrates the change in Edward I's approach to Caernarfon, from being a great fortress-palace in 1283, to a much simpler administrative and military facility after 1294. His cooks must have found this change particularly strange to work with, now that these excellent boiling furnaces, cisterns, doorways and drains were inconveniently, or quite uselessly, left stranded 3 feet (0.9m) above their working floor levels.

Conclusions

Having considered the service rooms at Conwy and Caernarfon, a number of factors emerge which may make it necessary to review a number of well-established opinions on how castles were designed and managed.

Since many earlier writers on this subject had military experiences, it was to be expected that they saw castles primarily as fully garrisoned forts with the capacity to man the perimeters and guardrooms at all times. Here, however, it is evident that the control of the service gates was primarily the responsibility of the administration, not the soldiery. At both castles the windows of the chief officers' chambers were deliberately positioned to view the portcullises of the water gates. From here they could give direct oral or visual instructions to those operating the gates and winches. If necessary, they could proceed directly to the winch rooms, via wall-top or mural passages. At Caernarfon, the portcullis in the Well Tower was operated from the counting house itself, not from a guardroom, again confirming the administrators' direct control of access through these service gates.

The role of castles as centres of both extra-mural and intra-mural administration has long been acknowledged, but it has yet to be recognized that rooms were designed and positioned for these purposes. One of the primary requirements for such rooms was a good source of natural light and sufficient space to sit in it for long periods when entering or transcribing the various rolls. Here, it is argued, broad window recesses lined with stone benches are frequently carrels for reading and writing, especially where they are in rooms that might otherwise be expected to have the usual narrow slit windows.

It is further argued that those rooms – usually basements – without mural access, little or no natural light and no direct access to a latrine, are not 'oubliettes' or 'bottle dungeons', as claimed by Gothick novelists and gruesome guidebooks, but secure storage rooms or treasuries. Trapdoors in their boarded or vaulted roofs could easily be disguised beneath floor coverings or furniture, so they remained virtually undetectable, or at least only accessible under the closest of supervision.

The design of castles is usually attributed to either the patron who commissioned the works, or the master masons/engineers mentioned in the building accounts. However, as the above studies of Conwy and Caernarfon show beyond all doubt, their designs are highly influenced by the needs of the administrators. The positioning of windows, doors and hatches to give them extensive visual supervision, the routing of passages to make sure that there were secure routes from stores to kitchens, kitchens to chambers and so forth, all show the workings of their minds. How this was achieved must be a matter of pure conjecture. Were there formal planning meetings, or did a discussion of administrators' needs take place before they agreed the mason/engineers accounts?

Whichever it was, the results were quite brilliant. Developing a three-dimensional understanding of the castles' structures and their use is difficult enough today, when they actually exist. It can only be with admiration and respect that we regard the minds of those thirteenth-century builders who were able to conceive these buildings as abstract forms and then convert them into stone and mortar.

Appendix

The Well Winch, Caernarfon Castle

The walls of the well in the Well Tower in the lower ward retain considerable evidence from which it is possible to reconstruct the probable form of the original well winch (Fig. 9.10). Working down from the top of the square shaft, which ascends to the first floor of the tower: the first features are two window-like openings into the staff kitchen, where it may have been possible (but seems unlikely) that water was drawn up using a bucket and

Figure 9.10: Caernarfon Castle: reconstruction of the winch in the Well Tower. Sockets in the walls suggest a wheel-and-axle winch operating a pair of counterbalanced buckets (top right). Once the buckets were raised, their contents were poured into a lead-lined sink (1) from which pipes carried supplies to the boiling house and lower ward? (2) and to a cistern in the kitchen (3) (P. Brears).

rope. Just below, sets of joist holes show where three timbers bridged the void, ideal for mounting a pair of pulleys over the well. Two further timbers were then set into the walls at right angles to the upper three. These, it is suggested, may have acted as stops to prevent buckets from fouling the pulleys described above. Sockets cut into the side walls of the well within a tall arched opening into the ground-floor well house were obviously intended to receive the bearing blocks of the winch itself. The left end of the back wall was cut away to receive a large wheel, the better-preserved evidence in the well house of the Granary Tower suggesting that this was some 7 feet (2.1m) in diameter and 1 foot 2 inches (0.35m) wide.

This evidence shows that the winch drew mechanized advantage from the long-established wheel-and-axle principle. This could have been achieved by turning the wheel as a treadmill, but it is too narrow for that, or by handles projecting from its rim, for which it is far too wide. This leaves just one option of passing a rope around its perimeter. The length of this rope may be readily estimated. If it is assumed that the axle was 1 foot (0.3m) in diameter, it would draw up some 3 feet 4 inches (1m) per revolution. As the well is 50 feet (15.2m) deep, it would require fifteen revolutions (50/3.3=15) to bring a bucket to the surface. Assuming that the drum of the pulley wheel was 6 feet in diameter, it would draw 20 feet (6.1m) per revolution; therefore, the fifteen revolutions would require some 300 feet (91m) of rope to be wound around it. In practice, this would have been extremely troublesome and dangerous. Every time the bucket was drawn up, the operator would find himself entangled in an uncontrollable mass of rope, but this could be avoided by making a much shorter loop of about 60 feet (18.3m) to pass just twice around the pulley, leaving sufficient extra for the operator to pull on.

Since the joists above the well suggest the existence of the two pulleys, it would appear that the winch operated a two-bucket system, one descending as the other ascended, which doubled the rate of extraction and greatly reduced the effort required, as each bucket and rope acted as a counterweight to the other. Given the suggested radius of the wheel (3 feet, 0.9m) and that of the axle (6 inches, 0.15m), this system would give a mechanical advantage of 1:6, so that only 20lbs (9kg) of effort would be required to raise a 120lbs (54kg) load, for example.

The well house is large enough for two men to work together conveniently. Since they should be able to heave the pulley rope at least 3 feet (0.9m) per second, it would only take two minutes to raise one bucket, and lower the other into the water. If each bucket held about 12 gallons (55l) of water (about 120lb, 54kg), a ten-minute session would easily raise some 60 gallons (273l), making it a very efficient system.

Large square sockets at each end of the brink of the well, show where a large sill beam was originally fixed. This would have formed a landing platform for the buckets, but may also have incorporated some form of safety barrier, or even a chute to convey the water from the buckets into the adjacent lead-lined cistern, but there is no evidence to confirm this.

Acknowledgements

I would like to record my great thanks to the late Richard Avent, Peter Humphries and Dr Diane Williams of Cadw and Dr Jeremy Ashbee of English Heritage for the invaluable discussion enjoyed at Conwy and Caernarfon, and also to John Kenyon of Amgueddfa Cymru – National Museum Wales for access to his transcription of the 1627 survey of Conwy.

Notes

1. The National Archives (TNA): PRO E 101/485/28.
2. TNA: PRO E 101 486/24, no.16.
3. TNA: PRO E 163/4/42, 17 Edward III (1343–1344) & TNA: PRO E 101 488/20, rot. 2, 488/31, 488/32, rot. 1, 489/9, 489/11, 489/14, 489/15 and 489/18.
4. TNA: PRO State Papers 16/89/25.
5. TNA: PRO E 101/13/32.
6. TNA: PRO E 163/4/42.
7. TNA: PRO E 101/485/28.
8. Marquess of Salisbury, Hatfield House Ms. CPM 1/62.
9. For further examples of under-floor storage rooms, see P. Brears, *Cooking and Dining in Medieval England* (Totnes 2008).
10. S. Thurley, *The Royal Palaces of Tudor England* (London 1993), 161.
11. M. Prestwich, *Edward I* (London 1988), 221–23.
12. A. J. Taylor, *Caernarfon Castle and Town Walls*, 6 edn (Cardiff 2004).
13. A. J. Taylor, *Caernarvon Castle and Town Wall, Caernarvonshire* (London 1953), 23.

The Landscapes of Edward's New Towns:
Their Planning and Design

Keith D. Lilley

It is well known that new towns were closely associated with the Edwardian castles in Wales. Indeed, it might be thought that there is little new to be said on this subject following Maurice Beresford's book, *New Towns of the Middle Ages*, in which he devotes most of the first chapter to this very topic.[1] Beresford's continuing influence is great and his book still highly influential judging by the number of times it is cited in accounts of Edward's activities in Wales. Beresford referred to these new towns as 'planted boroughs', seeing them in economic and constitutional terms, and says rather little about their layouts, or indeed the processes of design and planning that created them. He borrowed from T. F. Tout's earlier essay, *Mediaeval Town Planning*, in drawing parallels between the plans of the Edwardian towns in Wales and the bastide towns of south-west France, which have since been accepted and repeated without question by scholars.[2] It is the purpose of this paper to review such assumptions: to explore afresh the physical layout of the landscapes of Edward's new towns and to identify the processes and people that shaped them.

In contrast to the Edwardian castles, whose architectural structures and forms historians have carefully surveyed and scrutinized for many years, the surviving remains of the associated new towns have been mapped and analysed only superficially.[3] Studies of the towns' early histories are invariably accompanied by sketch plans or reproductions of historic town plans such as those by John Speed.[4] These provide little detail of the physical forms that the towns actually took, therefore missing the potential to explore their layouts and formation. Modern morphological study of urban landscapes, however, using detailed mapping and analysis techniques can provide a basis for comparing the forms of the new towns: to look for similarities and differences in street patterns and plot layouts, for example.[5] These techniques have been applied to Edward's new towns in Wales in a project, which, for

the first time, mapped out in detail their layouts and reconstructed their urban landscapes shortly after the towns were established in the late thirteenth century.[6] These maps have been published online in a digital atlas together with interpretive essays.[7]

Not only do these maps provide a basis for examining the forms of the new towns, but they also provide some insight into the processes that went into shaping them. As with the detailed architectural study of the castles, the analysis of the forms of the new towns helps to identify stylistic patterns between them, which reflect the processes of their initial design and planning. Moreover, since the towns are associated with Edward's castle-building enterprise, there are also written sources that touch upon these processes of urban formation, which, when studied alongside the physical forms, can help identify who was involved and what they did. By so doing, it is possible to begin to lay to rest the myth that the planning ideals of Edward's new towns in Wales were exotic imports from Continental Europe; instead, a much more interesting story emerges. The following discussion begins by looking at the physical forms of Edward's new towns and how they compare with each other; next, how the towns were formed through an extended decision-making process from their inception to their charters; and finally, what influences acted upon the designs of the new towns and where these may have come from.

A Comparison of Urban Form

There are of course no maps or plans of the new towns contemporary with their foundation. There is nothing exceptional about this: only one example of a manuscript map that appears to show a new town at its inception exists, a plan of Talamone in Tuscany dating to 1306.[8] For Edward's new towns the earliest cartographic representations are usually seventeenth century in date

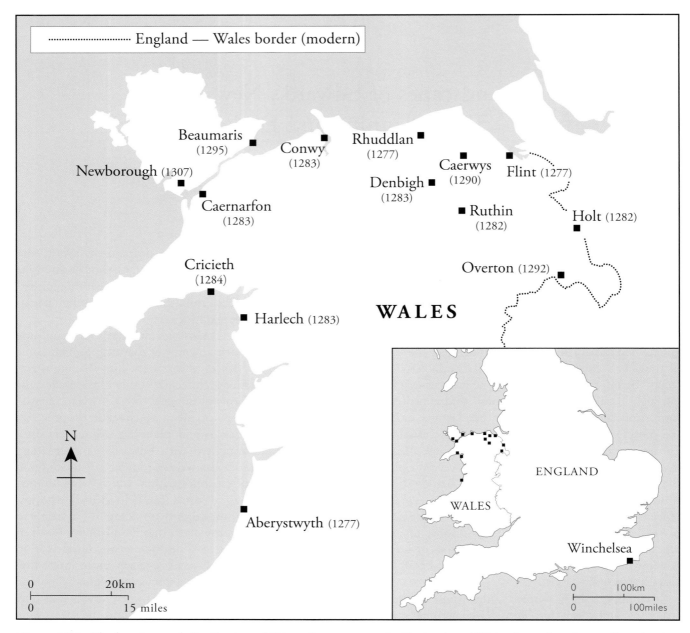

Figure 10.1: The location and distribution of Edward's new towns in England and Wales (note that dates reflect the time work began on the towns, and not necessarily when their charters were granted) (Keith Lilley).

or later. New maps, therefore, needed to be created. This was done using a geographical technique called town-plan analysis.[9] Large-scale nineteenth-century Ordnance Survey plans were used as the base maps. Modern accretions in the urban landscape were stripped away and using archaeological, topographical and historical evidence, maps were drawn to modern cartographic standards to show those elements that comprised the medieval urban landscapes.[10] This revealed a striking continuity

of certain townscape features, especially street and plot patterns. Space does not permit a full description of these methods in detail here. Suffice to say, the plans of Edward's new towns created this way provided a sound basis for the analysis and comparison of their morphological characteristics to provide some useful insights into how the urban landscapes were created in the first place.[11]

Those Welsh towns mapped in detail were all royal initiatives of Edward's reign: Aberystwyth, Beaumaris,

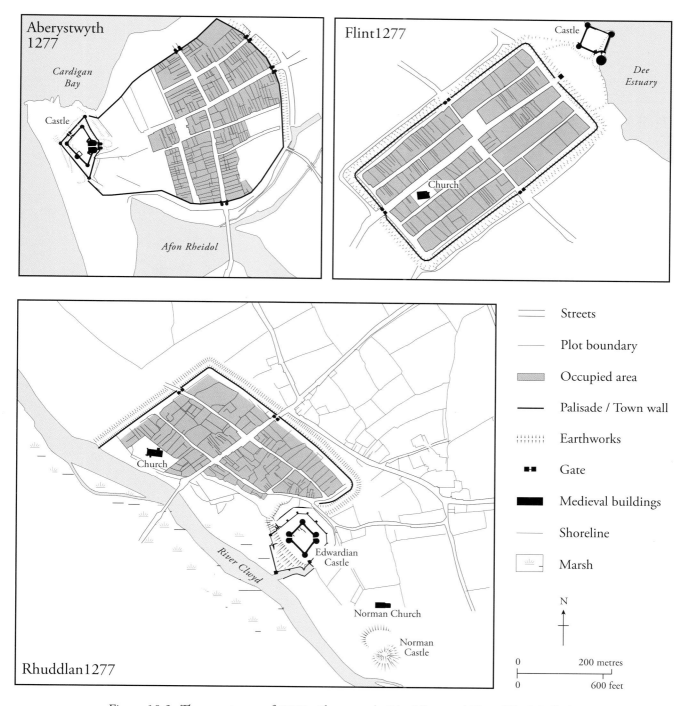

Figure 10.2: The new towns of 1277: Aberystwyth, Rhuddlan and Flint (Keith Lilley).

Caernarfon, Caerwys, Conwy, Cricieth, Flint, Harlech, Holt, Newborough, Overton, and Rhuddlan (Fig. 10.1). Winchelsea in Sussex, which was contemporary with the Welsh foundations, is also included for comparative purposes. Three of the new towns were established during the course of the first Welsh war: Aberystwyth, Flint and Rhuddlan; Caernarfon, Conwy, Cricieth, and Harlech followed the second war; Beaumaris and Newborough were later.[12] Certain interesting features begin to emerge when the plans of these towns are put side-by-side at the same scale (Figs 10.2–10.4). First, the wide variation in their relative overall physical size is striking. Some, such as

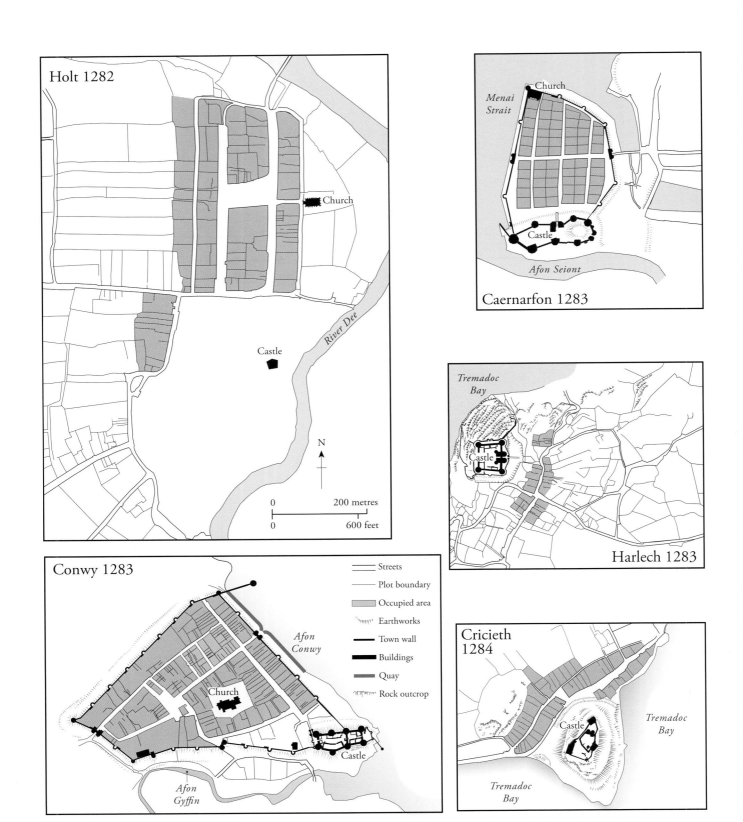

Figure 10.3: The new towns of 1282–84: Holt, Caernarfon, Conwy, Harlech and Cricieth (Keith Lilley).

Caerwys
1290

Church

Beaumaris
1295

Moat

Castle

Church

Overton
1292

Church

Newborough
1307

Church

Llys Rhosyr

Streets

Plot boundary

Occupied area

Town wall

Town ditch

Medieval buildings

N

0   200 metres
0   600 feet

Figure 10.4: The new towns of 1290–1307: Caerwys, Overton, Beaumaris and Newborough (Keith Lilley).

Cricieth and Harlech, are quite small, which is perhaps not surprising, but, so too is Caernarfon despite its significance as Edward's administrative centre in Gwynedd.[13] The first-phase towns of 1277 are all large castle-towns of similar size. This perhaps reflects a co-ordinated regional policy towards design and planning linked to the deliberate location of these towns around the perimeter of the Welsh stronghold of Snowdonia. Only after the second Welsh war were further towns established to complement Aberystwyth, Flint and Rhuddlan.

Overall, Edward's Welsh new towns look rather small in size, especially if they are compared with the contemporary new foundation of Winchelsea, though admittedly this was a *re*foundation of an existing and well-established port town on a new site (Fig. 10.5). Indeed, when the Welsh towns are compared, notable differences in built-up area are to be observed, despite all being established in a relatively limited time period (1277–1307), and within one region (north Wales). Even for those key Edwardian castle-towns, which shared the same principal functions, there are marked variations in relative urban area and size (Fig. 10.6).

But what of the new towns' forms and their characteristics? How much variation is there in their urban layouts? The maps make clear their common site characteristics. Typically occupying riverside or coastal locations with relatively unchallenging local topographies, most are castle-towns where town and castle have closely integrated forms, and thus dual commercial and military functions. Those places that lack this duality in form and function, such as Caerwys, Newborough, and Overton, are principally market towns (Fig. 10.4). Beyond these broad similarities, as the maps demonstrate (Figs 10.2–10.4), there are variations in the forms of the new towns, particularly in terms of their street and plot layouts. By no means is the grid street pattern a common trait, for example.[14] There is no standard blueprint to which the towns conform. To demonstrate this further, let us consider three pairs of new towns: Flint and Rhuddlan; Holt and Flint; and Conwy and Beaumaris.

Located some 20 miles (12km) apart, Flint and Rhuddlan were begun at the same time in the summer of 1277 and occupy similar sites.[15] Because of this it might be expected that the layouts of the two towns would share some common characteristics; for example, in their grid plans. But the two are quite different, despite the close integration of castle and town at both sites. At Flint the street pattern is 'orthogonal' in form, that is, made up of straight streets that intersect at right angles (Fig. 10.2). The streets are parallel, quite close together, with only one cross-street, which gives rise to narrow, elongated street-blocks that contain short, but regularly spaced plots. Compare this with Rhuddlan. Here, the street pattern is a skewed grid, with slightly bowed streets. There are fewer than at Flint, which gives rise to deeper street-blocks that contain largely irregular plots. Although both new towns were encompassed by defences linked with their castles, the overall shape of these circuits differ.

Despite being contemporary, the two new towns of Flint and Rhuddlan therefore display quite noticeable differences in layout. One explanation for this might be that their physical sites are not the same, which necessitated different urban layouts. Both towns, however, occupy sites with relatively flat topography so their locations are not *sufficiently* different to explain why Rhuddlan has a skewed grid plan and Flint does not. Building two contemporary castle-towns to a common ground plan was perhaps not high on the agenda of their planners, but in cases elsewhere (see below) equivalent comparisons suggest otherwise, and these make the contrasting layouts of Flint and Rhuddlan all the more intriguing.

Holt is not far from Flint. Situated on the banks of the river Dee, Holt was established as a castle-town several years later than Flint, on lands granted by Edward to his vassal, John de Warenne, earl of Surrey.[16] The circumstances of the town's foundation are uncertain, though the castle was begun in 1282 and probably, as A. J. Taylor says, 'with the services of the master of the King's Works'.[17] The adjoining town has certain similarities with Flint (Figs 10.2 and 10.3). The way the rectangular-shaped town extends away from the site of the castle at Holt is one obvious parallel. At both sites, the castle is in line with the central axis of the town, either side of which straight streets run in parallel to create elongated street-blocks. At Holt there is also one cross-street and, like Flint, the overall shape of the town is orthogonal. So although established at different times, possibly under different lords, Flint and Holt share similar plan characteristics and design traits. Does this point to a shared origin, or a common designer? Although little is known of those involved at Holt, the records of the King's Works for Flint provide clues about who was doing what, which may help to explain the differences between Flint and Rhuddlan – a point I will return to later.

Another pair of towns also offers scope for exploring who was doing what at their outset. Conwy and Beaumaris, like Flint and Holt, were established at different dates. Conwy, begun in 1283–84, and Beaumaris, begun in 1295–96, also share similar layouts that raise suspicions that there was a common hand behind them.[18] Again, a close look at their physical layouts makes their shared design clear (Figs 10.3 and 10.4). There are some basic

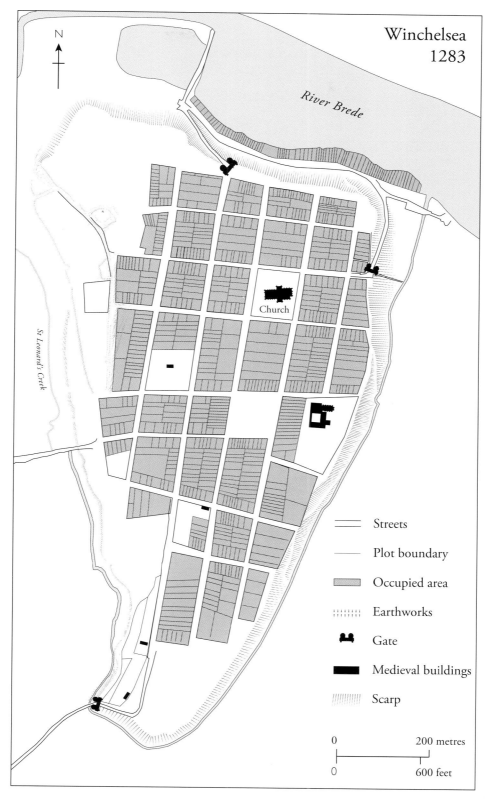

Figure 10.5: Winchelsea (Sussex) (Keith Lilley).

Town	Estimated urban area*	Urban dimensions*	Number of Burgages[†]	Number of Burgesses[†]	Number of Taxpayers[†]
Aberystwyth (chartered December 28 1277)	28½ acres/115,500m²	1,250 feet (Great Darkgate Street)/1,250 feet (Bridge Street/Pier Street) (380m/380m)	141½ in 1300–01		
Beaumaris (chartered September 15 1296)	28¾ acres/116,200m²	1,050 feet (Castle Street)/950 feet (Church Street) (320m/290m)	132¼ in 1305		
Caernarfon (chartered September 8 1284)	10⅓ acres/41,800m²	600 feet (High Street)/740 feet (Castle Street/Market Street) (183m/226m)	55 in 1298	57 in 1298	
Conwy (chartered September 8 1284)	22 acres/89,500m²	1,070 feet (Upper Gate Street/Chapel Street)/ 1,000 feet (Castle Street/Berry Street) (326m/305m)	112 in *c.*1295	99 in *c.*1295	
Cricieth (chartered November 22 1284)	4½ acres/18,700m²	1,000 feet (east/west)/220 feet (north/south) (305m/67m)	21⅓ in 1308–09		
Flint (chartered September 8 1284)	29 acres/117,800m²	1,500 feet (Church Street/Castle Street)/800 feet (Holywell Road/Chester Road) (457m/244m)			76 in 1292
Harlech (chartered November 22 1284)	6⅓ acres/25,800m²	780 feet (High Street)/440 feet (cross street, approx.) (238m/134m)	24½ in 1305		12 in 1292–93
Rhuddlan (chartered September 8 1284)	20½ acres/82,600m² (figure excludes the adjoining Norman town)	830 feet (High Street/Bridge Street)/1,250 feet (Parliament Steet/Gwindy Street) (253m/381m)			75 in 1292

* Urban areas (excluding castle) and overall dimensions based on field measurement and mapping undertaken by *Mapping the Medieval Urban Landscape* Project (see www.qub.ac.uk/urban_mapping/).

[†]Sources: E. A. Lewis, *Mediaeval Boroughs of Snowdonia*, 66; 'Extent of burgages, lands, etc, assigned for the castle of Beaumaris', *Original Documents*, 1, supplement to *Archaeologia Cambrensis*, 1 (1877), xiv–xix; *Merioneth Lay Subsidy Roll of 1292/3*, ed. K. Williams-Jones; J. Griffiths, 'Documents relating to the early history of Conway', *Transactions of the Caernarfonshire Historical Society* 8 (1947), 5–19; R. A. Griffiths, 'Aberystwyth', in *Boroughs of Mediaeval Wales*, ed. R. A. Griffiths (Cardiff 1978), 18–45; T. Jones Pierce and J. Griffiths, 'Documents relating to the early history of the borough of Caernarvon', *Bulletin of the Board of Celtic Studies*, 9 (1937–39), 236–46; I. J. Sanders, 'The boroughs of Aberystwyth and Cardigan in the early fourteenth century', *Bulletin of the Board of Celtic Studies*, 15 (1954), 282–93; K. Williams-Jones, 'Caernarvon', in *Boroughs of Mediaeval Wales*, 72–101.

For more information and discussion see individual entries for the towns see K. D. Lilley, C. Lloyd and S. Trick, *Mapping Medieval Townscapes: a digital atlas of the new towns of Edward I* accessed via http://ads.ahds.ac.uk/catalogue/specColl/atlas_ahrb_2005

Figure 10.6: Table showing variation in the size and extent of Edward's castle-towns in Wales (Keith Lilley).

similarities: both are castle-towns and both occupy coastal sites. But they also have a common T-shaped street plan, in which two perpendicular streets meet at a right angle. One of these streets stretches away (or towards) the castle entrance and is aligned with it. Even a visual inspection of the two town plans reveals these similar traits, but, by using a Geographical Information System (GIS), it is possible to go a stage further with the comparison.[19] The GIS plan of Beaumaris was reversed to create a mirror-image and reproduced at the same scale as the town plan of Conwy (Fig. 10.7). When the two plans are placed beside each other, the reversed GIS plan of Beaumaris shows a remarkable coincidence of features. The castles sit in the same relative position, as do the churches and quaysides. The orientation of the T-shaped street patterns also matches. Moreover, the street dimensions of Conwy match perfectly those of Beaumaris, both sharing a slight widening on their approach towards the castle entrances. The similarities in their plans are therefore very close.

Comparing the forms of Edward's new towns therefore not only demonstrates how different in size and shape they were, despite their common origins and circumstances, but also that they shared certain traits. These require explanation and investigation to determine whether the same design principles reflect the involvement of the same individuals. The differences are just as interesting and underline the importance of looking at the physical layout of each town in relation to those documented working on the sites in contemporary records. It is to this topic that we turn to consider the processes of urban formation and town planning and design.

Processes of Urban Formation

Although Europe experienced widespread and dramatic urbanization in the Middle Ages, very little was written down at the time about how urban landscapes were made, who was responsible for doing the work, and how they went about it.[20] This is especially true for towns and cities in Britain; Edward's new towns in Wales are unusually well documented for the period on account of the construction of their accompanying castles.[21] Nevertheless, the decision-making process for each place is not set out explicitly in contemporary sources, but referred to incidentally. This is why the physical layouts of the towns can help when trying to identify who was behind the design of Edward's new towns.

We talk of 'Edward's new towns', but of course the king's personal input into the process was partial, as with the castles. There were many others on site making decisions and doing the hard work, but these other individuals are often difficult to identify even though their influence may have been great. We know that Edward paid visits to the sites of some of the new towns, for example, Conwy, and witnessed work at Flint and Rhuddlan at an early date. He also undertook a tour of the towns in the autumn of 1284, starting at Flint and working his way round to Aberystwyth, a difficult journey at that time of year one might imagine.[22] How much initial input the king had into the design and planning process is questionable; such decisions were perhaps most likely left to those more expert in these matters. To identify these individuals, it is necessary to look again at the layouts of the new towns and consider their similarities and differences with reference to those who appear to have been shaping things locally on the ground, particularly in the initial stages of construction. Bear in mind that the time between when a town was first laid out physically and when it was granted a charter and gained townspeople, was sometimes a year or more, or indeed eight years in the case of 'new' Winchelsea.[23]

To return to Rhuddlan and Flint and their early stages of formation in summer 1277: rather than explain their different layouts as a result of their different sites, what evidence is there that their plans were due to the individuals who worked on them? In fact, somewhat paradoxically, it seems that work on both was overseen simultaneously by the *same* person. This is evident certainly in August when William of Perton, one of the king's clerks, was appointed as keeper of works at both places.[24] He was replaced in November by Nicholas Bonel, described as 'surveyor' of both Flint and Rhuddlan.[25] Of course, one person can devise two different designs for separate places, but we are more likely to interpret them as the product of two different minds rather than one. By August 1277, work had been underway at both places for more than a month. This involved diggers (*fossatores*) from eastern England, who were overseen at Rhuddlan by Master William of Boston, and at Flint by Master William of March.[26] Under their charge, the outlines of the town defences were probably the first elements to be set out. Since their defensive circuits are coincident with the internal configurations of the towns, we might suppose that the streets and plots were laid out at the same time, which would explain the differences between the two, discussed above. But were these men really likely to have the skills or expertise to lay out new towns? Evidence from Flanders suggests that the answer is yes. Here, the construction of new town defences at Ardres, in around 1200, was overseen by a Master Simon the Dyker whose activities are described by Lambert of Ardres. This is a vivid account in which Master Simon is described as 'learned in geometrical work' and working with surveying instruments, and therefore just the sort of person who would have been able to set out urban landscapes.[27] Of course, even if Masters William and William were involved in laying out Flint and Rhuddlan, this does not necessarily mean that they were responsible for the designs of the two towns. Others were no doubt involved, including Edward, who, as we have seen earlier, was present at both sites during the early stages of construction, a point that will be returned to later.

Clearly, it is not easy to pinpoint particular named individuals as key agents who influenced the layout of Edward's new towns. It is a question of placing the towns in the context of the known activities that took place in them early in their formation in relation to who is recorded doing relevant work. While there are clear continuities in the physical layouts of these towns through from their inception to the present, it is clear too that some suffered vicissitudes quite early on, which may have affected their physical forms. A case in point is Rhuddlan, which is known to have been considered as a future regional capital when it was conceived and planned in 1277. In the event,

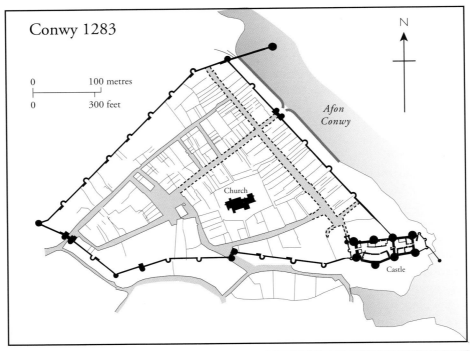

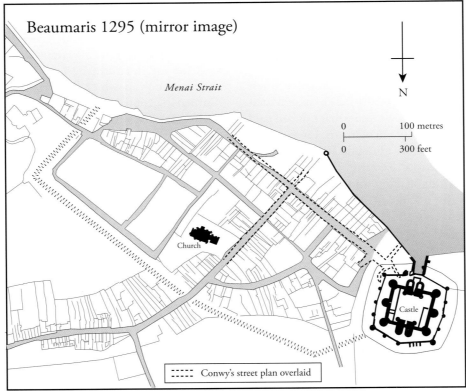

Figure 10.7: The plans of Conwy and Beaumaris compared. When overlaid, note how Conwy's T-shaped street plan (1283) matches exactly with the (mirror image) plan of Beaumaris (1295) (Keith Lilley).

it was overshadowed by Caernarfon in this capacity, and was also attacked and burned by the Welsh in 1282.[28] Rhuddlan's irregular plot patterns, which seem to be at odds with the town's regular (though skewed) street grid, may have resulted from these later events. It may be too that the initial take up of properties was slow, bearing in mind that the Edwardian new town at Rhuddlan was appended to an existing and earlier borough of Norman origin. This might explain the presence of William of Louth, who was the king's cofferer at the time he was sent to Rhuddlan, in July 1279, 'to view the void plots and other sites in that town, and assess and rent burgages in the same plots'.[29] Tout saw him as the surveyor of the new town, but Louth was there a full two years after work had first begun. Besides, burgages were already in place by February 1278 when Nicholas Bonel was instructed by the king to 'assess' burgages there.[30]

The evidence from Flint and Rhuddlan is not conclusive. Nevertheless, it is possible to make a 'best guess' based upon the evidence to hand. There were other individuals who no doubt also had an input into the process of creating new urban landscapes in Wales in the 1270s and 1280s. For example, as well as the king's men there were local officials, such as Howel, son of Griffin, a bailiff who helped in assessing the burgages at Rhuddlan.[31] And then there are those who had come from overseas, often highlighted in their roles in castle construction and engineering, such as Master Mannasser de Vaucouleurs who directed the excavation of earthworks at Caernarfon in 1283, and Otto de Grandson, in the king's retinue, who was also at Caernarfon.[32] And of course, Master James of St George, discussed in detail by Nicola Coldstream in this volume, who has traditionally been described as the king's chief architect in Wales.[33]

Despite the apparent complexities in urban planning and design at Flint and Rhuddlan, the evidence from Conwy and Beaumaris seems to point to an overall shared design and one designer. At Conwy and Beaumaris, both towns replaced existing settlements. At Conwy, however, the new town absorbed the site of the Cistercian abbey, whereas a new location at Beaumaris was chosen to replace Llanfaes. And yet, as we have seen, there are aspects of their plans that are strikingly similar, particularly the configuration of their streets and the relative placing of their castles and quaysides (Fig. 10.7). In Rhuddlan and Flint, Master James of St George had arrived late on the scene as far as the initial construction of the towns and castles was concerned, but at Conwy and Beaumaris he was there from the start.[34] Working alongside clerks of works, John of Candover at Conwy and Walter of Winchester at Beaumaris, it was Master James who managed the building

work and delegated tasks at both places. It was he who had an overall vision of the work taking place and, given their similarities, might well be seen as their designer.[35] The form of the principal street, gradually tapering as it leads towards the castle entrance in both towns, suggests an aesthetic sensibility: the attention of anyone in these main streets would be drawn to the castle.

As Jean Gimpel observed, such work was within the remit of medieval architects: 'life's vagaries led some of these architects to become town planners and thus they designed new towns'.[36] That Master James might have had sufficient expertise or interest in laying out new towns is perhaps revealed in the common forms of Conwy and Beaumaris. These two boroughs, however, appear to be the exceptions amongst Edward's new towns in Wales when it came to matters of urban design and planning. For the most part, it seems that these 'new towns' were not designed by one individual, but forged by many different hands in a negotiated and extended decision-making process that involved a wide variety of agents. This brings us back to consider what role Edward himself might have had in all this and what models or influences we can see in the layouts of his new towns in Wales.

Influences on the Formation of New Towns

The enduring myth that the Edwardian new towns derived from Continental models, in particular the bastide towns of south-west France, no doubt owes its popularity to the well-documented connections between Edward's dominions at home and abroad, and the simultaneous process of establishing towns in both (Fig. 10.8).[37] But the layouts of the new towns in north Wales do not share much in common with those of Gascony.

The orthogonal form of Flint, for example, has made it a prime candidate for those looking for Continental influences. Comparisons have been drawn with Aigues Mortes because Edward passed through here on his way to the Holy Land and because the Tour de Constance offers a superficial resemble to Flint's offset great tower.[38] But Flint's layout lacks some of the features usually expected with bastide towns, especially those of the English Agenais area of Gascony, and towns such as Monpazier and Beaumont-du-Perigord, which Beresford looks to.[39] For example, Flint's street pattern is based upon a series of longitudinal street blocks, with a single cross-street, and no central *place*; only its overall rectangular form makes it appear similar to Monpazier for instance.[40] None of the Welsh towns have the small narrow lanes called *carreyrous*, which is another distinguishing feature of the Agenais bastides. It may well be instructive to undertake a closer

Figure 10.8: Information board displayed on the town walls at Conwy drawing visitors' attention to the imagined parallels between the Welsh new towns and bastides of south-west France (Keith Lilley).

comparative morphological study of the English bastides of Gascony and the Edwardian 'new towns' of England and Wales, a research project that has obvious attractions, but from initial observations it seems the Gascon influence has been rather overplayed.

Instead, if models are to be sought for the Welsh towns then more convincing candidates can be found much closer to Wales. Two towns, in particular, seem to be cases in point: both date from the 1270s and are closely tied to the campaigns of Edward and his brother Edmund.

A much less exotic, but no less interesting model for Flint can be identified at nearby Chester. There are some good reasons why: Chester was the principal city in north-west England from which Edward, his men and his supplies, were channelled en route to Wales. Moreover, Flint was the first in the chain of new towns reached from Chester, the gateway to those others situated further west along the coast.[41] Chester's Roman origins and legionary importance may also have appealed to Edward's apparent imperial aspirations and it was a city he knew well from

his time as earl of Chester.[42] Indeed, its overall rectangular form, with a cross of streets and four gates, has some clear similarities with the layout of Flint.[43] Even if the inspiration for Flint's plan was not Edward's it may still have been influenced by Chester, for it would have been the nearest and most familiar English city to those involved on site at Flint in summer 1277. There is one further clue that hints that Edward had a role to play. He was given a copy of Vegetius's *De re militari* by his wife Eleanor in 1272.[44] Vegetius proclaimed that 'the mightiest nations and most renowned rulers could seek no greater glory than either to start new cities or to transfer those started by others into their name and improve them', a policy that seems to square with Edward's territorial ambitions in Wales.[45] But as well as rhetoric there was practical advice in *De re militari*, for example, on the construction of defences around encampments: it recommended them to be made four-square and enclosed with double bank-and-ditch earthworks.[46] At its outset, Flint was an encampment and is referred to as such in June 1277 when diggers were being recruited by Master William of Perton, the king's clerk, and funnelled via Chester 'to the camp at Flint'.[47] Flint also had two lines of defences with a space between them, as described by Vegetius (Fig. 10.2). So perhaps in the plan of Flint we see not only Edward's influence, but also a Roman one too – an imitation of the 'city of legions', built in accordance with advice from a handbook for Roman generals.

The second case where we might suspect an English model is Aberystwyth. Like Flint, it was a town that marked the gateway to Edward's territorial claims on Wales and was begun at the same time, in summer 1277. Here, the work was initiated under the direction of Edward's brother, Edmund, who had travelled from the south with his army.[48] *Brut y Tywysogyon* (*Chronicle of the Princes*) records that at Llanbadarn 'he began to build the castle'.[49] Again, we might try to point to parallels with the Gascon bastides. Indeed, Aberystwyth rather more than the other Welsh new towns perhaps has more in common morphologically with towns such as Créon.[50] But again a model can be found closer to Wales. Whereas Edward had come from Chester, Edmund's forces had come from Bristol, travelling across Ceredigion to what became the site of the new town of Llanbadarn. Looking at the layout of Bristol, especially the area within the inner circuit of defences (the earliest part of Bristol), we see features that are also present at Aberystwyth: the circular form of the defences, the cross of streets and the peripheral position of the castle (Figs 10.2 and 10.9). Moreover, Aberystwyth's street pattern also shares characteristics with Bristol, namely a distinctive configuration of a wider street

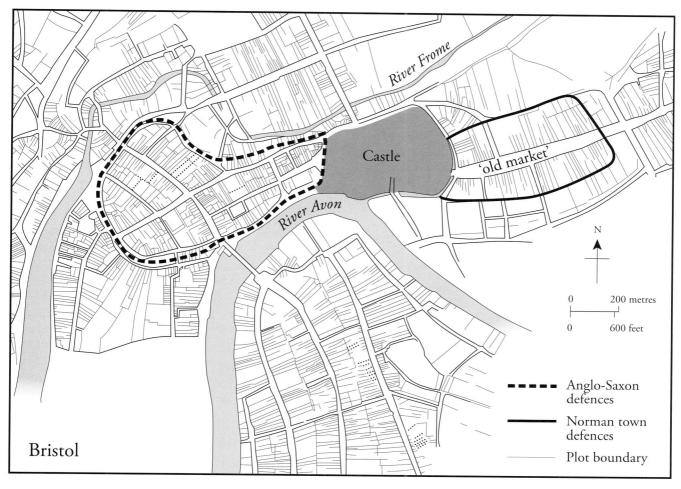

Figure 10.9: Bristol, the layout of the Anglo-Saxon town – a design for Aberystwyth? (Keith Lilley).

paralleled to the rear by a secondary street, which runs along only one side of each of the main street axes. This unusual pattern is difficult to explain using Continental models, but makes some sense when compared with Bristol. Again, as with Flint, it also seems to point to decision makers on site looking to familiar examples, though whether this was Edmund or one of his men is impossible to prove.

By looking at Flint and Aberystwyth in a wider comparative context, within and beyond Wales, some interesting possible influences begin to emerge. The possibility that Continental models were at play in the formation of the Edwardian new towns cannot be ruled out, but there is much to commend a more regional, more English, source for their designs; not least because those responsible for physically creating them were not from distant Gascony or Savoy, but from counties such as Gloucestershire or Lincolnshire.[51] Although key

individuals such as Edward or Master James were involved in the process of creating the towns, it seems likely that much of the hard work and local decision making was done by those recruited from England, such as Master William of Boston.

Conclusion
In the context of Edward's castle building in Wales, scholars have for too long neglected the new towns that were such an integral part of the construction programme. Here, I have tried to engage more comprehensively with the landscapes of Edward's new towns in Wales to show their range of plan forms, the processes that shaped them, and the possible influences that acted upon them. The need to look carefully at the layouts of these towns and to consider their plans is clear; so too is their context, especially their relationship with the adjoining castles. The processes by which these new urban landscapes

were being formed were by no means straightforward. The stages in the design and planning process are not easy to discern, and those who were involved are often not known. In one or two cases we can be a little more confident – perhaps with Conwy and Beaumaris, and even Flint and Rhuddlan. But for the most part, as Beresford pointed out, the landscapes of the towns themselves bear silent witness to the identity of those who shaped them.[52] To understand and appreciate them requires a synthesis of sources – cartographic, archaeological and documentary

– only then do some of the landscapes of these new towns begin to yield their secrets. There is certainly scope to draw comparisons between Edward's new towns in Wales and those elsewhere through the mapping of urban forms and a detailed study of their morphological features to identify similarities and differences. So doing will not only help expose the complexities of urban design and planning in Edward's realm, but also better place his new towns within a wider context of urbanization throughout Europe during this period of the Middle Ages.

Notes

1. M. W. Beresford, *New Towns of the Middle Ages: Town Plantation in England, Wales and Gascony* (London 1967).
2. T. F. Tout, *Mediaeval Town Planning* (Manchester 1934); J. Schofield and A. Vince, *Medieval Towns*, 2nd edn (London 2003); A. E. J. Morris, *History of Urban Form*, 4th edn (London 1994).
3. e.g. I. Soulsby, *The Towns of Medieval Wales* (Chichester 1983).
4. e.g. *Boroughs of Mediaeval Wales*, ed. R. A. Griffiths (Cardiff 1978).
5. K. D. Lilley, 'Urban landscapes and the cultural politics of territorial control in Anglo-Norman England', *Landscape Research*, 24 (1999), 5–23; K. D. Lilley, 'Urban planning and the design of towns in the Middle Ages: the earls of Devon and their 'new towns'', *Planning Perspectives*, 16 (2001), 1–24.
6. Arts and Humanities Research Council award B/RG/AN3206/APN14501. The *Mapping the Medieval Urban Landscape* Project ran from September 2003 to June 2005. Details available at http://www.qub.ac.uk/urban_mapping/
7. K. D. Lilley, C. Lloyd and S. Trick, *Mapping Medieval Townscapes: a Digital Atlas of the New Towns of Edward I* (AHDS Archaeology Data Service, University of York, 2005). Accessible via http://ads.ahds.ac.uk/catalogue/specColl/atlas_ahrb_2005
8. P. D. A. Harvey, 'Local and regional cartography in medieval Europe', in *The History of Cartography, I: Cartography in Prehistoric, Ancient and Medieval Europe and the Mediterranean*, eds J. B. Harley and D. Woodward (Chicago 1987), 488, fig. 20.27.
9. M. R. G. Conzen, 'The use of town plans in the study of urban history', in *The Study of Urban History*, ed. H. J. Dyos (London 1968), 113–30.
10. K. D. Lilley, 'Mapping the medieval city: plan analysis and urban history', *Urban History*, 27.1 (2000), 5–30.
11. See Lilley, 'Urban landscapes'; Lilley, 'Urban planning'.
12. For summaries of the new towns' early documentary histories see Beresford, *New Towns*, 534–35, 537, 544–46, 548–52, 558. Also, Soulsby, *Medieval Towns*, 69–72, 78–80, 88–92, 94–95, 110–15, 117–19, 135–37, 138–39, 144–47, 194–96, 211–12, 226–31. For fuller accounts see Lilley et al., *Mapping Medieval Townscapes, passim*.
13. On Caernarfon see, K. Williams-Jones, 'Caernarvon', in Griffiths, *Boroughs of Mediaeval Wales*, 73–101.
14. cf. Morris, *History of Urban Form*, 129–32.
15. A. J. Taylor, *The Welsh Castles of Edward I* (London 1986), 17–19, 27.

16. A. N. Palmer, 'The town of Holt, in county Denbigh', *Archaeologia Cambrensis*, 6 ser. 7 (1907), 9.
17. Taylor, *Welsh Castles*, 43.
18. For the dates see Taylor, *Welsh Castles*, 49–50, 103–5. Also *Calendar of Charter Rolls 1257–1300*, 276–77, 465.
19. See K. D. Lilley, C. Lloyd and S. Trick, 'Designs and designers of medieval 'new towns' in Wales', *Antiquity*, 81 (2007), 279–93. The methods are described in K. D. Lilley, C. Lloyd and S. Trick, 'Mapping medieval townscapes: GIS applications in landscape history and settlement study', in *Medieval Landscapes*, eds M. Gardiner and S. Rippon (Macclesfield 2007), 27–42.
20. K. D. Lilley, 'Urban landscapes and their design: creating town from country in the Middle Ages', in *Town and Country in the Middle Ages*, eds K. Giles and C. Dyer (Leeds 2005), 229–49.
21. As is revealed by the building accounts used by Taylor, *Welsh Castles*.
22. Taylor, *Welsh Castles*, 17, 18, 32; J. E. Morris, *The Welsh Wars of Edward I* (Oxford 1901), 126–35, 180, 199.
23. *Calendar of Patent Rolls 1272–81*, 414; *Calendar of Close Rolls 1279–88*, 509–10.
24. Taylor, *Welsh Castles*, 19.
25. *Calendar of Various Chancery Rolls 1277–1326* (London 1912), 160.
26. Taylor, *Welsh Castles*, 18, 27.
27. Lambert of Ardres, *The History of the Counts of Guines and Lords of Ardres*, trans. L. Shopkow (Philadelphia 2001), 190–91.
28. A. J. Taylor, 'Rhuddlan Cathedral: a 'might have been' of Flintshire history', *Flintshire Historical Society Publications*, 15 (1954–55), 43–51.
29. *Calendar of Various Chancery Rolls*, 178.
30. *Calendar of Various Chancery Rolls*, 165. Cf. T. F. Tout, *Chapters in the Administrative History of Mediaeval England*, II (London 1920), 65.
31. *Calendar of Various Chancery Rolls*, 165.
32. Taylor, *Welsh Castles*, 79–80, 81 n. 6.
33. See A. J. Taylor, 'Master James of St. George', *English Historical Review*, 65 (1950), 433–57; N. Coldstream, 'James of St George', this volume.
34. Taylor, *Welsh Castles*, 19–21, 28–29.
35. ibid., 46–49, 104.
36. J. Gimpel, *The Cathedral Builders*, trans. T. Waugh (London 1983), 121.

37. Tout, *Mediaeval Town Planning*, 18–25; Beresford, *New Towns*, 14–51; Schofield and Vince, *Medieval Towns*, 40–45; Morris, *History of Urban Form*, 123–26.

38. Beresford, *New Towns*, 40; cf. M. Prestwich, *Edward I* (London 1988), 121.

39. Beresford, *New Towns*, 28–35.

40. On Monpazier, see A. Lauret, R. Malebranche and G. Séraphin, *Bastides. Villes Nouvelles du Moyen Age* (Toulouse 1988), 205–07.

41. Taylor, *Welsh Castles*, 17, 18.

42. Prestwich, *Edward I*, 13.

43. See the description of Chester's cross-shaped urban form composed by Lucian writing in the late-twelfth century: cited in Lilley, 'Urban landscapes and their design', 243.

44. L. Thorpe, 'Mastre Richard, a thirteenth-century translator of the *De re militari* of Vegetius', *Scriptorium*, 6 (1952), 39–50.

45. Master Richard rendered this passage: 'E por ce, empereor trespuissant, les nacions ke sunt sacrez as princes ne quiderent nule major glorie ou de faire noveus citez ou a les citez ke furent jadis faites doner noun suz une amplificacion': see Thorpe, 'Mastre Richard', 50.

46. Thorpe, 'Mastre Richard', 41, 43, citing Vegetius, *De Re Militari*, book I, chapters 22–24, book IV, chapters 2–5.

47. Taylor, *Welsh Castles*, 17, citing The National Archives: PRO E 101/485/19.

48. ibid., 7.

49. *Brut y Tywysogyon or The Chronicle of the Princes. Red Book of Hergest Version*, trans. T. Jones (Cardiff 1955), 267.

50. On Créon see Lauret et al., *Bastides*, 286–87.

51. See the map showing the impressment of workmen for the King's Works in north Wales in Taylor, *Welsh Castles*, vi (Fig.1).

52. Beresford, *New Towns*, 146–47.

The Building Stones of the Edwardian Castles

Graham Lott

Introduction

The progress of Edward I across north Wales in his campaign to subdue the Welsh princes is clearly charted by the spectacular programme of castle building, which he began in 1277 with the construction of Builth Castle, and ended with the unfinished fabric of Beaumaris Castle begun in 1295. In all, fourteen castles were constructed or largely rebuilt.[1] The wide range of building stone used in these castles is a reflection of the complexity of the geology of the north Wales area, where the exposed geological units span a considerable part of geological time. They range from some of the United Kingdom's oldest rocks – the metamorphic Precambrian (Monian Supergroup) of Anglesey – to the relatively recently discovered sedimentary, clay-dominated Tertiary (Palaeogene) succession, seaward of the great Mochras Fault at Harlech (Plates 1 and 2). This lithologically varied rock succession (slates, sandstones, limestones and a wide variety of igneous and metamorphic rocks) provided an extensive palette of stones for building purposes many of which are spectacularly displayed in the castles (Plates 3 and 4).[2]

The present study was commissioned by Cadw as part of a research programme to inform the updating of the guidebooks produced for the castles. Earlier editions of the guidebooks contained very little information about the types and sources of the stones used in their construction. Four of the castles (Conwy, Harlech, Caernarfon and Beaumaris), built during Edward I's second campaign against the Welsh princes and perhaps representing, in terms of their size and complexity, the high point of medieval castle building in the United Kingdom, were revisited with a view to providing an updated assessment of the geology of the stones used. Further details of the results from these new assessments are contained in a series of British Geological Survey (BGS) reports.[3]

The Geological Succession in the North Wales Area

The geological succession in north Wales has been the subject of intensive study by the British Geological Survey and many university research teams over the last forty years and has resulted in major improvements in the mapping and understanding of these complex successions.[4] While it would be beyond the scope of this study to provide an in-depth discussion of the geological foundations upon which these castles were built, there are some aspects of the present geological coverage which do require some brief comments and explanations.

Our present understanding of the geological successions of the area is based on the work of numerous geological researchers, both amateurs and professionals, dating back as far as the eighteenth century. However, while the geological units described, in terms of their mineralogies, lithologies and textures are, as it were 'set in stone', the understanding, interpretation and particularly the stratigraphic nomenclatures used to identify the units, have been dramatically transformed (Plates 1 and 2). It is likely that anyone familiar with the geological succession as described in the area in maps and publications prior to the 1970s will probably not recognize a large proportion of the geological names, which subsequent researchers have now developed (and are still tinkering with). Nor perhaps would they recognize some of the terms under which the rocks themselves are now classified and described. In order to translate these old terms into their modern equivalents the British Geological Survey has constructed a *Lexicon of Named Rock Units* accessible via the internet at www.bgs.ac.uk.

The depth of knowledge we now possess concerning these rock units in north Wales and elsewhere has many advantages, not least of which is our improved technical ability to look in greater depth at the mineralogy, geochemistry and petrology of all these rock types in order to improve our understanding of their provenance or source areas. Petrographical analysis of modern thin sections prepared from samples (where accessible) of many of the principal rock types used in the construction of the castles (Plates 5 and 6), together with samples from the BGS archives, have been compared and used in this study to either confirm or, occasionally, raise questions regarding prior assertions as to their quarry sources.

The Building Stones of the Castles

Conwy Castle (1283–87)

The castle is sited at the mouth of the river Conwy on a rugged coastal ridge formed by rocks of Ordovician age (440–450 million years) from the Conwy Mudstone Formation, which includes the Conwy Castle Grit Member on which the castle sits (Plates 1 and 2). The unit consists of a lithologically heterogeneous succession of thin- and thick-bedded, dark blue and brown-grey, fine to coarse-grained, blocky, laminated and occasionally cross-bedded sandstones and limestones. The steeply dipping beds of this unit can be seen at outcrop in several locations beneath the castle walls. They exhibit a regular, closely spaced joint pattern, perpendicular to the bedding, which naturally breaks up the rocks into irregularly sized, tabular blocks, similar to those used to construct the castle walls. It is likely that much of the stone used in the construction would probably have come directly from the partial clearance of the original castle site and would therefore have probably required minimum dressing by the masons. Two contrasting uses of this stone in the castle's construction are clearly evident. The coursed stonework of the imposing eight round towers was constructed by selecting the larger stones from the thicker beds, while the intervening walls are of more irregularly sized, thinly bedded, tabular, blocks. The rubble wall fill throughout the castle is also a mix of these same lithologies.

In general, the natural limitations of the local sandstone at outcrop, notably its irregular bed thicknesses, laminated and well-jointed nature, meant that it could not be quarried in pieces large enough to provide freestone blocks suitable for structural, decorative or carved stonework. There are some exceptions where smaller window openings may have lintels made of large slabs of the local lithologies. However, for most such purposes, other more colourful sandstones were brought in for decorative use in both internal and external features such as arrowloops, windows, door jambs and chimney-pieces. In the early construction phases the stone selected for these apertures was still of comparatively local origin, having been quarried from sandstones cropping out across the estuary on the Creuddyn peninsula. These distinctive purple-red or mottled buff, medium- to very coarse-grained sandstones were probably quarried from the Gloddaeth Purple Sandstone Formation of late Carboniferous age (about 300–315 million years), and form the principal source of freestone used in all wall apertures in the castle, and to a lesser extent in the town walls (Plate 3: A). In thin section, samples of this sandstone comprise a framework mineralogy dominated by monocrystalline quartz grains with subordinate feldspars and sparse rock fragments. The pore-filling clay mineral, kaolinite, occludes much of the pore space in the sandstone. The principal cement in the sandstones is provided by the pervasive presence of narrow syntaxial quartz overgrowths.

Whilst the Gloddaeth sandstones proved adequate for the simpler requirements of this early phase of castle construction, the more sophisticated and finely carved architectural elements introduced in the fourteenth century, such as the expansive roof arches and grandly designed fireplaces and window tracery required a better quality and more decorative freestone. Documentary evidence suggests the vivid red sandstone used in these structures was quarried from the Helsby Sandstone Formation (Sherwood Sandstone Group) succession of Triassic age (about 200–250 million years). Red and variegated sandstones of this type crop out extensively in the Chester–Wirral area and could be transported relatively easily by sea to the castle. Only remnants of these, red-brown, cross-bedded sandstones now survive, but they present a colourful, and presumably deliberate contrast to the grey sandstones of the castle walls.

The grey sandstone and limestone lithologies used for the associated construction of the town walls of Conwy were, as in the castle, also largely obtained from the local Conwy Castle Grit Member. However, in the town wall and its towers along the estuary a significant proportion of large blocks of a hard, pale yellow, iron-stained igneous rock, known as rhyolite, were introduced into the fabric (Plate 3: B). These are finely crystalline igneous rocks, showing a distinctly banded internal structure. This structure resulted from the alignment of the crystals that formed in the molten magma as it was extruded across the ground surface as a lava flow. Rocks of this type crop out extensively in the Conwy Mountain area a few miles to the west of the castle, forming part of the Conwy Rhyolite Formation also of Ordovician age. Isolated blocks of this banded rhyolite can also be seen sporadically in the castle walls but many appear to be later inserts and perhaps not part of the original wall fabric.

One further point of note in the history of the building stones originally used in the castle and town walls is their common re-use as building materials in the older properties of the town. Stone from the ruins of both the castle and town walls has clearly been 'recycled' in later times and there are some examples where even the dressed purple and red sandstone blocks from the castle apertures have been reused in the town buildings.

Harlech Castle (1283–95)

The castle is sited on a rugged, fault-bounded cliff line composed of the hard sandstones and mudstones of the Rhinog Formation of the Harlech Grits Group (Cambrian 488–542 million years). From its craggy perch the castle looks westward over the low-lying marine platform area known as Morfa Harlech, almost 200 feet (60m) below. This location has garnered geological fame in recent decades when, during a deep drilling project at Mochras Island, it was discovered that the area to the west of this fault forms the eastern margin of an offshore Cardigan Bay Basin, in which several thousand metres of previously unknown, younger Mesozoic and Tertiary sediments are still preserved.

The building stone from which the castle is constructed is sourced principally from the hard grey-green and pebbly sandstone beds on which it sits (Plate 3: C). The lithologies found in the walls of the castle are varied, but most can be matched to beds in the surrounding Rhinog Formation. Petrographically the sandstones sampled are matrix-rich consisting of very poorly sorted quartz, feldspar and sparse polyminerallic framework grains in a pervasive micromicaceous clay matrix.

The stonework in the walls is generally coursed, but with varying block sizes, both within courses and from course to course. There is again a marked change in blocks sizes and 'quality' between the tower masonry and the linking walls. The towers are faced primarily with large, dressed, sandstone blocks and the walls with thinly bedded more irregular stones. The obvious irregularity of the surrounding topography suggests that much of this sandstone could probably have been quarried directly from the castle site and its surrounding ditch, or from quarries located very close by.

Despite the large block sizes seen in parts of the structure the local sandstones were not suitable as freestone for decorative detailing. Consequently, a paler, softer, yellow sandstone has been used for carved decorative and dressed stonework in window and door openings, fire surrounds and so forth (Plate 3: D). These sandstones are not evident in the local outcrop and are likely to have been obtained from further afield. Primary references quoted by Taylor[5] suggest that the source was the 'free quarry of Egrin'. The location of the Egrin or Egryn quarries has been the subject of considerable interest and research. Recent work by Palmer[6] and others has suggested that the quarries are located in the lower part of the Rhinog Formation, east of Egryn Abbey, which lies some distance to the south, just north of Barmouth. As yet no detailed examination and petrographic assessment of the sandstones at the potential quarry site has been published. It is, however, of note that surviving buildings in the farm complex at the Egryn Abbey site include elaborately carved medieval window dressings and plain door mouldings using a pale yellow sandstone of a similar character to that found at Harlech Castle. Again, as far as can be ascertained, no petrographic analyses of the sandstones used in the Egryn farm buildings, have been undertaken.

The yellow sandstone samples collected from the dressed stonework of Harlech Castle for petrographic analysis for this study confirm that these sandstones are likely to have come from the Harlech Grits Group. Although clearly different in colour to the typical green-grey sandstones of the castle walls, their general framework mineralogy and textures are comparable. They contain a lower proportion of the micromicaceous clay matrix and a higher proportion of detrital quartz framework grains – quartz-wacke sandstones (Plate 5: C, D and Plate 6: A). It seems very likely that the sandstone beds in the original quarries, if they were located at Egryn, were deliberately worked because of their distinctive colour. Their lower matrix content would probably have given them greater workability facilitating their use as decorative freestones.

Other lithologies that occur randomly within the walls of Harlech Castle include well-rounded quartzite boulders, probably sourced from the local beach, together with occasional thin, grey, cleaved metamorphic slate, probably derived from beds in the Llanbedr Formation (Harlech Grits Group), cropping out in the lower cliff face just south of the castle.

As at Conwy, it is also clear that a considerable proportion of stone from the castle walls has been subsequently recycled to build some of the older houses of the town.

Caernarfon Castle (1283–1330)

In contrast to Conwy and Harlech Castles, both constructed on ridges of hard resistant rock, the castle at Caernarfon occupies a flat-lying position at the mouth of the river Seiont, just where it enters the turbulent waters of the Menai Strait. The castle itself sits on steeply dipping, fissile, black, micaceous mudstones that form part of the Ogwen Group (Ordovician 443–488 million years), which can still be seen to crop out beneath the castle walls on its southern side. In contrast to Conwy and Harlech the unsuitability of these local mudstones for building purposes required that all of the stone used in the castle had to be imported to the site from further afield.

The stone used for most of the fabric is a pale grey, hard, occasionally fossiliferous, limestone quarried from the Lower Carboniferous (Visean) succession. The limestone of the castle walls principally comprises large regularly sized, coursed, blocks. Their consistent thickness reflects the relatively regular, well-bedded character of the limestone in its natural outcrop, which probably required only minimum dressing by the masons before use. Limestones of Lower Carboniferous age crop out extensively in the north Wales area – on the island of Anglesey, along both sides of the Menai Strait, at the Great Orme and in the Clwydian Hills further to the east and have been used extensively for building stone to the present day. Lithologically, with a few notable exceptions, the limestone beds show very little variation across the area. However, the closest and therefore most accessible outcrops occur in the Penmon–Benllech area of Anglesey and along the southern shoreline of the Menai Strait at Vaynol. Both of these areas had good access to the sea enabling shipment of the stone along the Menai Strait to the castle site. The sheer volume of building stone required for construction on this scale, however, would probably have required limestone (and sandstone) to be quarried from several of these local sources in order to maintain a continuous supply.

Although the scale alone of Caernarfon's massive grey, limestone ramparts are clearly meant to impress, the deliberate decorative use of variegated, pale, reddish or yellowish sandstone blocks for the quoins, window and door mouldings, and perhaps most recognizably in the four external decorative sandstone courses, suggests a clear desire to further showcase the high status of the building (Plate 4: A and B). Although the external sandstone courses were not directly accessible for petrographic sampling during this study, their general character under the hand lens shows that they are closely comparable with some of the more accessible sandstone dressings used inside the castle, which were sampled.

A wide range of sandstone lithologies was used in the castle and its towers (including the famous Eagle Tower statues). These include very coarse-grained, pebbly (occasionally conglomeratic) lithologies, quartz-cemented coarse-grained stone used for the walls and finer grained sandstones in the mouldings of the towers. They show a range of colours from off-white to greenish grey or yellow and pale reddish-brown. They may contain sparse or abundant, well-rounded or sub-angular, quartz pebbles and sometimes show prominent cross bedding. Some are hard and durable; others show signs of severe decay. In the internal walling to the north-east of the Eagle Tower a section of pale grey, very hard quartzite blocks form regular courses in the lower part of the wall. Despite this general variability, petrographically, samples of these sandstones suggest they are all probably of local origin, and could have been sourced from the Lower Carboniferous succession in either the Vaynol or Penmon areas (Plate 6: B, C, D). The subtle variations in colour shown by both the internal and external decorative sandstones can also be matched by the variegated sandstones that occur interbedded with the principal limestone beds in these local successions.

More rarely, cross-bedded, sparsely pebbly, red sandstone of Triassic age (Sherwood Sandstone Group) has been used in parts of the castle, most notably in the walling of the Queen's Tower. It has been suggested that some of these dressed blocks may have been recycled from Segontium Roman fort, which lies a few miles to the south-east of the castle. However, the wall remnants at the fort consist primarily of waterworn cobbles and boulders and the only visible large, dressed sandstone blocks are buff coloured, coarse and pebbly (?Lower Carboniferous). No red sandstones of unequivocal Triassic provenance were exposed so a direct comparison with the castle stones was not possible. The large buff sandstone blocks are similar in lithology to those used at the castle for walling, window and door mouldings and some may have been recycled from Segontium. Cobble and boulder grade material, clearly sourced from Segontium, is commonly recycled into the town walls at Caernarfon, but is not generally apparent in the castle fabric.

A small number of other lithologies occur randomly within the walls of the castle, some of which may be part of the original construction; others, however, are probably part of subsequent repair programmes to the wall fabric. Finely crystalline pale grey (and occasionally pink) granite blocks are present in the internal faces of the Black Tower wall section. These granitic blocks have been attributed to sources in Ireland in the Mourne Granite complex, possibly acquired as ships ballasts. More obvious recent repairs have used a finely grained grey granite probably sourced from the local Trefor Quarries on the Llŷn peninsula. A particularly distinctive contribution to the stonework is the presence of blocks of black chert banded limestones. These siliceous limestones, characteristic of deeper water sedimentation, are common in repairs to the upper walls and some towers. Limestone lithologies of this type are not uncommon in parts of the Lower Carboniferous succession cropping out in Anglesey.

Beaumaris Castle (1295–1330)

The castle at Beaumaris on the Isle of Anglesey is sited on a low-lying coastal plain of glacial till and soft sediments that mask large areas of the underlying rocks of the Monian Supergroup. It was the last castle to be built by Edward I in north Wales and it is constructed exclusively of stones from the geological successions of the island. As in the other castles described above, the lack of suitable freestone (sandstones or limestone) in the area meant that the architectural detail of the castle is plain and robust with very little elaborately carved stonework in evidence. In general the walls show an indiscriminate use of these local rock types, although occasionally the careful placement of large, pale coloured, squared sandstone and limestone blocks shows an attempt at deliberate decorative embellishment, for example, in the south-west tower of the inner ward (Plate 4: D).

The three principal rock types that have been used in the construction of the castle are limestones, sandstones and metamorphic schists. Three limestone lithologies commonly occur in the castle walls, the most common and distinctive of which are probably the thinly bedded blocks of brown to dark grey laminated limestone. These limestones are strongly ferruginous (pyritic) and have in places been badly affected by weathering and decay, commonly delaminating to create cavities in the wall fabric. The dark coloration and poor weathering characteristics of these limestones are likely to be a consequence of the presence of comparatively high proportions of detrital clay, iron and organic material. In sharp contrast to these dark laminated limestones are abundant, large squared blocks of hard, pale grey, smooth-textured, fine-grained limestone. These limestones form one of the more distinctive lithologies, particularly of the outer curtain wall. They show little evidence of decay, whether used on their bed or, as sometimes occurs, in a vertical position. In general these limestones have few large fossils; however, there are occasional blocks which are packed with large, spar-calcite replaced, thick-walled brachiopod shells. The third limestone lithology commonly found in the castle fabric comprises tabular blocks of pale grey to off-white, nodular and argillaceous limestone. Blocks of this limestone, which weathers to form a characteristic knobbly surface, frequently occur in the walls (for example, Gunner's Walk), but were also commonly used as lintels over some window and door openings (for example, the inner face of the south outer curtain wall).

A wide range of sandstone lithologies also occurs in the castle walls showing obvious variations in both grain-size and colour. Most commonly these include pale grey, coarse-grained, cross-bedded, pebbly sandstones. The pebbles are principally of white vein quartz, but occasionally green metamorphic schist and red jasper pebbles were also noted. The sandstone is silica cemented and therefore generally a very hard and resistant stone. Despite its very coarse-grained nature, this lithology is used throughout the castle both as block stone in the walls and, distinctively, around window openings, door frames and as lintels. The pale colour of the sandstone contrasts with the darker brown colours of the limestone. Other sandstones present include pale grey, pebble free, fine to coarse-grained, cross-bedded varieties, which are used sporadically in the simply carved decorative stonework of, for example, some fireplace surrounds. More rarely within the stonework, isolated blocks of ferruginous, red-brown to yellow brown, pebbly sandstone occur.

Among several other rocks types used in the walls are a number of variegated green and purple, metamorphic schistose lithologies commonly described as 'greenschist'. They are perhaps most evident in the lower courses (up to a level of 19 feet (6m) in places) of the inner curtain wall and are common in the rubble core-fills exposed in several parts of the castle (Plate 4: C). These hard, intractable metamorphic stones appear in the lower courses of the walls as large blocks of irregular shape and size and were clearly not easy for the masons to dress.

Other metamorphic lithologies present in smaller proportions include hard, green and purple, folded, fractured and foliated schist. Some blocks are cross-cut by white, calcitic veins. The strong green coloration is a consequence of the abundance of the clay mineral chlorite. Large blocks of pure white vein quartz occur sporadically in the walls. Igneous rock types are relatively rare in the wall fabrics, but are present as isolated blocks. They include hard, dark green to black finely crystalline dolerite and pale grey granites both of which may be later replacements during earlier consolidation work. Other rock types present include a number of well-rounded waterworn cobbles and boulders showing a range of lithologies, some clearly associated with 'recent' consolidation work. The presence of smooth-walled, ?mollusc borings in some of the limestone cobbles was noted suggesting they were perhaps sourced from the local beaches.

All of the building stone lithologies described above in the castle can be found in outcrops within 10 miles (16km) of the castle site. The three limestones used – the laminated brown limestones; the hard, pale grey, smooth-textured limestone blocks (subsequently known as the Penmon Limestone or Penmon Marble), and the pale concretionary limestones – can all be sourced from slightly further afield in the Lower Carboniferous, Visean (Asbian to Brigantian) limestone succession of the area to the north-east of the castle. Although each appears distinctly different, examples of similar lithologies can all be seen interbedded in the faulted Lower Carboniferous blocks of the Penmon and Benllech areas. Both areas have been the sites of extensive quarrying activity for many centuries, the remnants of which still characterize the landscape today. The importance of the Carboniferous succession for building purposes, both as building stone and probably for lime mortar production in the area, was enhanced by easy access to the sea. Moving the vast quantities of stone needed for both Beaumaris and Caernarfon Castles would have been greatly facilitated by using this sea route.

The variegated off-white to yellow-brown pebbly sandstone lithologies, which dominate much of the castle fabric, compare closely with the sandstones that form a series of moderately thick, channelized fluvial sandstone beds occurring at several levels within the limestone-dominated succession of the Benllech–Penmon outcrop.

The 'greenschist' lithologies were probably quarried from the local outcrops of Precambrian (Monian Supergroup >> 540 million years) rocks, which would also have provided most of the other metamorphic lithologies present.

The small proportions of other rock types present in the castle walls, as boulders and isolated blocks, can all be found in the local area either at outcrop or derived from the glacial deposits of the Quaternary succession.

Stone Procurement

Leaving aside the problems of mounting and co-ordinating a large castle-building programme within what was effectively a war zone, the erection of buildings on this scale clearly required a very large uninterrupted supply of both labour and building materials. In addition, this supply chain had to be maintained for the best part of twenty years. As is typical of large-scale building programmes of this period, the materials were sourced locally wherever possible to avoid the logistical and potentially ruinous financial costs of transporting heavy and bulky materials, like stone, over great distances. Even a king had to consider the cost.

The first requirement perhaps would be to recruit an experienced project manager. In this respect Edward I was fortunate in that he was already familiar with the skills and experience of the 'architect/builder', James of St George, whom he was to select eventually to supervise much of this vast building project. He was already an experienced castle builder having worked extensively on a number of European castles before he began working in north Wales. He had also supervised the reconstruction

of Builth Castle (1277) and advised on the construction of the castle at Aberystwyth.[7] At the same time, between 1277 and 1282, stone castles were being constructed in north Wales at Flint (Carboniferous Gwespyr sandstone) and at Rhuddlan (Carboniferous limestone, sandstone and red Triassic sandstone), where he was again present. Also under construction for the king around this time (from 1277) was Vale Royal Abbey, built of red-brown Triassic, Helsby Sandstone from Delamere Forest in Cheshire.[8]

Today, we are fortunate to have the benefit of many research studies on this magnificent stone-built heritage and access to the accumulated geological knowledge from over two centuries or more to enable us to locate the best building stone sources. How was James of St George able to deal with the supply of stone for the new castles? Did he or his emissaries travel the area to find suitable castle sites with a readily available stone supply or were the sites chosen without consideration of the local stone sources? Probably we shall never know the real answer to these questions. However, it is clear that in two of the four castles studied (Conwy and Harlech) the stones cleared from the sites or quarried very close to the site were used for most of the construction. Caernarfon and Beaumaris Castles, in contrast, took advantage of their coastal locations allowing limestone to be imported by sea from slightly further afield. It seems more than likely, in view of the earlier and on-going royal building activity noted above, that in his role as master of the King's Work's in Wales James of St George had probably already acquired a unique understanding of the building stone sources available to him in north Wales and its adjacent areas.

The magnitude of this castle-building programme in north Wales also required an 'army' of craftsmen and labourers to be impressed from several English counties.[9] The stone masons appear to have come principally from Somerset, Dorset, Gloucestershire, Shropshire, Derbyshire, Rutland, Lincolnshire and Yorkshire. These men would have brought with them a wide range of skills and experience of working many different stone types – Middle Jurassic limestones from Lincolnshire, Rutland, Gloucestershire, Somerset and Dorset; Triassic sandstones from Shropshire; Carboniferous limestones and sandstones from Derbyshire and Yorkshire. However, few would probably have had experience of some of the hard, more intractable stones from the Precambrian and Lower Palaeozoic rocks they were to use at Conwy and Harlech. In contrast, the Carboniferous limestones and sandstones (used at Caernarfon and Beaumaris) would almost certainly have been familiar to the masons from Derbyshire and Yorkshire, while the Shropshire masons would have known the softer Triassic sandstones of Cheshire well.

Conclusions

Any new research undertaken into the sources of the building stones used in Edward I's castles in north Wales will inevitably owe a considerable debt to the work of two geologists who spent much of their careers living and working in the north Wales area – Edward Greenly (1861–1951) and Ernest Neaverson (1885–1972). Greenly became a member of the staff of the Geological Survey of Great Britain in 1889 and learned his trade in the Highlands of Scotland working with some of the most famous geologists of the day. In 1895, however, Greenly resigned from the Geological Survey over concerns for the health of his wife. Scotland's loss in the Highlands was, however, Wales's gain as Greenly decided to settle in Anglesey and to continue his, now 'freelance', career by mapping and recording in great detail the geology of the island and adjacent north Wales coastal area. In 1919, after twenty-three years of 'unpaid' effort Greenly's epic memoir, *Geology of Anglesey*, was published by the Geological Survey. It made it very clear that the breadth of his knowledge of the geology of the area as a whole was then unequalled and is likely to remain so. Subsequently, Greenly pursued many other geological topics: he worked and published extensively on the geology of the Lower Carboniferous (limestones) of north Wales, which was a major source of building stone in the area from medieval times, and in 1932 he published his study on the stones of the castles of Beaumaris and Caernarfon.[10] Much of what was written by Greenly, regarding the geology and sources of the building stones of these castles, stemmed from his vast knowledge of the area and remains pertinent today. Subsequent studies, including this paper, have largely focussed on confirming, updating and improving the details of his work.

Further research and publications on the building stones of the castles of north Wales in general then had to await the deliberations of another long-lived career geologist, Ernest Neaverson. Neaverson, a Lincolnshire man, was a lecturer in palaeontology in the Geology Department at the University of Liverpool from 1920 to 1951. As a result of his studies, he also developed a particular interest in the building stones of the medieval (and earlier) castles and other buildings in the north Wales area, and this culminated in the publication in 1947 of his book, *Mediaeval Castles in North Wales*. Here again, his unrivalled knowledge of the local geology was used to determine the building stones used in a much wider range of buildings in the area. This publication remains the primary source of information on the building stones of the north Wales castles of all periods and summarizes unchallenged, and with due acknowledgment, Greenly's 'careful work' on Beaumaris and Caernarfon Castles.

Many of the identifications and conclusions reached by these two researchers concerning the probable sources of building stone used by Edward I and his 'architects' in his prolonged building campaign have remained unchallenged. However, modern techniques, most notably petrographic or thin section analysis, have perhaps allowed a more rounded picture of the stones used and their links to potential source areas to be better established.

Notes

1. A. J. Taylor, *The King's Works in Wales 1277–1330* (London 1974).
2. E. Greenly, 'The stones of the castles [Beaumaris and Caernarfon]', *Anglesey Antiquarian Society and Fields Club Transactions*, (1932), 50–56; J. Manley and W. Jones, 'From bedrock to battlements: the geology quarrying and construction of Caergwrle Castle, Clwyd', *North West Geologist*, 3 (1993), 11–42; E. Neaverson, *Mediaeval Castles in North Wales: a Study of Sites, Water Supply and Building Stones* (Liverpool 1947).
3. G. K. Lott, *The Geology and Building Stones of Beaumaris Castle (CR/04/113)* (Nottingham 2004); idem, *The Description, Identification and Sourcing of the Stones used in the Construction of Conwy Castle, Gwynedd* (Building Stone Assessment Report GR_114722_1) (Nottingham 2007); idem, *The Description, Identification and Sourcing of the Stones used in the Construction of Caernarvon Castle, Gwynedd* (Building Stone Assessment Report GR_119505_1) (Nottingham 2008); idem, *The Description, Identification and Sourcing of the Stones used in the Construction of Harlech Castle, Gwynedd* (Building Stone Assessment Report GR_1195095_2) (Nottingham 2008).
4. For a review of this work and for pertinent references, see M. F. Howells, *British Regional Geology: Wales* (Nottingham 2007).
5. Taylor, *The King's Works*.
6. T. Palmer, 'Egryn Sandstone: a lost and rediscovered Welsh freestone', *Welsh Stone Forum Newsletter*, 1 (2003), 7–9; idem, 'Egryn Stone: a forgotten Welsh freestone', *Archaeologia Cambrensis*, 156 (2007), 149–60.
7. Taylor, *The King's Works*.
8. R. A. Brown, H. M. Colvin and A. J. Taylor, *The History of the King's Works: the Middle Ages*, I (London 1963), 248–57.
9. Taylor, *The King's Works*.
10. E. Greenly, 'The stones of the castles'.

'Tŵr Dewr Gwncwerwr' ('A Brave Conqueror's Tower'): Welsh Poetic Responses to the Edwardian Castles

Dylan Foster Evans

Thomas Pennant's famous description of Caernarfon Castle as 'the magnificent badge of our subjection' implies that 'we' (the Welsh) know full well the symbolic meaning of Edward I's keystone fortress. But in Daniel Owen's novel *Profedigaethau Enoc Huws* (1891), the well-meaning Thomas Bartley asks the know-it-all know-nothing lead miner, Sem Llwyd, whether he is right in thinking that Caernarfon Castle – along with the Tower of London, Llanrwst Bridge, Rhuddlan Castle and many such things – was built by a stonemason called Indigo Jones. Sem is quick to correct his companion – those things, he says, were all built before the birth of Christ, thousands of years before Indigo's birth. This well-known example of Daniel Owen's penchant for comedy takes it for granted that the reader will know more about Caernarfon Castle and the architect Inigo Jones (1573–1652) than the foolish Sem Llwyd. But it also reminds us that the 'meaning' of Caernarfon Castle, as constructed by the educated (and Anglicized) Pennant, need not be that of all classes of Welsh men and women.[1]

We should not expect a unitary 'Welsh response' to the castles, despite the fact that the surviving literary sources from the first two or three centuries following Edward's conquest of Gwynedd (the period covered by this paper) direct our attention to a single stratum of Welsh society. This group consists of the men and women of the higher ranks of native Welsh society – the *uchelwyr* (singular *uchelwr*, literally 'high man'). In the decades following the Edwardian conquest, the poets who received the patronage of the *uchelwyr* developed a simple, but elegant, metre called the *cywydd* which, along with the traditional *awdl*, would be the medium for most of the high-status poetry composed between the fourteenth and seventeenth centuries.[2] This is not the only body of Welsh literature that may profitably be studied from the point of view of castle studies, as shown by Abigail Wheatley's work on the relationship between the prose tale *Breuddwyd Maxen* (Maxen's Dream) and Caernarfon Castle.[3] But it is by far

the richest such body, and references to castles by the poets of the *uchelwyr* are too numerous to list exhaustively in a relatively brief discussion such as this.

By contrast, the views of the lower ranks of society in medieval Wales are extremely difficult to discern. Few poems relating to them have survived, and they were naturally less likely than the *uchelwyr* to be office holders who would interact with the castles in an official capacity. We should, however, remember that the castles also served as gaols, and it is revealing that possibly the earliest reference to Caernarfon Castle in Welsh poetry is as a prison. In a famous poem, Dafydd ap Gwilym (*fl.* about 1340), miserably contemplating a fruitless wait under the eaves of his lover's house, grumbles: 'Ni bu yn y Gaer yn Arfon / Geol waeth na'r heol hon' ('There was never even in Caernarfon Castle / a dungeon worse than this street').[4] A few decades later the poet, Gruffudd Llwyd (*fl.* 1380–1420), gives us some medieval Welsh prison-slang by using 'Gwenllïan Hir' ('Tall Gwenllïan') as a misogynistic nickname for leg irons.[5] But the castle gaols were far from restricted to the lower classes, and although there is no record that Dafydd ap Gwilym ever fell foul of the law, his contemporary and fellow poet, Llywelyn Goch ap Meurig Hen, certainly did so, spending time imprisoned inside Harlech Castle in 1346 awaiting trial for killing a Welshman in the royal army.[6] And earlier in the same century, the influential soldier Sir Gruffudd Llwyd (d. 1335) had been imprisoned in Rhuddlan Castle: 'Ar llawr Caer Degeingl dygn a gystudd!' ('the warrior of Caer Degeingl [= Rhuddlan] suffers harshly!') said the poet Gwilym Ddu o Arfon.[7] So even prison life cannot guarantee us a glimpse of the poor man and woman's encounters with castles. It is difficult, however, not to get a sense of their experience from a sign that may be seen in a present-day Caernarfon street. In English 'Shirehall Street' and in Welsh 'Stryd y Jêl' ('Gaol Street'), the sign irresistibly replicates English authority on the one hand and its reception by the Welsh on the other.

A further factor that complicates our search for castles in the poetry is that they naturally shared their names with the towns built around them, so that it is not always obvious whether a reference to Caernarfon or Harlech, for example, is to the castle, the town or both. Things become clearer when the poets use one of the several Welsh words for a castle. The usual modern Welsh word, *castell*, comes from the Latin *castellum*, although its use was certainly influenced by the French and English forms of the same word.[8] But in describing castles the poets often use the word *tŵr*, from the French (or Middle English) *tour* 'tower'. This can refer to a single tower, but seems often to be used metonymically for the whole complex. Another term used is *caer*, a native Welsh word which is now normally translated as 'fort' but which had a wider semantic range in the Middle Ages, including both castle and walled town. 'Caer Ystwyth', for instance, was how Dafydd Nanmor and Lewys Glyn Cothi referred to fifteenth-century Aberystwyth.[9]

Despite the castle-building activities of Llywelyn ab Iorwerth, Llywelyn ap Gruffudd and others, native castles do not feature extensively in Welsh poetry from before 1282. A notable exception is Hywel Foel ap Griffri ap Pwyll Wyddel's plea to Llywelyn ap Gruffudd to release his brother Owain ap Gruffudd from imprisonment. That he was being held in a castle – probably Cricieth or Dolbadarn – is made clear by the poem's memorable opening line: 'Gŵr ysydd yn nhŵr yn hir westi' ('A warrior is a long-time resident in a tower').[10] Cricieth features prominently in post-conquest Welsh poetry, and although it was refurbished rather than established by Edward I, it will be one of the castles considered in this paper.

The response to the castles found in Welsh poetry is partly prescribed by the nature of that poetry. Praise poetry – including eulogies, elegies, poems composed to new buildings, and poems of request and of thanks – is the predominant mode. Since praise poetry often draws upon – and engenders – a positive outlook on life, it is not unexpected that the castles should themselves often be seen in a favourable light. The most obvious way in which a castle would seize a poet's attention is when the patron was the holder of an official position related to it. The earliest poem to an official and his castle is the famous *cywydd* composed around 1380 by Iolo Goch to Sir Hywel ap Gruffudd, known as Syr Hywel y Fwyall (Sir Hywel of the Axe, d. about 1381), a soldier who made his name in the French wars. Hywel was appointed constable of Cricieth in 1359, and held that position for some twenty years. Iolo's *cywydd* (which is noted in the Cadw guide to Cricieth) employs the prose tale *Breuddwyd Maxen* as a framing device.[11] It was composed at a time when fears of a French attack were palpable, and its depiction

of the castle and its constable is in many ways an early example of what might be called English nationalism expressed through the Welsh language. It is essentially a conservative poem, and as Dafydd Johnston has noted, its final lines, with their repeated use of the verb *cadw* (to keep), reinforce that message:

Cadw'r castell, gwell yw no gwŷr ...
Cadw'r mordrai, cadw'r tai, cadw'r tir,
Cadw'r gwledydd oll, cadw'r gloywdwr,
A chadw'r gaer – iechyd i'r gŵr!

(Keep the castle, he's better than a host of men ...
keep the sea-ebb, keep the houses, keep the land,
keep all the countries, keep the bright tower,
and keep the fort – health to the man!)[12]

A generation later, Cricieth was ruined by Owain Glyndŵr's forces, Harlech and Aberystwyth were taken, and other castles were damaged. The Crown's response to Glyndŵr's war reduced the opportunity for Welshmen to serve as constables, although men with Welsh blood did hold office in the garrison towns during the fifteenth century. These were often members of *advenae* families such as the Pulestons of Flintshire and Caernarfon. The Pulestons had originally come to Wales in the wake of Edward I's conquest – one of the first members of the family was hanged from the eaves of his own house in Caernarfon during the rebellion of Madog ap Llywelyn in 1294.[13] But the family married into Welsh stock and in a later generation one of its number, Robert Puleston, was a brother-in-law and supporter of Owain Glyndŵr.[14] The Pulestons were also important patrons of Welsh literature. In a poem composed to Siôn Puleston Hen (John Puleston the Elder) around 1500, Lewys Môn situates his patron 'yn Nhref Euda' ('in Eudaf's town'), thus identifying him with the legendary history of Caernarfon as found in *Breuddwyd Maxen*. He also calls the town by the name of 'Caersallog', as does Mathau Brwmffild in a poem to Siôn's son, and as did Rhys Goch Eryri a couple of generations earlier.[15] Caersallog was long thought to be an alternative name for Salisbury, the site of the infamous and treacherous murder of British leaders by the Saxons, as related by Geoffrey of Monmouth. But here in fact it seems to be another name for Caernarfon. The seventeenth-century copyist John Jones of Gellilyfdy made a note in one of his manuscripts which draws attention to Caernarfon's palimpsestic character: 'k[aer] Salloch. kaer Evdaf. kaer yn Arfon. Evdaf ai gwnaeth' ('Eudaf built it').[16]

Another family of English origins who became patrons of Welsh poetry were the Bulkeleys of Beaumaris. They were later arrivals in Wales than the Pulestons – the first member of the family to live in Anglesey was the Cheshire-born William Bulkeley (about 1418–90). He married the daughter of Gwilym ap Gruffudd of Penrhyn, Llandygái (who shall be discussed below), and was deputy constable of Beaumaris Castle in 1440, as mentioned by Lewys Môn in a poem to his son, Hugh (d. in or before 1507). When that poem was composed (during the reign of Richard III), Hugh had recently been relieved of his duties as deputy constable of Conwy Castle, but he refused to yield it to Richard's officers.[17] The poem shows an awareness of the racial tensions to be found in and around these colonial outposts (and which are encapsulated in part in the figure of Hugh Bulkeley himself):

> Y dre a'r wlad, yn ordr lân,
> yn un iaith a wnawn weithian.
> Gwiw nithiaist wŷr, gwnaethost well:
> gyrru heibio i'r gwŷr rhybell.
> Haws agor drws y gaer draw,
> nawcan hoes, na'u cynhwysaw.
> Huw'n agoriad hen gerrig;
> Huw, ni bo'r ail henw'n y brig.
> Agor ganwaith Gaer Gonwy:
> nedwch i mewn ond chwi mwy.[18]

(In good order, we'll now make the town and country into one nation.
You've sorted men, you've done better:
passing over outsiders.
It is easier to open the door of that fort
(nine hundred lifetimes) than it is to suffer them to come in.
Hugh is the key of old masonry;
Hugh, may no other name take over.
Open the fort of Conwy a hundred times:
henceforth don't let anyone in but yourself.)

In 1505 a Welshman called Huw Lewys was appointed constable of Harlech and was generously praised by Gruffudd ap Dafydd ap Hywel in a *cywydd* to ask for a pair of stocks from the men of Harlech on behalf of the men of Cricieth. Gruffudd calls Harlech 'Calais Gymru' ('the Calais of Wales') and 'Caer Gollwyn' ('Collwyn's Fort') after a local eleventh-century patriarch. Although he applauds both castles, he singles out Harlech for special praise, and its builders are even said to have laboured on 'tŵr Nimbrod Hen' ('Old Nimrod's Tower', namely the Tower of Babel).[19]

Poems to castles were not restricted to those about individuals who had an official role within their walls. Another relevant category of poems is that in which the castle is the basis of comparison, or of an extended metaphor. The simplest of these is when the castle, or its main tower, is used as a metaphor for the patron himself. The pre-eminent status of Caernarfon's largest tower is illustrated by the sixteenth-century poet Siôn Ceri in a poem to an *uchelwr* from distant Powys: 'Tŵr Eryr tir

Arwystl' ('the Eagle Tower of the region of Arwystli'). The Eagle Tower had a particular appeal to the poets, and only in north-east Wales did it have a rival – Chirk Castle's Adam's Tower.[20]

The castle could sometimes be used as a metaphor for a whole family. The earliest example of this is found in a poem by Owain Waed Da, probably composed early in the fifteenth century after Cricieth Castle had been slighted by Glyndŵr's forces. Although less famous than Iolo Goch's poem to Hywel y Fwyall, this poem gives us a more detailed picture of Cricieth by naming the towers each in turn. The poem itself is formally a eulogy to Hywel's nephew, Ieuan (or Ifan) ab Einion of Eifionydd, and his four sons:

> Ifan, awch darian, wych dŵr,
> Yw'r castell, wi o'r costiwr!
> Fab Einiawn yw'r mawrddawn mau
> A'i feibion, dewrion dyrau.
> Tŵr y Faner, torf uniawn,
> Yw Madog ddioriog ddawn;
> Hywel Fychan, gwiwran gŵr,
> Dihydwyll, yw'r deheudwr;
> Tŵr enwog mewn tair ynys,
> Parth yr haul, y porth yw Rhys;
> Tŵr dwynsiwn, pan draethwn, pwy?
> Gorau o Wynedd yw Gronwy.
>
> Llawenydd, bob dydd y daw,
> Llyna gastell llawn gostiaw![21]

(Ieuan, a shield of vigour, a fine tower,
is the castle; such a provisioner!
The son of Einion is my great gift
and his sons are worthy towers.
Madog of constant gifts and
a fine force is the Banner Tower;
Hywel Fychan – the man has a worthy inheritance
and is hard to deceive – is the South Tower;
famous in three realms,
the sun's home, Rhys is the Gatehouse;
who, when I would speak, is the Dungeon Tower?
Goronwy, the best from Gwynedd.

Happiness – it comes every day;
that is a fully-provisioned castle!)

Two generations later, Edward I's Caernarfon was the blueprint in an elegy for Edwart ap Dafydd of Chirkland and his son, Robert Trefor, by Guto'r Glyn:

> Llydan oedd gastell Edwart
> A'i dyrau gwych a'i dair gwart.
> Caerau Edwart gwncwerwr,
> Tyrau oedd ar gaerau'r gŵr.
> Tebyg o gerrig a gwŷdd
> I dwf Edwart ap Dafydd.

Dra adodd Duw i redeg
Edwart hael a'i dyrau teg,
Castell oedd ef i Drefawr,
A'i bedwar mab, dyrau mawr.
Aeth Duw ymaith â deuwr,
Y tad a'r pedwerydd twr.

Caer a gwart Edwart ydoedd,
Castell a meddgell ym oedd.
Twr abl oedd yntau Robert,
Twr y porth uwch tyrau pert.
Twr y wlad a'i phenadur,
Twr i'r Mars cyn torri'r mur.
Twr Edwart i'r tir ydoedd,
Twr yr Eryr ar wyr oedd.
Trithwr a ater weithian,
Tyrau i'r glod, trywyr glân.[22]

(Edward's castle was wide
with its splendid towers and its three wards.
The forts of Edward the conqueror–
there were towers on the warrior's forts.
[They were] similar, in masonry and timber,
to Edwart ap Dafydd's stature [or family].
While God let generous Edwart and his fair towers live,
he was a castle for Trefor, and his four sons were great
    towers.
God has taken two men away–
the father and one of the four towers.

Edwart was a fort and a [castle's] ward,
he was a castle and mead-store for me.
Robert was a fine tower,
the Gatehouse over fair towers.
The land's tower and its leader,
a tower for the March before the wall was broken.
He was Edwart's [or Edward's] tower for the land,
he was an Eagle Tower over men.
Three towers have now been left,
towers for poetry, three good men.)

Imagery of this kind proved popular, and Lewys Glyn Cothi took it further by embracing the latest technology, the siege gun. In a poem to a family of seven from the lordship of Hay, who had recently lost one of its members, Lewys accused God of firing a cannon ball from heaven to knock down one of the towers:

Castell oedd ar frig Gwestun
â saith dwr, e' saethwyd un;
torres un eto o'r saith
gan faen gwn o nef unwaith.[23]

(There was a castle above Weston
with seven towers, one has been shot down;
one of the seven was broken
by a single cannon ball from heaven.)

The poets could invoke castles in portrayals of both individual *uchelwyr* and their families, but it was more natural still that they should compare their patron's homes to Edward I's most famous creations. The fifteenth century saw a great upsurge in building, partly as a response to the destruction caused by Glyndwr's wars. Tudur Penllyn in the middle years of the century compared Huw Conwy's home at Bryneuryn to the Roman town of Caerleon as well as to Caernarfon's Eagle Tower. The same poet compared Gruffudd Fychan's house in Barmouth (y Twr Gwyn, which still stands) to an eclectic list of impressive buildings and towns, including Bristol, Calais, London and Cheapside, as well as the Eagle Tower, Twr Rheinallt (near Mold) and Troy. The house is also called 'Twr Bronwen a orffennwyd / Ferch Lyr o fewn Harddlech lwyd' ('the tower of Bronwen daughter of Llyr tower completed in grey Harlech').[24] This invokes the famous scene in which Brân (or Bendigeidfran), the brother of Branwen (or Bronwen) and the son of Llyr, king of Britain, is seated on the rock at Harlech at the beginning of the second branch of the *Mabinogi*.[25] Despite being built at a later date, Harlech Castle seems here to be comfortably absorbed into the world of early medieval Welsh narrative.

The most thoughtful poem in this class is Rhys Goch Eryri's *cywydd* (probably composed in the 1420s) which likens Caernarfon Castle to the hall of Gwilym ap Gruffudd at Penrhyn, Llandygái (the site of the present Penrhyn Castle).[26] The poem was composed in the wake of the Glyndwr rebellion, which had failed to capture the castle, and can in many ways be read as a response to that failure. Rhys praises the castle for its great strength and calls the Eagle Tower 'Twr dewr gwncwerwr' ('A brave conqueror's tower'). But as well as praising Penrhyn, Rhys undermines his poem's central concept by questioning the suitability of the castle as a metaphor. He asks whether Penrhyn should be compared to a king's castle, and his answer is that Gwilym's hall is far superior to it. For Rhys, the Eagle Tower contrasts sharply with the hall:

Y twr celffaint cyn teirawr,
Ochrog murdew corniog mawr,
A luniwyd dan ei linyn,
Gyrch dig, i gael gwarchae dyn,
Ac i ostwng ag ystyr
Calonnau a gwarrau gwyr.
A mawrdy talm, a murdew,
Mab Gruffudd, iôn gleifrudd glew,
A bair llawenydd bob awr
Ac urddas pob rhyw gerddawr.[27]

(The wizened tower,
angled, thick-walled, turreted, and big,
within three hours was built under a plumb line

in order to incarcerate (a harsh attack)
and with intent to force down
the hearts and necks of men.
But the thick-walled house for a throng,
belonging to the son of Gruffudd, a brave lord with a
       bloody pike,
causes merriment every hour
and honour for every poet.)

The oppressive strength of the castle is rejected by the poet in favour of the welcome found in Gwilym's hall, and he priviliges hospitality over the militarism of an earlier age. In fact, Gwilym had himself joined Glyndŵr's forces, but had left them at an early opportunity and had profited from the forfeited estates of his erstwhile companions. He may well have joined in the attacks against the castle, but he can now defeat it symbolically in another way. Another irony is that the English widow of Robert Parys, constable of the castle during the rebellion, has now become Gwilym's wife, and she is praised as such by the poet. The poem ends by decisively rejecting the comparison with the castle. Rhys states that Gwilym's hall may be likened only to God's court in heaven – he quickly asks the audience's forgiveness for such an audacious comparison!

The last category of poems for consideration relates to specific events. Many more poems have survived from the second half of the fifteenth century than from the first, and that fact, coupled with the Welsh involvement in the Wars of the Roses, means that a relative wealth of material has survived. These civil wars caused an increase in anti-English sentiment in Wales, and in one poem Ieuan Brydydd Hir enthusiastically foresees the destruction of castles (or fortified towns) throughout north Wales:

Pan ddêl dechrau rhyfel rhydd
Y curir gwŷr y ceyrydd:
Yng Nghaer a'i gwŷr anghywraint,
Y briwir swrn 'n Aber Saint.
Gwae o'r ymliw gaer amlwg
Gyffin a gaiff drin a drwg;
A chaer Ddinbych o'u haros;
A thân yn Rhuddlan a Rhos.[28]

(When open warfare begins
the men of the forts will be beaten:
in Caernarfon with its artless men
many will be injured at Aber-saint.
Because of the fighting, woe to prominent castle
of Conwy which shall have battle and harm,
and to the fort of Denbigh for standing against them;
and [there will be] fire in Rhuddlan and Rhos.)

The most famous siege of the period was the Lancastrian occupation of Harlech Castle, brought to an end by Yorkist forces in 1468. Dafydd ab Ieuan ab Einion, the de facto captain of Harlech for the Lancastrians against the forces of Edward IV, was praised by Dafydd Llwyd ap Llywelyn as the captain of 'Caer Branwen lle cair Brynaich' ('the fort of Branwen where there are Englishmen'), and the poet notes further that 'Ni bu ond Harddlech fechan / Gywir neb i'r goron wan' ('no-one but little Harlech has been true to the weak Crown').[29]

The imprisonment at Harlech of two Yorkist Welshmen, Henri ap Gwilym and Owain Llwyd, was the subject of a poem probably composed by the Cardiganshire poet, Gwilym ab Ieuan Hen. His feelings for Harlech are naturally antagonistic, and he calls for God to break the castle so that Henri and Owain may escape. He calls it an infernal cauldron and a long-turreted pigsty in which the devil himself shivers. Indeed, he constructs the castle as an alien feature of the Welsh landscape by comparing it to the outer limits of Iceland and by wishing that the castle and its five towers, and the rock upon which they stand, should be moved to the Mediterranean Sea! God, Mary and Jesus are called upon to destroy it, as is the most powerful Welsh Yorkist of the day, Lord William Herbert: 'Bâr dyrnod Herbard arnaw' ('may the anger of Herbert's fist strike upon it').[30]

And it was indeed William Herbert who took Harlech for the Yorkist cause. One of Guto'r Glyn's most famous poems gives an account of the campaign and the siege, which brought it to a close.[31] The Yorkist poet Hywel Dafi also describes the scene:

Tynnu â gwŷr tonnau gwin,
peiriannau fel mab brenin,
uchel ewri a chlariwns
a tharfu gwŷr â thwrf gwns.[32]

(Siege engines fired by men of the flowing wine,
like a king's son,
loud calls and clarions
and men frightened by the thundering of guns.)

Recently, an elegy by Huw Cae Llwyd has been identified as another poem relating to this siege. The slain *uchelwr*, Philip Fychan (or Vaughan) of Tyle Glas near Talgarth, was one of the few notable Yorkists killed in the campaign against Harlech. Despite winning fame as a lancer in the French wars, he was felled by a cannon ball, an irony remarked upon by the English chronicler, William Worcester.[33] Huw Cae Llwyd's elegy contains the most powerful expression in Welsh of the anger caused by the use of gunpowder weapons against noble horsemen:

Cyn lladd ein canllaw o un
Ef a laddai fil uddun.
Nid trwy wrolaeth saethu,
Troi brad fawr trwy bared fu.

Nid o rym neu ymwan,
Ond trwy'r twyll taro a'r tân;
Tân, llyfrwas, ytiw'n llofrudd,
Trwy'r carl a'i trawai o'r cudd.[34]

(Before our leader was killed by one enemy
he killed a thousand of them.
Shooting was not done bravely,
a great deceit was perpetrated through a barrier.
Not by strength or by fighting,
but by the trickery of striking with fire;
fire – a cowardly lad – is our murderer,
by means of the churl who struck him [*sc.* Philip] from
    a hiding place.)

This anger, aimed at the lowly gunner who has killed
a nobleman, has parallels in a host of other European
languages, and shows us a poet struggling to come to
terms with a changing world.[35]

The Welsh responses to the Edwardian castles are
ambivalent and as such are representative of Welsh
responses to the Edwardian settlement in general. The
uchelwyr on the one hand maintained a strong sense of
Welsh identity and sustained a thriving literary tradition,
while on the other they upheld English rule by serving as
Crown or Marcher officials. This apparently contradictory
position is perfectly illustrated in many of the poems to
English castles. Depending on circumstances, a castle such
as Harlech could be constructed as an alien imposition
on the landscape or construed as a building whose origins
lay deep in the Welsh legendary past. It is perhaps not
surprising that those castles built on sites that already had
a place in the Welsh psyche should be mentioned more
often than those, such as Beaumaris, that were built on
sites of less cultural relevance.[36] Yet poems to castles are
always products of specific circumstances, and are not
reflections of views that transcend events and time.

As a postscript, it is of interest that castles, Caernarfon
especially, have been a popular theme in the revival of
Welsh strict-metre poetry (and the *cywydd* in particular)
that has taken place since the late 1960s. The investiture
of Charles Windsor as prince of Wales in 1969 in
Caernarfon (the most Welsh-speaking town in Wales)
was a seminal event in the history of Welsh-language
culture, and the castle's symbolic role was reinvigorated.
In the late 1960s, for instance, Plaid Cymru's J. E. Jones
contributed a column under the pen name 'Tŵr yr Eryr'
('The Eagle Tower') to the weekly newspaper *Baner ac
Amserau Cymru*. There was also a strong medievalist
element in the poetry of this period, a feature which
persists today. Poets such as Gerallt Lloyd Owen (b.

1944) looked back to the Middle Ages for inspiration as
they called for direct action in the present to support the
Welsh language. The 600th anniversary of the Glyndŵr
rebellion again brought the castles to public attention.
In the volume of poetry and songs called *Syched am
Sycharth* ('Thirst for Sycharth', Owain Glyndŵr's home,
destroyed by Prince Henry's forces in 1403), leading
Welsh-language poets attacked what they saw as the
Anglocentric way in which the heritage of Wales (and
its castles in particular) is interpreted by public bodies.
In a poem entitled 'Pwy sy'n cadw...?' ('Who keeps...?'),
Iwan Llwyd (b. 1957) asks who decides which sites are
to be protected, and wonders whether those that relate
to Welsh defeats are privileged over those pertaining to
the success of Glyndŵr and to the vitality of Welsh-
language culture in general:

Pwy sy'n cadw Harlech? ai Brân
yn gwylio o graig y wylan,
neu gorrach yn graig o arian?[37]

(Who keeps Harlech? is it Brân
from the seagull's rock,
or is it a dwarf who is a rock of money?)

The Welsh-language responses to castles have, indeed until
recently, been given relatively little attention. But the
availability of new editions of poetry and recent shifts in
the field of castle studies itself make this an ideal time to
present the Welsh evidence to a wider public.[38]

Many lessons have been drawn from a contemplation
of Edward's mighty castles. For the sixteenth-century
Anglesey priest-poet, 'Sir' Dafydd Trefor, that lesson was
the brevity of life on this earth, and for him the fate
of the builder of Caernarfon Castle provided an ideal
exemplum:

P'le mae Edward, plwm ydych,
Y gŵr a wnâi'r gaer yn wych?
Mae'i ddelw, pe meddylien',
Wych yn y porth uwch ein pen,
Yntau'n fud, hwnt yn ei fedd,
Dan garreg dew yn gorwedd.[39]

(Where is Edward (you are made of lead)
the man who splendidly built the castle?
His fine image (if people would consider it)
is in the gatehouse above us,
but he himself is mute, away in his grave,
lying under a heavy stone.)

Edward is long gone, but his castles will continue to be
debated, reconsidered and reconstructed through the
medium of Welsh for many years to come.

Notes

1. T. Pennant, *A Tour in Wales. MDCCLXX*, II (London 1778–83), 214; D. Owen¸ *Profedigaethau Enoc Huws*, new edn (Caerdydd 1995), 134.

2. For the literature of the *uchelwyr*, see D. Johnston, *Llên yr Uchelwyr* (Caerdydd 2006), and (in English) A. O. H. Jarman and G. R. Hughes (eds), *A Guide to Welsh Literature, II: 1282–c.1550*, rev. edn ed. D. Johnston (Cardiff 1997).

3. A. Wheatley, this volume, and idem, *The Idea of the Castle in Medieval England* (Woodbridge 2004), 112–22, 139–41. On *Breuddwyd Maxen* and Caernarfon, see now *Breudwyt Maxen Wledic*, ed. B. F. Roberts (Dublin 2005), lxvii–lxix.

4. Text and translation from the on-line edition www.dafyddapgwilym. net, general ed. D. Johnston: 'Dan y Bargod' (98.27–8) [seen 10 April 2008]. Dafydd's *cywydd* 'Yr Wylan' ('The Gull', poem 45 in the on-line edition) refers to an unnamed castle, possibly either Aberystwyth or Cricieth. Unless otherwise indicated (as here), all translations in this chapter are my own. Translations of more than one couplet will be set out in lines as poetry. It should be noted, however, that they are not necessarily line-by-line translations of the Welsh.

5. D. Foster Evans, 'Gwenllïan Hir', *Llên Cymru*, 31 (2008), 188–90. Gwenllïan is a common Welsh girl's name.

6. A. D. Carr, 'The coroner in fourteenth-century Merioneth', *Journal of the Merioneth Historical and Record Society*, 11 (1990–93), 250–51.

7. *Gwaith Gruffudd ap Dafydd ap Tudur, Gwilym Ddu o Arfon, Trahaearn Brydydd Mawr ac Iorwerth Beli*, eds N. G. Costigan (Bosco) et al. (Aberystwyth 1995), 51 (6.16). Poems on the theme of a patron's incarceration are discussed in Johnston, *Llên yr Uchelwyr*, 310–12.

8. In the poetry composed to the native princes before the Edwardian conquest, the word *castell* 'occurs rarely and is used chiefly to refer to hostile Anglo-Norman castles'; see M. E. Owen, 'Literary convention and historical reality: the court in the Welsh poetry of the twelfth and thirteenth centuries', *Études Celtiques*, 29 (1992), 76.

9. On *castell*, *tŵr* and *caer*, see *Geiriadur Prifysgol Cymru* (Caerdydd 1950–2002), 438, 3660, 384 and cf. the discussion on the meanings of English *castle* and *tower* in Wheatley, *Idea of the Castle*, 19–43; *The Poetical Works of Dafydd Nanmor*, eds T. Roberts and I. Williams (Cardiff 1923), 59 (XX.56); *Gwaith Lewys Glyn Cothi*, ed. D. Johnston (Caerdydd 1995), 204 (89.1). These poems were probably composed when William Fychan (or Vaughan) of Rhydhelyg was serving as deputy to Walter Devereux (d. 1485), constable of Aberystwyth from 1463 to 1483.

10. *Welsh Court Poems*, ed. Rh. M. Andrews (Cardiff 2007), 25 (19.1).

11. R. Avent, *Criccieth Castle, Pennarth Fawr Medieval Hall-house, St Cybi's Well* (Cardiff 1989), 7.

12. *Gwaith Iolo Goch*, ed. D. R. Johnston (Caerdydd 1988), 8 (II.76, 80–82); English translation: *Iolo Goch: Poems*, trans. D. Johnston (Llandysul 1993), 8 (2.76, 80–82). For discussions, see D. J. Bowen, 'Cywydd Iolo Goch i Syr Hywel y Fwyall', *Llên Cymru*, 15 (1984–88), 275–88; D. Johnston, 'Iolo Goch and the English: Welsh poetry and politics in the fourteenth century', *Cambridge Medieval Celtic Studies*, 12 (1986), 86–87; A. C. Lake, 'Breuddwyd Iolo Goch', in *Ysgrifau Beirniadol XV*, ed. J. E. C. Williams (Dinbych 1988), 109–20.

13. A. D. Carr, *Medieval Anglesey* (Llangefni 1982), 56–57.

14. R. R. Davies, *The Revolt of Owain Glyn Dŵr* (Oxford 1995), 147.

15. *Gwaith Lewys Môn*, ed. E. I. Rowlands (Caerdydd 1975), 254 (LXXI.54, 59); *Gwaith Mathau Brwmffild*, ed. A. C. Lake (Aberystwyth 2002), 30 (6.6); *Gwaith Rhys Goch Eryri*, ed. D. Foster Evans (Aberystwyth 2007), 49 (2.3–4).

16. Quoted in E. P. Roberts ed., *Gwaith Siôn Tudur*, 2 (Caerdydd 1980), 216.

17. D. C. Jones, 'The Bulkeleys of Beaumaris, 1440–1547', *Transactions of the Anglesey Antiquarian Society and Field Club*, (1961), 1–7.

18. *Gwaith Lewys Môn*, 4 (I.53–62). Italicized word or phrases in quotations are the editor's emendations.

19. *Detholiad o Gywyddau Gofyn a Diolch*, ed. B. O. Huws (s. l. 1998), 69 (18.7, 8, 6).

20. *Gwaith Siôn Ceri*, ed. A. C. Lake (Aberystwyth 1996), 52 (13.6); D. J. Bowen, 'Tŵr Adam', *Llên Cymru*, 17 (1992–93), 142–43.

21. *Gwaith Madog Benfras ynghyd â Gwaith Eraill o Feirdd y Bedwaredd Ganrif ar Ddeg*, ed. B. J. Lewis (Aberystwyth 2007), 243–44 (15.25–38). For identification of the Welsh and English names of the towers, see 256.

22. *Gwaith Guto'r Glyn*, eds I. Williams and J. Ll. Williams, 2nd edn (Caerdydd 1961), 49 (XVIII.1–22). The poet plays on the names of the English king and the Welsh *paterfamilias*, both of which are 'Edwart' in Welsh.

23. Johnston, *Gwaith Lewys Glyn Cothi*, 394 (179.43–46) .

24. *Gwaith Tudur Penllyn ac Ieuan ap Tudur Penllyn*, ed. T. Roberts (Caerdydd 1958), 26 (15.31–32, 34), 27 (16.6, 9, 17, 19, 22, 26), 28 (16.38, 47–48).

25. *Branwen uerch Lyr: the Second of the Four Branches of the Mabinogi*, ed. D. S. Thomson (Dublin 1961), 1; *Mabinogion*, trans. S. Davies (Oxford 2007), 22.

26. On Gwilym ap Gruffudd, see Davies, *Revolt*, 314–16.

27. *Gwaith Rhys Goch Eryri*, 49 (2.6), 50–51 (2.69–78).

28. *Gwaith Ieuan Brydydd Hir*, ed. M. P. Bryant-Quinn (Aberystwyth 2000), 35 (4.35–42). The '[C]aer' mentioned here is probably Caernarfon, although it could perhaps be Chester.

29. *Gwaith Dafydd Llwyd o Fathafarn*, ed. W. L. Richards (Caerdydd 1964), 92 (38.16, 23–24).

30. *Gwaith Deio ab Ieuan Du a Gwilym ab Ieuan Hen*, ed. A. E. Davies (Caerdydd 1992), 102 (XVI.64). The poem is also attributed to Ieuan Tew Brydydd of Cydweli.

31. *Gwaith Guto'r Glyn*, 129–31 (XLVIII); translated in R. Loomis et al., *Medieval Welsh Poems: an Anthology* (Binghampton, NY 1992), 165–68 (89).

32. Quoted in E. D. Jones, *Beirdd y Bymthegfed Ganrif a'u Cefndir* (Aberystwyth 1984), 31. The poem is edited in full in W. G. Lewis, 'Astudiaeth o Ganu'r Beirdd i'r Herbertiaid hyd Ddechrau'r Unfed Ganrif ar Bymtheg' (unpublished PhD thesis, University of Wales [Bangor], 1982), 1, 165–68 (89).

33. William Worcester, *Itineraries*, ed. J. H. Harvey (Oxford 1969), 204.

34. *Gwaith Huw Cae Llwyd ac Eraill*, ed. L. Harries (Caerdydd 1953), 99 (XXXIX.13–20).

35. The Welsh reponse to gunpowder is discussed in detail in D. Foster Evans, '"Y carl a'i trawai o'r cudd": ergyd y gwn ar y Cywyddwyr', *Dwned*, 4 (1998), 75–105; idem, 'Gwlad y Gwn? Cymru, y canon a'r dryll', in *Cof Cenedl XVII*, ed. G. H. Jenkins (Llandysul 2003), 1–32.

36. Beaumaris is occasionally mentioned, including two references in poems to Hugh Bulkeley: *Gwaith Lewys Môn*, 3 (I.17; in the dialect form 'Duwmares') and *Gwaith Guto'r Glyn*, 253 (XCVII.14). The earliest known reference comes from an anonymous fourteenth-century satirical poem, see *Gwaith Prydydd Breuan, Rhys ap Dafydd ab Einion, Hywel Ystorm, a Cherddi Dychan Dienw o Lyfr Coch Hergest*, ed. H. M. Edwards (Aberystwyth 2000), 91 (7.27).

37. I. Llwyd et al*., Syched am Sycharth* (Llanrwst 2001), 58.

38. For a recent contribution to castle studies that emphasizes the cultural and symbolic roles of castles, see R. Liddiard, *Castles in Context: Power, Symbolism and Landscape, 1066 to 1500* (Macclesfield 2005).

39. *Gwaith Syr Dafydd Trefor*, ed. Rh. Ifans (Aberystwyth 2005), 84 (16.17–22). The statue in Caernarfon is of Edward II, and it seems that 'Sir' Dafydd credited him with building the castle. But equally, he may have thought that the statue was actually of Edward I.

Caernarfon Castle and its Mythology

Abigail Wheatley

Arnold Taylor's discussion of the building, design and symbolic significance of Caernarfon Castle has become the stuff of academic legend.[1] His article[2] combined acute architectural observation with ground-breaking documentary research and a keen awareness of political symbolism in a way that has captivated and inspired medievalists ever since. For many years it was cited as a unique example of imperial symbolism and/or literary resonances in castle architecture.[3] More recently, it has encouraged and guided many scholars, including myself, to look for similar symbolism and resonance in other castles.[4] This research has borne fruit, and a number of other castles, including the Tower of London[5] and Dover Castle,[6] can now be linked in similar ways to imperial and local legends. Taylor's analysis of Caernarfon Castle has, therefore, lost its uniqueness. Indeed, many of the phenomena he notes at Caernarfon are now known to have close parallels in other medieval castles.

While this additional evidence reinforces many of Taylor's arguments, and pays tribute to his pioneering approach, it also draws attention to certain elements of Taylor's work that are ripe for reassessment. This paper therefore seeks to amend a few of Taylor's details and to adjust some of his conclusions. Nevertheless, it remains very much indebted to, and supportive of, Taylor's work – both its spirit and its substance.

Taylor started his analysis of Caernarfon Castle by noting that Edward I sited it in the ancient centre of Gwynedd and close to the remains of the Roman fort of Segontium. He also highlighted the polygonal towers, instead of the more usual round towers, and the decorative treatment given to the curtain walls with the use of colour-banded stonework, achieved by the alternation of dark and light stone courses. Further, he remarked that the castle was built on and around a Norman motte; also that in the year the new castle was begun, the remains of a body were found on the site of Segontium and re-buried in the nearby church.[7]

Taylor noted that Segontium was linked to the Roman emperor, Constantine, in the influential ninth-century Latin text *Historia Britonum* (usually attributed to the Welsh author, Nennius)[8] and in later Welsh sources such as *Hanes Gruffydd ap Cynan*.[9] Taylor concluded that the incorporation of the Norman motte into the new castle was a material expression of continuity with the area's past, acknowledging the powerful symbolism of the ruins. He also cited documentary evidence to demonstrate that Edward I believed the body that had been discovered was that of the rebellious Roman general turned emperor, Magnus Maximus, who, in some medieval accounts, is identified as the father of Constantine the Great.[10] These imperial resonances were confirmed for Taylor by the medieval Welsh text *Breudwyt Maxen Wledic* (*The Dream of the Emperor Maxen*), part of the cycle of the *Mabinogi*, or *Mabinogion*, as the collection of works is usually called. Magnus Maximus appears in this text as the emperor, Maxen, who has a dream in which he sees a castle housing a beautiful maiden. Maxen believes the vision is real and sends out messengers to find the castle; they duly discover the castle of Aber Sein, situated at Arfon in Wales. Maxen marries Elen, the beautiful daughter of the castle's lord, and settles down to rule from Wales until he is called back to Rome to defend his title as emperor.[11]

From this accumulation of textual references and associations, Taylor was able to argue that the form and location of Caernarfon Castle, in Arfon at the mouth of the river Seiont, were chosen to make these legends into reality. He saw Caernarfon as a physical representation of the castle described in *Breudwyt Maxen Wledic*, situated at the mouth of a river and recreating the huge multi-coloured towers mentioned in the text.[12] Edward I's purpose in doing this, Taylor thought, was to appropriate the illustrious history that the Welsh associated with these local legends: to make himself a ruler of Wales in accordance with its own imperial mythography.

Taylor also saw the polygonal towers and polychrome

Figure 13.1: Caernarfon Castle from the south-west; Eagle Tower to the left (Cadw, Welsh Assembly Government: Crown Copyright).

stonework of Caernarfon (Fig. 13.1, Plate 13) as a complementary piece of imperial imagery: as a deliberate evocation of Constantinople, the city most famously associated with Constantine, the emperor whose name it bears and under whose rule it was the capital of the Roman empire.[13] Taylor supplied a striking visual comparison between Caernarfon Castle and the outer Theodosian land wall at Constantinople.[14] The statues of imperial eagles on the battlements of the Eagle Tower at Caernarfon (Fig. 13.2) were for Taylor further confirmation of this imperial imagery.[15] Caernarfon Castle, then, was an inspired invocation of all these imperial resonances and part of Edward's effort to transform himself into a new Constantine. For Taylor, the castle and town at Caernarfon were set up as another Constantinople: the Welsh capital of the king's new empire.

It is not surprising that this powerful account of Caernarfon Castle's imperial symbolism has proved so persuasive. However, on closer consideration, I believe that Taylor's very strong emphasis on Constantinople in Caernarfon's imperial imagery needs to be re-examined. Furthermore, his interpretation of the Welsh texts referring to Caernarfon may also need some revision.

To take the first point, Taylor's visual comparison between Caernarfon and the Theodosian land wall at Constantinople is very striking. However, careful inspection reveals that only one polygonal tower is shown in the foreground of Taylor's chosen shot of the wall: all the rest are orthogonal. In fact, unlike Caernarfon Castle, polygonal towers are in the minority along the Theodosian wall: most of its mural towers are orthogonal.[16] In short, although the polygonal towers are a striking feature of the walls of Constantinople, they are not as representative of them as Taylor perhaps implied.

This would not matter so much if it could be shown that there was a wide appreciation in medieval Britain, either by word of mouth or through literary or artistic sources, that the walls of Constantinople had polychrome-banded walls featuring polygonal towers. But Taylor comes up with only one figure associated with the court of Edward I who might have visited Constantinople,[17] and I have not been able to add to this. Furthermore, neither Taylor nor I could find any descriptions of Constantinople in crusading literature or art that feature either coloured banding or polygonal towers. It is dangerous to draw firm conclusions from absence of evidence, but clearly polychromy and polygonal towers do not seem to have been regarded as defining features of Constantinople by those who saw the city walls in the Middle Ages. So it seems likely that the vast majority of medieval visitors to Caernarfon cannot have appreciated any connection between the Welsh castle and the imperial city. The considerable expense of creating polychrome banding and the extra effort of introducing a strikingly new and distinctive shape for the towers, not seen in any of the other Edwardian castles in Wales, does not seem justified if it was intended to invite this particular comparison.

It is, however, possible that Caernarfon's distinctive appearance was created with reference to Roman architecture surviving closer to hand, in Britain. The banded appearance of the Theodosian land wall is formed by the standard Roman construction technique of 'tile-lacing', that is, building with alternate courses of masonry and Roman tiles.[18] The polychrome banding at Caernarfon is made up of cut stone of contrasting colours. Wide bands of pale sandstone alternate with thinner courses of red sandstone, which, as Taylor noted, does resemble tile-lacing, albeit on a giant scale. When the stone at Caernarfon was freshly cut, the resemblance must have been even more striking. However, Taylor did not draw attention to the fact that there are plenty of tile-laced Roman structures still standing in Britain. Interestingly, in *Historia Britonum*, just before the reference to the tomb of Constantine at Cair Segeint, the whole island of Britain is defined by its 'innumerable forts built of stone and tile'[19] – a reference perhaps to the prominent Roman remains visible throughout the land. No doubt British visitors to Caernarfon would have been reminded more forcefully of these local tile-laced Roman remains rather than those in far-off Constantinople, which most – or perhaps all of them – would never have seen.

Furthermore, in several British contexts, Roman tile-laced structures are closely associated with medieval castles that feature polychrome-banded stonework not identical to, but also not too dissimilar from that at Caernarfon. Therefore, although Taylor's statement that 'there were no English precedents'[20] for ashlar polychromy of the kind seen at Caernarfon was technically correct, there are in fact several British precedents for polychrome castle masonry, and these are often closely associated with banded Roman remains (Figs 13.3–13.6). With such strong British architectural precedents there seems little need to invoke the remote example of Constantinople. I will return later to these precedents in more detail.

Taylor's explanations for the imperial resonances at Caernarfon using local literary sources also require some reappraisal. Literary scholars have agreed that Taylor was quite right to regard Edward I's castle as an attempt to appropriate the local Welsh legends associated with the site.[21] However, it seems that Taylor, so deft at handling other types of medieval documents, perhaps underestimated the complexity of the literary sources he cited. For example, in *Historia Britonum*, the tomb of Constantine at Cair Segeint is specified as belonging not to Constantine the Great, as Taylor implied, but to his son.[22] The connection Taylor established between

Figure 13.2: Eagle Tower, Caernarfon Castle, from the south, showing detail of banded masonry (Abigail Wheatley).

Caernarfon and Constantine certainly existed, but was not as straightforward as perhaps he implied.

The way Taylor cited other sources suggests that he may not have been aware of the ease with which they could confuse and conflate different Roman or British characters with similar names (such as Constantius, Constans and Constantine, Maxentius and Maximianus, and Helena and Elen). In some of the Welsh sources, the princess whom Magnus Maximus marries becomes St Helena, finder of the True Cross and mother of Constantine the Great.[23] It is this version of the relationships on which Taylor's arguments relied, but the sources he cited do not always support it. Taylor cited the Latin chronicle, *Flores Historiarum*, to show that Edward I had found what he believed to be the body of Magnus Maximus.[24] However, the text need not be read in this way. Taylor implied that the phrase '*corpus maximi principis, patris imperatoris nobilis*

Constantini' should be translated as 'the body of Magnus Maximus, father of the noble emperor Constantine'. There is, however, no capitalization in the printed edition from which he took his extract; it seems that Taylor capitalized the initial letter of '*maximi*' to support his reading. A translation could instead read: 'the body of a great chief, father of the noble emperor Constantine'. There is thus no direct evidence to demonstrate that Edward I was aware of the connection between Segontium/Caernarfon and Magnus Maximus, though this passage does still show that Edward was aware of the site's imperial connections.

Of course, Taylor also cited the Welsh poem *Breudwyt Maxen Wledic*. This certainly does show that Segontium/Caernarfon was connected with Magnus Maximus in Welsh sources. However, Taylor seems to have misinterpreted the text a little. He made a specific connection between the polychrome-banded towers described in the poem and the appearance of the new castle at Caernarfon.[25] In fact, the huge, multi-coloured towers described in the poem belong to a city that Maxen 'sees' in his dream on the coast of mainland Europe, before he crosses the sea to Britain:

> *A pha hyt bennac y kerdei y velly ef a deuei y aber prif avon vuyhaf a welsei nep a phrif dinas a welei en aber er avon a phrifgaer yng kylch e dinas a phrif dyroed amyl amliwyauc a welei ar e gaer.*[26]

(After travelling in this way for a long time, he came to the mouth of a great river, the widest that anyone had seen, and he could see a great city at the mouth of the river, and a great wall around the city with many great towers of different colours.)[27]

The Welsh fortress Maxen 'sees', situated at the mouth of a river just below Mount Snowdon, has no multi-coloured towers:

> *Ac o'r menyd hwnnw avon a welei en redec ar draus a wlat en kyrchu e mor, ac en aber er avon ef a welei prifgaer decaf o'r a welsei den eryoet a phorth e gaer a welei en agoret ac e'r gaer y deuei.*[28]

From that mountain he saw a river crossing the land, making for the sea, and at the mouth of the river he saw a great castle, the fairest that anyone had ever seen, and he saw the castle gate was open, and he came into the castle.[29]

Recent work suggests that it was a third fortress, built at Arfon by Maxen for Elen as part of her maiden fee, that Caernarfon Castle may be intended to replicate.[30] This is described briefly at the end of the poem:

> *Hitheu a'e nodes val hynn: Enys Brydein a nodes y'u that o Vor Vd hyt Vor Ywerdon a'r teir rac enys a'e dale a dan amperauder Ruvein, a gwneithur teir prif gaer idi hitheu*

en e tri lle a dewissei en enys Brydein. Ac ena e dewissaud wneithur e gaer uchaf en Arvon idi[31]

He asked her to name her maiden fee. She listed thus: the Island of Britain for her father, from the North Sea to the Irish Sea, and the Three Adjacent Islands to be held under the empress of Rome; and three major forts to be built for her in three locations of her choice in the island of Britain. Then she asked that the prime fort be built for her in Arfon.[32]

Quite apart from the fact that Taylor seems to have conflated different passages of the poem, he also failed to note that *Breudwyt Maxen Wledic*, along with the other branches of the *Mabinogi*, was only written down in the fourteenth century.[33] Before that it was in circulation as an oral text, but it is not safe to assume that specific details, such as the particular terms of a description, were fixed in the exact form in which we now know them. So, although Edward I may well have encountered an oral version of *Breudwyt Maxen Wledic* in the thirteenth century, concrete links cannot be made between Caernarfon Castle and the poem in its present form.

Again, this negates the specific links that Taylor makes between the castle and the poem, but confirms a strong connection of a slightly different kind. *Breudwyt Maxen Wledic* can now be seen, not just as a local legend connected to Caernarfon Castle, but as a foundation legend for it: initially for the Norman castle and later deliberately renewed by Edward I's castle. From this perspective, the distinctive appearance of Edward's castle can be seen as a reconstruction of the fortresses built by the Romans in Britain, and specifically the fortress supposed to have been built by Maxen and Elen at Caernarfon.

From the first, Magnus Maximus – the Roman general who rebelled and was declared emperor, and ruled in Britain, Gaul, Spain and Italy, defeating various imperial rivals in the process – has held a special place in Welsh history.[34] Early accounts, including that of *Historia Britonum*, style him a tyrant and provide distinctly negative accounts of his role,[35] but by the time *Breudwyt Maxen Wledic* was composed, he was widely regarded in a favourable light as the last of the Roman emperors to rule from Britain,[36] in effect, the Welsh emperor. This role has been compared with that of King Arthur,[37] because like Arthur, Magnus Maximus led British troops to defeat the Romans in Italy. This allowed the Welsh to show that they had a local hero who had defeated the Romans.[38] Magnus Maximus was, therefore, a significant political figure and to appropriate his associations might have been an attractive prospect to Edward I. However, as the links between Caernarfon Castle and its imperial imagery are not as straightforward as they once seemed, it may be instructive to see how

Figure 13.4: Dover Castle keep from the north-west (David Robinson).

Figure 13.3: Roman pharos *at Dover Castle from the south-east, showing tile-laced construction (Copyright: English Heritage Photo Library).*

imperial foundation legends of this type were understood and invoked at other British castles.

As mentioned earlier, there are several other castle sites across Britain where Roman remains sit in close proximity to medieval polychrome masonry associated with imperial foundation legends. The circumstances are strikingly similar to those at Caernarfon. At Dover Castle, a tile-laced Roman *pharos* or lighthouse sits within the medieval castle walls, close to the massive twelfth-century keep, three sides of which are decorated with wide, alternating bands of light Caen stone and dark Kentish ragstone (Figs 13.3 and 13.4). Several medieval sources link Dover with Julius Caesar, and some go as far as to suggest that the castle was actually founded by him.[39]

The eleventh-century keep of Colchester Castle, on the other hand, is built directly on the tile-laced plinth of a Roman temple. The castle contains reused Roman materials, including tiles,[40] some of which are laid in neat bands (Fig. 13.5).[41] For Colchester, the links with Constantine the Great are through the mythical King Cole. In local legends, he was the builder of Colchester Castle and the father of St Helena, who, as we have seen,

is supposed to have found the True Cross and was believed to be the mother of Constantine.[42]

London's Roman tile-laced wall still stands to some height just outside the walls of the Tower of London (Fig. 13.6), and its banding may have been echoed by a water gate built around 1240. Recent excavations in the Tower moat suggest that the gate was faced with alternating courses of greeny-grey Purbeck marble and creamy Reigate stone.[43] Various medieval histories and chronicles suggest that the Tower of London was founded by Julius Caesar, or by Brutus, the legendary Trojan founder of Britain.[44]

At several important royal castles, medieval banded masonry is associated both with Roman remains and imperial foundation legends. There has been much discussion of the significance, or otherwise, of the reuse of Roman sites and materials in medieval contexts such as these and there now seems to be general agreement that convenience was one factor in their reuse. However, it is also possible to infer an intention to express the idea of *translatio imperii* or the transfer of empire, especially where a decorative finish was created with the reused material.[45] In cases like Dover, Colchester, London and Caernarfon, where literary evidence confirms a medieval awareness of imperial associations, the case for meaningful reuse becomes even stronger.[46]

Taylor did consider this possibility: he noted the

Figure 13.5: Colchester Castle keep from the south-east (Abigail Wheatley).

proximity of the Roman remains to Edward's castle and he also pointed out that a Norman motte had been incorporated into the new castle. This he interpreted as an attempt by Edward to assimilate the powerful associations of these older sites into his castle. There is also some suggestion that the Roman ruins of Segontium were robbed for use in Edward's castle.[47] So perhaps at Caernarfon, as at Colchester, actual reuse of Roman material was underlined by the use of banded masonry designed to recall the look of Roman tile-laced walls.

The distinctive polygonal towers of Caernarfon Castle can be seen in a similar light – as evoking ideas of *Romanitas* by alluding to Roman architectural forms. Although polygonal Roman towers are not as common in Britain as orthogonal or rounded ones, there are some still standing to this day.[48] The tile-laced Roman *pharos* at Dover, for example (Fig. 13.3), is hexagonal in plan and would certainly have been familiar to Edward, who knew Dover Castle well, not least from his imprisonment there during the Barons' War.[49] It may well have been this distinctive Roman-looking tower that led to medieval claims that Dover Castle had been founded by Julius

Caesar. These first appeared in the Anglo-Norman Chronicle written for Edward's daughter, Mary, by Nicolas Trivet, a Dominican friar, familiar at the king's court.[50] The *pharos* originally tapered inwards towards the top in eight neat steps, but these have been eroded over the years.[51] As it now appears, at half its original height, there is only one obvious step, which is somewhat reminiscent of the stepped plinth or batter that skirts the exterior wall surfaces at Caernarfon Castle.

It is therefore possible to argue that the striking appearance of Caernarfon Castle was intended to recall distinctive features of Roman architecture familiar to British observers. Interestingly, neither polygonal towers nor tile-banding seem to have been present at Segontium Roman fort itself.[52] In its current state, only the perimeter walls are still standing.[53] It is not clear what was left of the internal structures by the Middle Ages,[54] so it may not have been obvious to medieval observers exactly which Roman architectural features were present. More importantly, if the intention was to reproduce characteristic Roman architectural features, it may have been more important to choose features widely connected

Figure 13.6: London's Roman city wall at Tower Hill, showing tile-laced construction (Abigail Wheatley).

with Roman architecture, such as tile-banding, rather than match the remains at Segontium exactly.

The denuded state of Segontium Roman fort today might lead modern observers to doubt the strength of its impact on their medieval counterparts. It was, however, the largest of the Roman forts of its period in Wales, and its strategic location and size both suggest that the most prestigious Roman unit in Wales was located there.[55] This importance was reflected by the way the site was consistently featured in medieval texts, such as *Historia Britonum* and *Breudwyt Maxen Wledic,* as one of the most important forts in Wales.[56] Finds from the site probably played a part in this, too. Even when it was excavated in the 1970s, Segontium contained a huge number of Roman coins,[57] and it seems likely that coins and other Roman remains turned up regularly at the site during the Middle Ages. This not only provided material evidence of a Roman presence, but also some of the important imperial names that were associated with the fort in legendary histories.[58] Therefore, although the textual sources cited by Taylor were perhaps not quite as conclusive as he suggested, there are strong reasons for arguing that the banded castle at

Caernarfon was intended to refer to the nearby Roman remains and to appropriate their associations of past imperial grandeur.

In the medieval imagination, however, Roman remains not only inspired associations with the Roman past but also with King Arthur, especially in Wales. The Roman ruins at Caerleon inspired Geoffrey of Monmouth to reconstruct the glorious Arthurian city of Caerleon on Usk in his highly influential twelfth-century text *Historia regum Britannie*.[59] In this account, Arthur graces the city with his Whitsuntide crown-wearing ceremony and celebratory jousting.[60] It is perhaps no surprise that Segontium/Caernarfon, with its important Roman remains, also turns up regularly in medieval Arthurian literature.

We can only guess what Arnold Taylor would have made of this association. The great Arthurian scholar, R. S. Loomis, put forward his theory in a paper dated 1947, almost two decades before Taylor's famous article appeared, but there is no indication that Taylor was aware of this work. Loomis cited evidence to show that, from the early medieval period onwards, the whole area around Caernarfon – and more specifically the ruins of Segontium – were referred to by a variety of names cognate with 'Snowdon' (spelled in various different sources Sinadon, Snauedun, Isneldone, etc.). The names were used to describe a legendary ruined city, which appeared in various Anglo-Norman and Middle English Arthurian romances as a site of jousting, enchantment and intrigue.[61] Although this literary tradition began as early as the twelfth century, perhaps the most striking instance occurs in the fourteenth-century Middle English romance *Lybeaus Desconus*, named after its hero, the 'fair unknown' knight. Lybeaus and his companions encounter the enigmatic city after a hard ride:

> They rodyn ffaste as they maye
> Forthe on her jornaye
> On stedis baye and browne;
> Till on the third daye
> They saue a cite gaye:
> Men clepen hit Synadowne,
> With castelles high and wide
> And palysed proude in pryde,
> Worke of fayre ffacion [62]

Here Lybeaus jousts with a formidable adversary, enters a magnificent but deserted hall, which threatens to collapse about his ears, and meets a dragon with a woman's head who emerges eerily from a ruined wall. He allows the dragon to kiss him and, thus released from an evil enchantment, the dragon turns back into the lady of Synadowne, who marries the hero in gratitude to the general rejoicing of the city's population.

This kind of thrilling Arthurian romance, with its magic and monsters, seems a far cry from the dreamlike clarity of the historically inspired *Breudwyt Maxen Wledic*, yet both poems share a common ancestry. Their association with the site of Segontium/Caernarfon can be ascribed ultimately to the presence of the Roman remains there. Yet, strangely, although the connections between Caernarfon Castle and imperial heroes such as Constantine and Magnus Maximus are now widely cited, the castle's possible Arthurian overtones are rarely discussed (the notable exception is Richard Morris, whose paper of 1998 provides comprehensive coverage).[63] Even Loomis, a great believer in Edward I as an Arthurian enthusiast,[64] saw the probable use of material from Segontium in building Caernarfon Castle not as an attempt to establish continuity between the two sites, but as a robbing and diminution of the fort's legendary significance. For him, 'the magic departed' with the arrival of Edward's new castle.[65]

Yet, in a Welsh context, King Arthur was just as important a political and indeed imperial figure as Magnus Maximus. It fact, the parallels are so close that it has been suggested that the figure of King Arthur was originally based upon the literary figure of Magnus Maximus.[66] Like Maximus before him, it was Arthur who allowed the Welsh (also sometimes more generally the British) to show that they had measured up to and defeated the Romans. In Geoffrey of Monmouth's *Historia Regum Britannie*, it was Arthur who refused to pay the tribute demanded by the Romans since Caesar's conquest of Britain; he even declared war on them for these demands. He took his own troops to the Continent and was only prevented from conquering Rome by treachery at home.[67] Arthur was therefore a strongly imperial figure in his own right and it is no coincidence that stories of the legendary king cluster around British sites with impressive Roman remains and in some cases were directly inspired by them.

As I have noted, Geoffrey of Monmouth's seminal account of King Arthur and his court was inspired by the Roman remains at the important Welsh site of Caerleon.[68] It was there that Geoffrey set the significant scene where Arthur receives the Roman ambassadors demanding tribute and then rejects them.[69] King Arthur is also associated with many other Roman sites in Britain, not least those that boast later castles. Through this process many medieval castles acquired dual imperial connections: both Roman foundation myths and strong Arthurian legends. Dover Castle and the Tower of London are, once again, prime examples.

From the late twelfth to the early thirteenth centuries onwards, the Tower of London appears in French and then Middle English Arthurian romances as the site of a climactic siege leading to the tragic destruction of the Round Table.[70] While Arthur is engaged abroad, Guenevere is threatened with a forced marriage to Arthur's illegitimate and treacherous son, Mordred. The queen takes refuge in the Tower of London, which she garrisons and stocks with provisions, and manages to hold out against Mordred's siege. Arthur is then called back to Britain to defend his wife, and, in some Middle English versions, lands at Dover where he confronts Mordred in a decisive battle, during which Sir Gawain is mortally wounded.[71] Malory provides the final detail in his fifteenth-century *Morte D'Arthur*, noting that Gawain was buried in a chapel within Dover Castle, adding that 'there yet all men may se the skulle of hym'.[72] At both these great royal castles, Arthurian legends joined imperial foundation legends, both of which seem to have been inspired ultimately by the adjacent Roman remains.

The Arthurian scenes set at Dover Castle and the Tower of London name the castles specifically, thus linking the medieval castles to the ancient Arthurian past. However, the Arthurian material connected to Caernarfon works somewhat differently because there the heroes encounter ancient ruins and not the medieval castle. As Loomis points out, Arthurian scenes set amongst the ruins at Segontium/Caernarfon begin as early as the twelfth century and thus pre-date Edward I's castle considerably. This being the case, it is possible that the castle was built in the knowledge of the site's previous Arthurian associations.

Once again, evidence that Edward I knew of any Arthurian associations with Segontium or Caernarfon is far from explicit. The fact that he celebrated his conquest of Wales by holding a Round Table tournament only a few miles down the coast at Nefyn in 1284 is certainly suggestive.[73] It is not clear exactly what happened at events styled as Round Tables at this period, nor whether they carried overtly Arthurian connotations.[74] However, as Richard Morris points out, research by Martin Biddle and colleagues on the Winchester Round Table concluded that it may well have been built on the orders of Edward I to feature in a tournament he arranged at Winchester in 1290.[75] Appropriately enough, it was none other than Arnold Taylor who uncovered the documentary evidence for this previously unknown tournament: the volume published by Biddle and colleagues is dedicated to Taylor. It therefore now seems likely that Edward's other Round Table military games, such as the one at Nefyn, may also have featured explicitly Arthurian props and ceremonies. It is also certain that Edward was deeply involved with the legend of Arthur when he participated in the ceremonial reburial of the supposed remains of the king and Queen Guenevere at Glastonbury in 1287.[76] Perhaps it is no coincidence that this echoed Edward's reburial of the supposed father of Constantine the Great, at Caernarfon four years earlier.[77] On balance, it is certainly possible that Edward knew of the Arthurian associations with Segontium/Caernarfon and capitalized on them when he began his castle there.

If, as argued above, the coloured banding at Caernarfon should be understood as a reference to Roman masonry in general, and specifically as an announcement of symbolic continuity with Segontium, it could be seen as proclaiming dual imperial overtones – both Roman and Arthurian. Yet, although the sites of Segontium and Caernarfon had strong imperial and Arthurian associations at the time Edward I was building his castle, there is no explicit evidence that he intended either of these legendary

connections to be expressed in his distinctive castle. Although we know from the *Flores Historiarum* that he was aware of local imperial legends near Caernarfon,[78] there is nothing more conclusive about the appearance of Caernarfon Castle to be found in the records.

Evidence from the *Flores Historiarum* does, however, suggest that Edward I employed this combination of local imperial and Arthurian symbolism during his Welsh manoeuvrings to absorb Wales and its legendary past. In 1283, the year that Edward established Caernarfon Castle (and also the year in which the discovery and reburial of the supposed imperial body took place nearby), he received what was believed to be the Crown of Arthur from the Welsh and thus, as the chronicler put it, 'the glory of the Welsh was transferred to the English'.[79] In the same year, Edward also brought from Wales the Croes Naid, a supposed piece of the True Cross.[80] It was one of the most precious relics of the Welsh, and although little is known about it, it seems reasonable to make the connection with the Welsh legends of St Helena, who is believed to have found the True Cross and said to be the wife of Magnus Maximus and the mother of Constantine the Great. These two relics symbolized Edward's sovereignty over Wales[81] and allowed him to appropriate Arthur and Magnus Maximus, the two figures who more than any others stood for Wales's independence as a nation – and who were both strongly associated with Segontium/Caernarfon.

Perhaps it was exactly this combination of legendary references – the imperial and the Arthurian – that the coloured banding on Caernarfon Castle was meant to invoke. It can no longer be stated with certainty that Edward I was aware of the full range of legendary figures connected to Caernarfon when he commissioned his new castle. However, as Taylor originally suggested, it does still seem plausible that Edward was aware of the legendary associations of the site and that these inspired the distinctive Roman appearance of the castle. Caernarfon, therefore, should no longer be seen as the pre-eminent example of imperial imagery in castle architecture. Instead, it should take its place alongside other outstanding examples, such as Dover Castle and the Tower of London, where it seems highly probable that imperial, and possibly Arthurian, associations were expressed through polychrome banding in the medieval stonework.

Notes

1. A substantial portion of this article first appeared in A. Wheatley, *The Idea of the Castle in Medieval England* (Woodbridge 2004). I would like to extend my grateful thanks to Richard Morris for sharing his ideas on Arthurian symbolism at Caernarfon with me, and to Dylan Foster Evans for helping me to prepare the Welsh quotations included in this paper. Any errors are, however, entirely my own.

2. A. J. Taylor, 'Caernarvon', in R. A. Brown, H. M. Colvin and A. J. Taylor, *The History of the King's Works*, I (London 1963), 369–95; later reissued with minor revisions in A. J. Taylor, *The Welsh Castles of Edward I* (London 1986), 77–103.

3. See, for example, P. Binksi, *Westminster Abbey and the Plantagenets: Kingship and the Representation of Power, 1200–1400* (London 1995), 105, 139–40; M. Prestwich, *Edward I* (London 1988), 120, 211–14; P. Draper, 'The architectural setting of Gothic art', in *Age of Chivalry: Art and Society in Late Medieval England*, ed. N. Saul (London 1992), 60–75: 60, 62; R. K. Morris, 'The architecture of Arthurian enthusiasm: castle symbolism in the reigns of Edward I and his successors', in *Armies, Chivalry and Warfare in Medieval Britain*, ed. M. Strickland, Proceedings of the 1995 Harlaxton Symposium (Stamford 1998), 63–81: 65.

4. See, for example, T. A. Heslop, 'Orford Castle, nostalgia and sophisticated living', *Architectural History*, 34 (1991), 36–58; Morris, 'The architecture of Arthurian enthusiasm'; see also notes 5–6 below.

5. A. Wheatley, *The Idea of the Castle*, 34, 49–52, 57–8, 60, 69–71, 73–4, 76, 136–43; see also A. Wheatley, 'The White Tower in medieval myth and legend', in ed. E. Impey, *The White Tower* (London 2008), 277–88.

6. A. Wheatley, 'King Arthur lives in merry Carleile', in *Carlisle and Cumbria: Roman and Medieval Architecture, Art and Archaeology*, eds M. McCarthy and D. Weston, British Archaeological Association Conference Transactions 27 (Leeds 2004), 63–72: 67–70; Wheatley, *The Idea of the Castle*, 133–37, 142–44.

7. Taylor, 'Caernarvon', 369–70.

8. ibid., 369, n. 5 and 370, n. 2.

9. ibid., 369, n. 5.

10. ibid., 370, n. 2.

11. ibid., 370; see *Breudwyt Maxen Wledic*, ed. B. F. Roberts (Dublin 2005).

12. Taylor, 'Caernarvon', 370; the relevant extracts are quoted and discussed.

13. In what follows I will retain Taylor's description of the city by its earlier name of Constantinople (rather than Istanbul) as this expresses the connection with its founder, the emperor Constantine the Great, most succinctly.

14. Taylor, 'Caernarvon', pl. 15.

15. Taylor, 'Caernarvon', 371, and n. 1 on the same page.

16. See the plans in B. Meyer-Plath and A. M. Schneider, *Die Landmauer von Konstantinopel* (Berlin 1943); and more recent plans and photographs in M. Ahunbay and Z. Ahunbay, 'Recent work on the land walls of Istanbul: Tower 2 to Tower 5', in *Dumbarton Oaks Papers*, 54 (2000), 227–39.

17. Taylor came up with only one figure associated with the court of Edward I who might have visited Constantinople; moreover, Taylor himself admits that the famous medieval description of the walls of Constantinople by Villehardouin could not have spread knowledge of the appearance of the walls as it mentions neither polychromy nor polygonal towers, the features essential to Taylor's comparison of the two structures: Taylor, 'Caernarvon', 370 and n. 4 on the same page; see Geoffroy de Villehardouin, *Les Classiques de l'Histoire de France au Moyen Age: Villehardouin: La Conquête de Constantinople*, ed. E. Faral, II (Paris 1961), 32–35 for the brief and scanty description of the walls of Constantinople.

18. M. Greenhalgh, *The Survival of Roman Antiquities in the Middle Ages* (London 1989), 143; J. C. Higgitt, 'The Roman background to medieval England', *Journal of the British Archaeological Association*, 3 ser. 36 (1973), 1–15: 4.

19. '*In [Britannia] sunt viginti octo civitates et innumerabilia promuntoria cum innumeris castellis ex lapidibus et latere fabricatis*'. ('In [Britain] are twenty-eight cities and headlands without number, together with innumerable forts built of stone and tile.') *Nennius: British History and The Welsh Annals*, ed. and trans. J. Morris (Chichester 1980), 59, 18. Morris translates '*latere*' as 'brick', but 'tile' is the rendering given in the Medieval Latin Dictionary: J. F. Niermeyer and C. van de Kieft, *Mediae Latinitatis Lexicon Minus*, I (Leiden and Boston 2002), 762.

20. Taylor, 'Caernarvon', 370.

21. For example, B. F. Roberts, the most recent editor of *Breudwyt Maxen Wledic*, cites Taylor's article: *Breudwyt Maxen Wledic*, lxviii.

22. '*Constantinus, Constantini magni filius…ibi moritur, et sepulchrum illius monstratur juxta urbem quae vocatur Cair Segeint, ut litterae, quae sunt in lapide tumuli, ostendunt. Et ipse seminavit tria semina, id est auri, argenti aerisque, in pavimento supradictae civitatis, ut nullus pauper in ea habitaret unquam, et vocature alio nomine Minmanton.*' ('Constantine, son of Constantine the Great…died [in Britain]. His tomb is to be seen by the city called Caer Seint [i.e. Segontium], as the letters on its stonework show. He sowed three seeds, of gold, of silver, and of bronze, on the pavement of that city, that no man should ever live there poor; its other name is Minmanton.'): *Nennius*, 24, 65.

23. See J. F. Matthews, 'Macsen, Maximus, and Constantine', *Welsh History Review*, 11 (1982–83), 431–48: 439.

24. '*Apud Kaernarvan, corpus maximi principis, patris imperatoris nobilis Constantini, erat inventum, et rege iubente in ecclesia honorifice collocatum*' ('At Caernarfon, the body of a great prince, father of the noble emperor Constantine, was found, and was placed honourably in the church, to the joy of the king'). *Flores Historiarum*, ed. H. R. Luard, III (Rolls Series XCV, London 1890, repr. 1965), 59.

25. Taylor, 'Caernarvon', 370.

26. *Breudwyt Maxen Wledic*, 1–2, ll. 26–9.

27. *The Mabinogion*, trans. S. Davies (Oxford 2007), 103. This castle is described in both Maxen's dream sequence and in the journey of his emissaries as lying at the mouth of a river near the coast, but before the sea journey to Britain.

28. *Breudwyt Maxen Wledic*, 2, ll. 43–47.

29. *The Mabinogion*, 104.

30. *Breudwyt Maxen Wledic*, lxxviii–lxxx.

31. ibid., 8, ll. 225–29.

32. *The Mabinogion*, 108.

33. *The Arthur of the Welsh*, eds R. Bromwich, A.O.H. Jarman and B. F. Roberts (Cardiff 1991), 9.

34. Dumville identifies Maximus's importance in the work of Gildas, the sixth-century Welsh historian: D. N. Dumville, 'Sub-Roman Britain: history and legend', *History*, 62 (1977), 173–92: 180.

35. For example, see *Nennius*, 24–25, 65–66.

36. *Breudwyt Maxen Wledic*, lxiii–lxiv. See also Matthews, 'Macsen'; Dumville, 'Sub-Roman Britain', 180.

37. Dumville, 'Sub-Roman Britain', 181.

38. Maxen's role in this respect is widely discussed: see, for example, Dumville, 'Sub-Roman Britain'; D. N. Dumville, 'The historical value of the *Historia Britonum*', *Arthurian Literature* 6 (1986), 1–26; A. Gransden, *Historical Writing in England c. 550 to c. 1307* (London 1974), 10; Matthews, 'Macsen'.

39. '*Julius Cesar… en monstrance de la Conqueste faite sur la terre du Brutaine, q'ore est dit Engleterre, edifia le chastel de Dovre et de Caterburi et de Roncestre et de Loundres*' (Julius Caesar… in demonstration of the conquest made of the realm of Britain, as England was called, built the castle of Dover and of Canterbury and of Rochester and of London): Nicolas Trevet, 'The Anglo-

Norman Chronicle of Nicolas Trevet', ed. A. Rutherford (unpublished PhD thesis, University of London, 1932), pp.14, 52. *'Iulius Caesar fecit unam turrim in loco ubi nunc est castrum Doverr' ad reponendum illuc thesaurum suum. Quae quidem Turris nunc stat ibidem in Castro Doverr' iuxta ecclesiam'* (Julius Caesar built a tower in the place where the castle of Dover now is, to place his treasury in. This very same tower now stands in Dover Castle next to the church): Anonymous, *Cronicon Sancti Martini de Dover*, London, British Library Ms. Cotton Vespasian b. IX, fol. 72. Discussed fully in Wheatley, *The Idea of the Castle*, 142–44.

40. See P. J. Drury, 'Aspects of the origin and development of Colchester Castle', *Archaeological Journal*, 139 (1983), 302–419.

41. D. F. Renn, 'The decoration of Guildford Castle keep', *Surrey Archaeological Collections*, 55 (1958), 4–6; Higgitt, 'The Roman background', 4.

42. G. Rosser, 'Myth, image and social process in the English medieval town', *Urban History*, 23.1 (1996), 5–25: 8; Wheatley, *The Idea of the Castle*, 39–42.

43. E. Impey, 'The western entrance to the Tower of London, 1240–41', *Transactions of the London and Middlesex Archaeological Society*, 48 (1997), 59–75; 69.

44. Wheatley, *The Idea of the Castle*, 57–59, 70–76; Wheatley, 'The White Tower'.

45. See Greenhalgh, *The Survival of Roman Antiquities*; D. Stocker, 'Rubbish recycled: a study of the re-use of stone in Lincolnshire', in *Stone: Quarrying and Building in England, AD 43–1525*, ed. D. Parsons, (Chichester 1990), 83–101; T. Eaton, *Plundering the Past: Roman Stonework in Medieval Britain* (Stroud 2000).

46. I have discussed this more fully in chapter 4 of *The Idea of the Castle*.

47. This is implied, though not discussed or substantiated, in R. E. M. Wheeler, *Segontium and the Roman Occupation of Wales*, Y Cymmrodor 33 (London 1923), 94.

48. A Roman tile-laced polygonal tower, known appropriately as the Multangular Tower, still stands in York just outside the King's Manor. The Roman walls of Caerwent also feature several polygonal towers.

49. M. Prestwich, *Edward I* (London 1988), 47.

50. See note 39.

51. J. Coad, *Dover Castle* (London 1997, repr. 2001), 2.

52. The fort had orthogonal gate towers: see P. J. Casey and J. L. Davies, *Excavations at Segontium (Caernarfon) Roman Fort, 1975–1979*, Council for British Archaeology Research Report 90 (York 1993), Fig 1.2. Tiles excavated on site seem to have been used only for roofs and floors, with some specialist box tiles used in bathhouse walls and only occasional use of tiles in wall-building, for example in a drain: ibid., 229–30.

53. ibid., 16–17.

54. ibid, 17.

55. ibid., 10.

56. See *Breudwyt Maxen Wledic*, 8, ll. 225–29, quoted above.

57. Casey and Davies, *Segontium*, 122–64.

58. Loomis accepted that the account of Cair Segeint in *Historia Britonum* (see note 22 above) was inspired by a nearby inscription mentioning the name of Constantine, and by Roman coins found at the fort: R. S. Loomis, 'From Segontium to Sinadon – the legends of a *cité gaste*', *Speculum*, 22 (1947), 522. Coins inscribed with the names of Constantine, Helena and Maximian

were found in the most recent excavations at the site: Casey and Davies, 142–52.

59. J. S. P. Tatlock, *The Legendary History of Britain* (Berkeley 1950), 69–70.

60. Geoffrey of Monmouth, *The Historia Regum Britannie of Geoffrey of Monmouth, I, Bern, Burgerbibliothek, MS. 568*, ed. N. Wright (Cambridge 1985), 109–12.

61. Loomis, 'From Segontium to Sinadon', 520–33: 527–30. Please note the similarity between the form 'Sinadon' and the name 'Minmanton' cited as an alternative name of Caer Segeint in the ninth-century text *Historia Britonum*, cited in note 22 above.

62. *Lybeaus Desconus*, ed. M. Mills, Early English Text Society 261 (London 1969), 167, ll. 1520–32.

63. A notable exception is Morris, 'The architecture of Arthurian enthusiasm'.

64. R. S. Loomis, 'Edward I, Arthurian enthusiast', *Speculum*, 28 (1953), 114–27.

65. Loomis, 'From Segontium to Sinadon', 531.

66. Dumville, 'Sub-Roman Britain', 181.

67. Geoffrey of Monmouth, *Historia*, 116–29.

68. Tatlock, *Legendary History*, 69–70.

69. Geoffrey of Monmouth, *Historia*, 112–16.

70. H. O. Sommer, *The Vulgate Version of the Arthurian Romances, Edited from Manuscripts in the British Museum*, 6 (New York, 1861–, repr. 1979), 326–28; 'Stanzaic Morte Arthur', in *King Arthur's Death: the Middle English Stanzaic Morte Arthur and Alliterative Morte Arthure*, ed. L. D. Benson (Exeter 1986), 83–84, ll. 2994–3001; T. Malory, *The Works of Sir Thomas Malory*, ed. E. Vinaver, 2nd edn, III (Oxford 1967), 1228 ff.

71. 'Stanzaic Morte Arthur', 85–87, ll. 3042–3129.

72. Malory, *Works*, III, 1232.

73. *'Militia Anglicana et multi nobiles transmarini…apud Neuyn in Snoudonia in choreis et hastiludis rotundam tabulam celebrarunt.'* ('The English forces and many foreign nobles celebrated a round table at Nefyn in Snowdonia with dancing and jousting.') *Flores Historiarum*, III, 62.

74. Prestwich, *Edward I*, 120–21.

75. M. Biddle, 'The making of the Round Table', in M. Biddle et al., *King Arthur's Round Table: an Archaeological Investigation* (Woodbridge 2000), 337–92.

76. Prestwich, *Edward I*, 120.

77. See above and note 24.

78. See previous note.

79. *'Corona quondam famosi regis Britonum Arthuri regi Angliae cum aliis jocalibus reddebatur. Sic ad Anglicos gloria Walliensium… per Dei providentiam est translata.'* (The erstwhile crown of the famous Arthur, King of the Britons, was handed over with other jewels to the King of England. Thus the glory of the Welsh …was transferred to the English by the grace of God.'): *Flores Historiarum*, III, 59.

80. *'rex Edwardus…portionem Dominicae Crucis non modicam, ornatam auro et argento et lapidibus preciosis, quam de Wallia secum tulit, apud Westmonasterium cum solempni processione et concentu advexit.'* ('King Edward…brought a largish piece of the True Cross, ornamented with gold and silver and precious stones, which he had carried with him from Wales, to Westminster with a solemn procession and singing.'): *Flores Historiarum*, III, 63.

81. Prestwich, *Edward I*, 204.

The Conservation and Restoration of Caernarfon Castle 1845–1912

†*Richard Avent*

Today's visitor to Caernarfon Castle is faced with a great stately monument with battlemented walls dominating the seaward aspect of the town (Plate 13).[1] With the majority of the towers being roofed, the overall impression of an almost complete medieval fortress is only marred by the lack of surviving internal buildings. However, this picture might have been a very different one had an order to demolish the castle in 1660 been executed and had different decisions been made over the way its subsequent ruination was arrested with programmes of masonry consolidation. It will come as no surprise to many that the latter issue is the story of an uncomfortable marriage between restoration and the 'treat as found' tradition of masonry conservation.

Unusually for most monuments in State care today, Caernarfon Castle has always remained in the hands of the Crown. However, it is an unsuccessful attempt to effect a private purchase which provides us with one of the earliest pictures of the overall condition of the unconsolidated castle. On 20 February 1815, just four months before he was to lose a leg at the battle of Waterloo, Henry Paget, earl of Uxbridge (soon to become the first marquess of Anglesey), the then constable of Caernarfon Castle, wrote to the prime minister, the earl of Liverpool, expressing interest in purchasing the castle.[2] This resulted in the Commissioners of Woods, Forests and Land Revenues issuing a warrant to Robert Jones, a Caernarfon surveyor and architect, to report on the condition of the castle and undertake a valuation.[3] From his subsequent report, dated 9 November 1815, we learn that, 'The whole castle is in a most ruinous state … and great expence will be incured in putting the same into tolerable decent repair, the stairs and steps in the Towers and passages … are mostly broken down, and every part is in great dilapidated State, without any roofing'.[4] Six vaulted areas in the towers were in use: two for storing blasting powder, two for keeping ammunition, one as a guardroom for the local militia and the other was being used by the harbourmaster. There may

have been a separate occupier in the Eagle Tower[5] and one tenant occupied part of the castle ditch for an annual rent of £1 1s., a guinea. Jones valued the castle for a range of different lengths of lease, or for sale, at £500. Whichever option is adopted there would be 'powers for Building thereupon or converting the same to any other purpose'. The castle was spared these potential depredations by the commissioners' decision on 11 March 1816 that it should not, after all, be sold.[6]

Nearly thirty years later, on 8 January 1845, the mayor of Caernarfon, Thomas Evans, wrote to the commissioners drawing their attention to the recent collapse of the abutment to the arch of the Queen's Gate at the eastern end of the castle. Part of the masonry was now hanging in a precarious state above one of the main thoroughfares to the quay and railway.[7] Three days later the commissioners, in the persons of Alexander Milne and Charles Gore, wrote to the architect, Anthony Salvin, who had supervised work for them at other ruinous castles elsewhere in the country, asking him to visit.[8] By 24 March, John Provis, the commissioners' local agent based in Holyhead, was able to report that the emergency repairs to the arch of the Queen's Gate, which he had organized at the request of the commissioners, had been completed and the work had been extended to the walls on either side.[9] Despite being delayed by heavy snow from visiting earlier, a day later Salvin had completed his report (Fig. 14.1). He estimated that it would cost '£2,478 to make the castle safe with the work concentrating on repairs to the battlements and other areas where the stonework was at risk of collapsing, such as the two major breaches in the Chamberlain and Queen's Towers and precarious window and other openings'.[10] On 15 July, Gore put a submission up to the Treasury seeking authorization for the expenditure, which he received on 22 July.

Reading these papers, one is struck by the speed and efficiency of the response to the mayor's original plea. Even allowing for the benefits brought to the postal

Figure 14.1: A drawing of the interior of Caernarfon Castle by Anthony Salvin (RIBA Library Drawings Collection: PB277/5(8)).

system through the new railway link to Caernarfon, decisions are being made and instructions issued very promptly. Treasury approval within a week and without strings attached, to what was at the time very substantial expenditure, would be the envy of modern-day civil servants. Despite the passage of over 150 years, there are familiar aspects in all of this for those of us working in this business today, both in the process and in the technical language of Salvin's report, although the surviving official papers may not necessarily reflect the full story. A reference in Salvin's obituary in *The Builder* may be pertinent – 'The manner in which Caernarvon Castle has been kept from ruin may be credited to Salvin's influence in high quarters, and his enthusiasm for the work'.[11]

Salvin continued with the same local builder, David Williams, as originally employed by Provis considering that he had 'performed the work instructed to him in a most satisfactory manner'.[12] In May 1847 Salvin was able to report that Williams had completed his work and on 28

April 1848 he submitted an account showing that the total cost had been £1,875 0s. 5d.[13] Although Salvin's schedule included work to both the interior and the exterior of the castle, he seems to have concentrated on the external faces, where there was greatest risk to the public.[14]

With a sound knowledge of medieval military architecture, Salvin was the ideal architect for the work at Caernarfon. He had cut his teeth in this field in the mid-1830s when he had become involved in the very controversial re-facing of the twelfth-century keep at Norwich. Subsequently, the commissioners had employed him to work at the castles at Newark and Carisbrooke.[15] He clearly appreciated that the priority at Caernarfon was one of repair and consolidation, not restoration, although there is no reason to think that he would have been averse to the latter if asked. He summed up the situation at the beginning of his survey: '… there is sufficient detail to restore the whole of the external wall & Towers – these details are however in many instances fast disappearing, the quoinstones never having had much bond, in many places have fallen out, and parts of the walls have followed them, the same occurs to jambs of windows, doors & loops; the tops of the turrets are also much dilapidated & must be rebuilt, as also the parapets and battlements'.[16] Salvin's survey and the drawings he made at the time provide a useful record of the state of the castle before any repair work. One of his drawings, dated August 1848, illustrates the eastern half of the interior shortly after the completion of the work. This and photographs taken at various times during the second half of the nineteenth century indicate that he concentrated on urgent repair, leaving restoration to his successors (Fig. 14.2).

Very little serious conservation work appears to have taken place at the castle over the next twenty or so years although the deputy constable, John Morgan, commissioned Salvin to design new gates for the main entrance. Views differ about whether these were based on those at the castles of Alnwick or Carlisle, but Sir Llewelyn Turner claims that they were modified so that the wicket gate was sufficiently wide 'to freely admit ladies with crinolines'.[17] Turner, who was both godson and brother-in-law to John Morgan, claims that what work Morgan did commission turned out disastrously and had subsequently to be removed.[18]

Appointed deputy constable by the earl of Caernarvon in 1870, the year in which he was knighted, Turner (Fig. 14.3) set off immediately on a tour of other castles, 'carefully noting anything that was missing in Carnarvon Castle, and sometimes finding the missing link in castles far more dilapidated. Nothing struck me so much as the folly of allowing such buildings to remain unroofed and useless'. He believed that Caernarfon only required repairs to make it habitable: 'our ancestors did not build ruins … a castle restored to its pristine state will afford this and future generations an infinitely better idea of the life of our early kings and rulers than can be guessed from inspecting a ruin, of which there are plenty so badly decayed that they hardly admit of reparation'.[19] For the next thirty-one years, Turner applied this approach with vigour

Figure 14.2: The interior of Caernarfon Castle in the late nineteenth century (Archifau Gwynedd Archives).

funding practically all his building works from fourpence entry fees which had been introduced previously by John Morgan. After paying the gatekeeper, the average annual sum earned from the entrance charge between 1899 and 1902 was £175 7s. 2d., and out of this Turner paid for his mason, John Jones, other workmen and for all the necessary materials.[20] The Crown seems to have been content to rely on this local arrangement for future work at the castle. When agreeing to continue as deputy to the earl of Caernarvon's successor, Sir John Puleston, Turner made it clear that he did this on the basis that the castle's 'management should be entirely under my control; that no-one could apply for its use over my head; and that the repairs and structure should rest entirely in my hands'.[21]

One of Turner's first acts was to remove a low mound that occupied much of the upper ward of the castle. Water was running off the mound into the adjoining towers and wall passages causing damage and Turner had agreed with Salvin some years before that the mound should go. Finding himself with some cash in hand at the end of his programme of works, Salvin had obtained the commissioners' agreement to re-allocate some of these funds into a test excavation into part of the mound.[22] This appears to have revealed two distinctive stratigraphic levels interpreted as natural and artificial. A limekiln and vaults were found under part of the mound. It is possible that what was then interpreted as natural material might, if subjected to modern excavation techniques, have turned out to be the remains of the late eleventh-century motte constructed by Earl Hugh of Chester.[23]

Two other projects were undertaken by Turner during his first three years as deputy constable. The first was to try to tackle once and for all the running sore of what were known as 'encroachments' on the northern, townward, side of the castle. These were workmen's yards and temporary buildings constructed against the curtain over the filled-in castle ditch. Salvin had galvanized the commissioners into action in the 1840s and from then onwards there had been a constant stream of eviction notices, with varying degrees of success. The last straw came when a smithy was erected against the exterior of the Eagle Tower with smoke pouring up the side of the tower; a coal yard was established against the Well Tower and, as a final insult, a large enclosure was illegally created between the Eagle and Well Towers with a lavatory chute directing excrement into the Well Tower. After numerous attempts to evict the interlopers, Turner employed twenty-five railway navvies to clear the encroachments, re-excavated the castle ditch and walled the area. Although not endearing himself to the local citizenry, he had at least decisively resolved the problem.[24]

Figure 14.3: Sir Llewelyn Turner (Cadw, Welsh Assembly Government: Crown Copyright).

In terms of scale, Turner's most significant work at the castle also took place during this early period when he raised funds from a few of the local nobility and gentry for large-scale restoration of the fabric of the Queen's Tower and to roof and floor it. A little later, in 1877, the steps and newels were replaced in the turret of the tower. After the Eagle Tower, these were the finest apartments in the castle. The ground floor became a freemasons' hall, for which an annual rent of £12 was paid, and at some point the 'Volunteers' (presumably the local militia) took over the floor above. Turner converted the top floor to a museum, with the intention that it should one day house a national museum for Wales.[25] The campaign for a national museum within the castle walls was to gain momentum in the opening years of the twentieth century shortly after Turner's death but, by then, the Queen's Tower was no longer habitable and the aspirations of Lady Turner and Caernarfon Town Council moved on to the idea of reconstructing the great hall to full height from its surviving ground-level footings, something that Turner would have almost certainly found totally unacceptable. Fortunately, the commissioner of works rejected the proposal out of

Figure 14.4: Caernarfon Castle, with the restored Chamberlain Tower left centre (Cadw, Welsh Assembly Government: Crown Copyright).

hand pointing out that it would cause a storm of protest amongst archaeological and antiquarian bodies.[26]

Caernarfon's bid to house the National Museum of Wales in 1905, which made no mention of its existing museum, was centred on the statement that 'nowhere in the whole Principality are those National characteristics [of the Welsh people] more pronounced than in the Borough and County of Carnarvon, the historical, traditional, and natural centre of distinctively Welsh National Interests'.[27] The estimated cost for converting the castle's towers into a national museum was £10,000, half of which was to come from the rates, half from fundraising. The sum was based on a report by Walter Thomas, president of the Society of Architects. The Privy Council's decision, announced in June 1905, that Aberystwyth was to be the site of the National Library, with the National Museum going to Cardiff, was greeted with dismay in Caernarfon. The town clerk wrote to the Privy Council expressing his disappointment, whilst J. R. Pritchard, chairman of the county council, laid some of the blame on the councils of Conwy and Llandudno for their refusal to assist in the county's drive for additional funds.[28]

The 1870s saw the replacement of steps and newels to some of the stairs and work to the battlements of some of the towers and linking curtains of the upper ward. After the Queen's Tower, the largest restoration projects were to the Chamberlain (1890) and Well (1891) Towers. A substantial breach on the east side of the Chamberlain Tower was rebuilt along with the mullions and transoms of the lost windows (Fig. 14.4). Work on the Well Tower was altogether more adventurous. The upper part of the tower was not restored – it was built from new having been left unfinished in the fourteenth century. In 1896 the King's Gate 'was seriously taken in hand' (Figs 14.5 and 14.6) and the battlements of the curtain wall between the gate and the Well Tower on one side, and the gate and the Granary Tower on the other, were replaced. Turner's final work took place in 1901 on the Queen's Gate, bringing us back to where Salvin started fifty-six years earlier (Figs 14.7 and 14.8).[29] Turner does not appear to have carried out any major works on the principal structure of the castle, the Eagle Tower.

Sir Llewelyn Turner's death in 1903 marked the end of a major programme of work at the castle in which the

Figure 14.5: The King's Gate, Caernarfon Castle, before restoration (Cadw, Welsh Assembly Government: Crown Copyright).

three most ruinous towers had been restored, most of the battlements had been re-instated and public access greatly enhanced through extensive repairs to stairs and wall passages. Turner was succeeded in the post of deputy constable by his nephew, C. A. Jones, and discussions then seem to have taken place with the constable, Sir John Puleston, over the transfer of the castle's management to the Office of Works. A survey of the castle was undertaken in 1906, not long before its formal transfer in 1908, by F. A. Huntley, the district architect and surveyor for the Office of Works. He judged that much of the remaining fabric of the monument was in need of extensive re-consolidation and estimated that it would cost approximately £7,000 to put the ruins in 'a fairly good state of repairs' with the work being spread over three years. Within this cost 'no provision has been made for restoring: and suggestions to do so should, I think, be discouraged'.[30]

From Huntley's survey we learn that the Black and Watch Towers in the upper ward were in a particularly bad state of repair despite some steps and newels in the Black Tower having been replaced and the battlements restored by Turner in 1879.[31] Even more surprising are Huntley's comments about two of the restored towers. The upper part of the Chamberlain Tower is described as being 'in a dangerous and dilapidated condition'. Both this and the Queen's Tower, put up in the 1870s as part of Turner's most extensive restoration project in the castle, were judged to be very defective and probably in need of renewing. In the event, the roof and the floors of the Queen's Tower proved to be in such a poor state (a workman fell through one of the floors) that the tower could not be used during the 1911 investiture of the prince of Wales. Eventually it was completely re-roofed and re-floored by the Office of Works in 1912/13 at a

Figure 14.6: *The King's Gate, Caernarfon Castle, about 1920 (Cadw, Welsh Assembly Government: Crown Copyright).*

cost of £1,370. The main roofing beam, of Quebec oak, measured 44 feet (13.5m) in length and about four tons in weight.[32] Huntley described the masonry of the Eagle Tower as being in need of a major overhaul and pointed out that part of the tower had an unsightly temporary roof over the Volunteers' hall. His recommendation that this should be removed and the Volunteers relocated must have been followed for, by September 1912, this tower had been re-floored (Fig. 14.9).[33]

It is clear from Huntley's report and what we know of Salvin's and Turner's work that the castle had never been subjected to a thorough programme of masonry consolidation. Salvin had concentrated on making it safe and Turner on selective restoration. The main impetus for undertaking further work came with the need to make sure the castle was in a sufficiently sound state to host the investiture of the prince of Wales in 1911. In the run up to the investiture work seems to have been concentrated on the exterior walls with very large numbers of workmen being employed on this and other tasks associated with preparing for such a great event.[34] The clerk of works was retained to supervise a longer-term programme of work which involved fifty men in 1912 at a cost £2,192 (Fig. 14.10).[35] The overall approach and standards of

Figure 14.7: *The Queen's Gate, Caernarfon Castle, before restoration (Cadw, Welsh Assembly Government: Crown Copyright).*

Figure 14.8: *The Queen's Gate, Caernarfon Castle, after restoration (Cadw, Welsh Assembly Government: Crown Copyright).*

Figure 14.9: *An oak beam being brought into Caernarfon Castle from the quay (Cadw, Welsh Assembly Government: Crown Copyright).*

Figure 14.10: Grouting the walls of Caernarfon Castle in October 1912 (Cadw, Welsh Assembly Government: Crown Copyright).

workmanship are familiar to us today. Turner's policy of reconstruction was completely abandoned. The remaining battlements were to be conserved as found and little or no new stone was to be used in the repair of the walls. Old pointing, including that of Turner's masons, was to be replaced by a good quality lime mortar with the new pointing set slightly back from the face of the walling.

There was clearly a feeling in the Office of Works and probably other conservation circles that Turner had taken reconstruction too far at Caernarfon and that all future work should adhere to a more traditional conservation approach. This came to a head in a paper delivered to the Society of Antiquaries on 7 December 1911 by Sir Schomberg McDonnell, secretary to the Office of Works (1902–12), on the more general theme of the need for an Advisory Board empowered to recommend that certain monuments in danger should be taken into State care. Amongst a number of monuments, McDonnell cited Caernarfon as a castle for which the Office of Works

had to fight hard in order to bring it under its care. McDonnell was under the mistaken impression that it had been the constable, Sir John Puleston, rather than his deputy, who had overseen the restoration works. The mason, John Jones, had been allowed to go his own sweet way, restoring as he thought fit, 'There was nobody to say nay or to control him, and it is a fact that at this moment every one of the new battlements which deface the structure were constructed, not out of local stone, but out of York stone specially procured for the purpose'. He also felt that, had the castle not come under the control of the Office of Works, it would have been used for some totally inappropriate purpose.[36] The lecture was picked up by the national press and controversy raged over the next couple of months with an equal balance between Turner's defenders and detractors. While there is clearly some confusion over who did what and where the stone came from (it was actually sourced from Mostyn in Flintshire), the general message is clear and reflects the spirit of age

– reconstruction was no longer the done thing when it came to conserving ancient monuments and this has been the philosophy broadly adopted to the present day.

Acknowledgements (Richard Avent)

The idea for this paper originated in some notes on the conservation of the castle in the opening years of the twentieth century prepared by staff at the Royal Commission on the Ancient and Historical Monuments of Wales when compiling the Caernarvonshire Inventory and now lodged in the National Monuments Record for Wales, and I am grateful to the staff of the Royal Commission for their help when undertaking this research. I would also like to thank Philippa Martin at the Royal Institute of British Architects and the staff at the Gwynedd Archives Service for their assistance and for arranging for the photographs which illustrated the original paper. Finally, I am indebted to my colleague in Cadw, David McLees, for his helpful comments on my draft text.

John Kenyon is indebted to Penny Icke and Tricia Moore at the Royal Commission, Peter Humphries and Chris Kenyon at Cadw, and Lucy Rowe at the Victoria and Albert Museum regarding photographs and drawings of Caernarfon Castle.

Notes

1. This paper by the late Richard Avent first appeared in *The Modern Traveller to our Past: Festschrift in Honour of Ann Hamlin*, ed. M. Meek (Southport 2006), 344–52. John Kenyon has added supplementary material.
2. The National Archives: Public Record Office. Ministry of Works file no. AA86268/3A. The National Archives (TNA): PRO Works 14/9, f. 1.
3. ibid., f. 9.
4. ibid. The survey was originally accompanied by a plan which is no longer within the survey. A reference to 'The Tower' (identified as fig. 6 on the missing plan), which has been in the possession of John Griffith of Llanfair for 'upwards of fifty years' may be the Eagle Tower, the most prominent structure on the site.
5. ibid., f. 10.
6. TNA: PRO, Ministry of Works file no. AA86268/2. TNA: PRO Works 14/10, f. 2.
7. ibid., f. 9.
8. ibid., ff. 12, 18.
9. ibid., f. 25 and report.
10. ibid., ff. 33, 34.
11. Anon., 'The late Mr Anthony Salvin, architect', *The Builder* 41 (1881), 809.
12. TNA: PRO Works 14/10, f. 45.
13. ibid., ff. 56, 59.
14. Anon., 'A walk through Carnarvon', *Archaeologia Cambrensis*, 3 ser. 10 (1864), 177.
15. J. Allibone, *Anthony Salvin: Pioneer of Gothic Revival Architecture* (Cambridge 1988), 95–106; J. M. Crook and M. H. Port, *The History of the King's Works. 6. 1782–1851* (London 1973), 642–43.
16. TNA: PRO Works 14/10, f. 25 and report.
17. Anon., 'Miscellaneous notices: Caernarvon Castle', *Archaeologia Cambrensis*, 3 ser. 2 (1856), 188, refers to Alnwick Castle, while Turner refers to Carlisle Castle (Ll. Turner, *The Memories of Sir Llewelyn Turner* (London 1903), 388). Alnwick is the more likely, as there is no record of Salvin being associated with Carlisle.
18. Ll. Turner, *A Retrospect of the Work done by Sir Llewelyn Turner* (Caernarfon 1902), 7; Turner, *Memories*, 388–89.
19. Turner, *Retrospect*, 4.
20. ibid., 6. Turner had obtained the services of John Jones from the Paget family.
21. Turner, *Memories*, 393.
22. TNA: PRO Works 14/10, ff. 56, 60.
23. For further details and a section of the motte see, RCAHMW, *An Inventory of the Ancient Monuments in Caernarvonshire. 2. Central* (London 1960), 125, 127, Fig. 104.
24. Turner, *Retrospect*, 9–10.
25. Ll. Turner, 'Carnarvon Castle', *Archaeologia Cambrensis*, 4 ser. 5 (1874), 75–76; Turner, *Retrospect*, 7–8, 16; Works 14/10 includes a report 'Carnarvon Castle' by F. A. Huntley dated 5 October 1906. Huntley mentions that the first floor of the Queen's Tower is occupied by 'Volunteers'. Turner's 1902 booklet mentions on page 7 that forty new steps were placed in the Queen's Tower in 1887, but the copy in the Library of the National Museum of Wales has been corrected to 1877 in Turner's hand.
26. TNA: PRO Works 14/10 f. 146; Turner, *Retrospect*, 16–17.
27. Quoted in B. A. Campbell, 'The Battle of the Sites: a National Museum for Wales' (unpublished PhD, University of Leicester, 2005), 196.
28. ibid., 222.
29. Turner, *Retrospect*, 12–15 for details of this restoration work.
30. TNA: PRO Works 14/10, page 24 of Huntley's report (see note 25, above)
31. Turner, *Retrospect*, 8.
32. *The Times* for 6 June 1913, reproduced in Anon., 'Miscellanea: Carnarvon Castle – reconstruction of the interior', *Archaeologia Cambrensis*, 6 ser. 13 (1913), 344.
33. See copy of letter from William Weir to the Secretary of the Society for the Protection of Ancient Buildings, dated 11 September 1912, in the records on Caernarfon Castle in the National Monuments Record for Wales, Aberystwyth. Weir is critical of the ironwork used for such items as light brackets, and also of the use of 'American' oak for the floors, instead of English oak. He also mentions that the pointing in Turner's time had been done using Portland cement and black ash.
34. Article entitled 'Future of Carnarvon Castle' in the *Manchester Guardian* for 29 December 1911.
35. Anon., 'Miscellanea', 345.
36. S. K. McDonnell, 'The protection of ancient buildings and monuments', *Proceedings of the Society of Antiquaries of London*, 2 ser. 24 (1911–12), 21–22.

Arnold Taylor's Contribution to the Study of the Edwardian Castles in Wales

John R. Kenyon

Arnold Taylor will always be associated with the study of Edward I's castles in Wales (Fig. 15. 1). There was of course much more to his professional career than this alone, but it is for his towering achievement in combining the documentary and architectural analysis of the Welsh castles that he will be best remembered. It is also the reason for this collection of essays, which has given us the opportunity to review Taylor's work, discuss more recent approaches and consider new directions for the study of the Edwardian castles in Wales.[1]

Taylor joined the Office of Works in 1935 as an assistant inspector, following Bryan O'Neil's appointment as inspector of ancient monuments for Wales. However, it was on his return in 1946 from war service that he became closely associated with Wales and its castles, for by this time O'Neil had become chief inspector, and Taylor replaced him in Wales.

The study of the Edwardian castles was not new, of course. They had been attracting the attention of travellers and historians through the centuries, particularly from the eighteenth onwards, with descriptions by Francis Grose[2] and Thomas Pennant.[3] In the 1850s, within a few years of the founding of two of our national archaeological bodies, the Royal Archaeological Institute and the Cambrian Archaeological Association, the antiquary, Revd Charles Hartshorne, published papers on the castles of Caernarfon and Conwy.[4] Whilst his contemporary, that great castellologist, G. T. Clark, largely concentrated on the architecture of the castles,[5] Hartshorne transcribed a number of Edwardian accounts recording works' expenditure on the castles, including those for a group of buildings at Conwy known as Llewelyn's Hall, close to the upper gate of the town's defences.[6]

In 1903 the architect, Harold Hughes, was asked by the Cambrian Archaeological Association to survey the castles of Cricieth and Harlech. The study of Harlech duly appeared in 1913.[7] Hughes stressed the importance of the documentary evidence for understanding the architecture, but instead of utilizing primary sources he used information in J. E. Morris's book on the Welsh wars, a volume that has stood the test of time in the field of medieval military history.[8]

State involvement in the interpretation of the Edwardian castles began mainly when they passed into guardianship, though Conwy was an exception as we shall see.[9] It is not surprising that the first 'Ministry' paper was on Caernarfon, given the degree of interest in the conservation/restoration work that had been undertaken in the nineteenth and early twentieth centuries.[10] This was a substantial account by Charles Peers, chief inspector of ancient monuments, given in part in the summer of 1914 to members of the Honourable Society of Cymmrodorion at a special meeting held in the castle, in the Queen's Tower.[11] The first third of this paper is concerned with the documentation of the castle through to the seventeenth century, written in some detail, with the remaining two-thirds concerned with the analysis of the castle's architecture, a pattern to be followed by the Ministry's 'blue guides'.

In 1922 Peers was to follow his Caernarfon paper with a study of Harlech,[12] building on Hughes' account mentioned above. Some excavation, as well as a further study of the documents, allowed Peers to draw further conclusions about the history of the castle. In 1926 Wilfrid Hemp published a very detailed history and description of Denbigh Castle.[13]

It was not surprising that Conwy, with its castle and town walls, began to attract further academic attention. In the care of the local authority until 1953, two major papers were published in the 1930s. From 1928 until 1930 the architect, Arthur Henderson, surveyed Conwy for Harold Sands[14] and these drawings were published, with text by Harold Hughes, in 1938.[15] The castle historian and architect, Sidney Toy, also made a series of drawings of Conwy's castle and town walls, and read a paper to the

Society of Antiquaries in November 1936.[16] In the brief introduction to the documentary evidence Toy was assisted by the antiquary and historian, L. F. Salzman. Although not yet in State care, in 1939 Wilfrid Hemp, who had been appointed secretary to the Royal Commission on the Historical Monuments in Wales and Monmouthshire in 1928, carried out further work at Conwy to clarify some aspects of the castle's plan as part of the preparation of the county inventory.[17]

As a result of the majority of the Edwardian castles coming into State care in the first half of the twentieth century, detailed guidebooks were published by HMSO, the authors being former and existing members of the Inspectorate of Ancient Monuments. Although the majority appeared in the 1930s, that for Harlech was published in 1929, whilst Taylor's Rhuddlan was issued twenty years later.[18]

There were two other landmark papers in the first half of the twentieth century. The first was by Douglas Knoop and G. P. Jones, published in 1932. This was concerned with the character of the supply of labour, particularly with masons, and the role of the master mason in terms of his status and his role in the construction of the Edwardian castles.[19] The authors examined early fourteenth-century accounts for Beaumaris and Caernarfon and the mobility of masons between building sites, and two appendices list the names of the hewers (*cementarii*) and layers (*cubitores*) at the two castles and their pay.

The other landmark paper was J. Goronwy Edwards's Sir John Rhŷs Memorial Lecture given to the British Academy at the end of 1944.[20] Edwards examined the castles not from an architectural or military point of view, but as a building project, considering the time taken to build them, the labour involved, the cost, and, lastly, how the whole operation was financed. It was a seminal paper, one that heralded an era that was to culminate in the publication of the first two volumes of *The History of the King's Works* in 1963.

Although Taylor was familiar with the castles in Wales from boyhood holidays, his main tasks lay in England after his appointment in 1935.[21] His close involvement with the castles of Edward I, especially Conwy, began with his appointment as inspector of ancient monuments for Wales in 1946, a post he held until 1954 when he was promoted to the new post of assistant chief inspector. Bryan O'Neil, now chief inspector of ancient monuments, had always stressed the importance of documentary research in the interpretation of medieval buildings[22] and it was no doubt with this in mind that Taylor thought about Conwy when, in the same year, he saw the Savoyard castle of Saillon through a train window.[23]

Figure 15.1: Arnold Taylor on Conwy's town walls (By kind permission of Mrs Patricia Taylor).

It was during his time in Wales that the Royal Commission on the Historical Monuments in Wales and Monmouthshire continued to survey sites in Caernarvonshire; Taylor was later to become a commissioner. The first volume of the Caernarvonshire inventory, which included Conwy, was published in 1956, and in the same year the first Ministry guidebook to the castle and town walls appeared, written by Taylor.[24] Although forever associated with the Edwardian castles, this marked the beginning of a lifelong interest in Conwy Castle in particular and its associated town defences.[25]

Within a short time of taking up his post in Wales, Taylor had published a number of articles, besides the Rhuddlan guidebook. There was a note on Walter of Hereford at Caernarfon,[26] an examination of the career of the carpenter, Thomas de Houghton, who undertook work at a number of castles in England, Scotland and Wales,[27] and a note on the beginnings of Caernarfon Castle.[28] The visit of the Cambrian Archaeological Association to Harlech in 1949 led to a note detailing some revisions regarding the history of the castle, in which Taylor gave notice of his forthcoming paper on James of St George, emphasizing his disagreement with W. D. Simpson's view that Master James was the organizer of the King's Works in Wales, not the architect of the castles.[29]

Besides the documentary research in the Public Record Office, then in Chancery Lane, London – which was given fresh impetus by *The History of the King's Works* project commissioned in 1951 – it is the Savoyard connection with the Edwardian castles that is such an important aspect of Taylor's work. The connection was made as a result of several visits to Switzerland and Italy to consult documents and to study the Savoyard castles themselves. Even before this work had begun fully, Taylor published a paper on Master James of St George, the man whom he was to see as the architect of many of the Edwardian castles, as others had done before him.[30] Today, however, many would concur with Simpson and prefer to think of Master James as the man who implemented and oversaw the king's great design, instead of being the designer or architect of the buildings.[31] Nevertheless, in 1949, Taylor received the Reginald Taylor prize medal of the British Archaeological Association for his paper on Master James.

The results of Taylor's work on the Edwardian castles for *The History of the King's Works* began to come to fruition with a paper in *Antiquity* in 1952 on the construction date of Caernarfon. This was followed by a new guidebook for Caernarfon in 1953,[32] which replaced that by Peers published twenty years earlier. Work on the building accounts of the castle, as well as the fabric, enabled Taylor to show that the castle was not built in three distinct periods, as interpreted by Peers, but was conceived as a single design, although built in two phases, before and after the uprising of Madog ap Llywelyn in 1294. Peers had interpreted *muro inchoato circa mota castri* in a document of 1296 to mean the unfinished wall around the original Norman motte in the upper ward. However, Taylor showed that the words referred to the unfinished curtain wall above the ditch on the north side of the castle.

When Conwy's castle and town walls came into State care in 1953, it was the last of the great Edwardian castles to do so. Taylor was inspector for Wales and it is not therefore surprising that this was to become his favourite monument in north Wales. The conservation of the castle and town walls,[33] and especially the clearance of modern accretions in front of the walls, fully revealed their spectacular appearance, work that has been continued by Cadw to create greater access to the walled circuit. The site's recognition as a World Heritage Site in 1986 is in no small part due to Taylor's efforts.

The 1953 guide to Conwy was perhaps short on history, but went into considerable detail regarding the architecture. Master James is described here as 'the greatest military architect of the age',[34] an opinion held by Taylor throughout his life. Later editions appeared, and although the results of Taylor's work for *The History of the King's Works* were available, the documentary history of Conwy was never extended to beyond the general summary written for the original edition of the guidebook.[35] In the first two volumes of *The King's Works*, published in 1963 and covering the Middle Ages, Taylor contributed chapter 6 in volume one on the works in Wales, with a number of appendices in volume two. It was here that Taylor first championed the imperial link between the design of Caernarfon's towers and those at Constantinople.[36]

In 1963, Taylor returned to the architectural and personnel links between the Edwardian castles and Savoy, which he had championed in a number of publications in the 1950s.[37] The use of helicoidal and inclined scaffolds, the full-centred semi-circular arch and the design of latrine shafts and of windows can be seen at Harlech as well as in Savoy. A number of the features also appear in the other Edwardian castles, plus the embellishment of crenellations, which can be seen at Conwy.

In his retirement, Taylor continued to be involved with Edwardian castle studies. In 1980 his guidebooks to Harlech and Beaumaris were published, and two years later the third edition of the guide to Rhuddlan appeared.[38] He also took a great interest in the Cadw editions of his guidebooks; he revised and wrote new text and offered comments on the reconstruction drawings that so enhance the series. Taylor never wrote a guidebook to replace the anonymous Flint Castle booklet of 1946, but he contributed substantially to that written for Cadw by Derek Renn, first published (jointly with that on Ewloe Castle by Richard Avent) in 1991.

He was also able, in other publications, to go into more detail regarding some of the documents themselves. He examined the particulars accounts for Conwy for the period November 1285 to September 1286, and made a full transcript of this relatively scarce type of document, which described the Mill Gate and the town wall either side of it.[39] When Taylor was invited to contribute to a collection of essays to honour David Cathcart King, he decided to cast further light on the construction of Beaumaris by transcribing the building accounts for 1295–98.[40] Besides the actual details of expenditure, the accounts emphasized just how much of a major masonry castle could be constructed in a mere ten months, including the winter period. Taylor's involvement with Conwy continued well into the 1990s, with a paper on the great hall,[41] which examined whether what had been seen as one long room had actually been divided into three or more component parts, with a chapel at the east end, the hall in the centre, and another chamber at the west end, if not two, judging by the fireplaces.

Also in his retirement there came his crucial role in the controversy over the planned new route of the A55, which was intended to reduce traffic through Conwy and take the road away from the town. His campaigning was instrumental to the success of the tunnel option instead of a huge suspension bridge, which would have had a highly detrimental impact on the view of the castle from across the estuary. The public inquiry was held in 1974; the so-called 'preferred route' was rejected and in 1991 the A55 tunnel was duly opened. In every sense, Conwy truly stands as a monument to this great castellologist.

Taylor's contribution to the study of the Edwardian castles can never be equalled. He provided the foundation on which later students of the architecture and building accounts have built to understand further the design and construction of these castles. His was not the last word, nor would he have expected it to be so, just as we have seen with Jeremy Ashbee's work on Conwy's inner ward,

Peter Brears's review of the domestic arrangements and Nicola Coldstream's re-evaluation of the role of Master James of St George.[42] As fresh eyes explore the records in The National Archives and new editions of the Cadw guidebooks are published, additional information will come to light to further illuminate our understanding of the Edwardian castles in Wales.

Acknowledgements

I am indebted to Rick Turner for inviting me to contribute this paper to the volume as it enables me to pay tribute to a man who was always generous with his advice regarding various aspects of my castle studies. Also, as Honorary Secretary of the Society of Antiquaries of London, Arnold Taylor was one of the officers who appointed me to the post of Assistant Librarian in December 1969 and if it had not been for the Antiquaries, I would never have become involved in castle studies. Rick Turner also kindly commented on a draft text, as did Christine Kenyon and Derek Renn.

Notes

1. For an account of Taylor's life and work see A. Saunders, 'Arnold Joseph Taylor 1911–2002', *Proceedings of the British Academy*, 138 (2006), 363–81; A. Saunders, 'Taylor, Arnold Joseph (1911–2002)', *Oxford Dictionary of National Biography*, online edn (Oxford OUP 2006) [http://www.oxforddnb.com/view/article/77411]. See also R. Avent, 'Remembering Arnold Taylor, 1911–2002', *Heritage in Wales*, 24 (2003), 7–8. Many of Taylor's papers cited below were republished in his *Studies in Castles and Castle-Building* (London 1985).

2. F. Grose, *The Antiquities of England and Wales*, 7, new edn (London 1797).

3. T. Pennant, *A Tour in Wales MDCCLXX*, 2 (London 1783). It is here that Pennant was to describe Caernarfon Castle as 'the most magnificent badge of our subjection' (p. 223).

4. C. H. Hartshorne, 'Caernarvon Castle', *Archaeological Journal*, 7 (1850), 237–65; 'Conway Castle', *Archaeologia Cambrensis*, new ser. 5 (1854), 1–12. It was in the paper on Caernarfon that Hartshorne noted the connection between Conwy and Master James of St George (p. 240, n. 6).

5. G. T. Clark, *Mediaeval Military Architecture in England*, 2 vols (London 1884). Many of Clark's numerous papers were brought together in this book.

6. See A. Taylor, *The Welsh Castles of Edward I* (London 1986), 61, with documents in the National Archives: PRO cited. At the time of Hartshorne's study the relevant documentation was housed in 'the late Treasury of the Exchequer, in the Chapter House, Westminster' (Hartshorne, 'Conway Castle', 2).

7. H. Hughes, 'Harlech Castle', *Archaeologia Cambrensis*, 6 ser. 13 (1913), 275–316.

8. J. E. Morris, *The Welsh Wars of Edward I* (Oxford 1901), reprinted

with the same pagination by Alan Sutton Publishing (Stroud 1996), with a foreword by Michael Prestwich.

9. Caernarfon (1908), Denbigh (1914), Harlech (1914), Flint (1919), Beaumaris (1925), Rhuddlan (1944), Conwy (1953).

10. R. Avent, this volume.

11. C. R. Peers, 'Carnarvon Castle', *Transactions of the Honourable Society of Cymmrodorion*, (1915–16), 1–74.

12. C. R. Peers, 'Harlech Castle', *Transactions of the Honourable Society of Cymmrodorion*, (1921–22), 63–82.

13. W. J. Hemp, 'Denbigh Castle', *Y Cymmrodor*, 36 (1926), 64–120.

14. The Harold Sands collection of drawings and plans of a large number of castles is to be found in the collections of the Society of Antiquaries of London, although some of it is now with English Heritage in Swindon. Sands, a barrister by profession, had an amateur interest in castles, and wrote on some sites in Kent and Sussex early last century, for example, Bodiam.

15. H. H. Hughes, 'The Edwardian castle and town defences at Conway', *Archaeologia Cambrensis*, 93 (1938), 75–92, 212–25. Henderson's elevations continued to be used for many years afterwards, in Taylor's guidebook.

16. S. Toy, 'The town and castle of Conway', *Archaeologia*, 86 (1937), 163–93. Toy's reconstruction of the windows of the apartments in the inner ward still form the basis of the drawings in the current guidebook of the castle.

17. W. J. Hemp, 'Conway Castle', *Archaeologia Cambrensis*, 96 (1941), 163–74. The writer has an offprint of this paper, given to him by Arnold Taylor, containing a number of his pencilled corrections, annotations and a drawing. It seems that it was originally given by Hemp to Bryan O'Neil in 1942, as it contains a letter from Hemp to O'Neil dated 14 July 1939 referring to the 'good go' that

he had undertaken at Conwy in the week previous. RCAHMW, *An Inventory of the Ancient Monuments in Caernarvonshire. 1. East* (London 1956).

18. To the best of the writer's knowledge, the first State guidebooks to the Edwardian castles were as follows: W. J. Hemp, *Flint Castle* (London 1929); C. Peers and W. J. Hemp, *Harlech Castle* (London 1932); W. J. Hemp, *Beaumaris Castle, Anglesey, Wales* (London 1933); C. Peers, *Caernarvon Castle* (London 1933); W. J. Hemp and C. A. R. Radford, *Denbigh* (London 1935); A. J. Taylor, *Rhuddlan Castle* (London 1949).

19. D. Knoop and G. P. Jones, 'Castle building at Beaumaris and Caernarvon in the early fourteenth century', *Transactions of the Quatuor Coronati Lodge*, 45 (1932), 4–47. The Quatuor Coronati Lodge is the premier lodge of masonic research, having been founded in 1884.

20. J. G. Edwards, 'Edward I's castle-building in Wales', *Proceedings of the British Academy*, 32 (1946), 15–81. Edwards went on to examine the accounts for Flint in more detail, an account to which Taylor added a postscript: J. G. Edwards, 'The building of Flint', *Publications of the Flintshire Historical Society*, 12 (1951), 5–20; A. J. Taylor, 'The building of Flint: a postscript', ibid., 17 (1957), 34–41.

21. Saunders, 'Arnold Joseph Taylor', 365.

22. A. J. Taylor, 'Castle-building in Wales in the later thirteenth century: the prelude to construction', in *Studies in Building History: Essays in Recognition of the Work of B. H. St J. O'Neil*, ed. E. M. Jope (London 1961), 104–33.

23. A. J. Taylor, 'Castle-building in thirteenth-century Wales and Savoy', *Proceedings of the British Academy*, 63 (1977), 265–92: 270; Saunders, 'Arnold Joseph Taylor', 366.

24. RCAHMW, *An Inventory of the Ancient Monuments in Caernarvonshire*, 3 vols (London 1956 (East), 1960 (Central), 1964 (West)); A J. Taylor, *Conway Castle and Town Walls, Caernarvonshire* (London 1956).

25. See note 2. His contribution to the development of the Inspectorate of Ancient Monuments and Historic Buildings was also great, but that is a story told elsewhere, especially in Saunders' two accounts of Taylor's life.

26. A. J. Taylor, 'A note on Walter of Hereford, builder of Caernarvon Castle', *Caernarvonshire Historical Society Transactions*, 9 (1948), 16–19.

27. A. J. Taylor, 'Thomas de Houghton: a royal carpenter of the later thirteenth century', *Antiquaries Journal*, 30 (1950), 28–33.

28. A. J. Taylor, 'The birth of Edward of Caernarvon and the beginnings of Caernarvon Castle', *History*, new ser. 35 (1950), 256–61.

29. 'Harlech Castle', *Archaeologia Cambrensis*, 100 (1948–9), 278–80. Simpson originally published a study of Master James in 1928: 'James de Sancto Georgio, master of works to King Edward I in Wales and Scotland', *Anglesey Antiquarian Society and Field Club Transactions*, (1928), 31–41. He reiterated his view on the role of Master James as one of a civil servant, as opposed to an architect, in 'Harlech Castle and the Edwardian castle-plan', *Archaeologia Cambrensis*, 95 (1940), 153–68, especially p. 163, note 4. Simpson was librarian of the University of Aberdeen, and a prolific writer on castles, mainly those in Scotland, but also elsewhere. His work in Wales, part of a programme of research supported by a grant from the Carnegie Trust for the Universities of Scotland, has largely been overlooked in recent years.

30. Master James of St. George', *English Historical Review*, 65 (1950), 433–57, reprinted in Taylor, *Studies*, 63–87, with additional information and corrections provided on pp. 88–97. Morris, in his *Welsh Wars*, also saw Master James as the chief architect of the king's castles (p. 145).

31. Coldstream, this volume, and 'Architects, advisers and design at Edward I's castles in Wales', *Architectural History*, 46 (2003), 19–36.

32. A. J. Taylor, 'The date of Caernarvon Castle', *Antiquity*, 26 (1952), 25–34; *Caernarvon Castle and Town Wall, Caernarvonshire* (London 1953).

33. The special nature of Conwy's walls, and why they stand apart, was discussed by Taylor in his presidential address given in 1969 to the Cambrian Archaeological Association, as was the work undertaken since 1953: A. J. Taylor, 'The walls of Conwy', *Archaeologia Cambrensis*, 119 (1970), 1–9. Taylor also stressed what was needed in the future: 'There *must* be a long-term planning policy for Conway that puts the re-establishment of the whole circuit of the town walls in a dignified open setting high on its list of priorities.' The late Richard Avent and his colleagues at Cadw ensured that Taylor's work continued, thus making it possible for all to see that Conwy's town walls are truly amongst the finest in Europe.

34. A. J. Taylor, *Conway Castle and Town Walls, Caernarvonshire* (London 1956), 6.

35. Comparison of the Ministry of Works/Public Building and Works guidebooks with the four Cadw editions of the Taylor guidebook (1986, 1993, 1998, 2003) shows that there is very little difference between the texts of the history section.

36. R. A. Brown, H. M. Colvin and A. J. Taylor, *The History of the King's Works: the Middle Ages*, I–II (London 1963). Taylor's contribution on the Edwardian castles was later to be published twice as a separate publication: *The King's Works in Wales 1277–1330* (London 1974); *The Welsh Castles of Edward I* (London 1986). See Abigail Wheatley, this volume, on Taylor and the supposed links between Caernarfon and Constantinople's defences.

37. A. J. Taylor, 'Some notes on the Savoyards in north Wales, 1277–1300, with special reference to the Savoyard element in the construction of Harlech Castle', *Genava*, new ser. 11 (1963), 289–315. It is unfortunate that this very useful paper was not included in Taylor, *Studies*, seemingly for copyright reasons (ex inf. Derek Renn).

38. A. J. Taylor, *Harlech Castle/Castell Harlech, Gwynedd* (Cardiff 1980); *Beaumaris Castle/Castell Biwmares, Gwynedd* (Cardiff 1980); *Rhuddlan Castle/Castell Rhuddlan, Clwyd*, 3rd edn (Cardiff 1982). The Beaumaris guide provides a substantial description of Edward's last castle in Wales, but it is to be hoped that a future Cadw edition will include more detail, particularly of parts of the fabric largely omitted by Taylor, such as the Gate next the Sea and the Llanfaes Gate.

39. A. J. Taylor, 'The Conwy particulars accounts for Nov. 1285 – Sept. 1286', *Bulletin of the Board of Celtic Studies*, 30 (1982–83), 134–43.

40. A. J. Taylor, 'The Beaumaris Castle building account of 1295–1298', in *Castles in Wales and the Marches: Essays in Honour of D. J. Cathcart King*, eds J. R. Kenyon and R. Avent (Cardiff 1987), 125–42.

41. A. J. Taylor, 'The town and castle of Conwy: preservation and interpretation', *Antiquaries Journal*, 75 (1995), 339–63.

42. J. A. Ashbee, *Conwy Castle and Town Walls* (Cardiff 2007); J. Ashbee, 'The royal apartments in the inner ward at Conwy Castle', *Archaeologia Cambrensis*, 153 (2004), 51–72; P. Brears, this volume, N. Coldstream, this volume, and 'Architects'.

16

The Baronial Castles of the Welsh Conquest

John A. A. Goodall

The great baronial castles of the Welsh conquest rank amongst the most intriguing and ambitious architectural creations of the late thirteenth century. That this simple fact is not immediately apparent from much of the literature on castles in this period is a reflection of the competition they face. Flint, Rhuddlan, Conwy, Caernarfon, Harlech and Beaumaris – to name but six of the great royal castles central to the subject of this volume – are not only magnificent monuments, but they are also thoroughly documented and tie directly into the compelling narrative of Edward I's conquest of Wales. They are, it should be added, in the care of the State, and have consequently long been the object of well-resourced research. Their long shadow has cast the baronial castles that are the subject of this paper into a deep and unjustified shade.

As defined here, the baronial castles are a group of five buildings that came into being in common and specific circumstances: rather than receive all the newly conquered territories of Wales into direct royal ownership, Edward I parcelled out the estates of several members of the dispossessed Welsh nobility to a small circle of favoured English magnates. With one exception at Hawarden in 1281, all these royal grants were made in 1282 following the defeat of Llywelyn ap Gruffudd. They constituted the only major territorial distributions made by Edward I during his entire reign and they were to prove of great subsequent importance, serving to bind Wales into the dynastic politics of late medieval and early modern England.

In each case, the grant of lordship was associated with, or led to the erection of, a major castle: Hawarden, Denbigh, Ruthin, Chirk and Holt. Unlike their royal counterparts, these baronial buildings are not well documented (though accounts do survive for the start of works to Ruthin between 1277 and 1282 under royal direction) and little is known in detail about the progress of their construction. All that can be said with certainty is that they were all in existence and substantially complete by the first quarter of the fourteenth

century. Also, that the design and form of the new buildings related closely to those of the principal royal castles begun by Edward I.

The latter point was fully appreciated in the outstanding modern publication regarding the history of the royal castles, *The History of the King's Works*.[1] Indeed, this study moved outside the strict bounds of its subject in covering all these baronial buildings even though four of them were never in royal ownership. Considering the rigour with which it otherwise excluded sites, this coverage is a tribute to the perceived importance of their architectural relationship with the king's architectural projects. Yet this authoritative treatment has imposed a particular vision of the creative mechanics behind the castle construction of Edward I's conquest that distorts a full appreciation of them. It is a vision that requires delicate, but profound reappraisal.

In its analysis of the Welsh castles, *The History of the King's Works* (which rearticulates and expands on the ideas previously published by Arnold Taylor, one of its contributors) assumes the primacy of royal architectural projects over all others. In so doing, incidentally, it repeatedly prefers the claims of Edward I as a patron over those of his son. As a result, Edward II is not represented as making any meaningful conceptual contribution to the completion of castles such as Beaumaris or Caernarfon. In addition, the *King's Works* argues that the greatest of the royal Welsh castles were the culminating architectural creations of the English castle-building tradition. As a partial explanation for this, it represents the contribution of one individual – Master James of St George – as fundamental to the form of these castles. In this last respect, it deserves emphasis for present purposes that the accounts relating to the baronial castles have been scoured for references to James of St George as a way of inferring his direct involvement in their design.

It is with this last point that a reappraisal of the analysis presented in *The History of the King's Works* must begin. There are good reasons to suppose that the crucial influence on the design of the Welsh castles, both royal and baronial, was not James of St George but the body in which he worked: the King's Works. By the late thirteenth century the King's Works, though rooted geographically in the south-east of England with its effective home at Westminster, enjoyed a virtual monopoly on major architectural works across the kingdom. Moreover, in all their undertakings, the personnel of the King's Works in Edward I's reign were reformulating High Gothic architectural ideas first introduced to England in the early thirteenth century, during the later reign of John and the minority of Henry III.[2]

The degree to which the King's Works was centralizing architectural design by the mid-thirteenth century can be illustrated with reference to the castle buildings that can be attributed to one leading mason in Henry III's employment, Robert of Beverley (d. 1285). He is first documented in royal service at Westminster Abbey in 1253 and was eventually appointed to the post of 'King's Mason'. Amongst many other responsibilities, he took over control of the on-going reconstruction of the Tower of London in 1270. While working on this project, he constructed several towers distinctively designed with pairs of turrets projecting like ears to the rear. The largest and

most important of these towers with 'ear' turrets of this kind was erected during Edward I's reign, the Beauchamp Tower (1279–83) (Fig. 16.1).[3]

Significantly, this form of tower was not new within the castle and can be found, for example, in Broad Arrow Tower, which was built earlier in the remodelling process. Nor did the form fall out of use at his death: towers of this type continued to be erected in much later buildings, many of them linked with London masons. Most notable in Wales is Marten's Tower at Chepstow, erected by Ralph Gogun 'of London' in the 1290s (Fig. 16.2).[4] They also appear in completely different parts of the kingdom, as for example in the sophisticated early fourteenth-century remodelling of the great tower of Helmsley Castle (Yorkshire) (Fig. 16.3).[5]

In effect, it is possible to identify here a relatively unusual, but distinctive, tower form that was built by several different senior masons over a period of nearly a century. The fact that this particular design appears to be rooted in a royal project hints at the degree to which masons in royal employment were formulating, centralizing and controlling architectural design in this period. Nor is this example of what might be termed a canonic design of the King's Works isolated. Robert of Beverley can also plausibly be connected to the so-called

Figure 16.1: Beauchamp Tower, Tower of London (Jeremy Ashbee).

Figure 16.2: Marten's Tower, Chepstow Castle (Cadw, Welsh Assembly Government: Crown Copyright).

– and much-discussed – Tonbridge-style gatehouse: a residential gatehouse with two drum towers to the front and two stair turrets to the back. The name is taken from what can convincingly be represented on stylistic and circumstantial evidence to be the earliest surviving example of this building type at Tonbridge (Fig. 16.4).[6]

The detailing of the remarkably opulent Tonbridge gatehouse points to a connection with the Westminster Abbey works, which Robert was directing from 1260. Furthermore, Robert is documented as being involved in other castle-building operations in Kent, for example, at Leybourne in 1266.[7] Although documentary proof of his association with Tonbridge does not survive, it is very likely that he oversaw the construction of this exceptional building.

It is possible that the Tonbridge gatehouse was an original building, in the sense that it had no immediate predecessor and that Robert – or whoever designed it – literally conceived it for themselves. This seems unlikely, however, not least because the distinctive idea of pairing inward turrets, which is found in the Tonbridge gatehouse, is implicit in the 'ears' of the London towers that have just been discussed. Indeed, there is a possibility that Tonbridge was actually a copy of Henry III's splendid gatehouse at the Tower of London that collapsed in 1240.[8]

Figure 16.3: Helmsley Castle, great tower (Copyright: English Heritage Photo Library).

Whatever the case, if the Tonbridge-style gatehouse was a product of the King's Works, the subsequent popularity of this very distinctive gatehouse form in Wales is probably not to be explained through the Clare family connection with Caerphilly, as is now conventionally asserted. Indeed, some buildings in this form are more convincingly to be explained in relation to the King's Works than otherwise. The gatehouse at Llansteffan, for example, has been dated after 1270 on the presumption that it follows Caerphilly. Historical circumstances, however, equally allow that it could be slightly earlier, around 1265, which would be possible if the designs related to London instead.[9] One positive piece of evidence that there was such a connection with London is that Llansteffan presents in immediate juxtaposition the two building forms just discussed: the Tonbridge gatehouse and the tower with ear turrets (Fig. 16.5).

The most obvious way of explaining such a passage of ideas is through the exchange of architectural drawings. Virtually no medieval architectural drawings survive in England at all, but the case that they existed in quantity by the early thirteenth century is irresistible. Not only do they survive on the Continent, but the whole practice of masons in the Middle Ages was based on the skill of drawing. At the risk of stating the obvious, drawings allow designs to be created and approved remotely from a building site. They also served to store ideas and to encourage their exchange and conceptual development.

By this analysis, the King's Works brought into existence a reference collection of drawings that were accessible to its constituent masons. There are various ways of demonstrating this through points of technical analysis and comparison. In this context, however, it seems necessary only to invoke what seems to me the most striking feature of the Welsh castles as evidence for their existence: architectural variety. Viewed as a group, the royal castles begun between 1277 and 1295 do not develop one from another in a tidy evolutionary sequence. Instead, they play with a broad spectrum of ideas: Flint, with its great tower, Conwy with its corona of towers or Beaumaris with its pair of gatehouses. No Continental group of castles – and one good parallel for this would be the thirteenth-century works of the Teutonic Knights along the Baltic – offers such a diversity of planning. The only possible exception is the series of castles built by Fredrick II in Sicily.

The History of the King's Works and Arnold Taylor in his other published works went to great lengths to prove how the details of the Welsh castles spoke of the Continental training of James of St George, and in most points he was absolutely right. What he omitted to notice was

Figure 16.4: Tonbridge Castle, gatehouse (Jeremy Ashbee).

Figure 16.5: An aerial view of Llansteffan Castle (Cadw, Welsh Assembly Government: Crown Copyright).

that whatever their detail, their bones and body reflected a variety and sophistication of forms that cannot be explained without reference to the English architectural tradition of King John and King Henry III. That variety, I would argue, was inherited by James of St George and other masons active in the region through the agency of an archive of drawings in the King's Works.

All this is crucially important by way of assessing, understanding and appreciating the architecture of the baronial castles. If James of St George was an isolated genius, his ideas needed to be worked out in royal operations before they could be picked up, like scraps from a rich man's table, by the barons in their own castles. Moreover, when royal projects began to be starved of funds in the 1290s, then it necessarily followed that the creative boom driven by him began to slow down and lose vitality. But supposing that the royal castles and those of the barons derived from a common pool of designs, then the architectural operations undertaken by the king need not necessarily have primacy over those of his followers. Moreover, the architectural works of Edward I's reign can be understood in dynamic relationship to those of Edward II's.

To explain these ideas more clearly it is worth turning to consider perhaps the most celebrated of the baronial castles. Denbigh was correctly represented in *The History of the King's Works* as one of the outstanding architectural creations of the Welsh conquest (Fig. 16.6). This analysis assumed that the great triangular gatehouse on the site followed the design of its counterpart at Caernarfon (Fig. 16.7, Plate 13). It also argued that James of St George designed both gatehouses. In the case of Denbigh, it was

on the very slim evidence of Edward I's gift of £22 towards the forthcoming operations and a payment for 'clays' for the castle.[10] Finally, it implied by the silence on the subject that neither building had any progeny. Before addressing these ideas it is worth broadening the discussion a bit.

Caernarfon Castle actually possesses three very unusual buildings, each of which deserves comparison with the Denbigh gatehouse. The first of these, as is observed in *The History of the King's Works*, is the main gate, with its polygonal porch chamber and twin-towered façade. However, this building cannot be conclusively dated any earlier than Denbigh – 1295 – and therefore cannot certainly be claimed as a source for it. Moreover, it differs from Denbigh in that it can never have had a series of three towers on a triangular plan; the space in the castle simply does not physically allow it. Nevertheless, Caernarfon does possess two buildings begun before 1295 which could in combination have informed its gatehouse design: the Eagle Tower offers a convincing source for its polygonal forms, as does the Queen's Gate with its triangular plan.

In this sense, Denbigh seems most likely to have followed Caernarfon and to have taken its forms – and notably the combined triangular and polygonal plans – to a logical conclusion. Whether the Caernarfon gatehouse was begun before or after 1295, however, is impossible to say. A convincing case could equally be made that Caernarfon respects the ideas of an original plan established in 1283–92 or, alternatively, that it was designed contemporaneously with Denbigh and in accommodation of established physical constraints.

Quite as important in appreciating the close connection

between Denbigh and Caernarfon is the fact that their architectural ideas are reworked to brilliant effect in a third building, in Yorkshire. The great tower of Knaresborough (Fig. 16.8) was built by Edward II for his notorious favourite, Piers Gaveston, between 1307–15.[11] This remarkable structure was planned using two superimposed geometric forms lifted from the Eagle Tower at Caernarfon and the gatehouse at Denbigh: a triangle as defined by the three angle turrets and an octagon (or circle) as expressed in the shape of the basement chamber. Significantly, this building was almost certainly designed by a prominent London mason in the orbit of the King's Works, Hugh de Tichemers or Tichmarsh.[12]

At risk of confusing things, it is worth pointing out that both the Eagle Tower and the great tower of Knaresborough have perfectly convincing antecedents in much earlier architecture: both may well derive from the great tower built by Henry II at Orford, with which they share several formal points of comparison. Also, the fascination with polygonal forms – in other words complex geometry – the toy of the brilliant master mason, which the design of these buildings illustrate, is widely echoed in the church architecture of the mid-thirteenth century: it can be found, for example, in the chapter house of Westminster or the 1270s porch of St Laurence's church in Ludlow. The triangular plan of the Queen's Gate is likewise anticipated by such Henry III buildings as the outer gate of Tamworth or even the east end of Battle Abbey.

With these ideas in mind, it is worth considering briefly the other baronial castles in north Wales, jumping in a similar fashion between generations of building and regions. The design of Lions or Holt Castle (Fig. 16.9), built by John de Warenne, has been compared with that of Conwy.[13] This connection, while justifiable, does not acknowledge the existence of a more complex group of related designs with a richer architectural history.

The arrangements of Conwy with its corona of towers and the absence of a gatehouse are anticipated, for example in the inner bailey at Kidwelly. This is probably a work of the late 1270s undertaken by Payn de Chaworth with subventions of cash from Edward I.[14] And both Kidwelly and Conwy may derive in turn from the Henry III works to the Tower of London: the 1220s Lanthorn Tower looked very like the inner bailey towers at Conwy with a tall stair turret to the rear (this feature is unlikely to belong to the repairs undertaken in Henry VII's reign). According to one sixteenth-century survey there may, moreover, exist a parallel for Conwy's differentiation of towers in the inner and outer baileys (using stair turrets) with the scantily documented buildings at Ruthin, a castle begun under

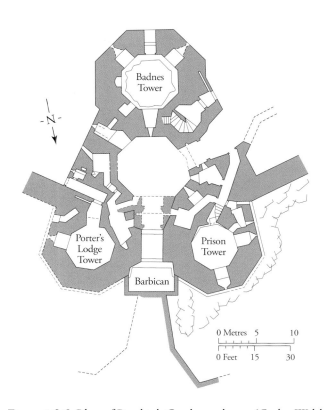

Figure 16.6: Plan of Denbigh Castle gatehouse (Cadw, Welsh Assembly Government: Crown Copyright).

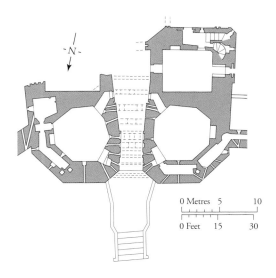

Figure 16.7: Plan of the King's Gate, Caernarfon Castle (Cadw, Welsh Assembly Government: Crown Copyright).

Figure 16.8: Reconstruction of Knaresborough Castle great tower (Illustration by Terry Ball; copyright: Country Life).

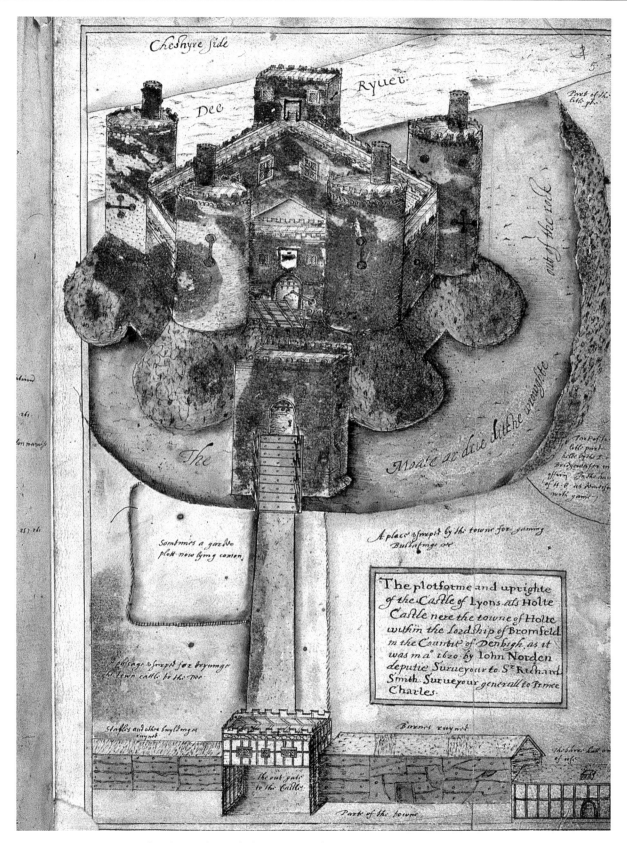

Figure 16.9: A survey of Holt Castle made by John Norden in 1620 (British Library, Harley Ms. 3696, f. 5).

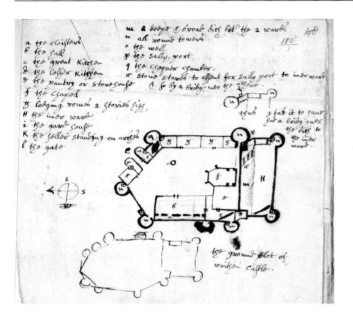

Figure 16.10: A survey of Ruthin Castle made by Randle Holme (British Library, Harley Ms. 2073, f. 110/1).

Figure 16.11: A bird's-eye view of Ruthin Castle in which the differentiation of towers between the inner and outer wards through the use of stair turrets is clear. From R. Newcome, An Account of the Castle and Town of Ruthin *(Ruthin 1829).*

royal patronage and handed over after 1282 to Reginald de Grey, justiciar of Chester (Figs 16.10 and 16.11).[15]

Similarly, the connection between Flint and Hawarden has been acknowledged in the past but never contextualized (Figs 16.12–16.14). Flint is a truly revolutionary building that deserves much more attention than it has received. The inspiration for creating such a massively conceived tower with a ring of chambers is probably to be found in the architecture of so-called shell keeps in the thirteenth century (there is no precedent for it in such cited French designs as the Tour de Constance at Aigues Mortes, which has no rings of mural chambers at ground- or first-floor level). One specific source might be the tower of the earl of Cornwall at Restormel, also under construction in the 1270s. The design of Flint possibly also reflects a thirteenth-century admiration for Romanesque great tower design, with its fascination for sophisticated mural chamber arrangements.

If Flint had a long architectural pedigree in England, its progeny also had a long future. It is not only probably the direct inspiration for the ring of wall chambers in the Eagle Tower at Caernarfon, but it is likely to explain a whole sequence of major buildings into the fourteenth century, such as the great towers of Wardour and Southampton. In the long term, the great tower of Flint was more admired (and therefore imitated) than any other castle begun by Edward I. It is a sad irony, therefore, that it remains amongst both scholars and visitors the least loved of all the royal castles.

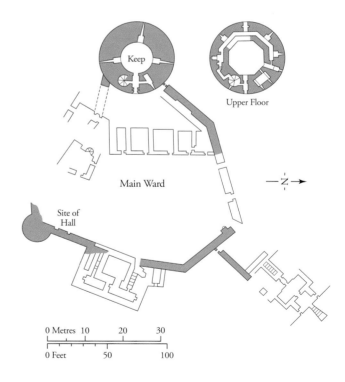

Figure 16.12: Plan of Hawarden Castle, after G. T. Clark ('Hawarden Castle', Archaeological Journal, *27 (1870), 239–54). Clark's plan was from a survey made in 1857 by James Harrison of Chester (Cadw, Welsh Assembly Government: Crown Copyright).*

Figure 16.13: The great tower, Hawarden Castle (John A. A. Goodall).

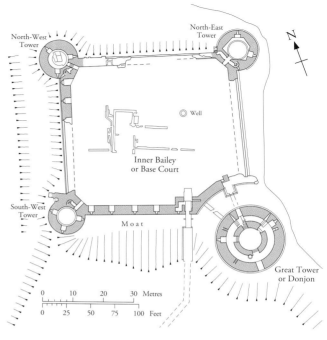

Figure 16.14: Plan of Flint Castle (Cadw, Welsh Assembly Government: Crown Copyright).

There can be little doubt in the circumstances that nearby Hawarden was modelled on this important and sumptuously finished building. It was probably begun by Roger de Clifford shortly after the castle that he had built on the site in breach of a treaty was sacked by the Welsh in the 1282 rebellion. The great tower at Hawarden closely copies the circular plan of Flint with a ring of chambers and passages in its disproportionately thick walls.

Two points of the Hawarden design are in striking contrast to those of its prototype however. First, the tower is built of shaped masonry, which is not regularly coursed. This type of construction is distinctive of Cheshire, as for example at Beeston in the works of the 1220s. It appears quite different from the beautifully cut ashlar of the great tower at Flint. Second, the tower stands on a motte (rather than within a moat). Overall, the Hawarden great tower seems like a straightforward attempt to reproduce a great building on a smaller budget irrespective of materials or location. Perhaps it was quite literally scaled down from a drawn plan of its model. Regardless of this detail, it has a direct bearing on our understanding of Flint. In particular, the form of Hawarden adds strength to the case that the central area of the tower at Flint was floored over rather than left open as a central light well.[16]

The last in the group of baronial castles briefly considered here is also the most exiguous. Chirk Castle

must have been begun by Roger Mortimer between 1282 and 1328 (Fig. 16.15). Unfortunately, however, there is no good documentary evidence to refine this dating. As it presently exists, the castle is a botched and incomplete structure. The present layout suggests that the original intention was to construct a rectangular enclosure with eight towers placed regularly around the perimeter. Only three quarters of this plan was realized and the fourth side of the castle was constructed much later on a reduced scale. This odd arrangement is supposed by some authorities to be the consequence of a structural collapse, but the tidy masonry break at the termination of the original build makes this seem very unlikely. Much more probable is that the original design was simply never realized.

It has been observed that Chirk bears a passing resemblance to the regularly planned inner ward of Beaumaris, begun in 1295. On the basis of this comparison, it was dated in *The History of the King's Works* slightly later than the royal building – which was assumed to be its source – to 'around 1300'. Aside from the absence of any gatehouse to command the entrance, this comparison between the two castles seems absolutely appropriate to make. The conceptual primacy of Beaumaris, however, cannot be accepted uncritically. Moreover, by relating the two Welsh buildings only to each other, the assessment of

Figure 16.15: North-East Prospect of Chirk Castle *by Thomas Badeslade, 1735 (Llyfrgell Genedlaethol Cymru – The National Library of Wales).*

Chirk ignores the possibility that both castle designs had a common architectural source elsewhere.

Such a putative common source is not difficult to find amongst buildings associated with the King's Works. Reconstructing the proposed reorganization of the Tower of London initiated by Henry III is fraught with difficulties. There is, however, a perfectly convincing case that as completed by Edward I, the castle was deeply indebted to the ill-fated building planned by his father in 1238 or 1239. In part, this broad continuity of design might be inferred from the long-term involvement of Robert of Beverley in the work. His service there not only bridged the two reigns, but his style of designing things – as we have seen in the case of 'ear-turreted' towers – was not individualist, but informed by the corporate memory of the King's Works.

If, for the purposes of argument, this broad continuity of design is accepted, then masons in the King's Works would have been aware of an exemplar for a regularly planned castle enclosed by an apron wall and a moat. It is such a plan that would – in my opinion – most logically have informed the design for Caerphilly in the 1260s: to all intents and purposes, Caerphilly could be analysed as a reduced version of Henry III's Tower of London plan, ripped-off from the King's Works in just the manner of the Tonbridge gatehouse. And – probably independently – so too are both Beaumaris and Chirk likely to have looked towards this London model for their inspiration. By extension, Chirk could be dated to the first foundation of the lordship in 1282 and precede Beaumaris.

What this paper has sought to argue is that the Welsh castles – both royal and baronial –were the products of a complex exchange of architectural ideas within the King's Works. It is this institution, not the politics of the conquest of Wales or the particular individuals employed by the king there, that hold the key to the development of castle architecture in the principality during the late thirteenth century. The paper has made this case in modification of an analysis that has – in one sense – isolated the royal castles by elevating them out of the context in which they were conceived and created. One way to rescue that context is to look again at the baronial castles that sprang up beside them and recognize them as more than just derivative buildings. These were a common product of a centralized architectural tradition in the King's Works, which, by the death of Edward I, was already emerging as the most admired and inventive in Europe.

Notes

1. R. A. Brown, H. M. Colvin and A. J. Taylor, *The History of the King's Works: the Middle Ages* (London 1963).

2. This idea is fully explored in my own forthcoming book, *English Castle Architecture, 1066–1640* (New Haven and London forthcoming), chapters 7–9.

3. C. Wilson, 'Beverley, Robert of (d. 1285)', *Oxford Dictionary of National Biography* (Oxford 2004) [http://www.oxforddnb.com/view/article/42212, accessed 31 Oct 2007].

4. R. Turner, S. Priestley, N. Coldstream and B. Sale, 'The New or Marten's Tower', in *Chepstow Castle: its History & Buildings*, eds R. Turner and A. Johnson (Almeley 2006), 151–66.

5. The raising of the tower is discussed in both J. Clark, *Helmsley Castle, North Yorkshire* (London 2004), 12–13 and G. Coppack, *Helmsley Castle, North Yorkshire*, 2nd edn (London 1997), 6–10.

6. Most recently discussed in D. Renn, 'Tonbridge and some other gatehouses', in *Collectanea Historica: Essays in Memory of Stuart Rigold*, ed. A. Detsicas (Maidstone 1981), 93–103.

7. *Calendar of Close Rolls, 1266–1272*, 144. The gatehouse is a building of the 1260s but connected to the 1220s works at Dover. See Goodall, *English Castle Architecture*, chapter 7.

8. *Matthaei Parisiensis Monachi Sancti Albani Chronica Majora*, III, ed. H. R. Luard (Rolls Series LVII, London 1876), 80.

9. P. H. Humphries, *Llansteffan Castle*, revised edn (Cardiff 1996), 1.

10. *King's Works*, II, 196–200.

11. P. Dixon, 'The donjon of Knaresborough: the castle as theatre', *Château Gaillard*, 14 (1990), 121–39 and J. Goodall, 'A royal gift: Knaresborough Castle', *Country Life*, 202.3 (2008), 72–74.

12. J. Harvey, *English Mediaeval Architects: a Biographical Dictionary down to 1550*, revised edn (Gloucester 1984), 299.

13. L. Butler, 'Holt Castle: John de Warenne and Chastellion', in *Castles in Wales and the Marches: Essays in Honour of D. J. Cathcart King*, eds J. R. Kenyon and R. Avent (Cardiff 1987), 105–24

14. J. R. Kenyon, *Kidwelly Castle*, 4th edn (Cardiff 2007), 9.

15. British Library, Harley Ms. 2073, f. 110/1. A facsimile is reproduced in the frontispiece of R. Newcome, *An Account of the Castle and Town of Ruthin* (Ruthin 1829), showing both a plan and bird's-eye view of the castle.

16. D. J. C. King, 'Hawarden Castle', *Programme of the 113th Annual Meeting at Chester, 1966* (Cambrian Archaeological Association, 1966), 28–29; idem, 'The donjon of Flint Castle', *Journal of the Chester and North Wales Architectural, Archaeological and Historical Society*, 45 (1958), 61–69; E. W. Gladstone, *Hawarden Old Castle* (privately published 1974).

Edward I's Building Works in Gascony

Marc Morris

As the legend on his great seal and the opening words of his writs and charters make manifest, Edward I bore not one title, but three (Fig. 17.1). King of England was, of course, the most important, but he was, in addition, lord of Ireland and duke of Aquitaine. To his Irish lordship Edward showed remarkably little attachment: between acquiring possession in 1254 and his death in 1307 he never saw sufficient reason to pay these lands a visit. On Aquitaine, by contrast, Edward lavished considerable amounts of time and attention. In the same period, 1254–1307, he travelled to the duchy on no fewer than

Figure 17.1: The great seal of Edward I (The National Archives).

five separate occasions, and altogether resided there for more than five of his sixty-eight years.[1] This paper exhibits the same wholesale bias, and devotes itself to the building works undertaken in Aquitaine by Edward during the half-century or so of his rule.

For Aquitaine, read Gascony, and vice versa: the two terms have been used interchangeably, if inaccurately, by Englishmen since the thirteenth century, so it seems too late to try to arrest the trend here. What they intended when they used either designation was the south-western corner of what is now modern France, but which was then a possession of the English Crown. To explain how this tenurial situation arose, one could venture as far back as the Norman Conquest; in a fundamental sense, the possession of Continental lands by English kings began when England's throne was seized in 1066 by a Norman duke. Gascony itself does not enter the picture until 1152, at which point Henry Plantagenet – count of Anjou, grandson of the Conqueror and hence soon-to-be King Henry II of England – married that most renowned of medieval heiresses, Eleanor of Aquitaine. The marriage handed to Henry the vast duchy inherited by his wife, extending the reach of his power (which would soon extend as far north as Hadrian's Wall) as far south as the Pyrenees. But this great agglomeration of lands – the Angevin Empire, as historians have dubbed it – was of only short duration. In 1204 Henry and Eleanor's incompetent son, King John, lost the ancestral heartlands of Normandy, Maine and Anjou to the king of France, and after John's death the collapse continued with the loss of Poitou during the minority of his successor. By the time Henry III came of age in 1227, the only part of the Angevin Empire that remained in English hands was its south-western rump – Gascony – and it was this diminished duchy that Henry in due course bequeathed to his own son, Edward I, in 1272.

Despite its diminished size, Gascony was a treasured and

jealously guarded possession. Merely from a meteorological perspective, it is not hard to imagine why its English rulers should wish to spend more time there than in Ireland, or, for that matter, northern England. Then as now, the principal attraction of this warm, sunny and fertile region was its wine. In the early years of the fourteenth century, over 80,000 tuns a year were being exported through the duchy's chief city, Bordeaux.[2] As the wine implies, this was a cultivated and cultured land. The English, and Edward in particular, considered the Gascons to be devious and wily, but they did not disparage them as they did the natives of Wales and Ireland.[3] The society of southern France was palpably civilized and ancient, as the Roman ruins in its towns and cities attested. The courts of the south had been the birthplace of troubadour poetry, as well as of several English queens. Edward's own mother, Eleanor of Provence, was the most recent southern match.

Against these attractions, however, Gascony presented several major problems. To begin with, obviously, it was the most distant of the English Crown's overseas dominions. To travel there overland via France took approximately three weeks, assuming the king of France was amenable, and to make the journey by ship took at least a fortnight, assuming the weather was clement.[4] Consequently, Gascony had to be ruled by a lieutenant or seneschal acting on the king's behalf. A greater problem still was the very limited authority that the English king (or his deputy) exercised in the duchy. Of old – well before the region had passed into English ownership – the dukes of Aquitaine had failed to establish themselves as powerful overlords. They held very little land of their own, and hence had very little income, and hence wielded very little power. As their successors, Henry III and Edward I were thus at a disadvantage if they wished to overawe their Gascon vassals, who were accustomed to managing their affairs by themselves. Lastly, Gascony was difficult to govern on account of its terrain. Except for the region south of Bordeaux known as the Landes, which until the nineteenth century was mostly desert, the duchy was thickly forested, hilly and (in places) mountainous. Rather like Wales, it was a landscape that encouraged local particularism and division, and militated against attempts at strong, centralized rule.[5]

The weakness of ducal authority and the fractiousness of local lords inevitably meant that civil strife in Gascony was not uncommon, and, indeed, it was civil strife that drew Edward to the duchy for the first time in 1254. Rebellion had been provoked by the overbearing rule of Henry III's ill-chosen lieutenant, Simon de Montfort, and stoked by the new king of Castile, Alfonso X. Henry saw off the threat of a Spanish invasion by agreeing that his eldest son should marry Alfonso's sister, which is why Edward was in due course married to Eleanor of Castile. As part of the deal, Alfonso stipulated that his new brother-in-law should receive lands worth 10,000 marks (£6,666), which is how Edward came to be granted Gascony: the duchy, along with the royal lands in Wales and Ireland, constituted the greater part of his new appanage.[6]

These developments, however, while they led to Edward's first visit to Gascony, did not mark the beginning of his rule there in any meaningful sense. Henry III retained the title 'duke of Aquitaine' and the right to review and overrule his son's decisions. By the end of 1255 Edward had returned home, where he was soon distracted by rebellion in Wales (1256) and revolution in England (1258). Thereafter his visits to Gascony were only brief, and the evidence of his involvement in its government is thin. When the crisis in England at length subsided in 1267, Edward's preoccupation was his impending crusade. Thus it was not until his return from the East in 1273, by which point his father was dead and his own rule had been proclaimed, that Edward was able to apply himself to Gascony in earnest.

The task he faced was shaped above all by one dominant factor, and that was a historic peace between England and France that had been agreed in 1259. Under the terms of the Treaty of Paris, Henry III had done homage to the king of France for Gascony, and at the same time abandoned his claim to the lost provinces of the Angevin Empire (Normandy, Anjou, et al.).[7] Modern commentators have tended to view this treaty in negative terms, dwelling on the legal and tenurial complexities it inevitably created, but in doing so they have missed the wood for the trees. All such considerations were outweighed by the great benefit that Edward derived from the treaty, which was a peaceful relationship with his most powerful neighbour. Unlike his Plantagenet predecessors, he did not have to worry about Gascony's external defence, and could concentrate on consolidating his rule within its borders. The need for such consolidation was pressing, not least because the Treaty of Paris ultimately led to a major increase in the duchy's size. In 1279, after much patient English diplomacy, King Philip III of France honoured the part of the treaty that promised Edward new lands on Gascony's eastern border. That year saw the transfer to English control of the Agenais, an extensive region around the city of Agen. Later, in 1286, Philip IV agreed to hand over southern Saintonge (i.e. the region south of the town of Saintes).[8]

With this background in mind, we may turn at last to Edward's building works, beginning with his castles. As the map shows (Fig. 17.2), by 1290 he was possessed

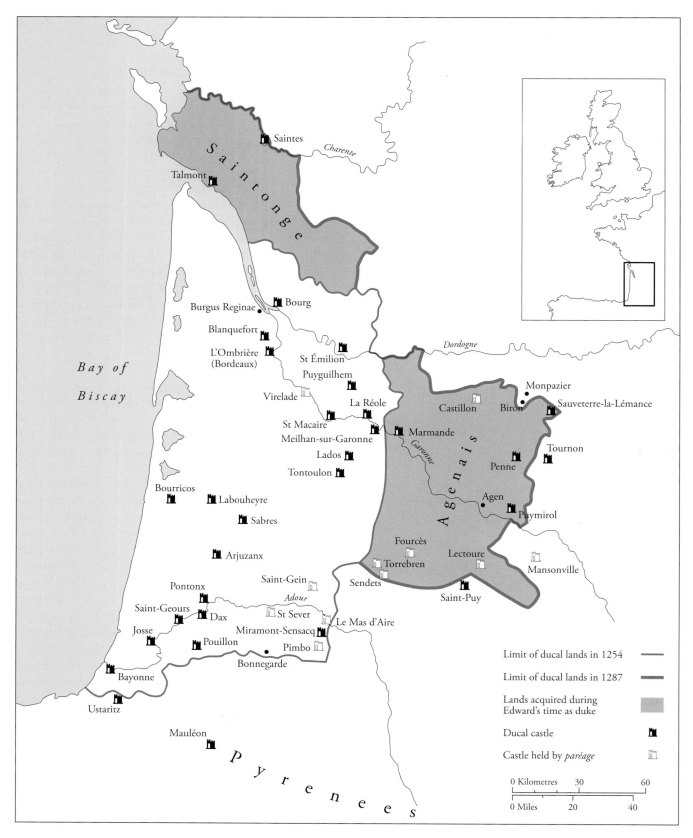

Figure 17.2: Map of Gascony (Cadw, Welsh Assembly Government: Crown Copyright).

with a goodly number of fortresses spread widely across the duchy. This simple picture, however, gives a misleading impression. Almost without exception, these buildings were nothing to brag about. The majority were ancient hand-me-downs, a far cry from the spectacular castles that the king created in Wales. It is fair to point out that the castles of Gascony have survived far less well than their Welsh counterparts – in many cases (for example, Arjuzanx, Bourg, Dax, L'Ombrière, Marmande, St Macaire, Saintes and Talmont) they have disappeared altogether – but this merely reinforces the impression that they were less durable and impressive buildings in the first place. Often they were no more than small towers or mottes. One of the better survivals is the donjon at St Émilion, apparently begun by Louis VIII of France and later finished by Henry III. As the picture shows (Fig. 17.3), it is an archaic and underwhelming affair.[9]

The very limited extent of ducal finances meant that Edward was hardly able to improve matters. At the start of his reign in England, the king began redeveloping the Tower of London on a massive scale. In Gascony, by contrast, a similar initiative to build a new stone castle at Bordeaux, perhaps ordered in an initial flush of enthusiasm, apparently proved abortive. The same constraints seem to have been felt elsewhere in the duchy around the same time. During his visit of 1273–74 Edward had to deal with the rebellion of his greatest vassal, Gaston de Béarn, and deprived the vicomte of several of his castles. One of these, Miramont-Sensacq, Edward subsequently ordered to be refortified, but, to judge from excavations there in 1881, it appears that the works were carried out in wood.[10]

As the recourse to tentative language and archaeological evidence suggests, the problem is not simply that the castles of Gascony are scrappy and ill preserved; they are also for the most part undocumented. Like their opposite numbers in England, Edward's officials in Bordeaux kept extensive records, but these were almost all lost when the duchy was occupied by French forces in 1294. As a result there is no equivalent to *The History of the King's Works* for Gascony; the best modern study is Jacques Gardelles' *Les Châteaux du Moyen Age dans la France du Sud-Ouest: La Gascogne Anglaise de 1216 à 1327*, which relies on archaeological evidence and the occasional orders concerning Gascony that emanated from England. Typically such orders were non-specific injunctions to the seneschal to ensure that the duchy's castles were kept in good repair: we hear little of specific building campaigns. Nevertheless, the paucity of documentary evidence should not lead us to make undue allowances. In general, the written and physical record suggests that Gascony witnessed little new building

Figure 17.3: The donjon at St Émilion (Copyright: Marc Morris).

during Edward's time as duke. Mend and make-do was the necessary *modus operandi*.[11]

To increase his stock of available castles, Edward could resort to other methods. One route was to purchase existing fortresses at a favourable rate. Talmont, for example, was bought for 1,322 *livres tournois* (about £330) in 1283, and Tontoulon for 3,500 *livres bordelais* (about £500) in 1290. In other cases they were obtained by exchange. Meilhan-sur-Garonne was acquired in this way in 1262, while the previous year Mauléon became ducal when its owner, Auger de Mauléon, was forcibly persuaded to exchange it for lands elsewhere. Sometimes Edward would content himself with only a partial share of a particular fortress. In 1275, for instance, he purchased a quarter share of the castles of Sendets and Torrebren from Guilhem-Raimond de Pins. At other times he settled for the acknowledgement of his right to use a castle on demand (so-called 'rendability'). Such power-sharing arrangements, known as *paréages*, were quite common in Gascony. Lesser lords liked them because having the duke as a shareholder was a good guarantee against aggression from powerful neighbours. From Edward's point of view, *paréage* offered another way of extending his seigneurial influence for comparatively little outlay.[12]

The most effective way for Edward to extend his

influence in Gascony, however, was not with castles but with new towns, or bastides. New towns, of course, were in themselves nothing new in the thirteenth century: in England they were being founded at a steady rate from the eleventh century onwards. But southern France, devastated by religious war in the early 1200s, lagged behind the rest of Europe in this regard, and consequently its urban redevelopment did not begin until Edward's lifetime. Following the example of the neighbouring count of Toulouse, who was laying out new towns from the 1240s, Henry III had established a handful of bastides in the last years of his reign. Once Edward had succeeded his father this piecemeal policy became programmatic. In 1274, the new king-duke instructed his seneschal to plant new settlements in the duchy wherever he saw fit, and as a result dozens sprang up in the two decades that

followed. In general, they were laid out to a far more rigid grid-iron pattern than the new towns Edward established in Wales. The only truly comparable site in Britain is the new town the king created at Winchelsea in Sussex after the original was swept away by the sea, and the similarity is not surprising: one of the men responsible for Winchelsea's foundation, Henry le Waleys, had earlier been entrusted with the design of half-a-dozen bastides.[13]

The creation of bastides served a two-fold purpose. Most obviously, they were a source of profit. Merchants who came to trade in their market places could be taxed at source by Edward's officials, while the increased economic activity that new towns encouraged across the duchy as a whole swelled the customs revenues at Bordeaux. Equally, and as we have already noted, they were a means of increasing ducal authority. Bastides, more so even than

Figure 17.4: Monpazier, a bastide founded by Edward I in 1285 and visited by the king the following year. At the centre of its rigid grid-iron of streets is a well-preserved arcaded market place (Copyright: Philippe Dufour).

castles, were typically founded by an act of *paréage*. It was local lords who put up the necessary land, in return for which they received the duke's protection and a share of the profits. To take just one example, the celebrated town of Monpazier (Fig. 17.4) was created by an act of *paréage* with the lord of nearby Biron.[14]

Edward's priorities in Gascony come into sharper focus during the period 1286–89. During these years the king was resident in the duchy – it was by far his longest stay – and the surviving records of his wardrobe and household shed some additional light on his building activities. We read, for example, that small works and repairs totalling £4 8s. were carried out at Bordeaux in the house of the city's archbishop, in which Edward and Eleanor apparently preferred to stay. To judge from the dates involved, these may well have been the same lodgings that witnessed a near catastrophe on Easter Day 1287, when the floor of a certain chamber in Bordeaux suddenly collapsed, causing the king and his companions to fall from a great height.[15]

There were also works carried out at Blanquefort, a ducal castle some 5 miles (8km) north-west of Bordeaux, which presents an interesting case study. Like other ducal castles, Blanquefort had been acquired in stages. Half of the castle and its lordship had been confiscated during the time of Henry III, the second half had been obtained by purchase by Edward's seneschal, Roger Leybourne, in 1270.[16] The desire to possess the whole of Blanquefort may have owed more to personal preferences than any pressing need for defence. Whenever Edward was in the neighbourhood of Bordeaux he tended to reside at Blanquefort rather than in the city. After his fall in 1287 – once he had recovered from a broken collar-bone – it was to Blanquefort that he retreated, and it was probably there that he took his second crusading vow a few days later.[17] What is notable, however, is that the works Edward commissioned at this favoured fortress were seemingly negligible. Arnold Taylor, in one of his later articles, suggested that there was 'a remarkable similarity' between the standing masonry at Blanquefort and the gatehouse at Rhuddlan, but this resemblance is entirely spurious.[18] What stands today at Blanquefort is a multi-towered donjon of a kind that cannot have been built before the mid-fourteenth century.[19] Whatever works Edward caused to be carried out there (they are alluded to once, in passing, in his household accounts) were almost certainly on a small scale, in keeping with the general tenor of his castle building in Gascony.[20]

Besides Blanquefort, there were two other locations at which Edward elected to spend long periods during his stay of 1286–89. During the spring of 1288 he spent several months at a site on the shore of the Gironde estuary, close to the point where the duchy's two main rivers, the Garonne and the Dordogne, converge. It seemed like a good location to plant a new town, and so a bastide was duly planted. Called Burgus Reginae in tribute to Eleanor of Castile, it was probably, as the name suggests, something of a self-indulgent exercise. Edward at the time was waiting for the wheels of international diplomacy to turn, and had little else to keep himself occupied. No doubt considerable sums were spent on the project, but no record of them has survived (the household rolls for the regnal year 1287–88 are not so complete). Certainly no trace of the town has survived into the present, beyond the name of the nearby village – La Bastide.[21]

The other location on which Edward expended much effort, and a comparatively large sum of money, was Bonnegarde, a settlement on the duchy's southern border. Bonnegarde (sometimes called Bellegarde) was also a bastide, and is often mentioned in academic discussion on the grounds of its apparently exceptional possession of a castle.[22] In this respect, however, the character of the site has been misunderstood. Bonnegarde's designation as a bastide was only a recent development in the thirteenth century (it was chartered as such in 1287). The elevated site on which it was laid out was far older, and seemingly prehistoric – something akin to an Iron Age hillfort. In south-western France such sites sometimes go by the name *castera*, and it is not difficult to see how this word could be misconstrued. The *castera* at Bonnegarde is formed of formidably steep earthworks and surmounted by a motte, which probably dates from the early Middle Ages, but it is not a castle in the true sense; rather it is an ancient fortification latterly converted into a new town. Edward's contribution during his stay of 1286–89 was to convert it yet again, by purchasing a sizeable plot of adjacent land from the neighbouring lord of Sault, on which a new lower but more extensive town was laid out.[23] This presumably freed up the *castera* itself for the king's own use, and, indeed, when Edward and his household ensconced themselves there in the winter of 1288–89, we read of all manner of new buildings being erected 'within the close (*clausturam*) of the motte of Bonnegarde'. New chambers were built for the king, the queen, their friends and their attendants; there was a new chapel dedicated to St Katherine, a kitchen for the use of 'the king's Dominicans', and 'other necessary buildings', which must have included lodgings of some kind for the leopard and lion that Eleanor of Castile had brought with her. The works were clearly considerable: plasterers, diggers and carpenters were in pay for a whole month before the royal party arrived, and construction continued for the duration of their stay. At the same time, it is clear that these new buildings were fashioned from timber. Bonnegarde was the biggest building expense recorded in Edward's household rolls during his visit of 1286–89, but even so the total cost of the new works there came to only £60.[24]

Figure 17.5: Sauveterre-la-Lémance, well sited on a spur of rock in a loop of river (Copyright: Philippe Dufour).

In overall terms, therefore, Edward's stay in Gascony in the late 1280s underlines the basic fact that, compared with those carried out in his other dominions, his Continental building projects were conducted on a very small scale.[25] To conclude, however, we may turn to consider what appears to be a major exception to this general rule, and a building that may furnish the only bona fide connection with the king's works in Wales.

At some point during the period 1287–89, Edward's celebrated Savoyard architect, Master James of St George, abandoned his castle-building activities in north-west Wales and set out to meet the king in Gascony. Arnold Taylor had naturally noticed this visit but was surprisingly uncurious about its nature, merely speculating in a footnote that it may have been 'for consultation about the works in Wales or in connexion with the building of bastides'.[26] Neither of these explanations seems very likely. Edward I may not always have been reasonable but he was by no means foolish; it would have made no sense to summon Master James from Wales to Gascony – a round trip of over 1,200 miles (1,920km) – simply for a consultation exercise. Likewise, it was hardly necessary to re-deploy the Savoyard, however great his skills, in order to advise the Gascons about the building of bastides: that really would have been to carry coals to Newcastle. It seems altogether

Figure 17.6: Sauveterre-la-Lémance: a closer view (Copyright: Philippe Dufour).

more likely that Master James was ordered south in 1287 for a more important and specific reason. Tentatively, I would suggest that the reason was the king's decision to establish a new castle at Sauveterre-la-Lémance.

Sauveterre-la-Lémance (Figs 17.5 and 17.6), which lies on what was Gascony's eastern frontier, is the only new castle to have been built in the duchy by Edward I. There is no record of precisely when it was started, but it is most unlikely to have been before 1279, for it does not feature in the survey of the Agenais undertaken that year, nor is it mentioned in any earlier document. The first we hear of its existence is in October 1289, when a new receiver was appointed for the Agenais, with additional responsibility for 'our bastide of Villefranche in the Périgord, near our castle of Sauveterre'. The town of Villefranche-du-Périgord had been acquired in 1287.[27]

If building work at Sauveterre began in the late 1280s, it was evidently well advanced by the time war broke out with France in 1294. We know this because, when peace was restored ten years later, a mason called William de Cosinges applied for the arrears of his wages for work carried out at the castle, 'as shown by a letter of John of St John' – seneschal of Gascony until the war's outbreak.[28] From this it would seem equally clear that William de Cosinges was the man responsible for Sauveterre's construction, not Master James of St George, who in any case looks to have been back in Wales by the summer of 1290.[29] But did Master James, one wonders, have a hand in the castle's origins? Sauveterre has no obvious architectural parallels with Edward I's Welsh castles, of the kind that Taylor discovered in Savoy.[30] Yet, as the king's only new fortress in Gascony, it must have been exceptional in every sense, built to guard a new frontier at a time when Anglo-French relations were already starting to show signs of tension. Who could be trusted to select the site, and to decide on the castle's layout and design? For a fortress of such signal importance, we might be tempted to assume that it was Edward himself, but there is no evidence that the king ever visited Sauveterre. Plausibly, therefore, it may have been to his greatest and most experienced castle builder that the king turned in 1287, and Master James may thus have come to Gascony to 'ordain' the new castle there, just as he had famously 'ordained' the castles in Wales.[31]

Notes

1. His visits were June 1254 to October 1255, December 1260 to March 1261, October 1261 to December 1262, September 1273 to April 1274 and September 1286 to June 1289. He is often said to have visited in 1262–63, but there is no evidence of this. R. Studd, *An Itinerary of the Lord Edward* (List and Index Society 284, 2000), 2–27, 54–56, 58–61, 64–66; E. W. Safford, *Itinerary of Edward I* (List and Index Society 103, 132, 135, 1974–77), I, 17–26, 228–72.
2. M. Vale, *The Angevin Legacy and the Hundred Years War, 1250–1340* (Oxford 1990), 141.
3. *Calendar of Close Rolls 1272–79*, 493.
4. J.-P. Trabut-Cussac, *L'Administration Anglaise en Gascogne sous Henry III et Edouard I de 1254 à 1307* (Geneva 1972), xvi–xvii.
5. J. Gardelles, *Les Châteaux du Moyen Age dans la France du Sud-ouest: la Gascogne Anglaise de 1216 à 1327* (Geneva 1972), 9–12, 27–28. Note, however, that ducal revenues had improved dramatically by the end of Edward's reign. Vale, *Angevin Legacy*, 142.
6. M. Morris, *A Great and Terrible King: Edward I and the Forging of Britain* (London 2008), 14–18.
7. For the text of the treaty, see *English Historical Documents, 1189–1327*, ed. H. Rothwell (London 1975), 376–79.
8. Morris, *A Great and Terrible King*, 172, 207.
9. Gardelles, *Les Châteaux*, 26, 44, 86, 105–06, 108, 130, 171–72, 213–16, 225–26.
10. R. A. Brown, H. M. Colvin and A. J. Taylor, *The History of the King's Works: the Middle Ages*, II (London 1963), 715–23; Gardelles, *Les Châteaux*, 28–29, 175–76.
11. S. Raban, *A Second Domesday? The Hundred Rolls of 1279–80* (Oxford 2004), 28; Gardelles, *Les Châteaux*, 28, 44.
12. ibid., 29–30, 172, 175, 223, 225, 228–29.
13. M. W. Beresford, *New Towns of the Middle Ages: Town Plantation in England, Wales and Gascony* (London 1967), 6, 14–15, 19, 28–29, 319–20, 351–59, 363–64; D. and B. Martin, *New Winchelsea, Sussex: a Medieval Port Town* (King's Lynn 2004), *passim*.
14. Beresford, *New Towns*, 359–62, 584; see also Vale, *Angevin Legacy*, 152–60.
15. *Records of the Wardrobe and Household, 1286–1289*, eds B. F. and C. R. Byerly (London 1986), nos 169, 255; Morris, *A Great and Terrible King*, 208–09.
16. Trabut-Cussac, *L'Administration Anglaise*, xx, 15n.
17. Morris, *A Great and Terrible King*, 208–09.
18. A. Taylor, 'Master Bertram, *Ingeniator Regis*', in *Studies in Medieval History Presented to R. Allen Brown*, eds C. Harper-Bill, C. J. Holdsworth and J. L. Nelson (Woodbridge 1989), 303. Taylor twice describes what he had seen at Blanquefort as 'a twin-towered gatehouse', when it was plainly nothing of the sort. There is no easy way to account for his error.
19. Gardelles, *Les Châteaux*, 102–03; see also A. Tridant, *La Forteresse de Blanquefort XIᵉ-XIIIᵉ-XVᵉ Siècle* (Blanquefort 1992), *passim*.
20. *Records of the Wardrobe and Household*, no. 304.
21. Morris, *A Great and Terrible King*, 212, 215.
22. e.g. Beresford, *New Towns*, 185, 187, 602; M. Prestwich, *Edward I* (London, 1988), 309.
23. J.-L. Blanc and J.-F. Massie, 'Le Castera de Bonnegarde', *Extrait du Bulletin de la Société de Borda*, (1977), *passim*. The documents used by Blanc and Massie were later published in *Records of the*

Wardrobe and Household, e.g. nos 544, 1372, 3049.

24. ibid., nos 1651 (£47), 1676 (£10), 2800 (leopard and lion); a further £2 7s. 6d. was spent in January on making a causeway (*chaucedi*) to the king's chamber from the gateway of the *castrum*. Ibid., no. 1699. After Edward's departure, the keeper of Bonnegarde was given £33 to build a new chapel there, which might imply masonry. Ten per cent of this money, however, was spent on drinks for the workers. Ibid., no. 2505.

25. For other expenditure on buildings during Edward's stay in Gascony, see ibid., nos 337, 475, 533, 1783, 1842.

26. A. Taylor, 'Master James of St George', in idem, *Studies in Castles and Castle-Building* (London 1985), 73. The evidence for Master James's visit is less certain than Taylor believed; the prest in Gascony was in fact paid to the unrelated Master S(tephen) of St George (*Records of the Wardrobe and Household*, no. 2128). Nevertheless, the payment made to Master James, 'going to the king in Gascony', and his disappearance from Wales at this time, strongly suggest that the visit did indeed take place.

27. Gardelles, *Les Châteaux*, 28, 220–22; *Rôles Gascons*, ed. F.-M. and C. Bémont, 4 vols, (Paris 1885–1906), ii, no. 1795; Beresford, *New Towns,* 588.

28. *Rôles Gascons*, iii, no. 4762.

29. Taylor, 'Master James', 72–73. Gardelles, *Les Châteaux*, 221, had no doubt that William de Cosinges was also the 'Master William of Geneva' who resumed work at Sauveterre around this time (1305). If so, it seems reasonable to assume that he was the man in charge of the project. Whatever the case, Master William's toponymic suggests that he, like Master James, was a Savoyard.

30. To the best of my knowledge, no detailed investigation of the site has been undertaken.

31. My thanks to Michael Prestwich for reading this paper in draft and making useful suggestions for its improvement.

Welshmen in the Armies of Edward I

Adam Chapman

As long ago as 1901, J. E. Morris established that Welsh infantry were invaluable to Edward I in all his military schemes after his first war against Llywelyn ap Gruffudd in 1277. Predominantly, the Welsh serving in his armies were drawn from the south of Wales and the March, where English influence and lordship were familiar if not always welcome facts of life. Despite, or perhaps because of, Morris's work, the role of the Welsh in the military successes (and failures) of Edward I is not one that has attracted significant attention from other historians, particularly in recent years. While Morris makes plain the role of Welsh troops in the success of Edward's eventual conquest of Gwynedd, and the affinity of the Welsh with Edward II is well known, little has been written about the rise of the Welsh foot soldier in English armies. This is despite their conspicuous presence in Edward's wars in Scotland.[1] In many respects, the involvement of Welsh infantry in other theatres of war is not surprising; it represents continuity from one prolonged military struggle, the Welsh wars, to others, first against the Scots, and later against the French. Even when parts of Wales rose in rebellion in 1287 and again on a larger scale in 1294, Edward made great use of the military resources within Wales to suppress the insurgents in their own land.

The military role played by the elite of Wales has fared a little better in the historiography, particularly in the context of the political machinations amongst the lords of Wales in the period immediately before the death of Llywelyn ap Gruffudd. The final conflict between Gwynedd and the English Crown was as much a conflict between Welshmen as it was between Welsh and English. In the first Welsh war in 1277, of the 15,000 men who served in the English army, some 9,000 were Welsh. As David Stephenson has demonstrated, the issue of control was at the heart of this conflict.[2] Llywelyn ap Gruffudd and Llywelyn ab Iorwerth before him sought to subordinate the rights of their fellow Welsh lords by acting as a conduit between them and the king of England. After 1277, two

Welsh lords on the boundaries of Gwynedd – Rhys ap Maredudd in west Wales and Gruffudd ap Gwenwynwyn in southern Powys – decided that their interests would be better served by retaining their lands as tenants-in-chief of the distant English Crown rather than in risking their gradual erosion under the influence of their neighbour, the prince of Gwynedd.

The decline of Welsh princely elites has been noted by R. R. Davies, R. A. Griffiths and A. D. Carr amongst others. In Edward's conquest there were opportunities for them, and these go a long way to emphasize the political and social divisions in Wales.[3] A significant number of the Welsh leaders of this period were from the north, but many of the soldiers were from the lands of south Wales. The shifting loyalties and varied fortunes of the princes of Gwynedd in the thirteenth century resulted in a Welsh elite that was increasingly familiar with the ways of England. Any disaffection within this elite was widely exploited by all parties in what became, in part, a competition between the resources of the two superior lords: Llywelyn ap Gruffudd, prince of Wales, and Edward I, the king of England. The wars of Edward I in Flanders, France and Scotland were an all important factor in the development of Wales following the conquest of Gwynedd and the settlement formalized in the Statute of Wales in 1284. The extraordinary numbers of Welsh infantry employed in the suppression of rebellions in Wales from 1287 and in England's wars from 1296 must have shaped the experience and attitude of generations of Welshmen, and the government of the lands of Wales throughout the rest of the fourteenth century.[4]

The main purpose of this paper is to describe the administrative mechanisms and personnel responsible for recruiting and leading the many thousands of Welshmen who served in Edward I's armies in Wales and abroad. Secondly, it seeks to give an impression of how military commissions were viewed by the existing Welsh elite and how, in turn, these were used by both the Crown and the Welsh themselves to reaffirm and to adapt existing social structures. Finally, the role played by the Welsh in Edward's wars and their role in the development of his use of infantry in his Scottish wars will be examined.

Important though the influence of Edward I was, the March and its English lords were a powerful force both politically and militarily in the period. The retinues drawn from the Marcher lords' Welsh lands were not wholly dependent upon their English tenants: Welshmen also served their English lords in war and peace. It was R. R. Davies who most convincingly highlighted the military importance of these estates and the role that their military resources played in the political importance of the Marcher lords on the English stage.[5]

Edward's wars in Wales brought with them significant developments in military organization. It is here that the role of Welshmen in English royal service first became apparent in a wider context. Edward's demands for soldiers were inevitably heaviest in the counties that bordered Wales and in the Marcher lordships within Wales. The men of these border counties were, in turn, willing to serve due to the threat of Welsh raids, or by coercion from their lords. In the English counties, Edward had access to the mechanisms of English government, the sheriff and his deputies, who were able to raise county levies of infantry, and therefore to lead them to the king's army. In the course of Edward's Welsh wars, however, the responsibility for recruitment and leadership evolved gradually. In 1277, the work was generally in the hands of the sheriffs; but by 1282, it had become usual to appoint officials – often household knights – specifically for the task.[6] Introduced simultaneously in Wales and England, this can be seen as the foundation of the system of commissions and the appointment of commissioners of array, a role which was to become almost that of professional recruiters by the end of Edward's reign in 1307.[7] Military recruitment changed from being an element within local government to a process which used the agency of local government as a tool. In due course, when the principality was fully shired after 1284, the organization of the levies was placed in the hands of the justiciars and their deputies rather than the county administration under the sheriff. In the principality of south Wales, the limited role of the sheriff in military recruitment was as much a result of the piecemeal conquest of the south as the decline in his importance in this area of administration. In the northern principality, however, where the role of sheriff was often held by prominent Welshmen, the situation was less clear cut.[8]

In the lordships of Wales, however, the king's writ did not run, a fact unchanged by the conquest of Gwynedd.

He could normally only request military assistance from the lords Marcher – who while in Wales were the king's equals and not merely his tenants-in chief – unless their lordships were in the king's hands. The concept of paid service was not the accepted element of military service that it became in subsequent decades. The king could and did request troops from the Marcher lordships by means of a writ to the individual lords; and the process of recruitment would be placed in the hands of the lord's steward, whose administrative responsibilities and position within the communities generally barred them from military service. The steward served the interests of his lord, rather than the military endeavours of the Crown.[9] The process, securely established by the time of Edward I's death, was that the justiciar – be he that of south Wales, north Wales or Chester – was responsible for the organization of the levies, and the funds to pay them were to be procured and disbursed by the chamberlain from the revenues he collected. The chamberlain's responsibility for payment of the levies extended beyond the bounds of the principality from at least as early as 1296. Like many offices in later medieval Wales, the actual work of recruitment was supervised by deputies of the justiciar appointed for the purpose of recruitment. The move away from sheriffs to commissioners of array can be seen as part of the beginnings of military professionalization. Sheriffs, with their annual terms of office, were less suited to the long campaigns of the Welsh and Scottish wars. In both Wales and England the king appointed officers whose standing and experience could be used repeatedly for the recruitment of royal armies.

The men who served as commissioners of array in Wales form an interesting group and reveal much about Edward's approach both to the elite of Wales and to the lords Marcher themselves. Moreover, they represent an important innovation in that they were, without exception, already important figures, by office or by standing in the communities from which they were recruited. They form three distinct – if not necessarily discrete – groups. The first was the Marcher lords themselves, and, more pertinently, their stewards and local officials. The second was the king's officials, the justiciar and his deputies in the lands of Wales. Generally these were Englishmen from the south-west of England or the counties of the Welsh border. Others were members of families who had followed the Marchers into the lands of south Wales and formed the backbone of royal administration in the region. For example, Warin Martyn, brother of the then bishop of St Davids, was appointed as deputy justiciar to Walter de Pederton between April and May 1298, with orders to levy 2,500 men from Cardiganshire, Carmarthenshire and Cemaes (Pembrokeshire) and to lead them thence to Carlisle.[10] The third group, which occasionally overlapped with the first two, was of prominent Welshmen. These men were either those who had proven themselves in royal service in the 1270s and 1280s, members of the royal household, or native lords who had declared their loyalty to Edward, such as the sons of Gruffudd ap Gwenwynwyn in southern Powys.

In many respects, the Welshmen who served as commissioners are the most interesting of the three groups, as the manner in which they came to be royal servants and leaders of the Welsh levies offers a valuable insight into post-conquest society, and particularly the nature of the Welsh elite. In the conquered lands of Gwynedd, and those lands forfeited by Rhys ap Maredudd following his rebellion in 1287, the royal influence that might be expected was balanced by the survival of the pre-conquest elite. The lineage of Ednyfed Fychan (d. 1246), steward (*distain*) of Llywelyn ab Iorwerth was perhaps the most conspicuous beneficiary of royal office. David Stephenson has suggested that there was a hereditary element to the office of *distain*, and, importantly, that it also carried military responsibility. The evidence for this is in part circumstantial: Ednyfed and his descendants were often called upon as military leaders. The privileged *wyrion eden* tenure they enjoyed made this service an explicit requirement, one that would have come their way in such a militarized society.[11] In Gwynedd, the *distain* replaced the office of *penteulu*, traditionally assigned to a member of the princely line, but which might constitute a danger in the attempts at dynastic consolidation under both Llywelyns in the thirteenth century.[12] In this light, it is interesting that the office appears to have survived in Powys well into the fourteenth century, though what its responsibilities were by the time that Owen de Cherleton obtained it in 1375 are unclear. The reasons for its survival, however, are rather more easily understood. Uniquely, the lordship of Powys passed to the Cherleton family, and thus into English hands by inheritance rather than conquest. It is quite possible – though it cannot be proved – that either William or Gruffudd de la Pole held this position in Powys in the later part of Edward's reign as the brothers were almost invariably appointed jointly as commissioners of array in this lordship.[13]

The descendants of Ednyfed Fychan came to dominate the administration of much of the principality of Wales in the fourteenth century and experienced a very different treatment from that of the remaining princes of Deheubarth and southern Powys. These princes had been successfully subdivided by the influence of Gwynedd and by incursions from the Marcher lords. Their survival

as 'Welsh barons' (*barwnaid*) had a particular military significance: they held their lands, in part by *tir pennaeth*, which is broadly defined in a later document as 'of the king in chief... by fealty and service of going with his men in the king's army when reasonably warned at the kings cost'.[14] While their general exclusion from administrative office has been long recognized, their status as recruiters and leaders of armies drawn from within the Welsh community has not been closely examined in this period. Their status was not the only qualification for such roles, however, as examination of their individual careers shows that personal service, favour and reward were at least as important as an individual's origins. Yet the importance of this class of society in providing both leaders of communities and the leaders of men was clearly recognized by English officials in the 1340s and must have been apparent in this earlier period.[15] The residual military bearing of the status of Welsh barony might even be said to have constituted some of the appeal of Owain Glyndŵr, himself a member of the *barwnaid*, more than one hundred years after the conquest.[16]

The role in public life, and particularly in military leadership, exercised by the descendants of Ednyfed Fychan suggests something more aggressive than the simple assumption of power under Edward's new regime. The dominance that this lineage displayed in the administration of north Wales, and Anglesey in particular, and from the reign of Edward II in south Wales through the person of Sir Rhys ap Gruffudd, is especially striking. The depiction of Sir Gruffudd Llwyd as the chief lord, guarantor and protector of Gwynedd in the poetry of Gwilym Ddu (admittedly from the reign of Edward II) makes use of forms and imagery more appropriate to the praise of a prince than of a lord not of royal stock. Implicit in these descriptions are Gruffudd's military pre-eminence as well as his and his family's socio-political dominance of north Wales.[17]

In the years after the conquest, Edward I made use of Welshmen as a personal bodyguard, and paid Welsh musicians to play at his court.[18] Their presence within his household presents some interesting questions. It might be seen as an extension of the presence of Welsh hostages and exiles within the royal household throughout the second half of the thirteenth century. After the conquest, the appearance of the '*Wallenses Regis*' at the English court may have carried a different, almost imperial, significance. Quite apart from the question of appearance, there is the military reputation of the Welsh in this period to be considered. The picture painted by Gerald of Wales of the Welsh warrior, fierce and proud, if lacking in discipline, is persistent and one which the wars of 1277 and 1282 can only have reinforced. The tactical effectiveness of the Welsh fighting man was questioned by Gerald and by other chroniclers throughout the twelfth and thirteenth centuries. Sean Davies's recent analysis presents a more complex picture than the shorthand remarks of chroniclers, and one which concurs more easily with that which emerges from the period following the conquest.[19]

Only a relatively small number of Welshmen entered Edward's military household for any period of time. Cynwrig Sais offers perhaps the most consistent example, serving as a squire of the household in the rebellion of 1294–95 and in Scotland in 1300.[20] Similarly, Sir Gruffudd Llwyd of Tregarnedd, Anglesey, appears to have been brought up within the queen's household, and his father and uncle served in the king's armies in 1282. As a descendant of Ednyfed Fychan, and by virtue of his marriage to Gwenllian, daughter of Cynan ap Maredudd, his status in Anglesey and north Wales did not rely purely upon royal patronage. It is also the case, however, that his and his family's influence was a necessity in securing the consent of the Welsh community to English rule. It is no accident, therefore, that he was the most significant military leader and royal agent in north Wales from the late 1290s until his death in 1335.[21]

Gruffudd Llwyd is perhaps the best known of the Welsh leaders of Edward I's reign, but he was by no means alone. A man frequently overlooked is Sir Hywel ap Meurig, who served the interests of the earls of Hereford as lords of Brecon and also Roger Mortimer, as well as acting as constable for the king at Builth and leading levies from the middle March in 1277. His sons and their descendants remained prominent in Marcher affairs until the end of the fourteenth century.[22] The most interesting case in many respects is that of Morgan ap Maredudd who led the rebellion of the men of Glamorgan and Morgannwg in 1294–95. His life and career demonstrate the political sensitivity of the March in English affairs and the ability of Welshmen to exploit them. He first appears in the historical record attempting to claim his father's lands in Machen, in the lordship of Newport, by litigation. These lands had seemingly been appropriated by Gilbert, earl of Gloucester and lord of Glamorgan, while Edward I was on crusade. The litigation was unsuccessful, and the appropriation was formalized. Later, it seems he was briefly allied to Dafydd ap Gruffudd in his last doomed rebellion, but for the next ten years he disappears from view.[23] The leaders of the revolt of 1294–95 were treated relatively leniently, though some suffered forfeiture or long-term imprisonment (but at least one is evident among the Welsh squires serving in Flanders in 1297). Morgan emerged with both lands and liberty intact. The description of

the Worcester chronicler, to the effect that he submitted himself to the king's peace against the wishes of the earl, suggests that the men of Glamorgan and Morgannwg were truthful in their description of their revolt as being against their earl rather than against their king.[24]

Edward's Wars in Scotland and Flanders

Edward's aim in using his Welsh levies appears to have been to provide a mass army of paid infantry in support of mounted men-at-arms raised by feudal means. As such, they were dependent upon the king's finances and largely independent of the great magnates. Though the concept of paid infantry armies was far from new, they were a political tool as much as a military force.[25] While the men were recruited at the discretion of their lords, they were paid out of the revenues of the Crown from the time they mustered. From a commander's perspective, an army with significant military experience from the decades of conflict in Wales that would fight for wages, and could be led by men with something to gain from their loyalty and service, had a definite appeal. The nature and effectiveness of these men are debatable, yet this is an argument that can be applied to infantry forces of any origin during Edward's reign. What evidence there is, however, suggests that the Welsh made good, if occasionally ill-disciplined, soldiers who were far less prone to desertion than their English colleagues.

The numbers apparently employed are staggering. If Prestwich's estimates based upon incomplete records are correct, then the Welsh foot soldiers recruited for Edward's Scottish campaigns between 1296 and 1298 are particularly impressive. As many as 10,000 Welsh troops may have served at the battle of Falkirk, and similar numbers two years earlier. These numbers on their own were comfortably larger than those of the vast majority of medieval armies. As a proportion of the Welsh population at this date – perhaps 200,000 – it exceeded any number recruited for any conflict before or since, reflecting perhaps half the men of fighting age living in Wales at the time.[26] While these were probably the largest Welsh levies ever employed by Edward I, they are in other respects representative. On occasion, the numbers and availability of the Welsh foot soldier enabled Edward to undertake military operations that would otherwise have been impossible. The expedition of 1297 is perhaps the clearest – and certainly the best documented – example of this: of the maximum strength of 7,800, almost 5,300 of the infantry were Welsh (though perhaps only ten of the cavalry).[27] Their continued use throughout the Scottish wars appears to suggest that Edward was not only interested in sheer force of numbers in his campaigns, but also used Welsh soldiers as a matter of policy. Just as in England, the military burden in Wales was far from equally distributed. Areas under royal lordship were employed far more consistently and in greater numbers than the lordships of the March. Since they had served in significant numbers from the first Welsh war in 1277, there was not only a pool of valuable military experience and skill, but also, as time went on, a tradition of military service amongst Welshmen.

Their equipment has been a matter of some contention. Morris's doubts that the Welsh of north Wales 'ever practised archery' before the conquest are impossible to confirm, but it appears unlikely given the way in which infantry drawn from north Wales was used in Edward I's wars. The only reference in historical writing to the difference in armaments between the northern and southern Welsh is found in the writings of Gerald of Wales, who states that south Wales was the land of the bow and north Wales that of the spear. Such delineation sounds unlikely by the late thirteenth century given the way in which foot soldiers were specified and described in the reigns of Edward II and Edward III. Almost invariably, the form of commissions of array specifies an equal mix of men armed with spears and with bows. There are exceptions, but these are generally concerned with the ratio between types of troops rather than weapons. The likelihood therefore is that men from all parts of Wales – a heavily wooded country in the Middle Ages – bore both styles of weapons and had always done so.

The Depiction of the Welsh (Figs 18.1 and 18.2)

The common impression of the Welsh in the Middle Ages was one almost of barbarians, without the trappings of civilization, tough and wild. This well-known trope can be found throughout medieval literature and administrative documents and has its place as late as the seventeenth century.[28] It is likely, however, that for most Englishmen and certainly for most observers from the Continent, their encounters with the Welsh were in times of war and, most probably, as soldiers. The well-known illustrations apparently used as a filing aid by English chancery clerks give us the clearest impression of what Welsh soldiers looked like in this period. They depict both an archer (Fig. 18.1) and a spearman, also armed with a long knife of the sort later described by Froissart in his account of the Welsh at Crécy (Fig. 18.2), both wearing only one shoe. Their appearance is distinctive: the long hair, bare legs and thin cloaks suggest a distinct absence of civilized dress and behaviour to contemporary English eyes, an

Figure 18.1: An English chancery clerk's impression of a Welsh archer reproduced from enrolled letters concerning Wales – Littere Wallie (The National Archives: PRO E 36/274).

impression which is confirmed by English and Scottish chroniclers. Moreover, it accords well with the account of the appearance of Welsh foot soldiers provided by the Flemish chronicler, Lodewyk van Veltham, relating to 1297:

> Edward, king of England, came to Flanders. He brought with him many soldiers from the land of Wales, and also some from England. He came to Ghent… There you saw the peculiar habits of the Welsh. In the very depth of winter, they were running about bare legged. They wore a red robe. They could not have been warm. The money they received from the King was spent on milk and butter. They would eat and drink anywhere. I never saw them wearing armour. I studied them very closely, and walked

Figure 18.2: Like his counterpart, the archer, this marginal drawing from calendared correspondence concerning Wales from the second half of the thirteenth century depicts a spearman wearing only one shoe (The National Archives: PRO E 36/274).

among them to find out what defensive armour they carried when going into battle. Their weapons were bows, arrows and swords. They also had javelins. They wore linen clothing. They were great drinkers. Their camp was in the village of St Pierre. They endamaged the Flemings very much. Their pay was too small and so it came about that they took what did not belong to them.[29]

The picture presented by van Veltham is one of rowdy, under-armoured but relatively well-armed foot soldiers, much in accordance with the illustrations. Their behaviour in Flanders, alluded to above, is well recorded in chronicles, particularly in that of the abbey of Bury St Edmunds. The fractiousness of Edward's alliance with the Flemings, particularly with the citizens of Ghent, is evident, as is the effectiveness in siege-craft of the English army which, as noted earlier, was more than two-thirds Welsh. One episode, describing an individual act of reckless bravery by a Welsh soldier who swam a river, climbed a palisade, killed three defenders and returned to his fellows displays much of what English documents often termed 'light-

headedness'. That he was apparently rewarded with 100s. at the order of Edward himself shows that this was not always regarded as an undesirable quality. Their experience of what might today be termed 'guerrilla tactics' was equally clearly recognized in this period, though ironically in the course of a campaign when the Welsh were largely absent. The *Annales Regis Edwardi Primi*, in its description of the battle between the English and the Scots immediately after the successful siege of Caerlaverock, laments their absence. In what was termed a reward for their earlier service, no Welsh foot soldiers were raised for this expedition, and that was considered to have handicapped the pursuit over the mountains and moors of Scotland.[30]

Another characteristic of the armies of Welshmen gathered by Edward I was the number of standards the Welsh brought with them to war. In part, these badges of identity can be identified with the Marcher lordships, and the desire of these lords to express their power by their ability to raise men. The numbers employed suggest that they signified bonds of community as well as those of lordship and leadership. Another detail drawn from the Bury St Edmunds chronicle suggests that Edward I may have made some use of these emblems in Flanders, though the number of standards carried by the Welsh is unrecorded for this campaign. This seemingly unchivalric trick – using large numbers of banners to make the army appear more impressive than it actually was – had been employed with captured French banners at Evesham in 1265 and was again used in Flanders.[31]

'Since the King [was] extraordinarily clever he sent in advance his Welshmen, numbering up to thirty thousand, with lances erect and pennons attached. Therefore the French scouts were terrified by so many colours… and believed that the force of Englishmen was as large as they supposed it to be from the number of banners.'[32]

The vast numbers of foot soldiers raised for Edward I by his commissioners of array would not have been possible without the significant contribution of the Welsh. With the exception of the counties immediately adjacent to Wales and Scotland, the English shires could not supply large numbers of experienced foot soldiers and proved unreliable when called upon to do so. Moreover, those Englishmen raised in areas away from the March of Scotland seemed prone to desert in a way that the Welsh were not. This may have been a consequence of language; a Welshman on the borders of Scotland would be all too easy to identify. It might equally have been a result of the quality and status of their leaders who, as we have seen, exerted authority and obligation far greater than those of royal office holders.

The development of the military and administrative

infrastructure of England was accelerated by the Welsh wars. Edward required men to be available for prolonged periods of time and this required flexibility of organization, numbers and tactics. Aside from the numbers of experienced, able and inexpensive foot soldiers that the Welsh provided in the wars in their own country and in the later conflict with the Scots, their chief impact was organizational. The experience of the Welsh in Edward I's wars was a defining one for several generations of Welshmen and, arguably, for the population of Wales as a whole. It was not simply a period of antagonism, but part of a more complicated process of acceptance and adaptation by a pragmatic population.

Perhaps more importantly for Wales in the fourteenth and fifteenth centuries, if not later, Edward's conquest preserved a large proportion of the pre-conquest Welsh elite with a remnant of their lands and liberties. In the case of the descendants of Ednyfed Fychan, their power and prestige were increased by their service to the English Crown, and by the Crown's dependence upon them. While the experience of what some have termed colonial rule may not have been equitable, it did offer significant opportunities, particularly in the military sphere. If nothing else, from 1282 until the death of Edward I (and indeed beyond), it should be remembered that the 'English foot soldier' was more than likely a Welshman.

Acknowledgement

I should like to thank Professor Anne Curry, Dr Adrian Bell, and Dr David Simpkin for their extremely helpful comments and corrections; any remaining errors are therefore my own. I would also like to thank Rachel Evans both for her excellent translation of 'Buchedd a moes y Cymry' and her encouragement and patience. *Diolch yn fawr.*

Notes

1. J. E. Morris, *The Welsh Wars of Edward I* (Oxford 1901).
2. J. B. Smith, 'Edward II and the allegiance of Wales', *Welsh History Review*, 8 (1976–77), 139–71.
3. D. Stephenson, *The Governance of Gwynedd* (Cardiff 1984).
4. R. R. Davies, 'Colonial Wales', *Past and Present*, 65 (1974), 3–23; R. A. Griffiths, *The Principality of Wales in the Later Middle Ages: the Structure of Personnel and Government I, South Wales, 1277–1536* (Cardiff 1972); A. D. Carr, 'An aristocracy in decline: the native Welsh lords after the Edwardian conquest', *Welsh History Review*, 5 (1970–71), 103–29.
5. For examples of such effects, see R. A. Griffiths, 'Gentlemen and rebels in later mediaeval Cardiganshire', *Ceredigion*, 5.2 (1965), 143–67.
6. For the attitude of Marcher lords to military recruitment, R. R. Davies, *Lordship and Society in the March of Wales 1282–1400* (Oxford 1978), 80–84.
7. M. Powicke, *Military Obligation in Medieval England: a Study in Liberty and Duty* (Oxford 1962), 118–33; see also, M. Prestwich, *War, Politics and Finance under Edward I* (London 1972), 99–100.
8. Prestwich, *War, Politics and Finance*, 100.
9. For the sheriff and steward in the southern principality, see Griffiths, *The Principality of Wales*, 47–52. Outside Wales, less than six per cent of sheriffs served as arrayers of infantry *while* they were in office as sheriff between 1300 and 1400: R. Gorski, *The Fourteenth Century Sheriff: English Local Administration in the Late Middle Ages* (Woodbridge 2003), table 5.5, 147.
10. For the role of the steward and the complexity of government in the March see Davies, *Lordship and Society*, notably chapter 9, 'The management of lordship', 199–216.
11. Griffiths, *The Principality of Wales*, 94.
12. G. Roberts, "Wyrion Eden': the Anglesey descendants of Ednyfed Fychan in the fourteenth century', in *Aspects of Welsh History: Selected Papers of the late Glyn Roberts* (Cardiff 1969), 179–214.
13. D. Stephenson, *The Governance of Gwynedd*, 11–20, and A. D. Carr, 'Teulu and penteulu', in *The Welsh King and his Court*, eds T. M. Charles-Edwards, M. E. Owen and P. Russell (Cardiff 2000), 65–81.
14. Madog ap Gruffudd of Glyndyfrdwy successfully petitioned for the office during the temporary disposition of John de Cherleton in 1322: *Calendar of Patent Rolls 1321–24*, 373; the original petition is The National Archives (TNA): PRO SC 8/51/2534. The office of *penteulu* was awarded to Owen de Cherleton for life on 12 April 1375. *Calendar of Patent Rolls 1374–77*, 148–49.
15. From an inquisition into the holdings of Madog ap Gruffudd Fychan of Glyndyfrdwy, 1320. *Calendar of Inquisitions Post Mortem*, VI (London 1910), 150, no. 256.
16. *Calendar of Ancient Correspondence Relating to Wales*, ed. J. G. Edwards (Cardiff 1935) ; D. L. Evans, 'Some notes on the history of the principality of Wales in the time of the Black Prince (1343–1376)', *Transactions of the Honourable Society of Cymmrodorion*, (1925–26), 25–110.
17. For the most recent work on his early career in arms in English service, see the web-pages of the AHRC funded 'The Soldier in Later Medieval England' Project: http://www.medievalsoldier.org/som.php
18. See for example, M. T. Davies, 'The rhetoric of Gwilym Ddu's Awdlau to Sir Gruffydd Llwyd', *Studia Celtica*, 40 (2006), 155–72.
19. TNA: PRO E 101/351/17 and other references to musicians can be found in C. Bullock-Davies, 'Welsh minstrels at the courts of Edward I and Edward II', *Transactions of the Honourable Society of Cymmrodorion*, (1972–73), 104–22.
20. S. Davies, *Welsh Military Institutions 633–1282* (Cardiff 2004).
21. The cognomen 'Sais' (Englishman) refers to his allegiance rather than his ethnic origins. For 1294, *Book of Prests of the King's Wardrobe for 1294–5*, ed. E. B. Fryde (Oxford 1962); for 1300, London, British Library Add. Ms. 35291, f. 97v.

22. J. G. Edwards, 'Sir Gruffydd Llwyd', *English Historical Review*, 30 (1915), 589–601. For his supposed upbringing in Queen Eleanor's household, ibid., 598, n. 57.

23. J. B. Smith, 'Marcher regality: *Quo Warranto* proceedings relating to Cantrefselyf in the lordship of Brecon, 1349', *Bulletin of the Board of Celtic Studies*, 28 (1979), 267–88; W. T. Waugh, 'The Lollard knights', *Scottish Historical Review*, 11 (1914), 55–92.

24. Morgan ap Maredudd appears among the witnesses in two charters of Dafydd ap Gruffudd concerning the *cantref* of Penweddig, May 1283. *Littere Wallie Preserved in Liber A in the Public Record Office*, ed. J. G. Edwards (Cardiff 1940), 74–75 (no. 139) and 133 (no. 235).

25. *Annales Monastici*, IV, ed. H. R. Luard (Record Commission, London, 1869), 526, and *Calendar of Ancient Petitions Relating to Wales*, ed. W. Rees (Cardiff 1975), 217–18 (no. 6389).

26. See for example, S. D. Church, 'The 1210 campaign in Ireland: evidence for a military revolution?', in *Anglo-Norman Studies, 20: Proceedings of the Battle Conference in Dublin 1997*, ed. C. Harper-Bill (Woodbridge 1998), 5–57. My thanks to Dr Church for reminding me of this reference.

27. J. C. Russell, *British Medieval Population* (Albuquerque 1948), 319–52.

28. In general, see M. Prestwich, *War, Politics and Finance*, 93–94. The accounts for the 1297 campaign are BL Add. Ms. 7965; see also N. B. Lewis, 'The English forces in Flanders, August–November 1297', in *Studies in Medieval History Presented to F. M. Powicke*, eds R. W. Hunt, W. A. Pantin, R. W. Southern (Oxford 1948), 310–18. For Welsh presence in the horse valuations (and thus as cavalry), see H. Gough (ed.), *Scotland in 1298. Documents relating to the Campaign of King Edward the First in that Year, and especially to the Battle of Falkirk* (London 1888), 56–66.

29. The most vivid and comprehensive summary of the perception of the Welsh in the Middle Ages is R. R. Davies, 'Buchedd a moes y Cymry' [The manners and morals of the Welsh]', *Welsh History Review*, 12 (1984–85), 155–79. See also, W. R. Jones, 'England against the Celtic fringe: a study in cultural stereotypes', *Journal of World History / Cahiers d'Histoire Mondiale / Cuadernos de Histor. Mundial*, 13.1 (1971), 155–71.

30. Evans, 'Wales in the time of the Black Prince', 25–110, (46, n. 1).

31. *Willelmi Rishanger, quondam monachi S. Albani, et quorundam anonymorum, chronica et annales, regnantibus Henrico Tertio et Edwardo Primo*, ed. H. T. Riley (Rolls Series XXVIII/II, London 1865), 442.

32. For a later example of the Welsh and their use of standards, see: N. M. Fryde, 'Welsh troops in the Scottish campaign of 1322', *Bulletin of the Board of Celtic Studies*, 26 (1976), 82–89. For the attitude of Marcher lords to military recruitment, Davies, *Lordship and Society*, 80–84.

33. *The Chronicle of Bury St. Edmunds 1212–1301*, ed. A. Gransden (London 1964), 143–45.

Scottorum Malleus: Edward I and Scotland

Chris Tabraham

Edward in Scotland

On 7 July 1307 King Edward I of England breathed his last at Burgh by Sands, beside the Solway Firth, 6 miles (10km) north-west of Carlisle (Fig. 19.1). He had just turned sixty-eight and was wracked by illness, yet there he was preparing once more to invade Scotland – his sixth attempt in eleven years. It would have been his seventh had ill health not prevented him from leading his army in the invasion of 1306. Edward's contemporaries knew him as 'Longshanks' because of his commanding height. In Scotland today he is better known by the soubriquet painted on his tomb in Westminster Abbey in the sixteenth century – *Scottorum Malleus*, 'Hammer of the Scots'. But hammer as hard as he might, the king who secured Acre for the Crusaders and conquered the Welsh, could not crack the Scots. In the end, all his hammering came to naught (Fig. 19.2).

Edward spent a combined total of three of his last eleven years on earth on Scottish soil. The reasons behind his obsession with Scotland are long and complex, and are explained elsewhere in full.[1] Suffice to say it was sparked into life by the unexpected deaths, in relatively quick succession, of King Alexander III (1286) and seven-year-old Queen Margaret, 'Maid of Norway' (1290), the latter without an obvious heir. Edward of England, their brother-in-law and great-uncle respectively, was invited by the Guardians of the Scottish realm to adjudicate in the succession process, referred to from the eighteenth century on as the 'Great Cause'. In November 1292 Edward gave his verdict in the great hall of Berwick Castle – John Balliol, lord of Galloway, would be the new king of Scots. King John was duly enthroned at Scone, on the ancient Stone of Destiny, on St Andrew's Day (30 November) that same year.[2]

It seems, however, that right from the outset Edward

Figure 19.1: The stone memorial to Edward I of England at Burgh by Sands, beside the Solway Estuary, with Scotland in the distance (Copyright: Historic Scotland).

Figure 19.2: Edward I of England, seated on his canopied throne, flanked by Alexander III of Scotland (left) and Llywelyn, prince of Wales (right) (The Royal Library, Wriothesley Ms. Quire B; The Royal Collection © 2009, Her Majesty Queen Elizabeth II).

sensed an opportunity to end, for once and for all, the ambiguous relationship between the crowns of England and Scotland that had rumbled on for more than 200 years – really ever since that day in 1072 when King Malcolm III of Scotland had bent his knee to William the Conqueror at Abernethy, beside the river Tay east of Perth, and become 'his man'. It was not long before Edward, in his self-declared role as 'chief lord of Scotland', was undermining the authority of King John at almost every turn.

By 1295 the Scots had tired of Edward interfering in their affairs. This interference had included an impudent demand the previous year for King John and his senior nobles to join Edward for his forthcoming military campaign in Gascony against the French king, Philip IV. In July 1295 the Scottish parliament relieved Balliol of his kingship, and thereafter proceeded to negotiate a treaty of mutual assistance with the French. Edward decided enough was enough. On 16 December he summoned his magnates to muster on 1 March 1296 at Newcastle upon Tyne followed by an order on 23 January 1296 for the army to comprise 1,000 men-at-arms and 60,000 infantry. When the Scots finally ratified the treaty in February 1296, war was inevitable.

The war effectively began when Edward crossed the border at Coldstream on 28 March and marched on Berwick-upon-Tweed, then Scotland's chief commercial town and port. There he presided over the killing of most of the burgh's male population. A month later he defeated a Scottish army at Dunbar, then spent the next four months touring eastern Scotland, during which he secured the abdication of King John, the fealty of countless Scots, and possession of the Stone of Destiny, which he removed from Scone Abbey and took to London as the ultimate trophy of war. When he himself crossed back over the border in late August, leaving behind an English administration and heavily garrisoned castles, he clearly felt that the task of conquering Scotland was all but complete, for he was soon planning his next military campaign for the following year – in Flanders.

But Edward had not anticipated determined resistance, and certainly nothing on the scale that erupted in 1297 under the leadership of William Wallace and Andrew Moray. The fight-back reached its climax on 11 September when the Scottish host overwhelmed Edward's feudal army at Stirling Bridge. The encounter, which saw the English army annihilated whilst attempting to cross the bridge, must have evoked in Edward's mind memories of the debacle at Bangor Bridge in 1282.[3]

Edward returned to Scotland in 1298 bent on avenging this slight. He was duly successful at Falkirk, and after some summary executions, headed south once more thinking that the job was complete. But the resistance would not go away. In 1300 he entered Galloway in strength. In 1301–02, he returned once more to familiar territory, eastern Scotland, wintering at Linlithgow. In 1303 he was back again in eastern Scotland, virtually reprising his first invasion tour of 1296. This time he stayed for fully fifteen months, during which time he secured the general surrender of the Scots at Strathord, north of Perth, and the capture of the strategic castle of Stirling. When he finally crossed back into England on 25 August 1304 he was not to know it would be the last time he would set foot in Scotland.

Edward probably thought that he would never have need to journey to Scotland again. He was by now aged sixty-five and not in the best of health. Any minor Scottish problems hereafter could be addressed by his son, Edward, prince of Wales, to whom he had already entrusted command, of a sort, since the campaign of 1301–02. Then in March 1306 came the unexpected and the deeply disturbing news that his erstwhile ally, Robert Bruce, earl of Carrick, had come out in rebellion and been enthroned as King Robert at Scone. The date of the coronation was 25 March, which, ironically, marked the tenth anniversary of the outbreak of Edward's Scottish wars. Edward was forced to act. Alas, this time the ageing sovereign was unable to make it back into the saddle, and the young prince led the feudal army for the summer invasion of 1306. When that too achieved little, King Edward summoned up his strength to lead his countrymen again in the summer of 1307. If he was still able by the time he reached Burgh by Sands on 6 July, he would have caught his last glimpse of Scotland, lying tantalizingly close across the shimmering waters of the Solway Firth.

Edward's Building Works in Scotland

One might be forgiven for thinking that Edward, having spent all this time in Scotland, might have left behind a considerable military legacy, such as he did in north Wales. He did not: other than a few grassy humps and bumps, and perhaps the odd bit of masonry, nothing tangible remains today of Edward of England's eleven-year attempt to conquer Scotland.

That Edward did not build anything on the scale of Caernarfon or Conwy is surely down to one thing – he was too busy fighting. The Lanercost chronicler summed up Edward's predicament perfectly: 'Whatever he gained in summer, he lost in winter.'[4] More crucially, the cost of raising and sustaining large campaign armies, year on year, was prohibitively expensive. Most of the £77,000 paid out by the Wardrobe in 1298 went to finance Edward's Scottish campaign;[5] the Galloway campaign of 1300 is estimated to have cost between £40,000 and £50,000, and the 1303–04 campaign as much as £80,000.[6] These were monies that Edward's royal coffers just did not have. Time and again, soldiers deserted or refused to follow orders because they were not paid. But lack of money did not prevent Edward from single-mindedly pursuing his goal. In 1304 he ordered the building of three new stone castles, all beside the river Forth. Two were to be near the formidable royal castle at Stirling, at Polmaise and Tullibothwell (modern Tullibody), both of which had direct access to the sea, something Stirling itself lacked. The third was to be at Inverkeithing, close to where the Forth Bridge now stands. Although there is documentary evidence to suggest that work apparently started, no trace of any of them exists today.[7]

It seems that Edward was never able to get beyond the repair and strengthening of existing castles. Moreover, any new build was overwhelmingly confined to structures built of earthwork and timber. This made them far easier to destroy, which is precisely what Robert Bruce did in the years after becoming king in 1306. The Lanercost chronicler tells of Bruce systematically destroying them one by one: 'lest the English should ever again be able to lord it over the land by holding the castles.'[8] This helps to explain why Edward's fortifications today are conspicuous by their absence.

Edward's Peles

Mention the word 'pele' to the townspeople of Linlithgow, midway between Edinburgh and Stirling, and the vast majority will think only of the attractive parkland at the heart of their town. The word, from Ancient French *pel*, meaning stake, derives from the timber fortresses that Edward of England erected around the twelfth-century royal residence in 1301 and 1302. A pele, in this Edwardian context, was a largely earthwork and timber fortification added to an existing castle or fortified place to provide further secure accommodation for an expanded permanent garrison, as well as temporary space for a campaigning army, its ordnance and other munitions. Linlithgow pele was used as a supply base for Edward's assault on Stirling Castle in 1304.

There were in fact two separate peles built at Linlithgow, or at least two separate building episodes.[9] The first, hastily constructed in the autumn of 1301 prior to Edward wintering there, involved 100 carpenters and eighty ditchers building a pele around the castle. The second, and much more elaborate construction, was begun

following Edward's departure early in 1302 and took almost the entire year to build. It also involved Edward's favourite master of works, Master James of St George, summoned to Scotland by the king specially to oversee its construction.

This second pele consisted of a twin-towered central gatehouse, a curtain wall of whole logs to either side of it, and two towers at either end right beside the loch. In front, there was a great water-filled moat. A less substantial moated palisade was built to protect the complex from attack via the loch. Master James was assisted in this work by Thomas of Houghton and Adam of Glasson, master carpenters, and Master Adam the Fleming of Bury St Edmunds, in charge of the ditchers. The workforce at its height comprised sixteen stonemasons with their 'servers' (assistants), forty carpenters and 240 ditchers, the latter including 140 women, who received less pay than the men. In addition, 100 soldiers from the garrison provided labour, whilst a man with a horn received 5s. for blowing his instrument to call the men to work. The entire operation cost Edward around £900, roughly one-tenth of what he had paid Master James for Harlech Castle.[10]

Nothing now remains of Edward's great pele at Linlithgow, at least on the surface. We know from documents that it must have included the burgh kirk of St Michael's within its walls, indicating that the water-filled moat lay between the kirk and the burgh, and excavations have found traces of a great ditch in this area, which might just belong to Edward's pele.[11] We have to be mindful, however, that another, later would-be English conqueror of Scotland, Oliver Cromwell, ordered major construction works at Linlithgow in the 1650s.

Similarly, nothing, or at least nothing definite, now survives of Edward's other major peles built at royal castles. The pele constructed at Dumfries Castle in the autumn of 1300 cost as much as Linlithgow and involved well over 200 ditchers, eighty carpenters and fifteen masons, who were inspected by Edward himself during the building work. The pele built at Selkirk Castle in 1302 cost almost £1,400, suggesting it was more elaborate than either Linlithgow or Dumfries. Even so, this did not prevent it from being captured by the Scots in the following year. The pele built at Dunfermline in 1303 prior to Edward wintering there involved some sixty carpenters and 200 ditchers. Unfortunately, the records are almost entirely lacking for the substantial outer defensive works carried out at Berwick Castle in that same year.[12]

There was one pele, however, that was different from the others – Lochmaben. Edward visited Lochmaben Castle, 8 miles (13km) north-east of Dumfries and just 24 miles (38km) north-west of Carlisle, twice (Fig. 19.3).

Figure 19.3: Aerial view of Lochmaben showing the Bruce motte-castle (A) and the site of Edward's pele (B) (Crown Copyright: Royal Commission on the Ancient and Historical Monuments of Scotland).

The first occasion was in the summer of 1298 during his victory tour of south-west Scotland that followed his rout of Wallace at Falkirk, and second in the summer of 1300, during his lightning campaign in Galloway. But Edward knew Lochmaben's importance well enough without him having to visit it, for it was the *caput*, or chief seat, of the powerful lords of Annandale, the Bruces. Robert Bruce 'the Competitor', grandfather of the future King Robert I and the man who had vied with Balliol for the throne of Scotland in the Great Cause of 1291–92, breathed his last at Lochmaben in 1295 shortly before Edward invaded.[13]

Edward had no need to seize Lochmaben in 1296, for Robert Bruce, son of 'the Competitor', was firmly on his side. The father of the future king of Scots was not only lord of Annandale and earl of Carrick, but also the lord of a great estate in England at Writtle in Essex. He owned a house in London and a manor in the pleasant suburb of Tottenham. At the very moment that Edward crossed the Tweed into Scotland, this Robert Bruce was serving the English king in his capacity as constable of Carlisle Castle, and in that role beat off a fierce Scottish counterattack on the fortress in the early days of the invasion. By 1298, the situation had changed: the elder Robert Bruce continued to remain loyal to Edward; his son, however, the future king, had thrown in his lot with the patriots. This probably persuaded Edward to seize Lochmaben. He ordered Sir Robert Clifford to build a pele there and twelve carpenters and forty-eight ditchers, guarded by twenty-six crossbowmen, were duly despatched from Carlisle to carry out his orders. This makes the Lochmaben pele doubly significant, for not only was it the first of Edward's peles built in Scotland, but it was also the only one that records tell was built at a baronial, as distinct from a royal, castle.[14]

There is, however, a complication. There happen to be two castles at Lochmaben – the motte-and-bailey castle beside Kirk Loch, next to the town of Lochmaben itself, and the stone castle beside Castle Loch 1 mile (1.6km) to the south-south-east. The former was definitely the Bruce family's castle, built very probably around 1200 to replace their original *caput* at Annan, badly damaged by floods. The upstanding stonework of the second castle dates from the reign of Edward III (1327–77), by which date the castle was serving as the sole remaining English garrison base in the Scottish West March. But this second castle is also known as the Peel of Lochmaben and has traditionally been identified as the site of Edward I's 1298 pele. If so, it would be unique among Edward I's Scottish peles as the only one built on a greenfield site.[15]

The archaeological excavations carried out at the second Lochmaben castle in the 1960s and 1970s discovered nothing to confirm beyond reasonable doubt that the site originated in 1298.[16] The evidence, however, indicated that the site was in use by the early fourteenth century. Received wisdom suggests that the first thing Edward's men did was to relocate and build from scratch there the new pele at the greenfield site, effectively abandoning the Bruce castle.[17] However, the record of the erection of the first fortification specifically refers to 'an enclosure outside the castle, made strong by a palisade' ('*clausi extra castrum palitio firmati*'), suggesting that the intention initially was to strengthen the existing castle.[18] This would accord with normal practice. A possible scenario is that at some point early in the English occupation of Lochmaben, a decision was taken to abandon the Bruce family castle and build a new construction by Castle Loch. Lochmaben was in a highly strategic position, for forest and marsh forced those coming north from Carlisle to travel by way of Annandale, before either branching off westward into Galloway or heading north-east towards Edinburgh. That Lochmaben continued to be the single most important English garrison stronghold in the Scottish West March throughout the fourteenth century, until its eventual recapture by the Scots in 1384, confirms that all three English Edwards appreciated its pivotal position.

Just when this decision to relocate was made is not known. We do know that young Robert Bruce, the future king, attacked his father's castle in 1299, without success, but that as a result the English carried out further works to strengthen their position. Could this have been the time when the decision to relocate to Castle Loch was made? A report filed by the constable in 1301, that '7000 Scots had burnt our pele toun and assailed our pele', certainly seems to suggest that by this date we are dealing with a purpose-built defensive pele rather than a strengthened castle.[19] Unfortunately, the Wardrobe accounts are silent on the matter.

Edward in Camp

Edward spent altogether three years campaigning in Scotland. From Ayr in the west to Arbroath in the east, from Kirkcudbright in the south to Kinloss in the far north, 'Longshanks' took respite from the struggle in castles and monasteries, towns and villages the length and breadth of the land. However, there would have been many an occasion when the king had to rest in his pavilion tent, which is what he did on the night of 5 July 1300, during the siege of Caerlaverock Castle, the stronghold of the Maxwells, lords of Nithsdale, beside the Solway Firth (Fig. 19.4). The anonymous herald in King Edward's entourage, who penned the wonderful *Le Siege de Karlaverock* recording the two-day investment, writes that:

> There was many a cord stretched,
> Many a peg driven into the ground.

referring to the establishment of Edward's pavilion encampment in which he and his eighty-seven knights would stay that night. This doubtless included his portable chapel.[20]

After capturing mighty Caerlaverock, Edward headed west into Galloway. He spent several nights in the parish of Girthon, beside the Water of Fleet, north-west of Kirkcudbright, at a spot perhaps now known as Palace Yard, near Gatehouse-of-Fleet. This enigmatic site, to which it seems neither prehistorians nor medievalists wish to lay claim, comprises a simple oval, measuring about 350 feet by 195 feet (107m by 60m), and defended by an earthen bank and broad ditch (Fig. 19.5).[21] Constructing such a simple earthwork would not have been difficult for Master Thomas of Houghton and Master Adam the Fleming, and their carpenters and ditchers.

In the eastern Borders, another enigmatic site continues to baffle archaeologists. It lies beside that icon of the later medieval Anglo-Scottish border, fifteenth-century Smailholm Tower. The sub-circular enclosure, also banked and ditched, is a little smaller than Palace Yard (243 feet by 170 feet; 74m by 52m), but otherwise it is remarkably similar (Fig. 19.6).[22] We know that Edward spent the night

Figure 19.4: Edward I besieging Caerlaverock Castle in the summer of 1300: an artist's impression by David Simon (Copyright: Historic Scotland).

Figure 19.5: The earthwork known as 'Palace Yard', near Gatehouse-of-Fleet, Dumfries and Galloway (Copyright: Chris Tabraham).

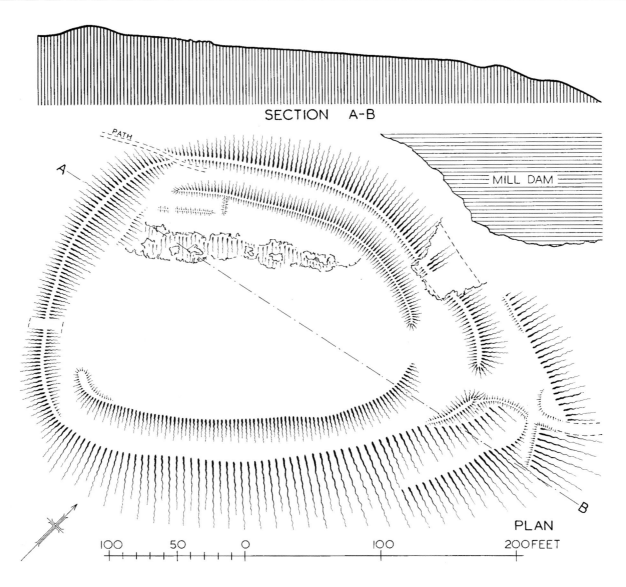

SECTION A-B

PLAN

Figure 19.6: Ground plan of the earthwork beside Smailholm Tower, Scottish Borders (Crown Copyright: Royal Commission on the Ancient and Historical Monuments of Scotland).

of 30 May 1303 at Smailholm. Could this be the spot? And if so, how many other temporary resting places of Edward I remain to be discovered the length and breadth of Scotland?

The Kildrummy Conundrum

Master James of St George not only oversaw the construction of the great pele at Linlithgow in 1302, he also orchestrated the great siege of Stirling Castle in 1304. However, he has also been identified more recently as the

man responsible for building the once great gatehouse at Kildrummy Castle, in Aberdeenshire.[23] The evidence for this claim is based on two premises – the one architectural and the other documentary.

Regarding the architectural premise, there is no doubting the marked similarity in size, shape and layout, between the ground plans of the gatehouse at Kildrummy and that at Harlech, which Master James was responsible for building (Fig. 19.7). The only discernible difference is that Kildrummy lacks the two circular stair towers at the rear. If the similarity between the two-light windows inserted into the Warden's Tower in Kildrummy and those in the courtyard elevation of Harlech's gatehouse is factored in, as well as the similarity between the sole remaining fireplace in the Kildrummy gatehouse with ones in Conwy, also one of Master James's construction works, there certainly seems a convincing case for thinking that the same guiding hand was behind both (Fig. 19.8).[24]

The documentary evidence supports this premise, rather than being persuasive in its own right.[25] We know that King Edward visited Kildrummy twice, in 1296 and 1303. We also know that on his second visit he was accompanied by Master James, who whilst there received a payment of £100 from Edward for work undertaken, but not specified. There is now no way of knowing what that £100 was for. It need not necessarily have had anything to do with Kildrummy; it could just as easily have been belated reimbursement for works at Linlithgow, which are known to have then been seriously in arrears. By way of comparison, each of the corner towers at Harlech cost in the region of £115, in which case if the payment was for the gatehouse at Kildrummy, Edward was getting good value for money.[26]

One further thought: a close inspection of the upstanding masonry at Kildrummy demonstrates that the gatehouse was not built in isolation, but formed part of a larger construction that took in the stretches of curtain wall to either side and very probably the two adjacent angle towers also.[27] If Master James of St George was supervising building works at Kildrummy, it involved not just the construction of the gatehouse, but other elements of the defensive circuit, and quite possibly the refurbishment of existing structures elsewhere also.

The Day Edward Stopped Hammering

Edward I's eleven-year quest to become 'chief lord of Scotland' failed on 7 July 1307, the day he breathed his last beside the Solway salt-marsh. A contemporary poem expressed what the Scots felt at his passing:

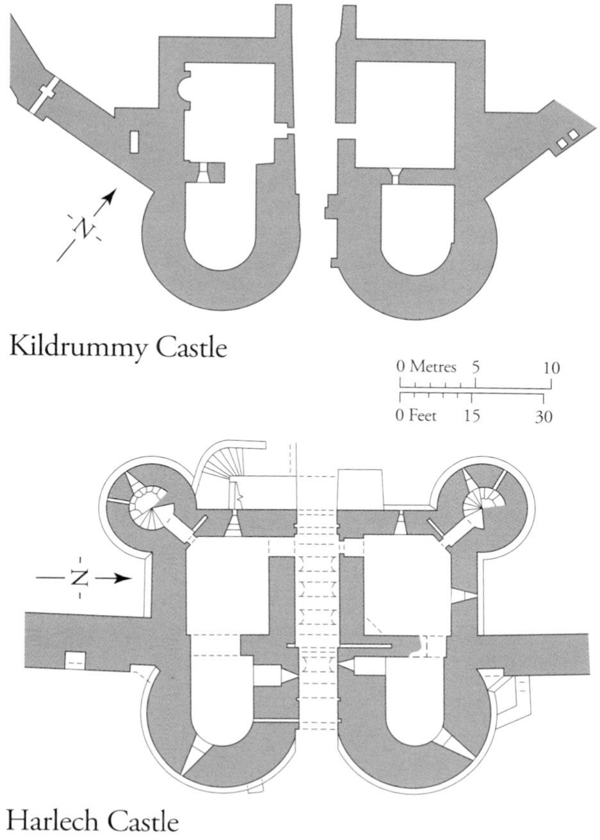

Kildrummy Castle

0 Metres 5   10

0 Feet   15   30

Harlech Castle

Figure 19.7: The ground plans of the gatehouses at Kildrummy and Harlech (Copyright: Historic Scotland and Cadw, Welsh Assembly Government).

Figure 19.8: The Warden's Tower (right) at Kildrummy Castle. The two two-light windows in the upper storeys are not dissimilar to windows in the courtyard elevation of the gatehouse at Harlech Castle (Crown Copyright: Royal Commission on the Ancient and Historical Monuments of Scotland).

You will count one thousand three hundred and seven
years in the world.
On the day of the Translation of the ever-blessed Thomas
the martyr
In Burgh by Sands, where the borders of the kingdom
end,
Edward died, who evilly killed Scots.
His entrails were buried with his brain at Holm [Holm
Cultram Abbey].
War-monger who lashed the English with dire scourge.
He trampled their proud necks underfoot,
He defiled the world, and cheated the Holy Land.
He invaded the Scots, broke up the realm by fraud,
He laid waste their churches, shut up their prelates in
prison,
He killed Christ's folk and seized the gold of the tithe.
His sins are well known in all the world.
England will weep when at last it lies in ruin.
Scotland, clap your hands for the death of a covetous
king.

Thanks be to God that Robert has been made king,
Whom the rod of salvation controls with the might of
virtue.[28]

So died one of the greatest military commanders of the thirteenth century, and undoubtedly the greatest threat to Scotland's independence at any point in the later Middle Ages.

Postscript

Almost three hundred years following King Edward I's death, one of the greatest ironies in British history took place. On 25 July 1603, a new king of England was crowned in the Gothic splendour of Westminster Abbey. He was seated on the golden coronation chair made at Edward I's instruction to house the ancient Scottish Stone of Destiny stolen by him from Scone Abbey in 1296. The new sovereign, however, was no Englishman but James VI, king of Scots.

Notes

1. For a full account of the life of Edward I, see M. Prestwich, *Edward I* (London 1988).
2. For detailed accounts of events leading up to the outbreak of war in 1296, and of the subsequent campaigns waged by Edward, see Prestwich, *Edward I*, 356–75, G. W. S. Barrow, *Robert Bruce & The Community of the Realm of Scotland* (Edinburgh 1988), 1–68; E. L. G. Stones and G. G. Simpson, *Edward I and the Throne of Scotland*, 2 vols (Oxford 1978); F. Watson, *Under the Hammer: Edward I and Scotland 1286–1307* (East Linton 1998). Maps charting Edward's various Scottish campaigns are in *Atlas of Scottish History to 1707*, eds P. G. B. McNeill and H. L. MacQueen (Edinburgh 1996), 86–90.
3. J. E. Morris, *The Welsh Wars of Edward the First* (Oxford 1901, reprinted Stroud 1997), 179–80.
4. *Chronicon de Lanercost* (Bannatyne Club 1839), 200.
5. *Calendar of Documents relating to Scotland*, ed. J. Bain, II (London 1884), E 372/144.
6. Prestwich, *Edward I*, 514.
7. R. A. Brown, H. M. Colvin and A. J. Taylor, *The History of the King's Works: the Middle Ages*, I (London 1963), 418–19; Watson, *Under the Hammer*, 199–200.
8. *Chronicon de Lanercost*, 223.
9. For fuller details, see *King's Works*, I, 412–15.
10. ibid., 359.
11. L. R. Laing, 'Excavations at Linlithgow Palace, West Lothian, 1966–67, *Proceedings of the Society of Antiquaries of Scotland*, 99 (1966–67), 111–47.
12. For fuller details on these, see *King's Works*, I, 409–22.
13. For details of the Bruces of Annandale and Lochmaben, see Barrow, *Robert Bruce*, 20–38.
14. For fuller details, see *King's Works*, I, 409–11.
15. For detailed descriptions of the two castles, see Royal Commission on the Ancient and Historical Monuments of Scotland, *Inventory of Monuments in Dumfriesshire* (Edinburgh 1920), 148–53. For the Peel of Lochmaben, see R. C. Reid, 'Edward I's Peel at Lochmaben', *Transactions of the Dumfriesshire and Galloway Natural History and Antiquarian Society*, 3 ser. 31 (1952–53), 58–73.
16. A. D. S. Macdonald & L. R. Laing, 'Excavations at Lochmaben Castle, Dumfriesshire', *Proceedings of the Society of Antiquaries of Scotland*, 106 (1974–75), 124–57.
17. See Royal Commission on the Ancient and Historical Monuments of Scotland, *Eastern Dumfriesshire: an Archaeological Landscape* (Edinburgh 1997), 203–07.
18. J. Stevenson, *Documents Illustrative of the History of Scotland, 1286–1306*, II (Edinburgh 1870), ii, quoted in *Inventory of Monuments in Dumfriesshire*, 53.
19. Stevenson, *Documents*, 432.
20. *The Roll of Caerlaverock*, ed. T. Wright (London 1864). For the reference to the portable chapel, see *Calendar of Documents relating to Scotland*, II, 409, no. 1580.
21. RCAHMS, *Inventory of Monuments in the Stewartry of Kirkcudbright* (Edinburgh 1914), 93, no. 176.
22. RCAHMS, *Inventory of Monuments in Roxburghshire*, 2 (Edinburgh 1956), 418–19, no. 925.
23. W. D. Simpson, 'James de Sancto Georgio, master of works to King Edward I in Wales and Scotland', *Anglesey Antiquarian Society and Field Club Transactions*, (1928), 31–41.
24. For a recent review of thirteenth-century double-towered gatehouse castles in Scotland, including Kildrummy Castle, see G. Ewart and D. Pringle, '"There is a castle in the west": Dundonald Castle excavations 1986–93', *Scottish Archaeological Journal*, 26 (2004), whole issue (x, 166p.).
25. A. J. Taylor, 'Master James of St George and the works of Kildrummy', *Proceedings of the Society of Antiquaries of Scotland*, 96 (1962–63), 220–21.
26. *King's Works*, I, 361.
27. C. Tabraham, *Kildrummy Castle and Glenbuchat Castle* (Edinburgh 2008).
28. *Scotichronicon, by Walter Bower*, ed. D. E. R. Watt, 6 (Aberdeen 1991), 333–35.

A Research Agenda for the Edwardian Castles

Robert Liddiard

The organizers of the conference upon which this volume is based and the editors responsible for bringing the papers to publication deserve congratulation for putting together such a comprehensive study, which not only takes our knowledge of the Edwardian castles forward, but also informs the study of castles in the British Isles. The breadth of scholarship contained in the essays brought together here means that offering some thoughts towards a research agenda is no easy task. This short concluding piece will consider why the Edwardian castles are so important and discuss some broad themes that emerged from the conference, before making some concluding comments about future work.

If many of the papers in this volume offer a critique of some long-held ideas then it also reflects and acknowledges the groundbreaking scholarship that has led us to where we are today. It is entirely appropriate that even where there are scholarly disagreements or differences of emphasis, nowhere is Arnold Taylor – whose groundbreaking work did so much to advance the study of the Edwardian castles – set up as a straw man. Indeed, it is fitting that his achievement is the subject of a contribution in its own right. At the same time, this volume also demonstrates that as far as the study of the Edwardian castles is concerned we are at a new phase historiographically, with new questions and ideas. That this should be the case is a reflection of changing attitudes in castle studies on a general level, as scholars have sought to broaden lines of enquiry primarily based on architectural remains and embrace the conclusions of archaeological theory, landscape history, literature and art history.[1] In common with castle studies as a whole, scholarship on the Edwardian castles will advance in three main ways: by addressing understudied aspects of the buildings and their environs (which exist in some number), by fully integrating new work with the conclusions of studies undertaken elsewhere in Europe and by forging links with other disciplines. This volume is a timely example of what can be achieved.

Conference Themes

The Edwardian castles are important for a number of reasons. The concentration of military architecture in north Wales is unparalleled in the British Isles. Furthermore, a substantial number of the Edwardian castles are preserved to an exceptional degree, which permits architectural analysis in a detail that is often not possible for earlier secular buildings. Their royal patronage is also important; not simply because it allows the architectural remains to be discussed within the context of the well-known history of royal works, but also because of the survival of documentary evidence that furnishes a considerable body of information on the process of construction. In addition, the Edwardian castles are not monuments that exercise a presence solely in the study of the past; their significance as markers of identity (be it British or Welsh or English) has been reworked by successive generations and as World Heritage Sites they continue to exercise an influence on the cultural landscape today.

Perhaps the most obvious way of interpreting the Edwardian castles is to relate them to the wider context of castle building in the thirteenth and fourteenth centuries. The most noticeable conclusion to be drawn from such an analysis is that many of the architectural features seen at the Edwardian castles can be found at other thirteenth-century castles and that the influence of the Edwardian buildings on subsequent castle design was limited. Such an observation gives weight to, and is inextricably bound up with, the idea that the Edwardian castles represent high points in medieval military architecture, the culmination of over a century of evolutionary struggle between attacker and defender as castle planning responded to an ever-increasing sophistication in siege warfare. Thereafter, in a long drawn-out process, the castle lost its military purpose and eventually evolved into the country house, ultimately when the sophistication of artillery necessitated purpose-built fortifications.[2] To some, the Edwardian castles therefore symbolize the 'apogee' of English castle building, an idea given added significance by the seeming hand of a master designer in their construction and the patron's apparent interest in ideas of *imperium*, which combined to add both a distinctive Continental and a metaphorical edge to their sophistication.

The interpretation that sees a military rise of the castle up to 1300 and then subsequent decline has been subject to considerable argument and counter-argument and does not need extended discussion here, but it is fair to say that the place of these buildings in the broader history of military architecture has sometimes been seen in the past as unusually or particularly significant.[3] That significance is neatly summed up by Richard Morris who in 1992 commented that 'the impression is firmly given of an elite group of men-of-war, long-standing comrades in arms of the king, indulging in an orgy of military architectural expression on an almost unlimited budget'.[4] The body of scholarly literature upon which Morris reflected goes to the heart of a series of issues that recur throughout this volume. The first is that the Edwardian castles have a degree of unity that means they can profitably be studied as a group, the second that astronomical sums were wasted on them in some kind of proto Star Wars programme and thirdly, that the military architecture was somehow excessive or unusual.

The importance of the Edwardian castles is tied up with a somewhat banal point, but the implications of which are significant, in that the 'principal' Edwardian castles (Conwy, Caernarfon, Harlech and Beaumaris) are those that also happen to be the best preserved. One could almost say that they survive too well and, albeit implicitly rather than explicitly, distort the picture of castle building across the region. Similar comments could be made about the long periods in which these sites have been in State guardianship; it has facilitated scholarly research on their fabric, perhaps at the expense of other monuments. It would, of course, be utterly foolish to suggest that castle studies would be better served if Conwy was preserved like Aberstwyth or that our knowledge would be more informed if the scholarly effort expended on Caernarfon had been applied to Castell y Bere, but it is to say, as both Ashbee and Goodall point out in this volume, that the sum of historical research together with patterns of preservation and destruction, can sometimes distort our picture of castle building in the late thirteenth century and perhaps unduly raise the significance of the Edwardian castles. This is not to deny their importance or their splendour as monuments, but it is to say that our view of these buildings might be different if, say, Ranulf of Chester's Beeston had been brought to completion in the 1220s or that royal Montgomery had not been slighted

during the Civil War. When viewed within the context of the pattern of baronial building from the late thirteenth to the early fourteenth centuries and the melting pot of ideas that was the institution of the King's Works, then the importance of the Edwardian castles is not diminished, but the idea that they represent a 'high point' of architectural development becomes very much open to question.

Within a framework that interprets the Edwardian castles as the high point of medieval military architecture in the British Isles, it is those elements that appear unusual that have often been invested with particular significance: the role of Master James of St George as designer and his Savoyard connections, for example, or the use of banded masonry and polygonal towers at Caernarfon in imitation of the Theodosian walls at Constantinople. Of course, it has long been known that many of the architectural elements found in the Edwardian castles can be found elsewhere, but the proceedings here shed new light on those elements deemed in the past to be particularly unusual, and in turn suggest perhaps more mundane, albeit no less important, motivations. Wheatley suggests a more generic idea of the Roman past at Caernarfon rather than specific imperial imagery and Coldstream emphasizes the English antecedents for the form of the castles themselves. Such conclusions do not diminish the importance of the Edwardian castles, but rather add important evidence to the placing of these buildings within a wider framework of the motivations and practicalities behind castle building and design in medieval Britain. For the Edwardian castles themselves this process is of some importance, as future work must be rooted in the mainstream of thinking on castles in general, rather than seeing these buildings as somehow existing in their own context.

Of course, the geographical concentration and the short period of construction give a historical unity to the Edwardian castles and to their study, but ideas of a particular degree of unity to the buildings that justifies them as a special group, especially driven by the hand of an individual designer, are more open to question. While the Edwardian conquest may have been, in Prestwich's words, 'exceptional in its totality', a following episode of castle building was not unusual and the peculiar circumstances of conquest did not result in a blueprint either for the castles themselves or their attendant urban centres. Moreover, the sums expended on their construction were not, in relative terms, excessive, but were roughly equivalent to a single major military campaign. A number of the contributors have sought to disentangle the roles played by the king and his lieutenants in the process of planning and design and in so doing have not minimized the role of Edward I or Master James of St George, but rather placed the building projects within a larger network. The importance of individuals such as Richard the Engineer is a reminder that there are wider social ripples of the Edwardian conquest – and a wider archaeology – that would repay further investigation.

None of this is to take anything away from the fact that what we see in north Wales today represents a fantastic testament to what an English medieval monarch could achieve in a short space of time and, of course, their chronological and geographical context invites a certain kind of regional research. But it is to refuse to push the Edwardian castles into a special group of 'The Edwardian Castle' and to recognize that much of their form can be explained with reference to earlier buildings, just in the same way as the campaign that led to their construction had its roots in earlier English efforts against the Welsh.

Ultimately, however, whatever else they may have represented to people at the time or for generations since, the Edwardian castles are, of course, monuments to conquest. As Michael Prestwich makes clear, however, Edward I did not foresee a complete conquest of north Wales in 1277 and had no plans for war in 1282. The castles that eventually resulted were certainly not on some kind of kingly wish list that Edward was waiting to unleash on an unsuspecting vassal. Likewise, Gwynedd itself was not a static kingdom waiting to be conquered, but one that was undergoing profound social and economic changes; it can only help our view of continuity and change in north Wales over the 1280s to have more detailed and comparative work elsewhere in Wales on the themes pursued by David Stephenson in order to assess the impact of castle building on native Welsh society. Such work would be best served within a broader research agenda, which would not only further our knowledge of the Edwardian castles themselves, but contribute significantly to wider issues in castle studies.

Future Work

The papers in this volume highlight the importance of interdisciplinary work and the value of bringing together the approaches of scholars from a variety of backgrounds working on different, but complementary, material. For the Edwardian castles, any research agenda or future work must not be pursued in isolation, either from other castles (both regional and national) or from broader currents of academic thinking on the subject. Priorities for future work on the Edwardian castles should not necessarily be governed by the intellectual fashion of any particular time, but should be closely related to those 'mainstream' topics currently of interest to castle scholars across Europe.

In essence, the challenge for the Edwardian castles is the same for castellology as a whole 'to develop a distinctive, coherent and forward-looking agenda of its own, but also, perhaps more importantly to nurture interplay with complementary fields of research'.[5]

As several of the contributions demonstrate very clearly, there are some important insights to be gained by studying those structures placed in the immediate vicinity of the castle buildings. The most obvious forms of landscape manipulation visible today are the attendant boroughs of castles such as Beaumaris and Caernarfon, but the documentary evidence for gardens at places like Conwy and Rhuddlan points to the possibility of wider schemes of landscape 'design'. The identification of such landscapes, which often involved the heightening of the visual effect by schemes of water manipulation and parkland, has been a major theme of landscape studies in the past decade and the potential existence of such landscapes at the Edwardian castles must rank as a research priority. Certainly the idea that the 'military' context of the Edwardian castles' construction precludes the possibility of landscape manipulation can be discounted, as there is now a considerable body of evidence for such design schemes existing in what are often thought of as 'militarized' contexts; indeed, it is possible that some of the best archaeological remains are to be found in such areas.[6] Where it exists, the evidence at the Edwardian castles is suggestive, but it remains to be seen how far, for example, the mill pond below the gate at Harlech or the similar pond at Caernarfon were simply utilitarian in purpose or part of a wider scheme of design. It is in this light, too, that some architectural features might benefit from re-examination. At Denbigh, for example, the highly elaborate and spacious postern gate and attached walkway seems inappropriate for a simple postern; rather, the fact that it would have led to the contemporary deer park might raise issues of a possible connection with hunting ceremony and ritual.

If gardens were considered female spaces in the Middle Ages then several of the papers here draw attention to the activities, or possible activities, of women at castles in north Wales. The potential of this area for study has been highlighted recently by studies examining the existence of female space within great medieval buildings and the potential at sites such as Conwy is made clear from Ashbee's contribution in this volume on royal apartments.[7] Such work can only be taken forward on a comparative basis, integrating what is found in north Wales with comparative information from elsewhere. It is a testament to the scholarship of Arnold Taylor that few new insights in this volume have come from re-reading of the documentary sources; rather, most have come from the integration of architectural analysis with insights and comparison with other places, something that clearly shows the way forward.

In addition to the study of the Edwardian castles themselves, there is a real need for thematic investigations into the broad range of medieval monuments in the regional landscape. The effects of the Edwardian conquest were not just felt in the landscapes of Conwy and Beaumaris, but also in Cheshire and beyond. Turner's analysis of the archaeological legacy of Richard the Engineer is a case in point and one cannot help but wonder about other individuals involved in the building programme who, on the back of profits gained through service in the King's Works, returned home and constructed moated sites, manor houses and gardens. It goes without saying that the Edwardian castles represent the 'high end' of the market in terms of settlement, but the wider archaeological legacy of the conquest remains to be seen, yet this is vital before the place of the Edwardian castles in the settlement hierarchy of north Wales can be fully addressed.

A greater understanding of the native Welsh lordly sites both before and after the Edwardian conquest would also be of enormous benefit. The contribution by Dylan Foster Evans points up one vital area of research that would repay future work: the Welsh perspective on the Edwardian castles. While much discussion has taken place about the English character of these monuments, their Welsh dimension is perhaps easy to overlook. Lawrence Butler's contribution to this volume points the way forward to much needed work on the buildings and landscapes of the Welsh princes. The potential for archaeological investigation on native Welsh sites is undoubtedly strong, especially on those sites not subject to twentieth-century clearance and where good archaeological deposits are likely to remain. Realistically speaking, the possibilities for research excavation on any scale are presently limited, but there remains, for example, scope for metal detector survey and the analysis of small finds. Where such studies

have been conducted on medieval monuments elsewhere, the results can often shed important light on the function of spaces or on the 'social zoning' of particular areas such as enclosures or baileys.[8] Together with work on the sites of buildings, field survey of the wider environs of Welsh residences is likely to yield much material and there is probably enough work in this field to occupy a generation of scholars. Again, our current knowledge in this area is partial, but to judge from limited fieldwork and praise poetry such as Iolo Goch's *Sycharth* there is considerable potential for reconstructing the landscape context of *llysoedd* and castle sites.

In a volume that adds substantially to the sum of knowledge about the Edwardian castles and which draws out their significance to the history of castle building in the British Isles as a whole, ultimately some consideration must be given to their function, be it intended or actual. This is not to enter the timeworn arguments about the military role of the castle, but to point up some of the possible ambiguities and enigmas that remain. Conwy exhibits one of, if not the first, example of stone machicolation in the British Isles, the design of the arrowloops at Caernarfon represent some of the most up-to-date military engineering of its day; yet, at the same time, this highly sophisticated architecture is found at castles that did not see mechanisms put in place to provide for maintenance, garrisoning, financial support and which were often, probably routinely, left undermanned. If there is a tension and ambiguity here concerning the prima facie purpose of the architecture on the one hand and its actual use on the other, and in this the Edwardian castles are far from unique, then it is not for this volume to provide a definitive answer, but to act as a platform for future work. Whatever direction research takes, the Edwardian castles will continue to provide not just a corpus of well-preserved and documented architectural remains for academic study and public display, but also a tangible and vivid reminder of a conquest that is still, for some, contested.

Notes

1. It is instructive to compare the approach taken in R. A. Brown, *Castles* (Princes Risborough 1985) and O. H. Creighton and R. A. Higham, *Medieval Castles* (Princes Risborough 2003).
2. R. A. Brown, *English Castles*, 3rd edn (Batsford 1976). For a different view see P. Dixon and B. Lott, 'The courtyard and the tower: contexts and symbols in the development of late medieval great houses', *Journal of the British Archaeological Association*, 146 (1993), 93–101 and C. Coulson, 'Fourteenth-century castles in

context: apotheosis or decline?' *Fourteenth Century England* 1, ed. N. Saul (Woodbridge 2000), 133–51.
3. C. Coulson, 'Peaceable power in English castles', *Anglo-Norman Studies, 23: Proceedings of the Battle Conference 2000*, ed. J. Gillingham (Woodbridge 2001), 69–95 ; P. Marshall, 'The ceremonial function of the donjon in the twelfth century', *Château Gaillard*, 30 (2002), 141–51; P. Dixon, 'The myth of the keep', in *The Seigneurial Residence in Western Europe AD c 800–1600*, eds G. Meirion-Jones, E. Impey and M. Jones, BAR

International Series 1088 (Oxford 2002), 9–13.

4. R. K. Morris, 'The architecture of Edwardian enthusiasm: castle symbolism in the reigns of Edward I and his successors', in *Armies, Chivalry and Warfare in Medieval Britain and France*, ed. M. Strickland, Proceedings of the 1995 Harlaxton Symposium (Stamford 1998), 63–81.

5. O. Creighton and R. Liddiard, 'Fighting yesterday's battle: beyond war or status in castle studies', *Medieval Archaeology*, 52 (2008), 161–69.

6. T. O'Keeffe, 'Were there designed landscapes in medieval Ireland?', *Landscapes*, 5 (2004), 52–68; P. Everson, 'Medieval gardens and designed landscapes', in *The Lie of the Land: Aspects of the Archaeology and History of the Designed Landscape in the South West of England*, ed. R. Wilson-North (Exeter 2003), 24–33.

7. R. Gilchrist, *Gender and Archaeology: Contesting the Past* (London 1999); A. Richardson, 'Gender and space in medieval royal palaces c. 1160–c. 1547: a study in access, analysis and imagery', *Medieval Archaeology*, 47 (2003), 131–65.

8. In a monastic context see T. Pestell, *Landscapes of Monastic Foundation* (Woodbridge 2004); and discussion in a secular context in D. Austin, *Acts of Perception: a Study of Barnard Castle in Teesdale* (Durham 2007), 2 vols.

21

King Edward I's Castles in North Wales – Now and Tomorrow

Alun Ffred Jones AM, Minister for Heritage, Welsh Assembly Government

Cadw and their collaborators, Bangor University and the Castle Studies Group, are to be congratulated on this collection of essays. It shows they are at the forefront of continuing academic research and interpretation. However, this volume would not be complete without discussion of contemporary attitudes. They therefore invited me to close the collection with an essay dealing not only with attitudes to the castles today, but also pointing a direction for Cadw's own future work.

Figure 21.1: The King's Gate, Caernarfon Castle, dominates the street frontage looking towards the town and combines strength with display (Cadw, Welsh Assembly Government: Crown Copyright).

This is a task that requires considerable sensitivity because, at least for some in Wales, medieval conflicts continue to resonate. In 1983, the Wales Tourist Board launched 'Cestyll 83', a festival of castles in Wales. They were taken aback by the response. Although welcomed by many, the festival was branded 'Insult 83' by Cofiwn, a group dedicated to commemorating events in Welsh history. A coffin representing the death of the Welsh nation was carried to the main gate of Caernarfon Castle. Protests also took place at other castles. Cofiwn attacked the festival for celebrating the 700th anniversary of the start of the major Edwardian castle-building programme, and the castles' role in the conquest.

It would be easy to dismiss such protests as the actions of a tiny, unrepresentative minority, which on one level they clearly were. The truth is more complex. The Wales Tourist Board's official evaluation of 'Cestyll 83' commented that 'while this vandalism was the work of a tiny hothead minority, and the number of vociferous critics was small, it seems fairly clear that a rather larger number of people in North Wales felt some unease about celebrating the anniversary'.[1] This assessment seems about right. Many Welsh people feel no sense of discomfort with King Edward's castles and, sadly, are uninterested in them. But some still see them as castles of conquest. These feelings are naturally strongest in Gwynedd, and are most marked in the case of Caernarfon, where one of the most strongly Welsh-speaking towns is watched over by the grandest and most symbolic of King Edward's castles (Fig. 21.1). The ambivalence that lies behind such feelings was perhaps most eloquently encapsulated by Thomas Pennant in the eighteenth century when he described Caernarfon Castle as 'the most magnificent badge of our subjection'.[2] Pride, admiration and resentment jostle closely together here.

All of this must be very hard for many English people to understand. For instance, the Tower of London, built by Norman invaders in the wake of 1066, is now a symbol of the power and authority of the English medieval monarchy.

The beheadings it witnessed give it grim associations, but it is as English as anything in London. People might well therefore ask why Welsh people should feel differently about the castles of *le roi Edouard*, as a conquering first-language French-speaker in Wales. There are two answers, one general, one specific. The first is that England eventually absorbed its French-speaking conquerors into an English-speaking state, something that Wales was never in a position to match. The second is that Caernarfon in particular was thrust into the spotlight twice in the twentieth century as the venue for the constitutional theatre of the 1911 and 1969 investitures.

The historical significance of the investitures has been analysed by John Ellis of the University of Michigan in a major recent book.[3] I am grateful to him for sharing his manuscript prior to publication. In the limited context of this essay, two points about 1911 need to be made.

The first concerns the way in which the investiture in 1911 successfully handled the potentially ambivalent attitudes towards Caernarfon Castle. It did so not by trying to downplay the medieval conflicts of its origin, but by celebrating them. In a way that is alien to us now, it was an age of romanticized rhetoric. Owen Rhoscomyl, one of the foremost Welsh champions of the investiture, writing in *The Western Mail* on 13 July 1911, conjured up the image of the 'fire and sword and ravage of the thousand thronging armies that swore to wipe out this scanty folk from the roll of nations fading into baffledness' in the glory of the investiture. Journalists depicted Caernarfon Castle as a means of subjugating Wales, but also as a tribute to the tenacity of the Welsh. W. Llewellyn Williams wrote: 'the old castle of the oppressor is in its ruins: the national spirit is stronger than ever it was before'.[4] The Welsh language paper *Y Tyst* soared into hyperbole on 9 July. In English translation, it said that the investiture showed that 'we have won the day over the English and have conquered totally their cruel attempt and traditional policy to weaken and destroy Welsh nationality. We have at last grasped the sword from our enemy and buried it in his own heart'. Caernarfon Castle was moreover widely seen not merely as testament to the strength of medieval Welsh resistance, but also as the scene of reconciliation, the location where King Edward had offered his son as prince of Wales. With the benefit of Lloyd George's strong support, the investiture was seen by the Welsh-speaking *gwerin* as an affirmation of Welsh nationality. Keir Hardie was one of the very few vocal critics, attacking the investiture from a perspective that was at once patriotically Welsh, pacifist and internationalist; and support for it was muted in the industrial valleys of south Wales.[5]

This leads to the second revealing aspect of the 1911 investiture – the way in which Caernarfon was selected as the venue. It was not an automatic choice. Cardiff and Caernarfon were backed by rival campaigns. Caernarfon won with the support of English opinion and the subsequent backing of the Westminster Government. Lloyd George's position as the local MP was no doubt influential. The investiture helped to consolidate his standing in Welsh-speaking Wales after the disappointment of the failure of the Cymru Fydd movement. But John Ellis argues that the choice of Caernarfon had a wider significance. In his view, it played well with English stereotypes of the Welsh as impractical romantics, avoiding the bustling modern commercialism of Cardiff in favour of the medieval symbolism of Caernarfon. Whatever the truth in this, Caernarfon clearly was a safe distance from the industrial valleys of south Wales, riven by the industrial conflicts of 1910 and 1911.

The 1969 investiture was, like 1911, popular with a majority of Welsh people, but exposed painful divisions particularly in Welsh-speaking Wales in a way that 1911 did not. Confidence in Wales's political future, and in the very survival of the Welsh language, was for many at a low ebb, and frustration was correspondingly high. There is a tendency for the bombing attempts of that year to receive undue attention. What was perhaps more significant was the way in which opinion within the Urdd – Wales's leading Welsh-language youth organization – was polarized by the sentiments expressed in Gerallt Lloyd Owen's award-winning poem about the investiture, 'Fy Ngwlad'. For the critics, the choice of Caernarfon Castle as the venue made the symbolism of the occasion more, not less, awkward. The castle was the scene of several protests, and the image of Llywelyn ap Gruffudd and his death in 1282 was central to the anti-investiture campaign. The way in which the castle was targeted for symbolic protests in 1983 can only really be understood in the light of the feelings aroused in 1969.

The continuing symbolic power of Edward's castles should hardly surprise us. Recent years have seen a shift in emphasis in how medieval castles are understood. No longer are they seen as purely military in design and function. Rather, increasing attention is being paid to their role in communicating status and authority. The precise mix of roles depended on particular local circumstances. The military function of the Edwardian castles in north Wales clearly ranked highly, but equally, impressing and overawing the native Welsh population was an intrinsic part of their political role. In the case of Caernarfon, the polygonal design of the towers, the coloured bands of masonry, and the gratuitous height of the walls are recognized as a deliberate evocation of Roman imperial power. In Harlech and Conwy, towers were built in places where walls would have been sufficient defence. Turrets on top of towers, and finials on battlements, were not strictly utilitarian. The way in which Edward's castles express domination to some today simply shows how brilliantly they still have the potential to communicate their original message.

There is a revealing contrast here with the castles built by the native Welsh princes. Symbolizing power and authority was an equally important part of their function – perhaps an even bigger part, as mountains, woods and marshes were the real defensive assets of the Welsh. Native Welsh castles were built on a fraction of the budget that Edward was able to lavish on his, and relied heavily on dramatic natural settings for much of their visual effect. Now weathered into romantic ruins, and set against the background of Snowdonia, Cadair Idris or the river Tywi, it is natural that they inspire a different set of feelings today (Figs 21.2 and 21.3, Plates 15 and 16).

All this has left Cadw in a tricky position at times. The Edwardian castles and their walled towns are in architectural terms the outstanding medieval monuments of Wales, our proud World Heritage Sites. But if history is written by the victor, still more is it built by him. Showcasing Edward's castles is rightly central to Cadw's work, but at times there have been accusations that this comes at the expense of other aspects of Wales's medieval story. The rest of this essay points a way forward in response.

First, I hope that as the devolution story unfolds, and as we build a new, confident and inclusive Wales, we can as a people increasingly come to terms with our troubled medieval history. This is important if we are to foster the unity that Wales needs to meet future challenges. If this happens, one by-product will be that the ambiguity of the feelings that some still harbour for Edward's castles will fade.

Coming to terms with the past does not, however, mean forgetting it. Rather, it means getting the past right, and viewing it in as coherent and balanced a way as we can. Cadw has a key role to play in this. There is always a danger that visitors can tend to see 'ancient monuments' in isolation. The challenge for Cadw is to help them see

Figure 21.2: Castell y Bere set on a rocky hillock in the southern foothills of Snowdonia (Cadw, Welsh Assembly Government: Crown Copyright).

historic buildings in the context of the history and historical geography that made them – and to tell the story of the defeated and the poor as well as that of the rich and victorious whose building record was inevitably stronger.

As part of this, Cadw will continue to invest in the visitor centres for the main Edwardian castles, but will also tell more fully the story of the native Welsh princes. Owain Glyndŵr has a significant profile in the popular consciousness in Wales, and through its investment in the visitor centre at Harlech, Cadw will tell the story of the role that the castle played as his court. But the Edwardian castles would have never been built had it not been for the threat posed by the attempts of Llywelyn Fawr and Llywelyn ap Gruffudd in the thirteenth century to create a unified native Welsh polity, and popular understanding of this in Wales is far weaker. Few understand, for instance, that the title 'prince of Wales' was not created by Edward I, but goes back to the Treaty of Montgomery in 1267, when Llywelyn ap Gruffudd was formally recognized as prince of Wales not only by the English Crown but also by the Papacy, the overarching authority of medieval Christendom.

In redeveloping the visitor centre at Conwy, Cadw will therefore give a special place to telling the story of Llywelyn Fawr and Llywelyn ap Gruffudd. This will, among other things, help visitors to see Conwy Castle in context, by bringing out the significance of Aberconwy Abbey and Deganwy Castle that preceded it. At Beaumaris, Cadw will explain the way in which the Edwardian town took over from the developing native urban centre of Llanfaes. In addition, Cadw will give extra profile to the story behind the castles built by the two Llywelyns: Dolwyddelan, Dolbadarn, Deganwy, Cricieth, Ewloe, Dolforwyn, Carndochan, Castell y Bere and the 'castle beyond Brecon' (identified as Sennybridge by David Cathcart King[6]). Thanks to the work of the late Richard Avent, they have been rescued from the condescension of history. Now that castles are no longer interpreted simply in terms of their military effectiveness, these castles can now be seen for what they were – a carefully calculated network of centres of political and administrative authority supporting the nascent thirteenth-century Welsh state.

Cadw recognizes the importance of symbolism. In September 2000, the 600th anniversary of Glyndŵr's proclamation as prince of Wales, Cadw flew his flag from the castle in Caernarfon, just as it flew in the streets of the town (Fig. 21.4). Actions such as this count. They all help to ease the feelings of ambivalence that some still hold. Cadw intends to continue this sensitive approach, and will also use the arms of the princes of Gwynedd to increase recognition of the castles that they built.

It is also important to raise public awareness of other

Figure 21.3: This finely carved head, believed to represent Llywelyn ab Iorwerth (Llywelyn Fawr), was recovered from Deganwy Castle and is indicative of the high quality work that the princes of Gwynedd were able to commission (Copyright: Amgueddfa Cymru – National Museum Wales).

sites not in Cadw's guardianship that have a special place in Wales's medieval story. Cadw will, for instance, be seeking to work in partnership with landowners and local authorities to raise awareness of, and improve levels of interpretation at Deganwy, Carndochan, Cwm-hir Abbey, the ford at Montgomery, and Glyndŵr's courts at Sycharth and Glyndyfrdwy. In addition, Cadw is working in collaboration with the National Trust to help people to understand the significance of Dinefwr Castle to the story of Deheubarth.

Finally, Cadw is committed to strengthening links with local communities in the places where it has major sites, especially the Edwardian castles. It has a role to play as 'remembrancer of a place' in a broader sense than simply telling the story of a particular building in isolation. So, for instance, in Caernarfon, there is a role for Cadw to work in partnership with Gwynedd Council to tell the story of the town through the ages, how for instance its evolving character was shaped by its role as a port. Helping people to understand the inter-relationship between the Edwardian castles and their towns is something that Edward himself would have understood, given the way in which each castle and town was originally planned as an integrated whole. Cadw will, as part of this, seek to mount special events to

Figure 21.4: The flag of Owain Glyndŵr flying at Caernarfon Castle on 16 September 2008 (Cadw, Welsh Assembly Government: Crown Copyright).

Figure 21.5: A performance of the Mabinogion *at Harlech Castle (Cadw, Welsh Assembly Government: Crown Copyright).*

attract local people to visit the castles. There is real scope here to foster a much greater sense of 'local ownership' of the great Edwardian castles (Fig. 21.5).

This paper has reflected on the continuing potential of Edward's castles to act as symbols, and the continuing resonance of their medieval story today. Our challenge is to understand and to educate others in the past as truthfully and coherently as we can. In doing that we not only do justice to the past, but also have a better chance of working out what it is to be citizens of Wales in the twenty-first century.

Notes

1. John Brown, 'An Appraisal of the Impact of Cestyll 83: The Festival of Castles', (unpublished report to the Wales Tourist Board, 1984).
2. T. Pennant, *A Tour in Wales*, II (London 1783), 214.
3. J. S. Ellis, *Investiture: Royal Ceremony and National Identity in Wales, 1911–1969* (Cardiff 2008).
4. W. Ll. Williams, 'Historic ceremony in a historic place', in *Morning Leader,* 12 July 1911.
5. E. Hughes ed., *Keir Hardie's Speeches and Writings from 1888 to 1915* (Glasgow 1927?), 144.
6. D. J. C. King, 'Camlais and Sennybridge Castles', *Brycheiniog,* 21 (1984–85), 9–11.

Index

The numbers in italics refer to illustrations

Plate 1

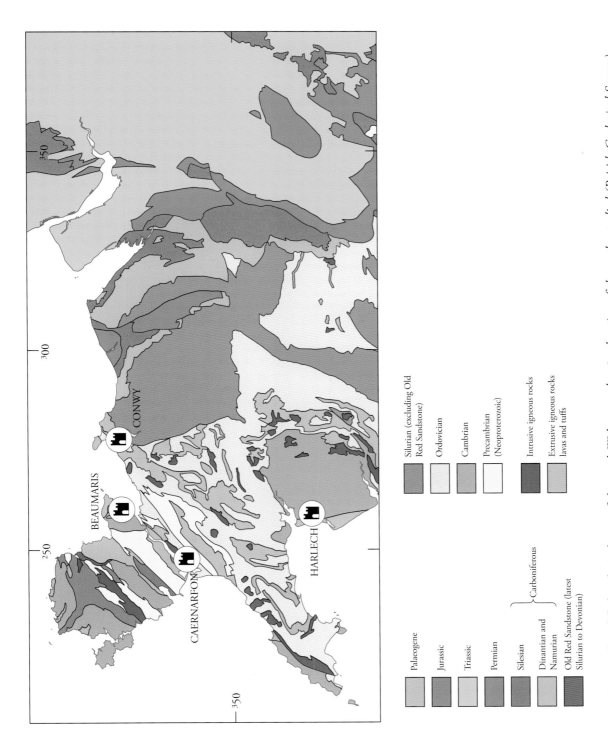

Plate 1: Simplified geological map of the north Wales area showing location of the castles studied (British Geological Survey).

Plate 2

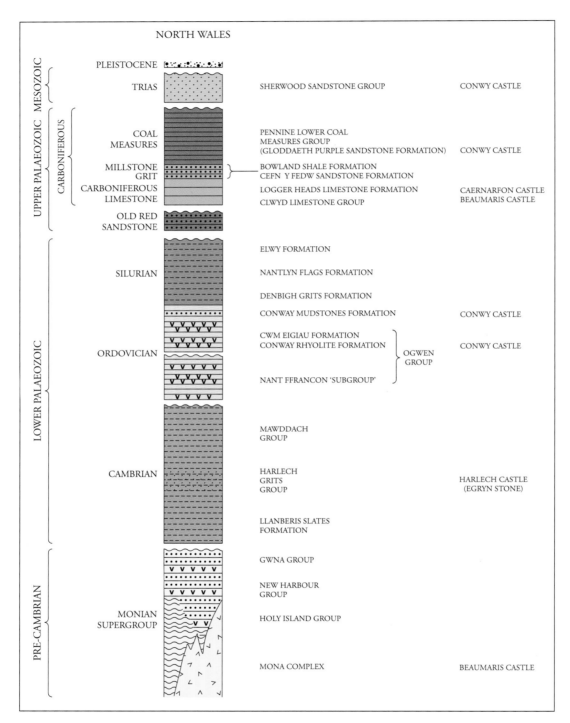

Plate 2: Simplified geological succession for the north Wales area showing the principal lithological units from which the building stones used in the castles' construction were sourced (British Geological Survey).

Plate 3

A: *Conwy Castle – Door and window openings throughout the castle are outlined with variegated, purple-red and buff coloured cross-bedded, sandstones of the Gloddaeth Purple Sandstone Formation (Carboniferous).*

B: *Conwy – Pale coloured, banded rhyolite blocks dominate parts of the town walls and its towers (Ordovician).*

C: *Harlech Castle – The massive walls and towers of the castle are constructed solely of greenish-grey sandstones of the Rhinog Member of the Harlech Grits Group (Cambrian).*

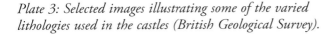

Plate 3: *Selected images illustrating some of the varied lithologies used in the castles (British Geological Survey).*

D: *Harlech Castle – Pale yellow-brown 'Egryn Sandstone' (Cambrian) is used in door and window openings, and quoins.*

Plate 4

A: Caernarfon Castle – Pale grey, coursed, limestone walls with contrasting, variegated sandstone courses, window and door openings, all sourced from the local Carboniferous successions.

B: Caernarfon Castle – Variegated, medium- to coarse-grained cross-bedded Carboniferous sandstone mouldings occur throughout the castle.

C: Beaumaris Castle – Dark green blocks of chloritized, foliated 'greenschist' (Precambrian) occur randomly within the Carboniferous limestone stonework.

D: Beaumaris Castle – Large squared, pale grey limestone blocks contrast with the tabular brown limestone of the rest of the wall fabric (Carboniferous).

Plate 4: Selected images illustrating some of the varied lithologies used in the castles (British Geological Survey).

Plate 5

A: Conwy Castle (south-west tower window opening – PP). Fine- to medium-grained, moderately well-sorted quartz framework grains, porosity patchily occluded by pore-filling kaolinite. Weakly cemented.

B: Conwy Castle (hall range – PP). Fine-grained, moderately well-sorted quartz framework grains, porosity partially occluded by kaolinite. Weakly cemented.

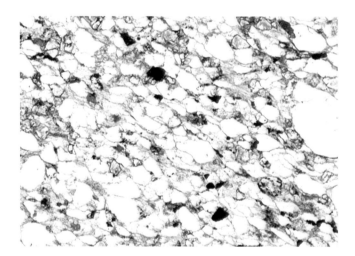

C: Harlech Castle ('Egryn Stone', fallen block – PP). Poorly sorted quartz grains, feldspars and rock fragments in a micromicaceous matrix/cement. Compacted fabric.

D: Harlech Castle ('Egryn Stone', carved sandstone moulding fragment – XP). Poorly sorted quartz grains, spars feldspars and rock fragments in a micromicaceous matrix/cement.

Plate 5: Selected thin section images of the rock types used (field of view 3mm left to right in each image; PP – plane polarized light; XP cross-polarized light; blue dye impregnation showing porosity) (British Geological Survey).

Plate 6

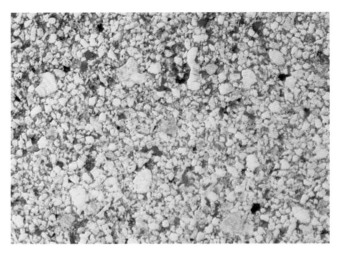

A: Harlech Grit Group (outcrop sample, near castle car park – XP). Poorly sorted, quartz grains, feldspars and rock fragments in a micromicaceous matrix/cement.

B: Caernarfon Castle (Queen's Tower, weathered internal wall – PP). Moderately well-sorted, fine- to medium-grained quartz with sparse feldspar and rock fragments. Weakly cemented. Good open porosity.

C: Caernarfon Castle (Black Tower – internal wall – PP). Very poorly sorted coarse to very coarse polycrystalline quartz grains with sparse feldspars. Quartz cemented. Good open porosity.

D: Caernarfon Castle (Eagle Tower – external door moulding fragment – PP). Poorly sorted very fine- to fine-grained, quartz with patches of ferruginous clay matrix. Mica moderately common. Rare feldspars. Moderately cemented. Patchy open porosity.

Plate 6: Selected thin section images of the rock types used (field of view 3mm left to right in each image; PP – plane polarized light; XP cross-polarized light; blue dye impregnation showing porosity) (British Geological Survey).

Plate 7

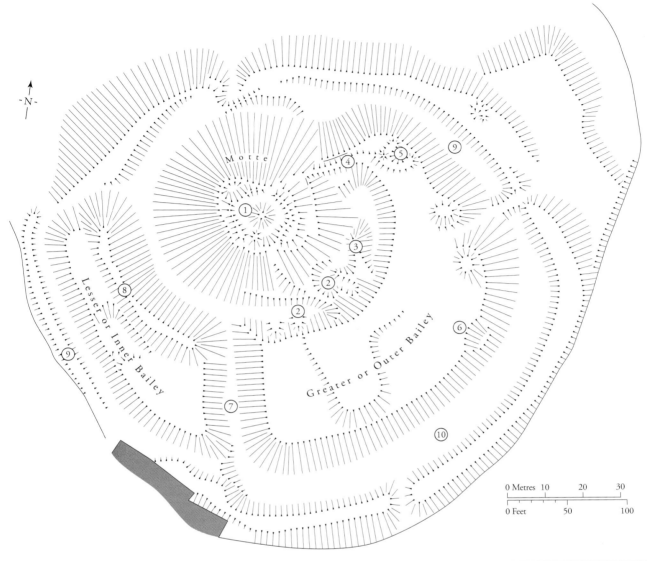

Motte

Lesser or Inner Bailey

Greater or Outer Bailey

① ② ③ ④ ⑤ ⑥ ⑦ ⑧ ⑨ ⑩

-N-

0 Metres 10   20   30

0 Feet   50   100

Plate 7: Plan and aerial view of Builth Castle (Cadw, Welsh Assembly Government: Crown Copyright and © Crown Copyright: Royal Commission on the Ancient and Historical Monuments of Wales; NPRN 92025; GTJ25808).

Plate 8

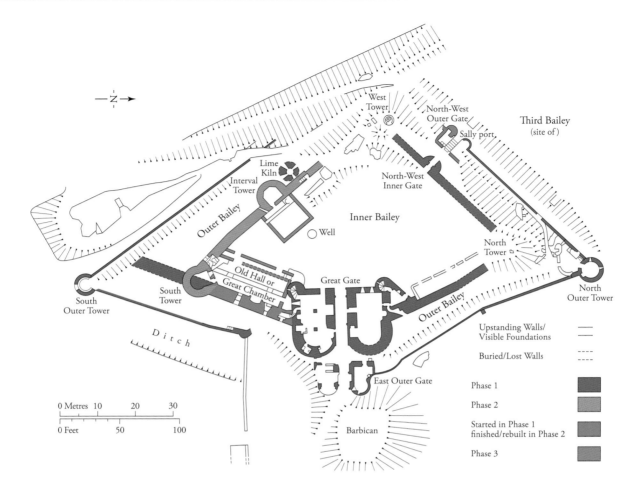

Plate 8: Plan and aerial view of Aberystwyth Castle (Cadw, Welsh Assembly Government: Crown Copyright and © Crown Copyright: Royal Commission on the Ancient and Historical Monuments of Wales; NPRN 86; DI2008_0928).

Plate 9

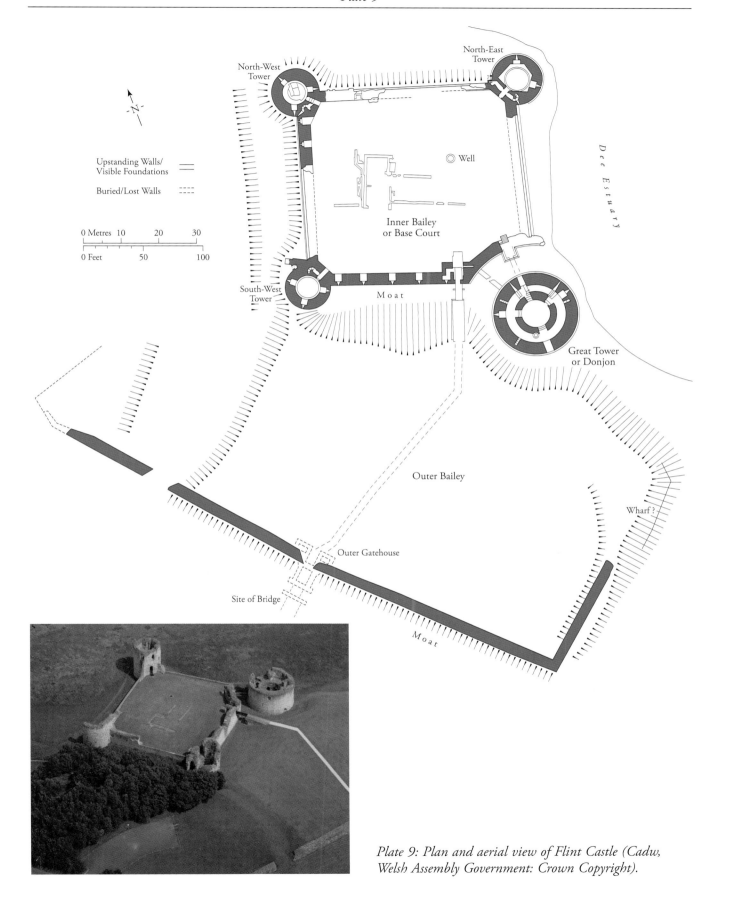

North-East Tower

North-West Tower

Dee Estuary

Upstanding Walls/
Visible Foundations

Buried/Lost Walls

0 Metres 10   20   30

0 Feet   50   100

Well

Inner Bailey
or Base Court

South-West
Tower

Moat

Great Tower
or Donjon

Outer Bailey

Wharf ?

Outer Gatehouse

Site of Bridge

Moat

Plate 9: Plan and aerial view of Flint Castle (Cadw,
Welsh Assembly Government: Crown Copyright).

Plate 10

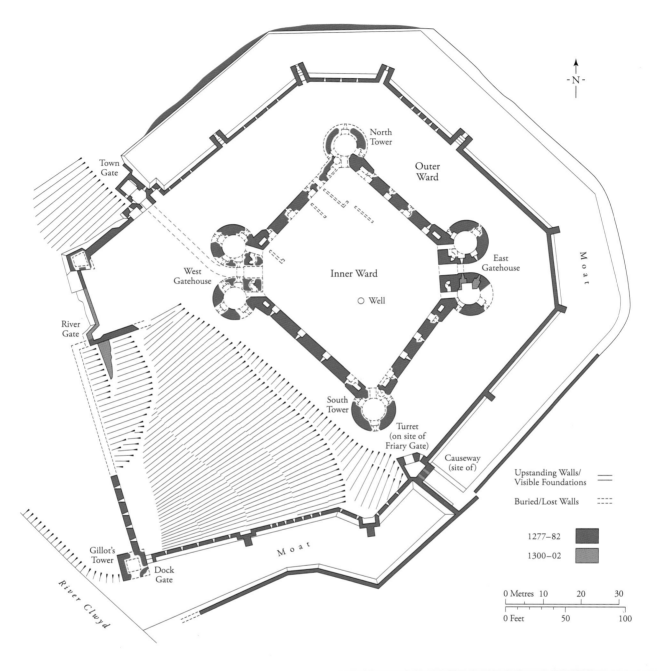

Town Gate

North Tower

Outer Ward

-N-

West Gatehouse

Inner Ward

East Gatehouse

River Gate

Well

South Tower

Turret (on site of Friary Gate)

Causeway (site of)

Upstanding Walls/ Visible Foundations ———

Buried/Lost Walls - - - -

1277–82

1300–02

Gillot's Tower

Dock Gate

M o a t

River Clwyd

0 Metres 10   20   30

0 Feet   50   100

Plate 10: Plan and aerial view of Rhuddlan Castle (Cadw, Welsh Assembly Government: Crown Copyright).

Plate 11

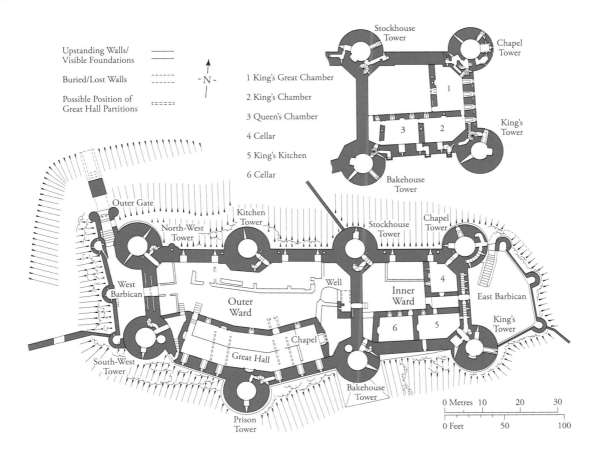

Upstanding Walls/
Visible Foundations

Buried/Lost Walls

Possible Position of
Great Hall Partitions

- N -

1 King's Great Chamber

2 King's Chamber

3 Queen's Chamber

4 Cellar

5 King's Kitchen

6 Cellar

Stockhouse Tower

Chapel Tower

King's Tower

Bakehouse Tower

Outer Gate

Kitchen Tower

North-West Tower

Stockhouse Tower

Chapel Tower

West Barbican

Outer Ward

Well

Inner Ward

East Barbican

King's Tower

South-West Tower

Great Hall

Chapel

Bakehouse Tower

Prison Tower

0 Metres 10 20 30

0 Feet 50 100

Plate 11: Plan and aerial view of Conwy Castle (Cadw, Welsh Assembly Government: Crown Copyright).

Plate 12

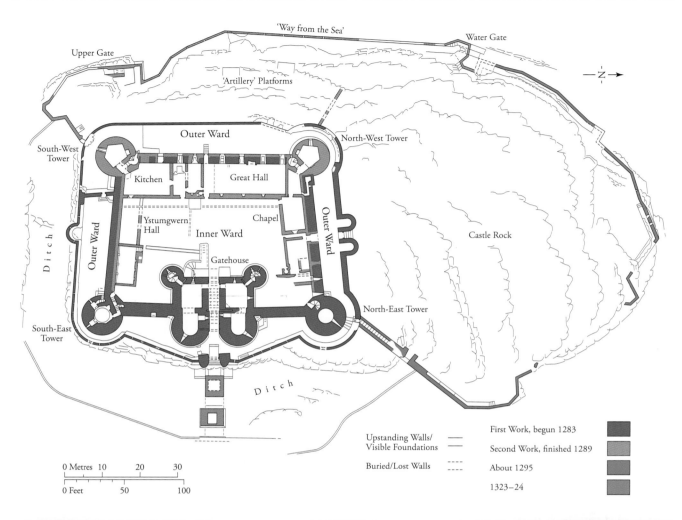

Upper Gate

'Way from the Sea'

Water Gate

—Z→

'Artillery' Platforms

Outer Ward

North-West Tower

South-West Tower

Kitchen

Great Hall

Ditch

Outer Ward

Ystumgwern Hall

Chapel

Outer Ward

Inner Ward

Castle Rock

Gatehouse

South-East Tower

North-East Tower

Ditch

Upstanding Walls/ Visible Foundations	——	First Work, begun 1283	■
Buried/Lost Walls	----	Second Work, finished 1289	■
		About 1295	■
		1323–24	■

0 Metres 10 20 30

0 Feet 50 100

Plate 12: Plan and aerial view of Harlech Castle (Cadw, Welsh Assembly Government: Crown Copyright).

Plate 13

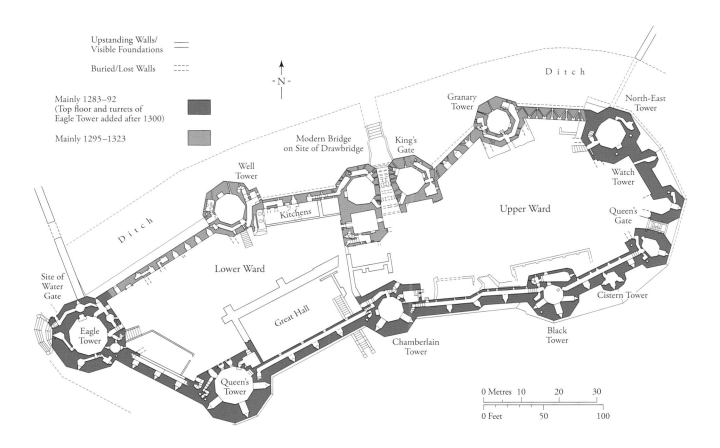

Upstanding Walls/
Visible Foundations

Buried/Lost Walls

Mainly 1283–92
(Top floor and turrets of
Eagle Tower added after 1300)

Mainly 1295–1323

- N -

D i t c h

Granary
Tower

North-East
Tower

Well
Tower

Modern Bridge
on Site of Drawbridge

King's
Gate

Watch
Tower

Kitchens

D i t c h

Upper Ward

Queen's
Gate

Lower Ward

Site of
Water
Gate

Great Hall

Cistern Tower

Eagle
Tower

Chamberlain
Tower

Black
Tower

Queen's
Tower

0 Metres 10   20   30

0 Feet   50   100

Plate 13: Plan and aerial view of Caernarfon Castle (Cadw, Welsh Assembly Government: Crown Copyright).

Plate 14

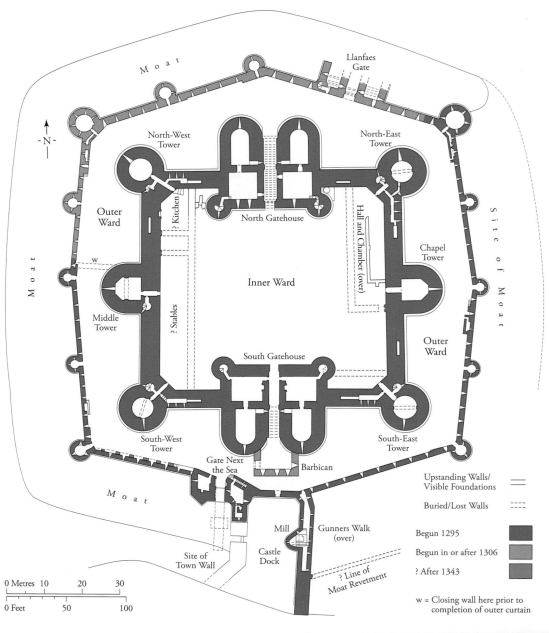

M o a t

Llanfaes Gate

North-West Tower

North-East Tower

Outer Ward

? Kitchen

North Gatehouse

Hall and Chamber (over)

Chapel Tower

M o a t

S i t e   o f   M o a t

Inner Ward

w

? Stables

Middle Tower

Outer Ward

South Gatehouse

South-West Tower

South-East Tower

Gate Next the Sea

Barbican

M o a t

Site of Town Wall

Castle Dock

Mill

Gunners Walk (over)

? Line of Moat Revetment

-N-

Upstanding Walls/ Visible Foundations		———
Buried/Lost Walls		- - - -
Begun 1295		■
Begun in or after 1306		■
? After 1343		■

w = Closing wall here prior to completion of outer curtain

0 Metres 10   20   30

0 Feet   50   100

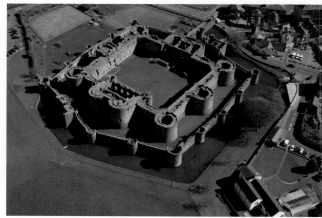

Plate 14: Plan and aerial view of Beaumaris Castle (Cadw, Welsh Assembly Government: Crown Copyright).

Plate 15

Plate 15: Aerial views of Cricieth Castle (top) and Dolbadarn Castle (bottom) (Skyscan Balloon Photography for Cadw and Cadw, Welsh Assembly Government: Crown Copyright).

Plate 16

Plate 16: Dolwyddelan Castle (top) and Dolforwyn Castle (bottom) (Cadw, Welsh Assembly Government: Crown Copyright).